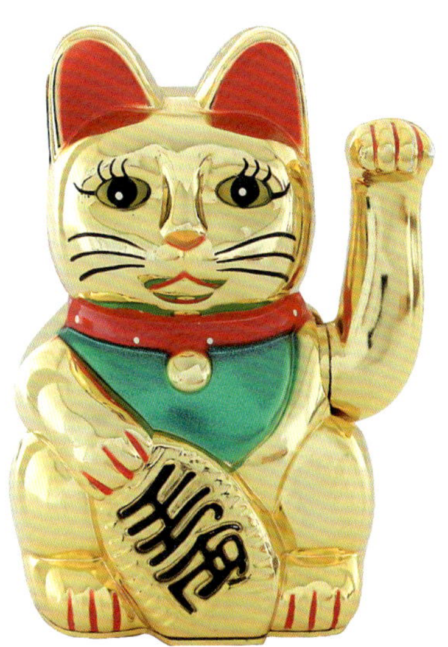

"An exceptionally well-written
and insightful book, shot through with
Hanson's decades of experience
with the public image of the pussy."

— *LA Weekly*

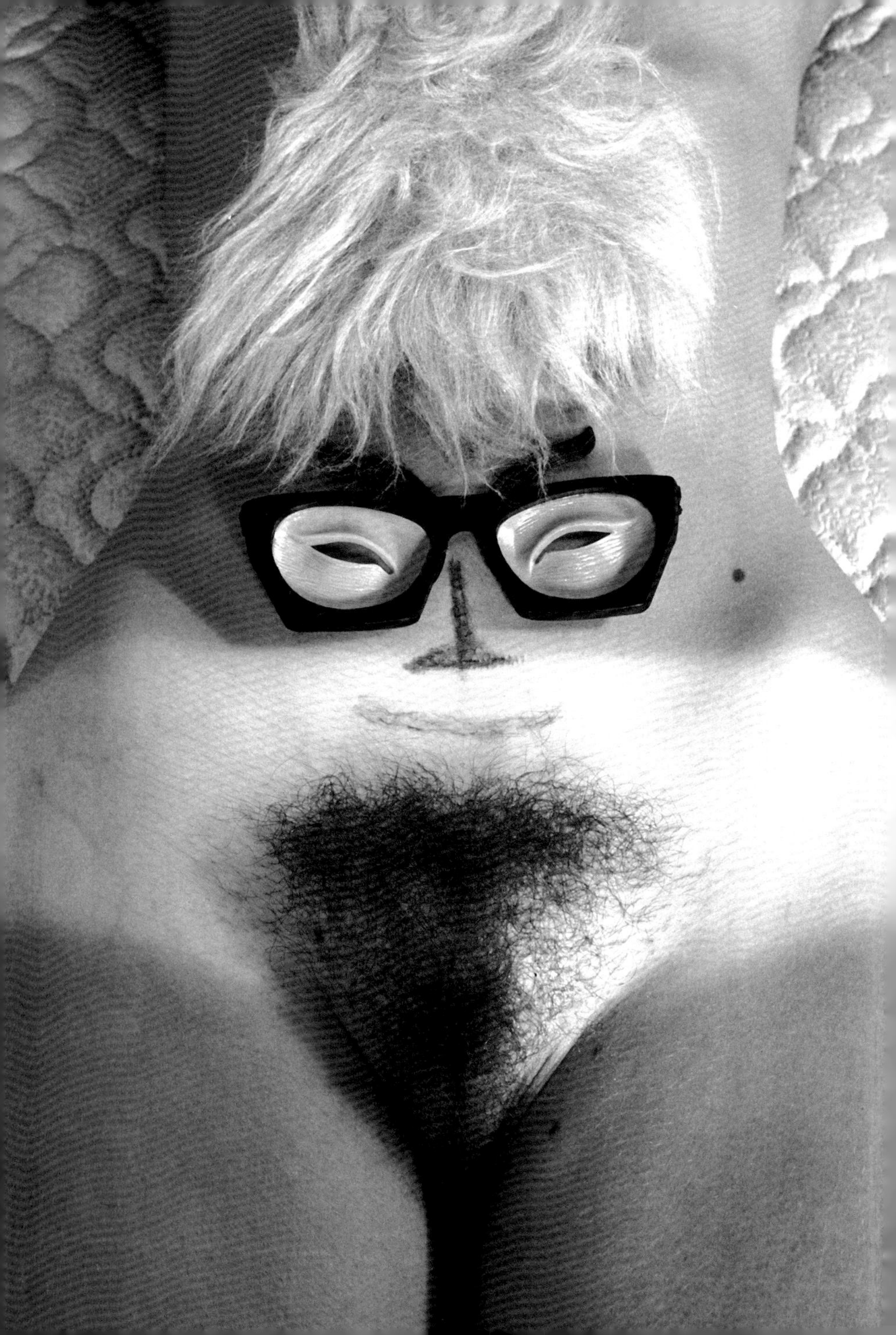

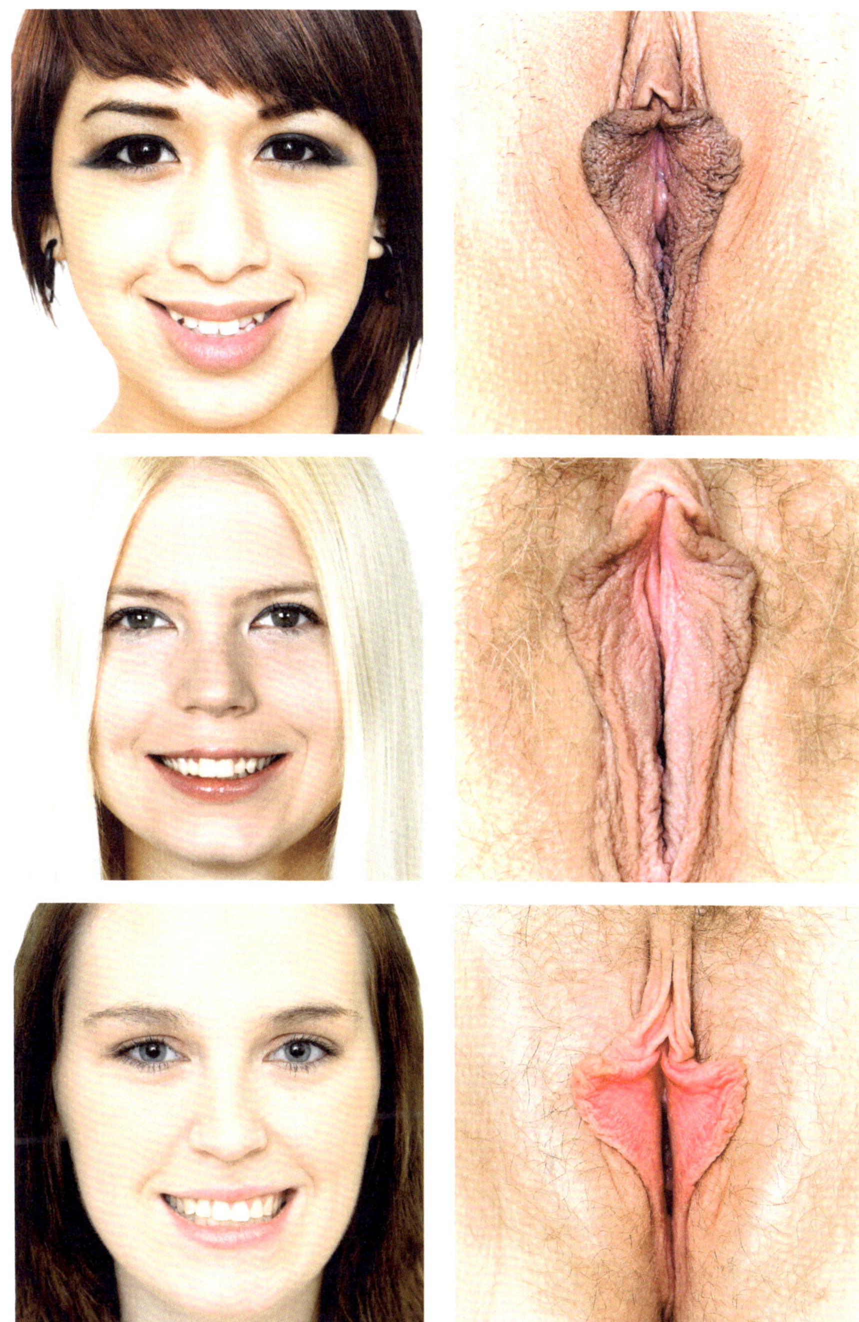

DIAN HANSON

THE LITTLE BIG BOOK OF
Pussy

A Lilliputian Library
of Labial Loveliness

TASCHEN

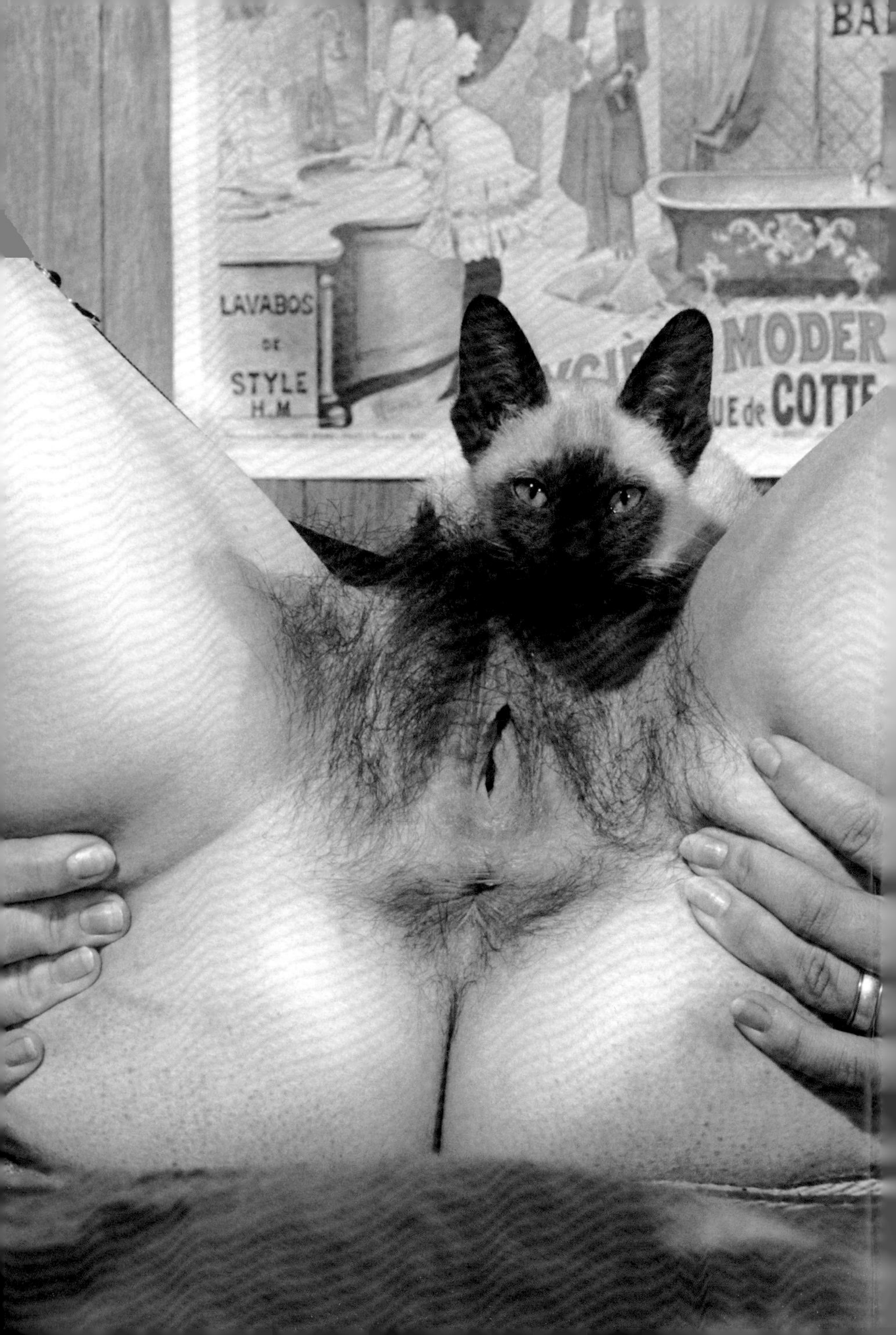
BAI
LAVABOS
DE
STYLE
H.M
MODER
UE de COTTE

Here, Kitty, Kitty!

BY DIAN HANSON

Pity poor pussy, so loved, hated, and feared. How can the penis be a source of unequivocal fascination, while its counterpart causes such consternation? The poem above, picked up in Alabama, sums up the conflict surprisingly well.

I grew up thinking my pussy was both a golden treasure all men wanted and a nasty dirty thing; the boys, it seems, got a similar message. While they proudly declared themselves breast, leg, or butt men, no guy wanted to be a pussy man. Porn actor/director David Christopher, aka Pussyman, confirms: "Say that, and everyone thinks you *are* a pussy." Anathema even to Christopher, who admits pussy forms the center of his personal universe. Better to be a dick, or an asshole — unflattering, but still manly — than that castrating epithet *pussy*.

The simple truth is: Whether you prefer sweet endearments like pussy, kitty,

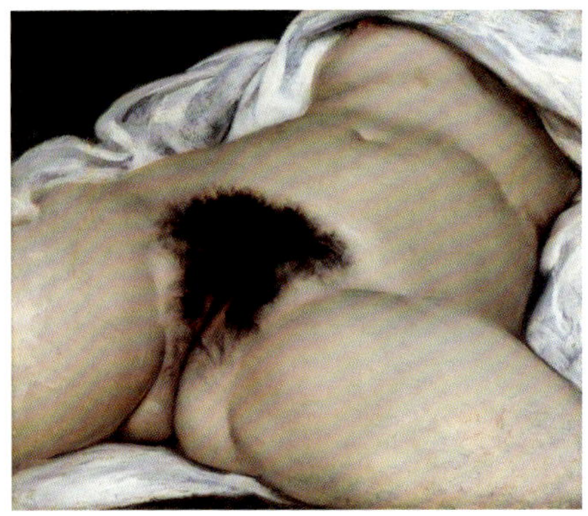

yum yum, lady parts, muff, honey pot, and golden furrow, or slander like gash, fuckhole, stench trench, cumbucket, fish taco, and hairy axe wound, this orifice has such power to tip the gender balance that no man approaches it lightly. One day you're just friends with benefits; the next, the trap snaps, and you're brought to ground by the wily vagina. No wonder the player is such a powerful male icon: To roll in the pleasures of pussy without falling under its spell is a dream as old as mankind, if one seldom realized. In fact, there's evidence that before Vishnu, Buddha, Yahweh, Jesus, Allah, or Kim Kardashian, mankind actually worshipped pussy.

Paleolithic cave paintings found across Europe include triangular shapes with a central cleft that can only be interpreted as pussy. The Cave of Vulvas, found within the Tito Bustillo cave in Spanish Cantabria, is decorated with hundreds of crimson painted pussies. At Chufin Cave, in the same district, vulvas surround every hole in the rock.

A half world away, the walls of Australia's Carnarvon Gorge are engraved with egg-shaped vulvas, each centered with what looks like an exclamation point. The long dash and dot have been interpreted as the vaginal slit with the urethra below, representing a woman lying on her stomach, though the dot seems as likely the anus of a woman on her back. Either way, they're so numerous that the gorge has been named The Wall of One Thousand Vulvas.

Prehistoric pussy is also found in the caves of India, Thailand, South Africa, and Patagonia — in short, on every continent except Antarctica — and even in such far-flung outposts as Easter Island, where vulvas are the second-most-common theme in rock art. More surprising than this abundance of ancient pussy is the paucity of same-period penis: Paleolithic phallic symbols are largely confined to small, talismanic carvings. The phallus gained in popularity with the rise of patriarchal religion in succeeding centuries, and the pussy went back to being that 1% of the female anatomy most loved and feared by men.

And so it remained for centuries until the nasty old 1970s once again put pussy

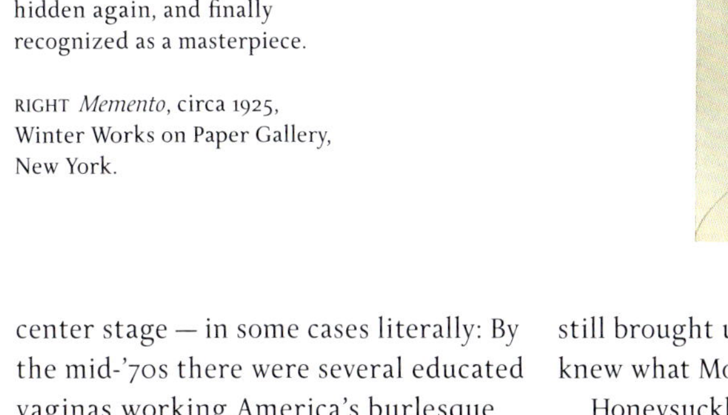

PAGE 4 Teresa Mather and friend, circa 1975.

OPPOSITE *L'Origine du monde* (The Origin of the World) by Gustave Courbet, 1866, was hidden, stolen by the Nazis, hidden again, and finally recognized as a masterpiece.

RIGHT *Memento*, circa 1925, Winter Works on Paper Gallery, New York.

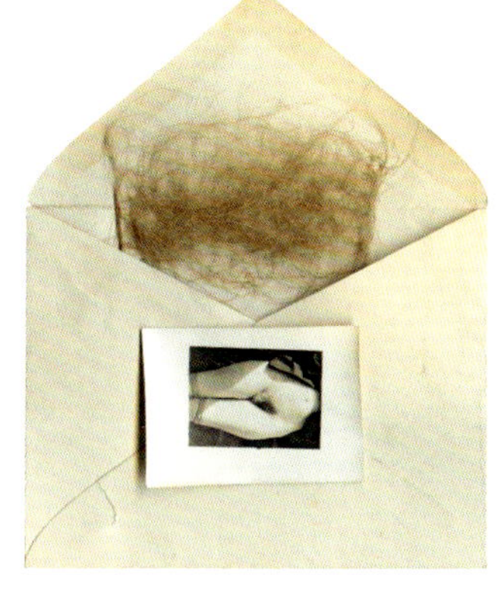

center stage — in some cases literally: By the mid-'70s there were several educated vaginas working America's burlesque stages. Monica Kennedy and Honeysuckle Divine were the two to beat, and really, no one dared try.

Monica's act was sold as performance art. A pretty light-skinned African American in a platinum-blonde wig, she was discovered and promoted by Rod Swenson, a Yale arts grad credited with inventing granola, and later with managing punk legend Wendy O. Williams, before turning to the study of environmental entropy. It's said Swenson was developing his scientific theories at the time he managed Monica, and on a good night she was, like entropy, a pure expression of disorder.

Monica lay on the stage and let fans eat her pussy. She fucked and sucked up to 10 audience members in a single show. She pissed in their faces, and even, when the mood struck, shat on a plate and offered it as a souvenir. Everything was done with warmth and good humor, and a muddled political subtext, but experienced fans still brought umbrellas, as one never knew what Monica might unleash.

Honeysuckle had no promoter and few pretensions to art. She called herself a comedian and most often played the down-trodden 42nd Street Playhouse, arriving with a shopping cart of props, dressed like a bag lady. For three shows a day she mopped the floor, queefed out *Jingle Bells*, tooted a variety of wind instruments, smoked cigarettes, shot autographed ping-pong balls to the back rows, and belched geysers of Jergen's hand lotion with her muscular vagina. Her most notorious trick, resulting in endless arrests, was serving lunch. She'd slather her puss with peanut butter and wipe it onto white bread, then pop out a pickle to complete her "pussy-burger." Her legions of fans lined up to eat it. "With relish?" you ask, to which I answer, "Aren't the pickle and peanut butter *enough*?"

That was the '70s for you: one crotch-crazed decade, a time when flashing your pussy was not only groovy, but politically relevant, like when Germaine Greer hooked her heels behind her ears for a full-page photo in *Suck, First European Sex Paper*. Only in the '70s could a feminist do that and *increase* her credibility, at least with impressionable young girls like me. In fact, I nominate that photo of Greer grinning through her thighs to represent the 1970s. It'd look just great on a stamp.

The groundwork for audacious *Suck*, and all that followed, was laid in 1965, when Sweden's Berth Milton launched *Private* magazine, with pussy spread cover to cover. The same year an American publisher introduced pussy-positive *Jaybird* magazine, exploiting a legal loophole that allowed pubic hair in nudist magazines. Both publishers were arrested, and both prevailed in court, leading to an outpouring of hardcore in Northern Europe, and to flagrant pussy in America's sex shops. Then, in its April 1970 issue, *Penthouse* magazine, sold on public newsstands all over the United States, printed a tiny photo of a girl showing a square millimeter of black bush. Two months later *Playboy* published a similar photo, and when the world didn't end, all American men's magazines followed suit.

After *Playboy, Penthouse, Gallery, Genesis, Modern Man*, and *Mr.* sprouted hair, Larry Flynt parted it. *Hustler's* first pink centerfold was Patti, December 1974, a natural redhead posed with labia exposed, and open. In subsequent issues *Hustler* Honeys held their labia apart in what came to be called a spread shot, the flesh accentuated by a narrowly focused, pink-filtered strobe nicknamed a pussy spot. Within the year most American men's magazines emulated *Hustler*. In just five years we'd gone from a hint of hair to blatant pink. The sheer volume of sexual imagery was intoxicating, and it wasn't just men who were high on pubic liberation.

Most of the photos in this book were taken between 1967 and 1979, and you can see the mood of the day reflected in the models' faces. The women look almost giddy flashing their newly legal parts.

By the end of the '70s the mood was shifting; porn was big business and pussy now commonplace. What once was a shock had become a carefully groomed and depilated component, just another part of the commercial package, along

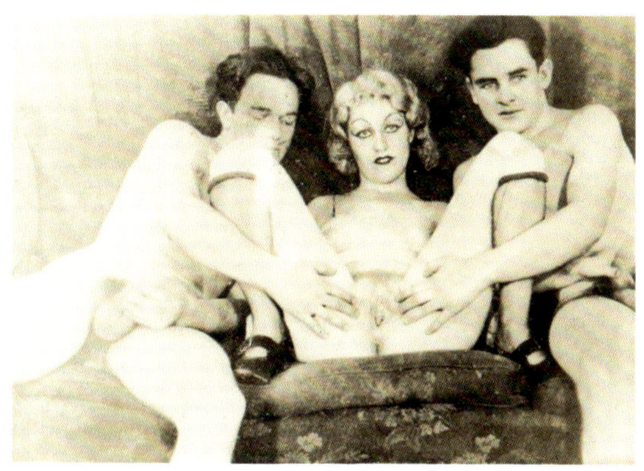

with perfected breasts and practiced facial expressions.

In the '90s porn director John "Buttman" Stagliano would tell Martin Amis that "pussies are bullshit" to explain America's growing obsession with anal sex.

The trend continued into the 2000s, as commercial porn explored extreme themes in its battle with the Internet. If fans would no longer pay for anal gang bangs, who could expect them to pay for something as quaint as pussy?

Today, among the carefully topiaried crotches of a porn industry long past its prime, in a business struggling to survive Pornhub and unlimited free streaming content, a '70s-style backlash has emerged. Hairy pussy is the hot new Internet niche, and as such, the first porn trend to celebrate vulva in nearly two decades. Most hairy sites are still amateur, but young pros like Raven Rockette, Simone Delilah, and Keira Croft have updated their 'dos to include more hair, alarming the shaved generation.

When Sasha Grey appeared on the TV show *Entourage* in August 2010 sporting a natural pubic triangle, Twitter went wild with posts of "Eww!", "disgusting," "sicko BUSH," and "This is 2010!". Unfazed, Grey tweeted back "…that's what a grown woman looks like…I'm happy to contribute to making it ok again :) All 'fashions' have their cycles!"

Could it be that a post-porn generation is coming of age—a group, even within the industry, that refuses to conform to the tired expectations of artificial glamour? Since the popular stars above also have natural breasts, lips, and hair color, the signs are hopeful. Perhaps the new century *can* be more pussy positive than the last … few thousand. Not Paleolithic positive, but better.

As an owner, I'd like to think so, and offer a closing poem, written in 1830 to teach children to respect their pets, as a kinder model of the long misunderstood, secretly adored, pussy:

I love little pussy
Her coat is so warm
And if I don't hurt her
She'll do me no harm

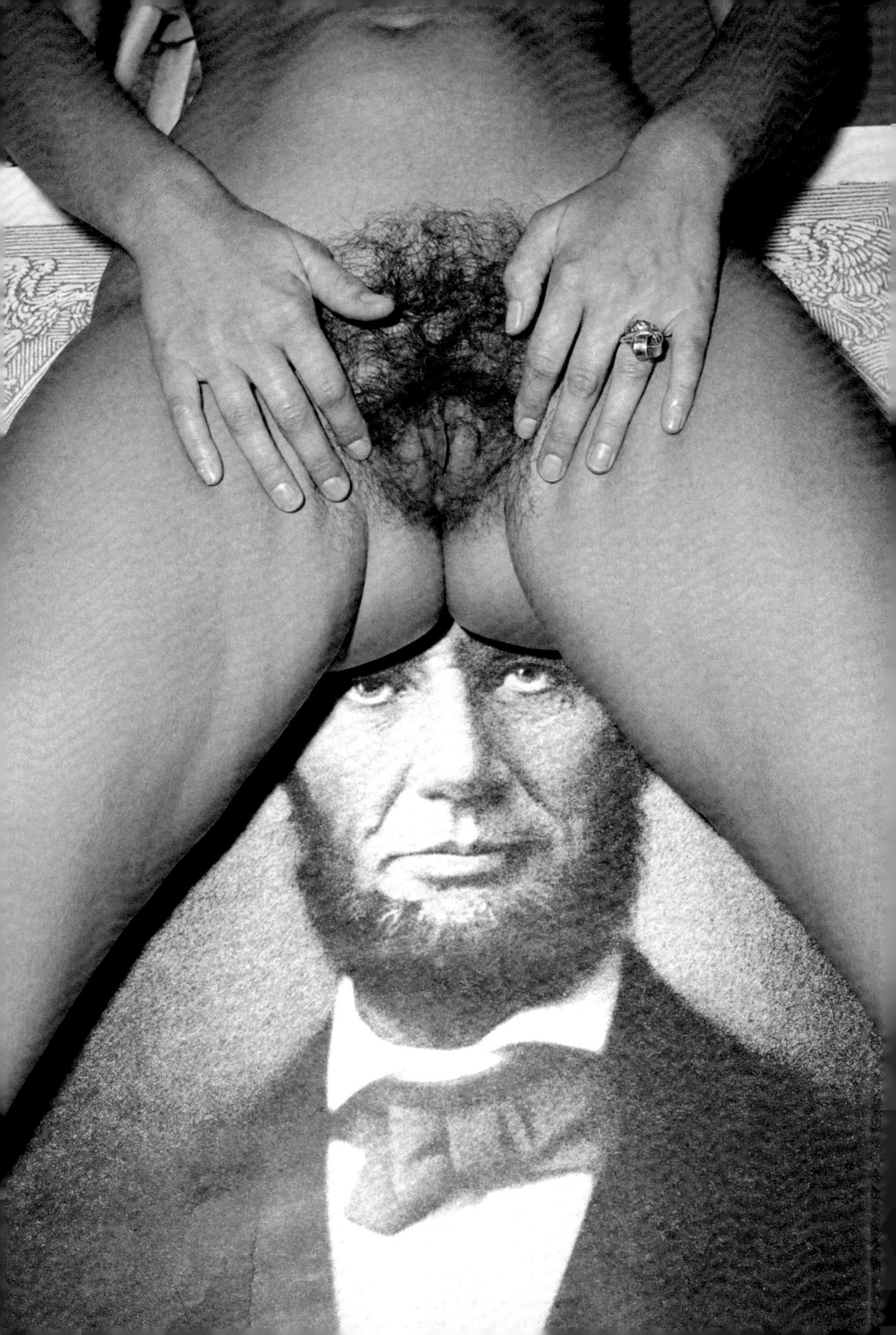

Kitzlige Kätzchen

VON DIAN HANSON

Arme, kleine Muschi – so geliebt, so gehasst und gefürchtet. Wieso ist alle Welt vom Penis fasziniert, während sein Gegenstück derartig betroffen macht? Das oben zitierte Gedicht aus Alabama bringt den Zwiespalt gut auf den Punkt. Als Heranwachsende dachte ich einerseits, meine Muschi sei ein Goldschatz, auf den es alle Männer abgesehen hätten, andererseits glaubte ich, sie sei ein ekliges, schmutziges Ding. Die Jungs verstanden es ähnlich. Stolz erklärten sie, sie stünden auf Brüste, Beine oder den Hintern eines Mädchens,

keiner wollte ein Muschi-Liebhaber sein. David Christopher alias Pussyman, Pornodarsteller und -regisseur, bestätigt das: „Wenn du so was von dir behauptest, dann *bist* du für alle gleich eine Muschi." Lieber lässt man sich als Schwanz oder Arschloch bezeichnen, als dass man mit diesem kastrierenden Schimpfnamen bedacht wird. Die schlichte Wahrheit ist: Ob man Koseworte wie Muschi, Pussy, Mjammjam, Pflaume, Honigtöpfchen und Goldenes Vlies oder abwertende Begriffe wie Spalte, Fickloch, Riechritze, Spermakübel, Fisch-Taco

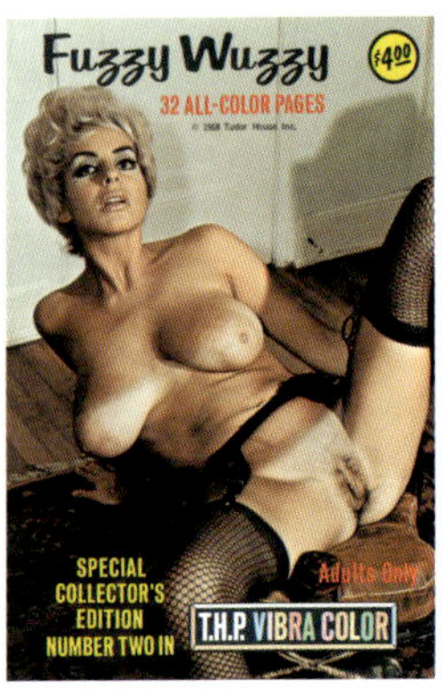

PAGE 10 Unknown model tantalizes Abraham Lincoln, circa 1975.

LEFT *Fuzzy Wuzzy* magazine, 1968, the year American sex shops first carried magazines with graphic depictions of pussy.

OPPOSITE LEFT *Young Beavers*, 1970.

OPPOSITE RIGHT *Hair To Spare*, circa 1974, celebrated extra hairy pussy.

oder behaarte Axtkerbe bevorzugt – diese Körperöffnung hat eine so große Macht, das Gleichgewicht der Geschlechter ins Wanken zu bringen, dass kein Mann die Sache auf die leichte Schulter nimmt. Sich den Vergnügungen der Muschi hinzugeben, ohne sich ihrem Zauberbann zu unterwerfen, ist ein Traum, der so alt ist wie die Menschheit, doch in die Tat umgesetzt wird er selten. Tatsächlich gibt es genügend Belege, dass die Menschheit – noch vor Vishnu, Buddha, Jahwe, Jesus, Allah oder Kim Kardashian – einer Anbetung der Muschi frönte.

Paläolithische Höhlenmalereien in Europa zeigen dreieckige Formen mit einer zentralen Spalte, die nur als Abbildungen des weiblichen Geschlechts interpretiert werden können. Die in der Tito-Bustillo-Grotte entdeckte „Höhle der Vulven" im spanischen Kantabrien ist von Hunderten purpurfarben gemalten Muschis bedeckt.

In die Wände der Carnarvon-Schlucht in Australien, auf der anderen Seite des Globus, sind eiförmige Vulven geritzt, deren Mitte jeweils von einem Symbol ähnlich einem Ausrufezeichen verziert ist. Es wurde als Vaginalschlitz mit der darunter befindlichen Urethra einer auf dem Bauch liegenden Frau gedeutet, obgleich der Punkt eher den Anus einer auf dem Rücken liegenden Frau darzustellen scheint.

Prähistorische Muschis sind auch in Höhlen in Indien, Thailand, Südafrika und in Patagonien zu finden. Selbst in den Felsbildern der Osterinseln sind Vulven das zweithäufigste Motiv. Überraschender als diese Fülle an uralten Muschis ist der Mangel an Penisdarstellungen in denselben Epochen: Paläolithische Phallussymbole beschränken sich weitestgehend auf kleine, talismanartige Schnitzereien. Mit dem Aufkommen patriarchalischer Religionen in den folgenden Jahrhunderten gewann der Phallus an Popularität, während die Muschi wieder auf jene zwei Prozent der weiblichen Anatomie reduziert wurde, die Männer so sehr lieben und fürchten. Und dabei blieb es für Jahrhunderte, bis die Muschi in den schmuddeligen 1970er-Jahren wieder im Blickpunkt stand: Mitte der 1970er-Jahre gab es eine Menge geschulter Vaginen, von denen viele auf den Varieté-bühnen Amerikas arbeiteten. Monica Ken-

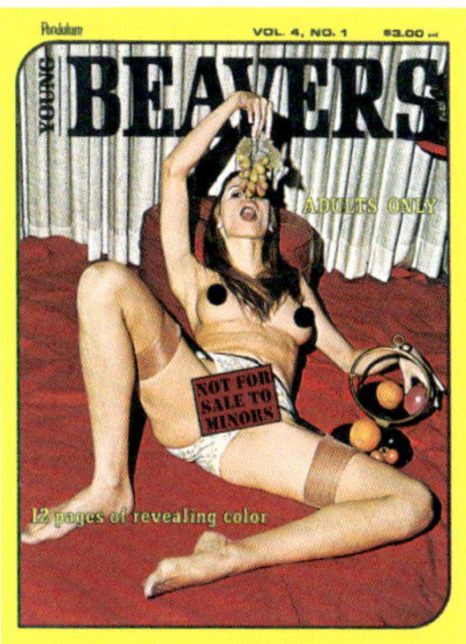

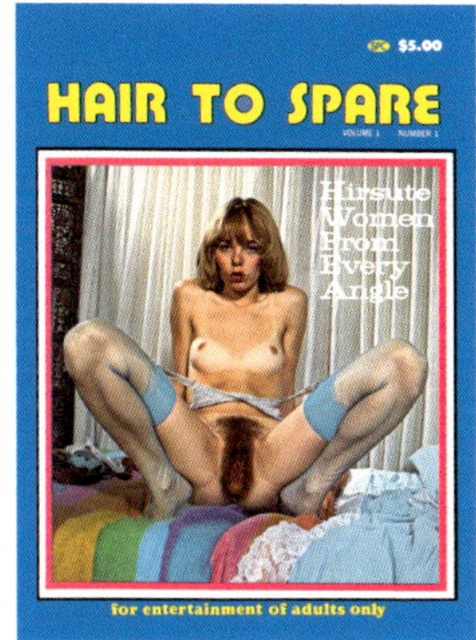

nedy und Honeysuckle Divine hießen die beiden Damen, denen man erst mal das Wasser reichen musste.

Monicas Vorstellung wurde als Performance-Kunst verkauft. Sie war eine hübsche Afroamerikanerin mit platinblonder Perücke und wurde entdeckt und promotet von Rod Swenson, einem Yale-Absolventen und Künstler. Später hat er die Punklegende Wendy O. Williams gemanagt, bevor er sich dem Studium der Umweltentropie zuwandte. Monica legte sich auf die Bühne und ließ sich von ihren Fans die Muschi lecken. Während einer Show fickte und lutschte sie bis zu zehn Männer aus dem Publikum. Sie pisste in die Gesichter ihrer Bewunderer, und wenn ihr danach war, kackte sie auf einen Teller und bot dieses Arrangement als Souvenir an. Alles, was sie tat, vollführte sie mit herzlicher Geste, in bester Stimmung und versehen mit einem ungereimten politischen Subtext. Gleichwohl brachten erfahrene Fans Schirme mit, denn man konnte nie wissen, was Monica als Nächstes vom Stapel ließ.

Honeysuckle bezeichnete sich selbst als Komödiantin und trat häufig in einem heruntergekommenen Theater an der 42. Straße auf. Für ihren Auftritt schob sie, gekleidet wie eine Stadtstreicherin, einen Einkaufswagen voller Requisiten auf die Bühne. In drei Shows täglich wischte sie mit ihrer muskulösen Vagina den Boden, furzte mit ihr „Jingle Bells", trötete damit auf Blasinstrumenten herum, rauchte mit ihr Zigaretten, feuerte signierte Pingpong-Bälle in die hinteren Reihen oder stieß mit ihr wie ein Springquell Unmengen von *Jergens*-Handlotion aus. Ihre berühmteste Nummer, derentwegen sie immer wieder verhaftet wurde, war die Darreichung eines Imbisses. Sie schmierte sich die Muschi mit Erdnussbutter ein, wischte sie dann mit einem Stück Weißbrot ab, garnierte das Ganze mit einem Gürkchen – fertig war der „Pussyburger". Die Legionen ihrer Fans standen Schlange, um einen davon essen zu können.

So war das in den 1970ern, einem Jahrzehnt, das ganz närrisch nach allem war, was mit dem Schritt zu tun hatte, einer Zeit, in der es nicht nur als cool, sondern auch als politisch relevant galt, die Muschi mal kurz aufblitzen zu lassen, so wie

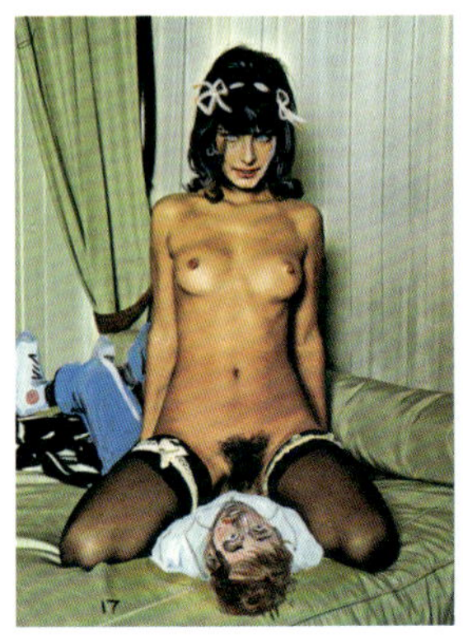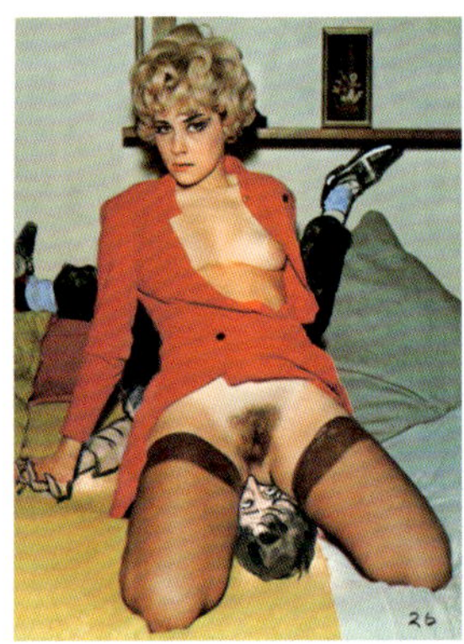

Germaine Greer, die sich für ein ganz-seitiges Foto in *Suck*, der „ersten europäischen Sexzeitung", ihre Stöckelschuhe hinter die Ohren klemmte. So etwas konnte sich eine Feministin nur in den 1970er-Jahren leisten und damit sogar noch ihre Glaubwürdigkeit erhöhen.

Die Grundlagen für gewagte Publikationen wie *Suck* und alle anderen, die noch folgten, wurden 1965 geschaffen, als der Schwede Berth Milton *Private* auf den Markt brachte, ein Magazin, in dem von der ersten bis zur letzten Seite klaffende Mösen zu sehen waren. Im selben Jahr brachte ein amerikanischer Verleger das muschifreundliche Magazin *Jaybird* heraus und nutzte dabei eine Gesetzeslücke, die Abbildungen von Schamhaar in Nudistenmagazinen erlaubte. Beide Verleger wurden verhaftet, und beide gewannen ihre Prozesse, woraufhin in Nordeuropa ein wahrer Schwall an Hardcore-Veröffentlichungen hervorbrach und in Amerikas Sexshops schamlos Muschis dargeboten wurden. Schließlich veröffentlichte das Magazin *Penthouse* in seiner Ausgabe vom April 1970 ein winziges Foto des „Schätzchens des Monats", auf dem ein Quadratmillimeter schwarzen Schamhaars zu sehen war. Im Januar-Heft 1971 zog dann der *Playboy* mit einem ähnlichen Foto nach.

Nachdem *Playboy*, *Penthouse*, *Gallery*, *Genesis*, *Modern Man* und *Mr.* die Schamhaare sprießen ließen, machte sich Larry Flynt daran, sie gewissermaßen zu scheiteln. Das erste doppelseitige Bild in *Hustler*, auf dem Rosiges zu sehen war, zeigte im Dezember 1974 Patti, ein von Natur aus rothaariges Model, das seine Labien offen zur Schau stellte. Auch in den folgenden Ausgaben hielten die *Hustler*-Zuckerschnecken ihre Schamlippen auseinander. Noch im selben Jahr eiferten die meisten amerikanischen Männermagazine *Hustler* nach. Innerhalb von nur fünf Jahren war der Schritt von nur angedeutetem Schamhaar zu bleckendem Rosa vollzogen. Allein schon die Masse an Sexbildmaterial wirkte berauschend, und es waren beileibe nicht nur Männer, die von der Befreiung des Intimbereichs ganz benommen waren.

Die meisten Fotos in diesem Buch wurden zwischen 1967 und 1979 aufgenommen, und wie die Stimmungslage war, kann man

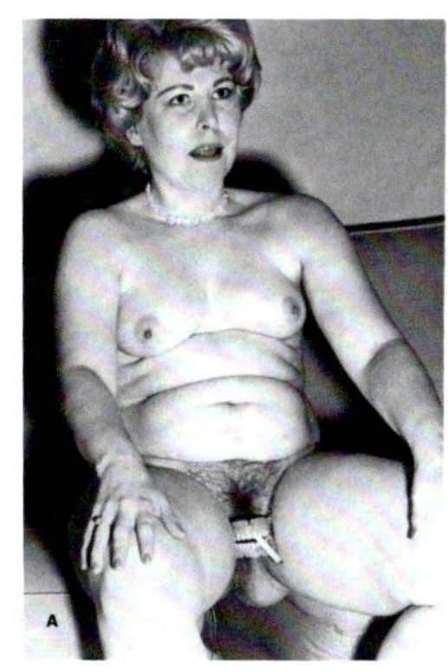

an den Gesichtern der Models ablesen. Es sieht fast so aus, als wäre den Frauen regelrecht schwindlig davon, dass sie ihr Juwel ganz legal aufleuchten lassen durften.

Gegen Ende der 1970er-Jahre wandelte sich die Stimmung, Porno war inzwischen das große Geschäft und eine Muschi nichts Besonderes. Was einst noch schockierte, war zu einem festen Element geworden, zusammen mit vollendeten Brüsten und routiniertem Gesichtsausdruck nur noch Teil des kommerziellen Gesamtpakets.

In den 1990er-Jahren ließ Pornoregisseur John „Buttman" Stagliano, um die wachsende Analsexbesessenheit der Amerikaner zu erklären, Martin Amis wissen, Mösen seien „Mist". Der Trend setzte sich, als die Pornoindustrie im Konkurrenzkampf mit dem Internet extremere Themen erprobte, bis in unser neues Jahrtausend fort. Wenn die Fans keine Lust mehr hatten, für Anal-Gangbangs zu zahlen, wer konnte dann erwarten, dass sie Geld für so etwas Putziges wie eine Muschi ausgeben würden?

In unseren Tagen macht sich unter all den sorgfältig zurechtgestutzten Genital-

frisuren einer Pornoindustrie, die ihren Höhepunkt längst hinter sich hat und gegen Pornhub und den unbegrenzten Zugang zu kostenlosen Videoseiten ums Überleben kämpft, eine Gegenreaktion bemerkbar, die sich am Stil der 1970er-Jahre orientiert. Behaarte Muschis sind die neue heiße Nischennummer im Internet und als solche der erste Pornotrend seit 20 Jahren, der der Vulva huldigt. Die meisten der mit Behaartem aufwartenden Webseiten bieten noch Amateurmaterial, doch junge Profis wie Raven Rockette, Simone Delilah und Keira Croft haben ihre Seiten mit mehr Bildmaterial ihrer behaarten Muschis aktualisiert und damit die Depilationsgeneration alarmiert.

Als Sasha Grey im August 2010 in der Fernsehshow *Entourage* mit natürlich gewachsenem Schamhaar auftrat, lief die Twitter-Adresse der Sendung heiß mit Posts wie „Igittigitt!", „Ekelhaft", „Ist ja krank, dieser BUSCH" oder „Das ist 2010!". Unbeeindruckt twitterte Grey zurück: „... so sieht eine erwachsene Frau nun mal aus ... Ich bin froh, einen Beitrag dazu leisten zu können, dass

„**Die polynesische Legende erzählt von
dem Gott Maui, der auf der Suche nach
dem ewigen Leben zurück in die Vagina
seiner Mutter krabbelte, dabei jedoch
in zwei Hälften zerbissen wurde.**"

dies wieder okay ist :) Alle ‚Moden' haben ihre Phasen!"

Ist es möglich, dass die Postpornogeneration erwachsen wird, wenn eine Gruppe, die sogar in der Pornoindustrie tätig ist, sich weigert, den ausgelutschten Ansprüchen nach künstlichem Glamour gerecht zu werden? Da die oben erwähnten populären Stars auch natürliche Brüste, Lippen und Haarfarben haben, gibt es Hoffnung. Vielleicht kann unser neues Jahrhundert muschifreundlicher werden als … die letzten Jahrtausende. Als Frau und Muschi-In-haberin gefällt mir diese Vorstellung, und so zitiere ich zum Abschluss ein 1830 verfasstes Gedicht, das Kindern Respekt vor ihren Haustieren beibringen sollte und als liebenswerteres Abbild der lange Zeit verkannten, insgeheim jedoch angebeteten Muschi gelten mag:

*Ich liebe das kleine Kätzchen,
sein Fell ist so kuschelig warm.
Und wenn ich ihm nicht wehtu,
macht's auch keine Mätzchen.*

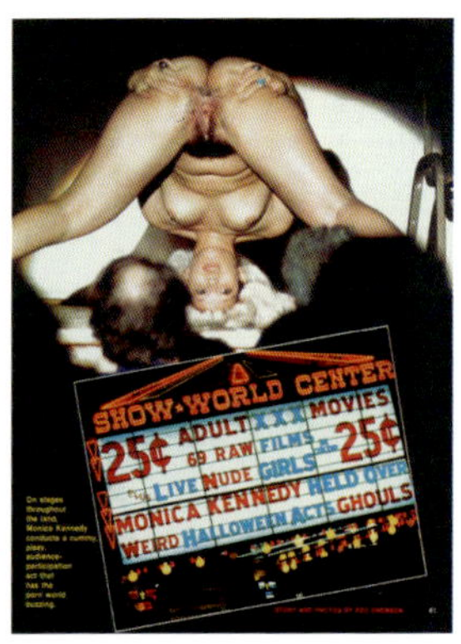

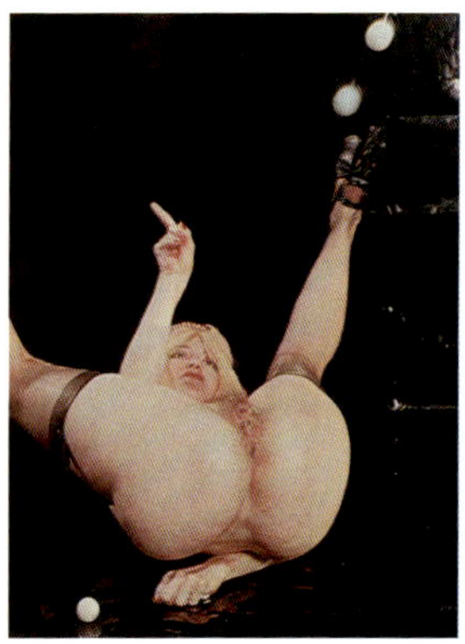

FAR LEFT Monica Kennedy onstage in New York City, 1976, offering her pussy for cunnilingus.

LEFT Vaginal performance artist Honeysuckle Divine shooting ping-pong balls, 1976.

OPPOSITE Unknown models, circa 1968.

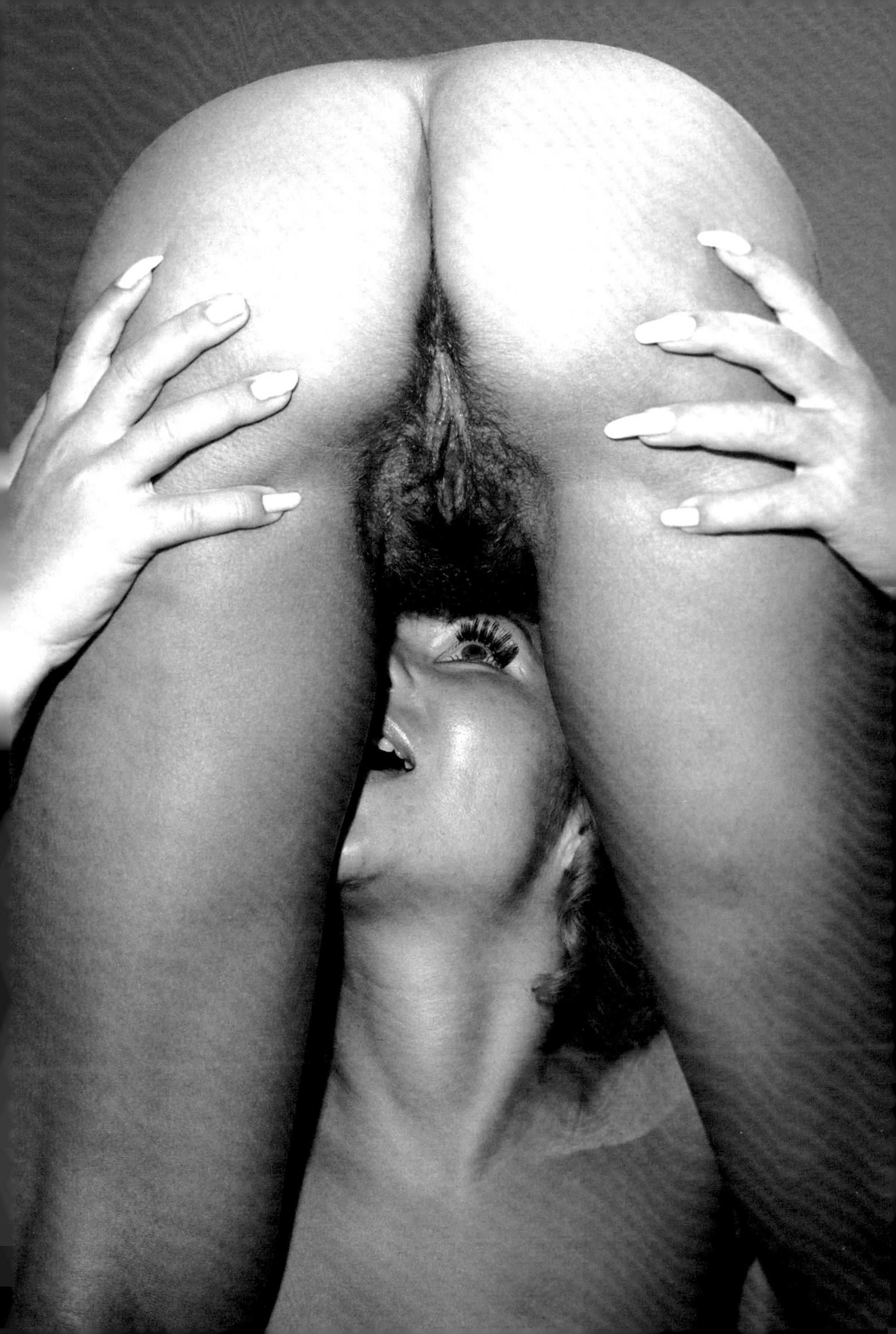

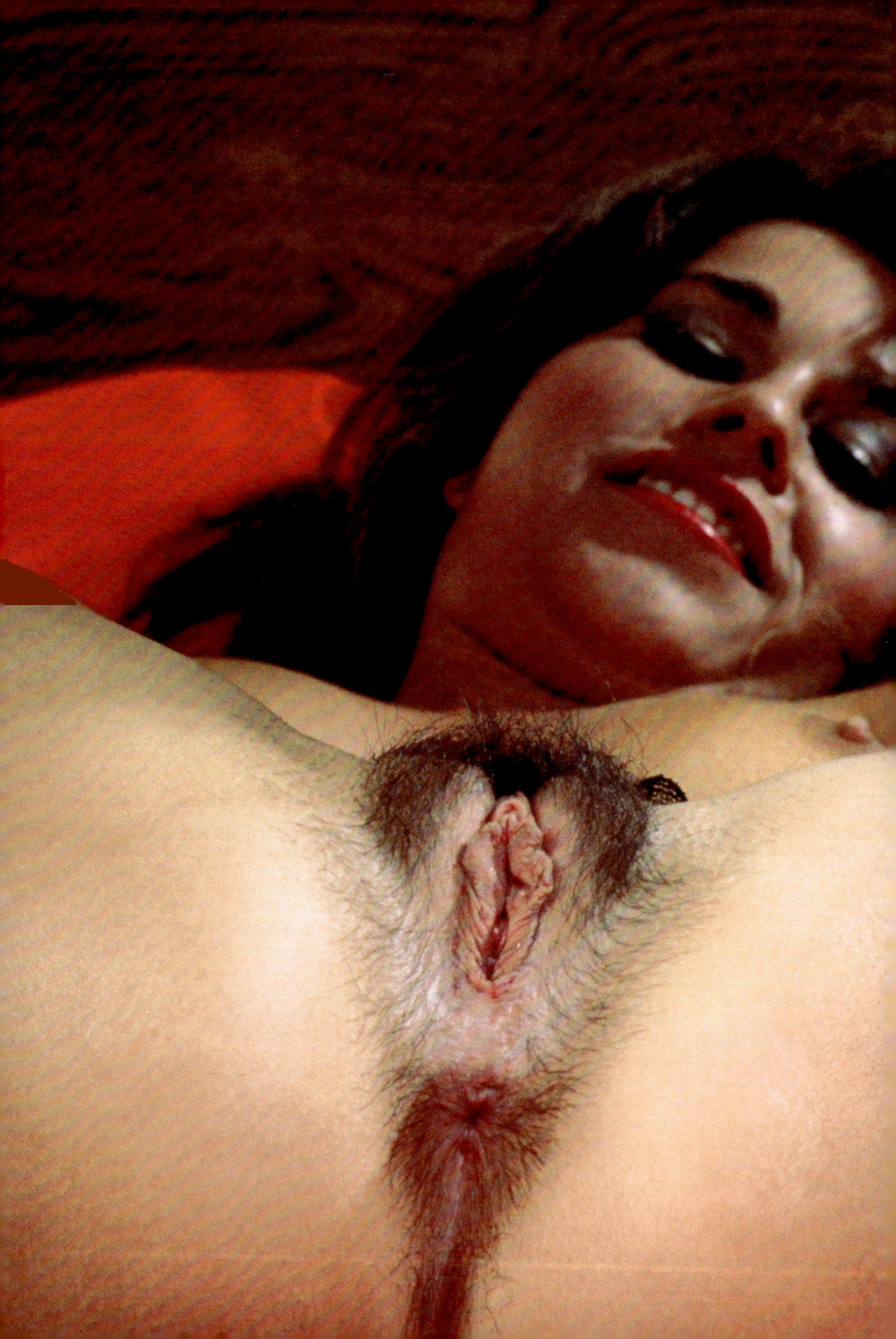

Viens, minou, minou!

PAR DIAN HANSON

Pauvre petit minou, tant adoré, tant haï, tant craint. Comment se fait-il que le pénis soit l'objet d'une fascination univoque tandis que son équivalent féminin ne provoque que consternation? Le poème cité ci-dessus, glané en Alabama, résume bien cette divergence de perception. J'ai grandi en pensant que ma chatte était à la fois le plus précieux des trésors, convoité par tous les hommes, et un truc sale et honteux; il semblerait que les garçons aient perçu un message similaire. Alors qu'ils n'hésitent pas à se vanter d'adorer les seins, les jambes ou les fesses, aucun ne s'enorgueillit d'être un homme à chattes. L'acteur et réalisateur de porno David Christopher, alias «Pussyman», le confirme : «Si vous dites ça, tout le monde vous prend pour une mauviette.» Mieux vaut être traité de bite ou de trou du cul – épithètes peu flatteurs mais encore à peu près virils – que de mauviette (*pussy* en anglais), éminemment castrateur. La vérité, la voici: que vous préfériez les mots doux à tendance puérile comme chatte, foufoune, abricot, coquillage, zézette, pot

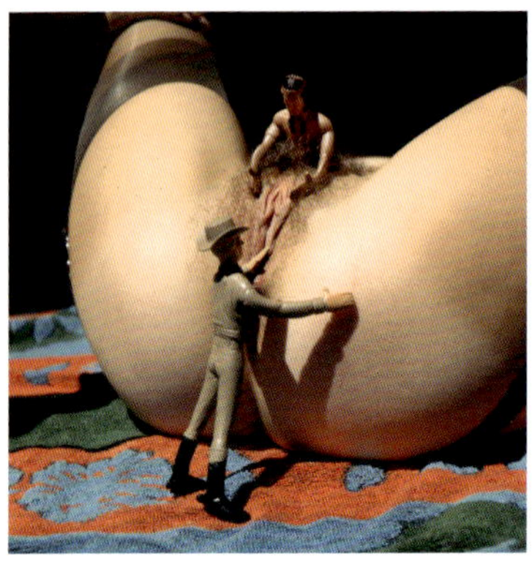

à miel et autres moumounes, ou les termes plus crus, souvent diffamatoires comme chagatte, con, moule, fente, touffe, pissette, garage à bites ou trou à crinière, cet orifice a une telle capacité à perturber le fragile équilibre entre les sexes qu'aucun homme ne l'aborde à la légère. Un jour, on n'est que des amis avec bonus, et le lendemain, voilà que le piège se referme, imparable : le malicieux vagin vous met à genoux. Pas étonnant que le joueur soit une icône masculine si répandue : se vautrer dans les plaisirs de la vulve sans tomber sous son emprise est un rêve vieux comme le monde. Les chercheurs ont même prouvé qu'avant Vishnou, Bouddha, Yahvé, Jésus, Allah ou Kim Kardashian, l'humanité vouait un culte au sexe féminin.

Parmi les peintures rupestres trouvées dans les grottes paléolithiques européennes figurent des formes triangulaires fendues en deux qui ne peuvent représenter qu'une vulve. La caverne des Vulves, découverte dans la grotte de Tito Bustillo, dans les Asturies espagnoles, est décorée de centaines de chattes rouge vif. À l'autre bout du monde, en Australie, les parois de la gorge de Carnarvon sont gravées de vulves en forme d'amande, dont le centre est occupé par une sorte de point d'exclamation. Ce point surmonté d'un trait a été interprété comme l'urètre et la fente du vagin d'une femme couchée sur le ventre, même si, à mon avis, il peut aussi bien représenter l'anus d'une femme allongée sur le dos. Peu importe. Ces symboles sont si omniprésents que la gorge a été rebaptisée le Mur au Millier de Vulves.

Des vulves préhistoriques ont aussi été retrouvées dans des grottes d'Inde, de Thaïlande, d'Afrique du Sud, de Patagonie et jusqu'aux confins de la Terre, sur les sculptures monumentales de l'île de Pâques, où la vulve est le deuxième thème le plus traité. Cette abondance de foufounes antiques est d'autant plus étonnante que les pénis datant de la même époque sont très rares. Les symboles phalliques paléolithiques étaient généralement cantonnés à de petites statuettes à valeur de talisman. Avec l'avènement des religions patriarcales, au cours des siècles suivants, le phallus a gagné en popularité, tandis que la vulve endossait un rôle plus obscur.

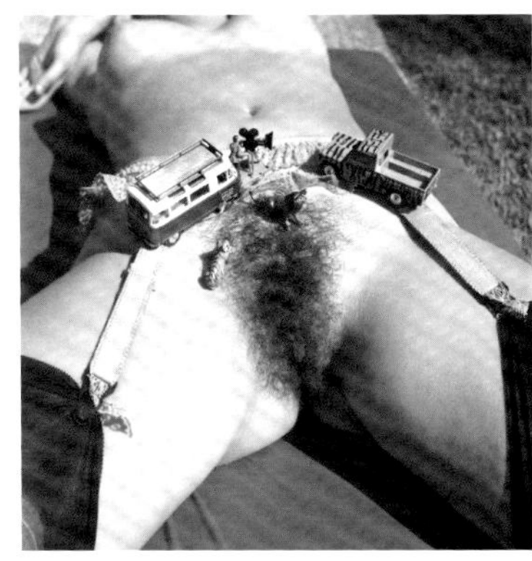

Pendant des siècles, elle ne fut que ces 2% du corps féminin les plus adorés et abhorrés des hommes, jusqu'aux bonnes vieilles années 1970, où elle revint sur le devant de la scène… au sens propre. Au milieu de cette décennie merveilleuse, les dresseuses de vagin étaient légion, notamment sur la scène du théâtre burlesque américain. Monica Kennedy et Honeysuckle Divine étaient les deux femmes à abattre dans ce domaine et pour être franche, personne ne s'y serait risqué.

Le numéro de Monica était présenté comme une performance artistique. Cette jolie fille à la peau café au lait portant une perruque blond platine fut découverte et lancée par Rod Swenson, un diplômé en arts sorti de Yale connu pour avoir inventé le muesli et servi d'agent à la légende punk Wendy O. Williams, avant de se consacrer à l'étude de l'entropie environnementale. Il paraît que Swenson développait ses théories scientifiques au moment où il s'occupait des affaires de Monica, ce qui ne manque pas de logique, puisque dans ses bons soirs, Monica était, comme l'entropie, une pure expression du chaos. Mo-

nica s'allongeait sur la scène et laissait ses fans lui lécher le minou. Elle baisait et suçait une dizaine de membres du public chaque soir. Elle leur pissait au visage et même, quand l'envie lui prenait, elle chiait dans une assiette et l'offrait en souvenir. Tout était fait avec générosité, bonne humeur et un message politique sous-jacent, bien que confus.

Honeysuckle travaillait seule et n'avait aucune prétention artistique. Elle se qualifiait de « comique » et se produisait le plus souvent dans un cabaret de la 42e Rue, où elle arrivait en poussant un caddie rempli d'accessoires, habillée comme une vagabonde. Trois fois par jour, elle montait sur la scène pour balayer le sol, péter *Jingle Bells*, souffler dans une série d'instruments à vents, fumer des cigarettes, projeter des balles de ping-pong sur le dernier rang et cracher des geysers de lotion Jergen avec son vagin particulièrement musclé. Son truc le plus réputé, lequel lui a valu un nombre incalculable d'arrestations, était de servir le déjeuner. Elle badigeonnait son minou de beurre de cacahuète qu'elle tartinait ensuite sur des tranches de pain

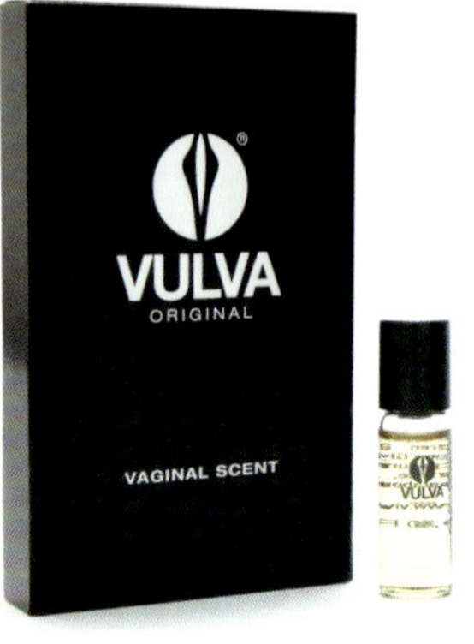

LEFT Vulva Original vaginal scent, marketed by a German website as "The real erotifying vaginal scent of a desirable woman," for men to sniff off the backs of their hands.

OPPOSITE LEFT From hippie sex magazine *Escape*, 1971.

OPPOSITE RIGHT The same theme explored in *Cinema Scorchers*, 1970.

blanc, et pour parachever son « pussyburger », elle y déposait un cornichon sorti de son vagin.

C'étaient les années 1970, une décennie folle de la chatte, une époque où montrer son sexe était non seulement tendance et cool, mais aussi pertinent politiquement, à l'image de Germaine Greer collant ses talons derrière ses oreilles sur une pleine page dans *Suck, The First European Sex Paper*. Il n'y a bien que dans les années 1970 qu'une féministe pouvait gagner en crédibilité en posant ainsi, en tout cas aux yeux des jeunes filles impressionnables comme moi. Je choisirais d'ailleurs cette photo de Greer souriant entre ses cuisses ouvertes pour représenter les années 1970.

Les origines de cette publication audacieuse, et de toutes celles qui se sont engouffrées dans la brèche ensuite, datent de 1965, année où le Suédois Berth Milton a lancé le magazine *Private*, dont le sexe féminin était le fonds de commerce. La même année, un éditeur américain a lancé le magazine *Jaybird*, en profitant d'une niche juridique autorisant les magazines naturistes à montrer des poils pubiens. Les deux rédacteurs en chef ont été arrêtés et tous deux ont gagné leurs procès, ce qui a permis la floraison de dizaines de titres pornographiques en Europe du Nord et de vulves montrées sans pudeur dans les sex-shops américains. Puis, un jour d'avril 1970, le magazine *Penthouse*, vendu en kiosque dans tout le pays, a inséré une toute petite photo de son « Pet of the Month » qui laissait voir un millimètre carré de touffe noire. En janvier 1971, *Playboy* publiait une photo similaire de la playmate Liv Lindeland, et comme la Terre ne s'est pas arrêtée de tourner, l'ensemble des magazines masculins d'Amérique leur ont emboîté le pas.

Une fois que *Playboy*, *Penthouse*, *Gallery*, *Genesis*, *Modern Man* et *Mr.* eurent montré du poil, Larry Flynt franchit un nouveau cap. En décembre 1974, Patti fut la première double page centrale rose de *Hustler*, une rousse naturelle posant vulve offerte et éclose. Dans les numéros suivants, les chéries de *Hustler* écartaient jambes et lèvres, exposant leur chair la plus intime à un stroboscope équipé d'un filtre rose particulier surnommé le *pussy spot*. En l'espace de cinq ans, les magazines masculins amé-

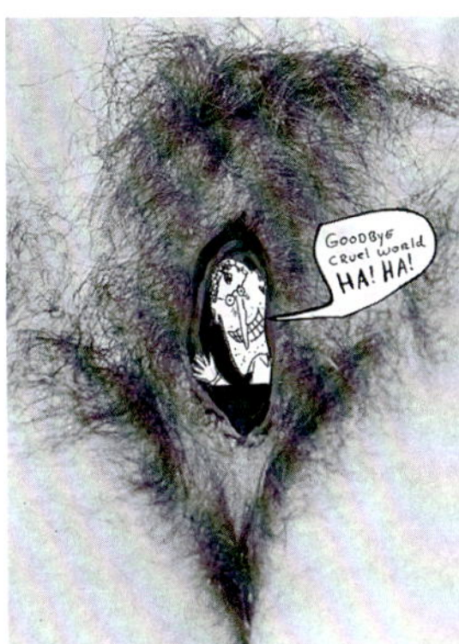

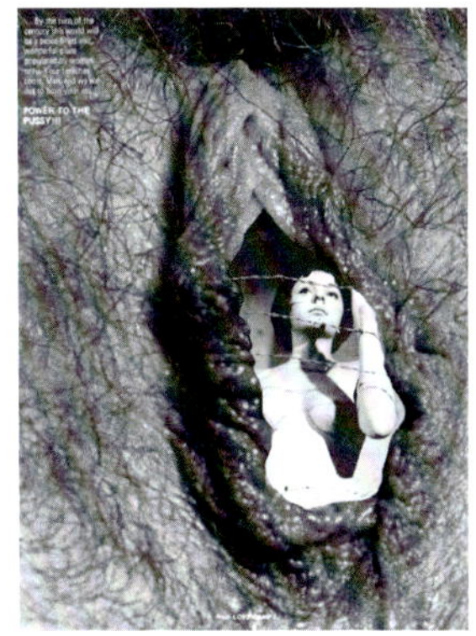

ricains sont passés d'une petite touffe noire au rose vif, pour aboutir à un marché où l'iconographie sexuelle est devenue intoxicante. Précisons que les hommes ne sont pas les uniques fomenteurs de cette libération pubienne.

La plupart des photos contenues dans ce livre ont été prises entre 1967 et 1979, et l'état d'esprit de l'époque se reflète sur le visage des modèles. À la fin des années 1970, cependant, l'humeur change. Le porno est devenu une industrie tentaculaire et rentable, et la chatte un lieu commun. Ce qui était choquant quelques années plus tôt n'est plus qu'un ingrédient de la recette, avec les seins gonflés et l'expression interchangeable et étudiée du visage.

Dans les années 1990, le réalisateur de porno John « Buttman » Stagliano affirmait à Martin Amis que le vagin était « du pipi de chat » pour expliquer l'obsession croissante de l'Amérique pour la sodomie. Cette tendance a perduré dans les années 2000, quand le porno commercial s'est mis à explorer les thèmes extrêmes dans sa bataille contre la toute-puissance d'Internet. Si les amateurs ne voulaient plus payer pour voir des gangs-bangs anaux, il semblait évident qu'un petit minou suranné, aussi épilé et musclé soit-il, n'éveillerait pas leur intérêt.

Aujourd'hui, en réaction contre les entre-jambes cliniques et esthétisés d'une industrie pornographique en perte de vitesse, qui tente de survivre au succès de concurrents comme Pornhub – avec ses contenus en accès gratuit et illimité –, il semble que nous vivions les prémices d'un retour à l'esprit des années 1970. Les chounes poilues sont la nouvelle niche en vogue sur Internet, la première célébration de la vulve par le porno depuis près de vingt ans. De jeunes professionnelles comme Raven Rockette, Simone Delilah ou Keira Croft ont opté pour des pubis duveteux, provoquant la panique chez leurs consœurs adeptes de l'épilation intégrale. Quand Sasha Grey a fait une apparition dans la série télé *Entourage* en août 2010 en arborant un triangle pileux naturel, Twitter s'est trouvé saturé de commentaires du type « Beurk ! », « Répugnant », « Oh ! Le barbichu de barbare ! » ou « C'est ça, 2010 ! ». Déboussolée, Grey s'est fendue d'une réponse sur le même réseau social : « C'est à

ça que ressemble une femme adulte…
Je suis heureuse de contribuer à ce
que ce soit à nouveau accepté :-) La
mode fonctionne par cycles ! »

Se pourrait-il qu'une nouvelle généra-
tion post-porno soit en train d'émerger,
des gens raisonnables qui, même au sein
de l'industrie, refusent de se plier aux
exigences d'un soi-disant glamour entiè-
rement artificiel ? Peut-être le siècle à ve-
nir sera-t-il plus fana de foufoune que ne
l'a été le précédent… millénaire, ce d'une
façon toutefois moins obsessionnelle et
brutale qu'au paléolithique. En tant que
propriétaire de minou, j'aime à le penser,
et je vous offre pour conclure cet autre
poème, écrit en 1830 pour apprendre aux
enfants à respecter leurs animaux domes-
tiques, et par extension le minou de l'âge
adulte, trop longtemps incompris et se-
crètement adoré :

J'adore les petits minous
Leur fourrure est si chaude
Et si je les traite bien
Ils ne me feront aucun mal

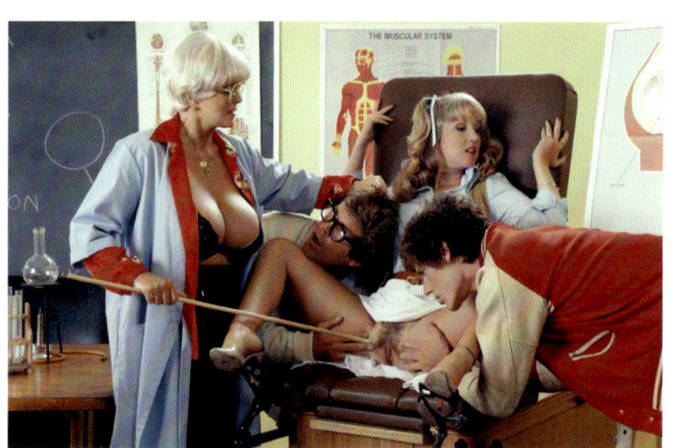

LEFT Adult star Candy Samples
poses as a sex education teacher,
circa 1988. Photo by Tommy
Malibu.

OPPOSITE Photographers have
never been able to resist liken-
ing the vulva to the mouth, as
in the poem that opens this
introduction. Circa 1985.

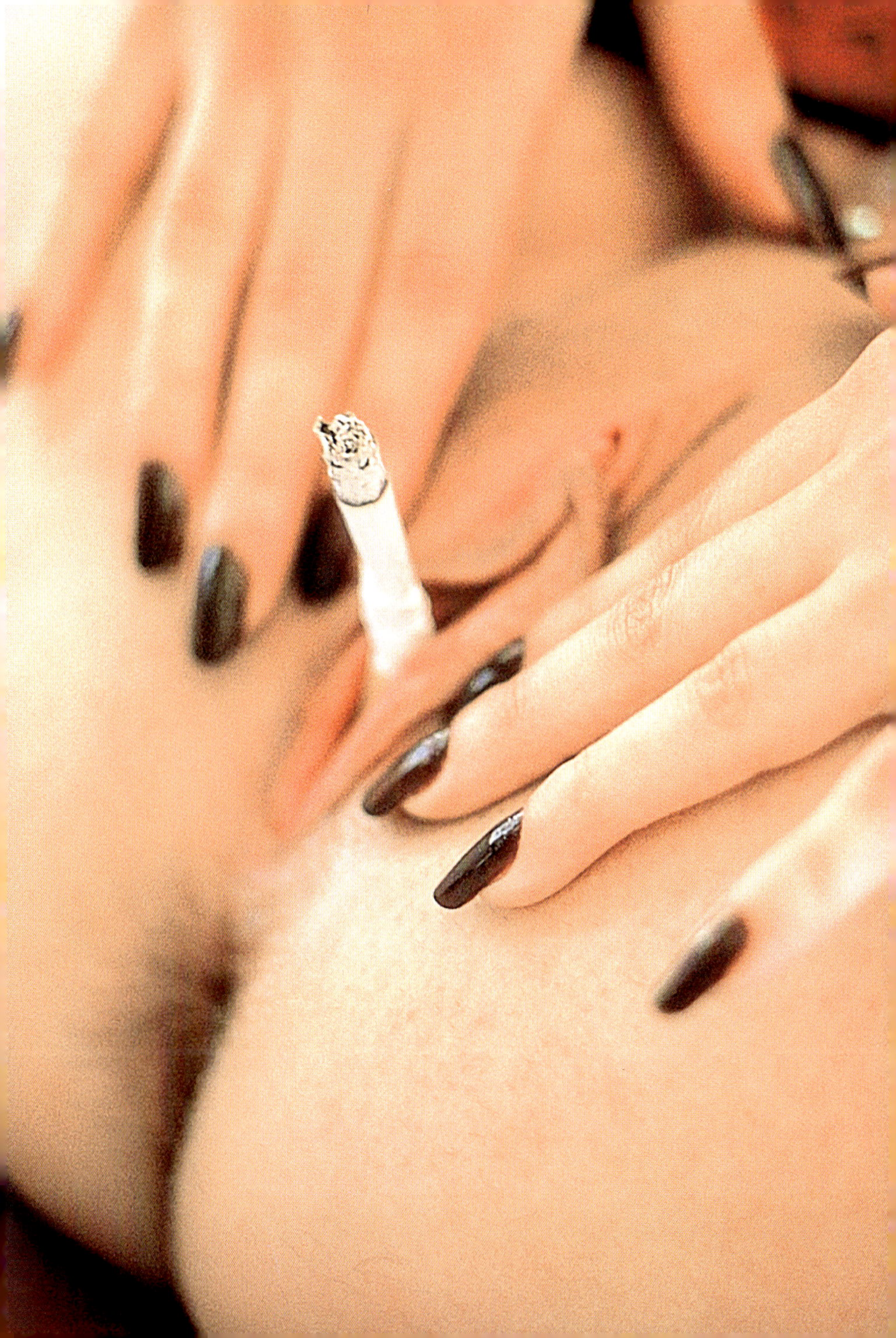

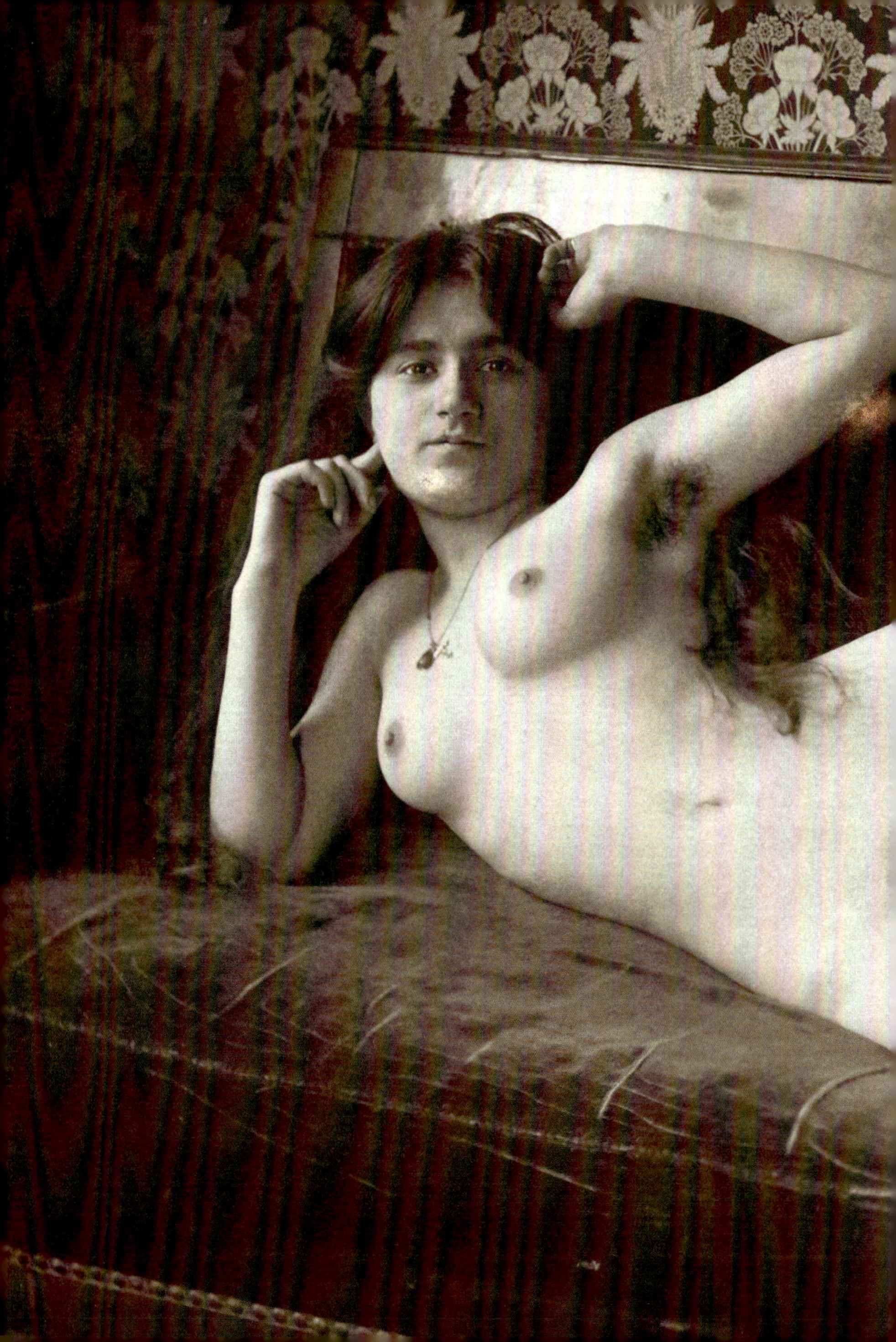

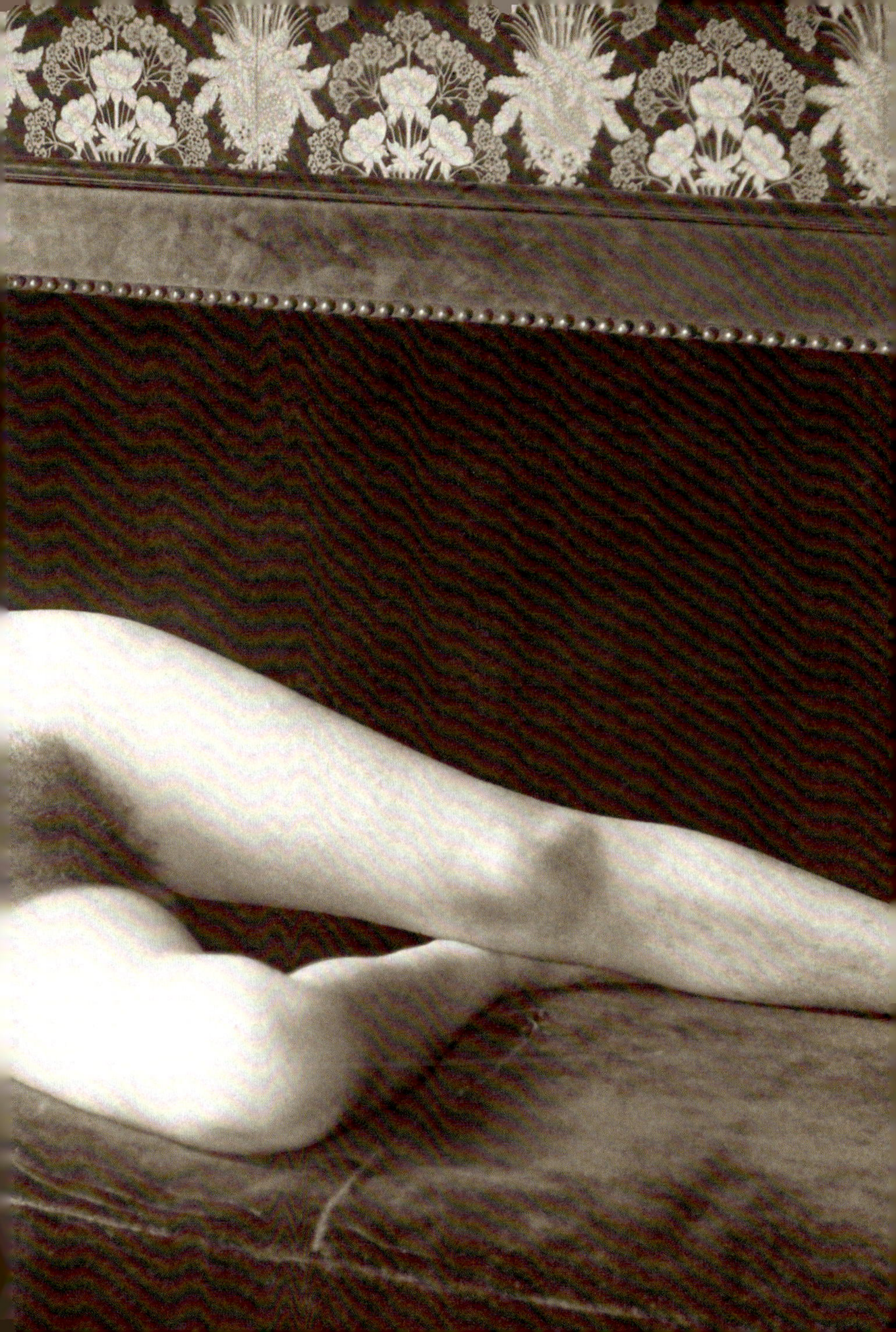

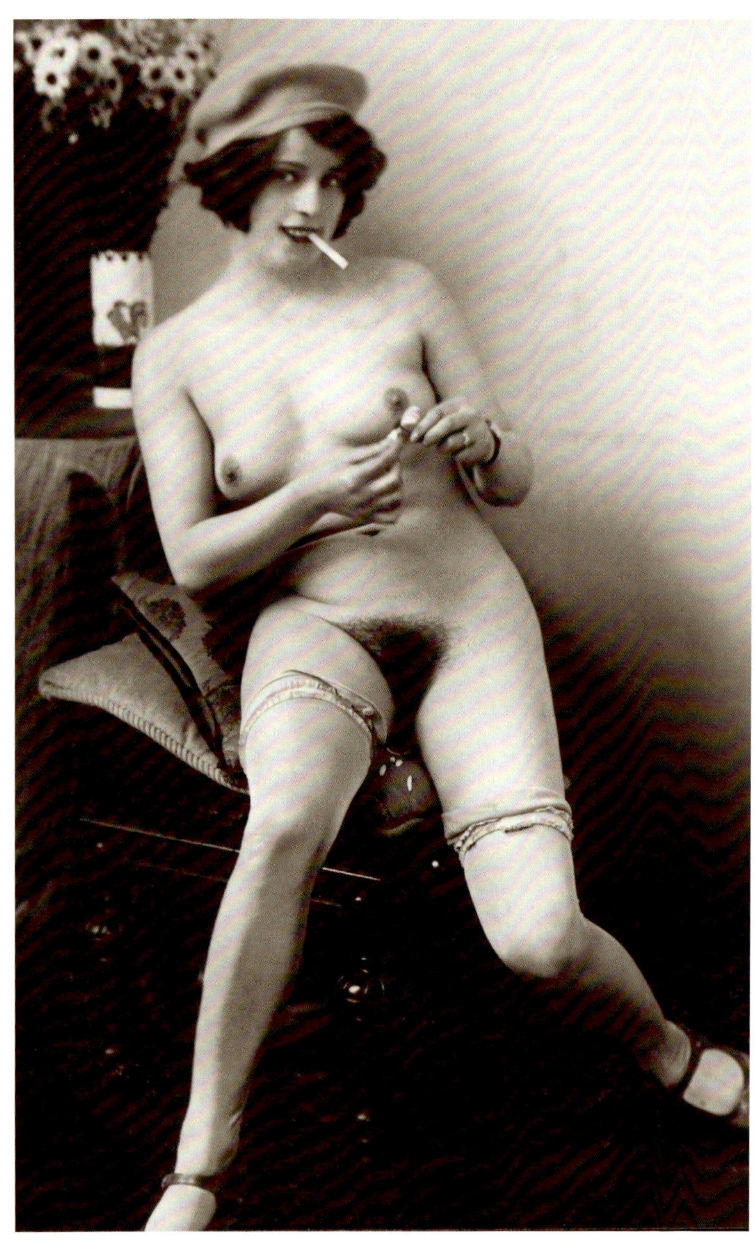

PAGES 26-27 **Unknown**

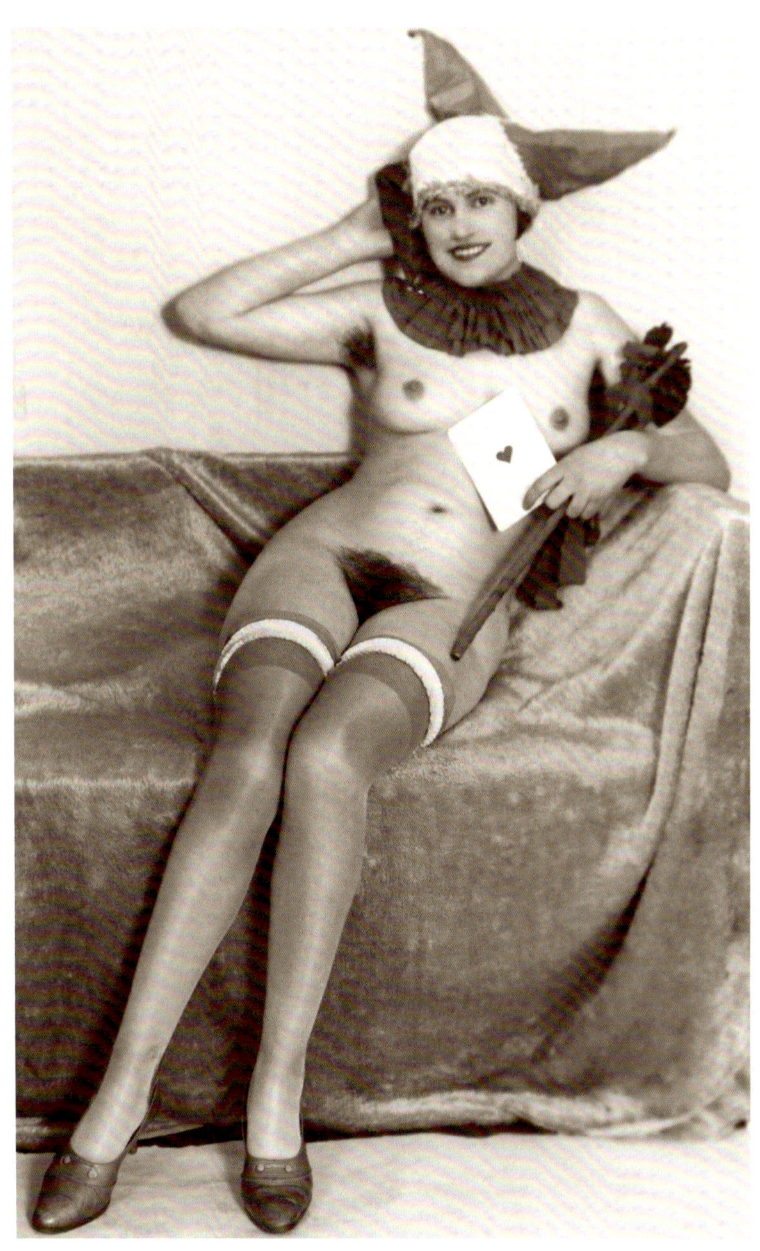

OPPOSITE AND ABOVE **French postcards made for the German market**

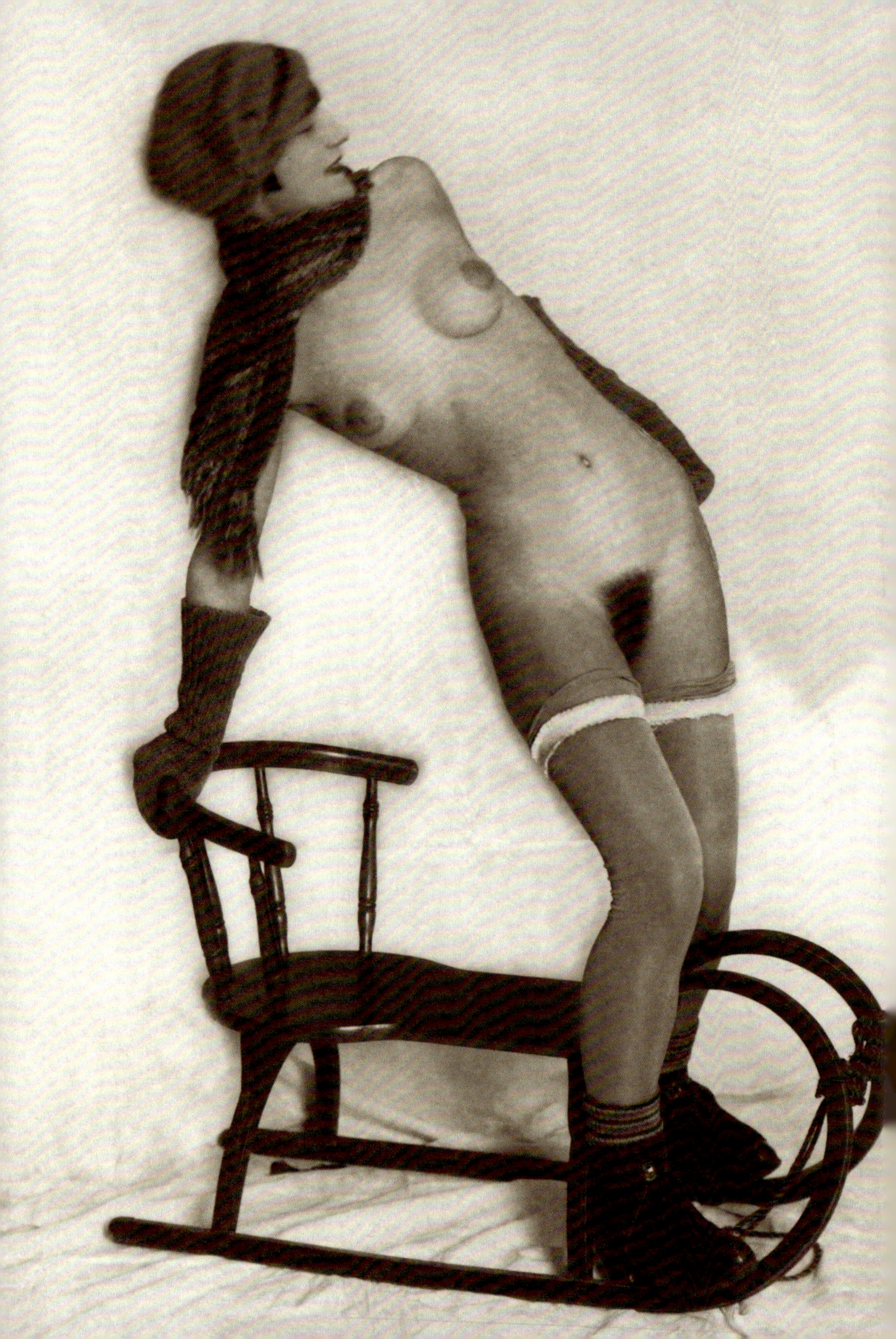

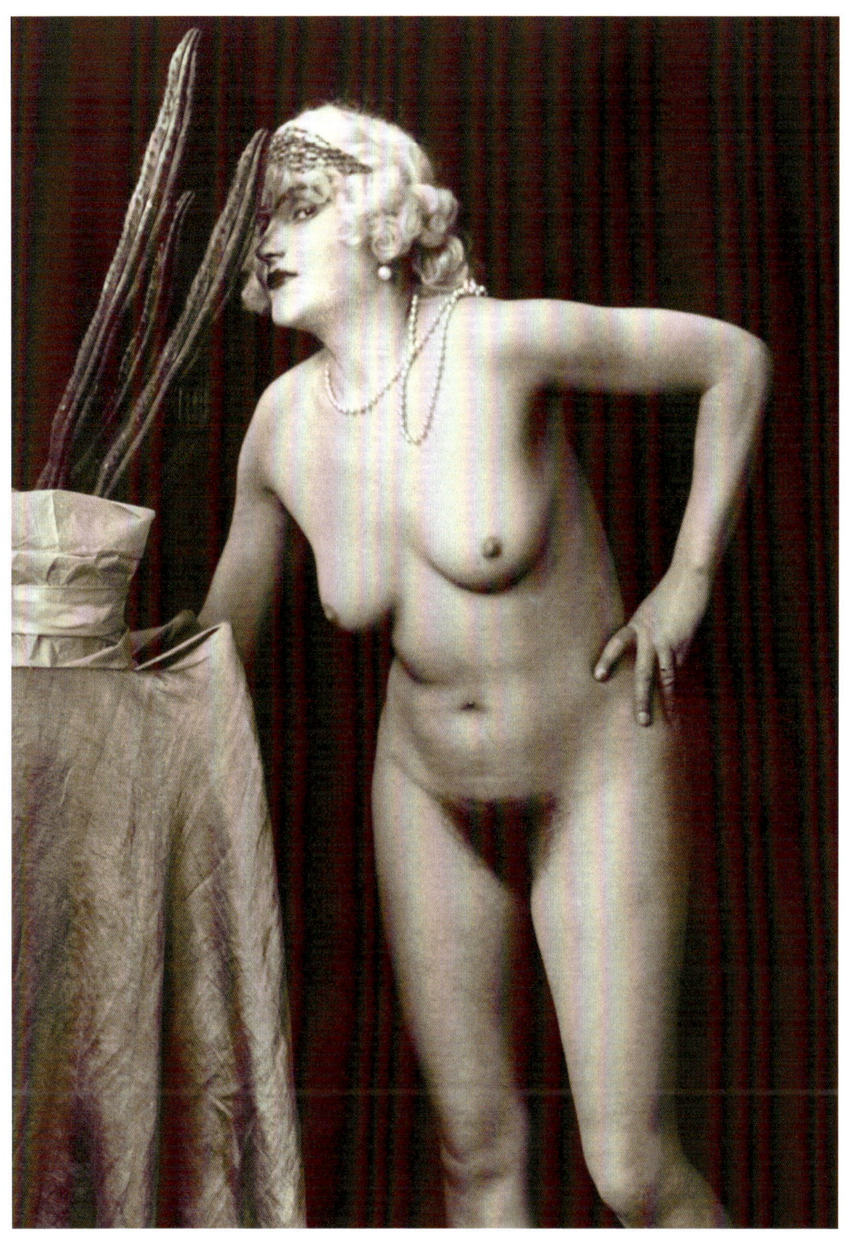

OPPOSITE AND ABOVE **French postcards made for the German market**

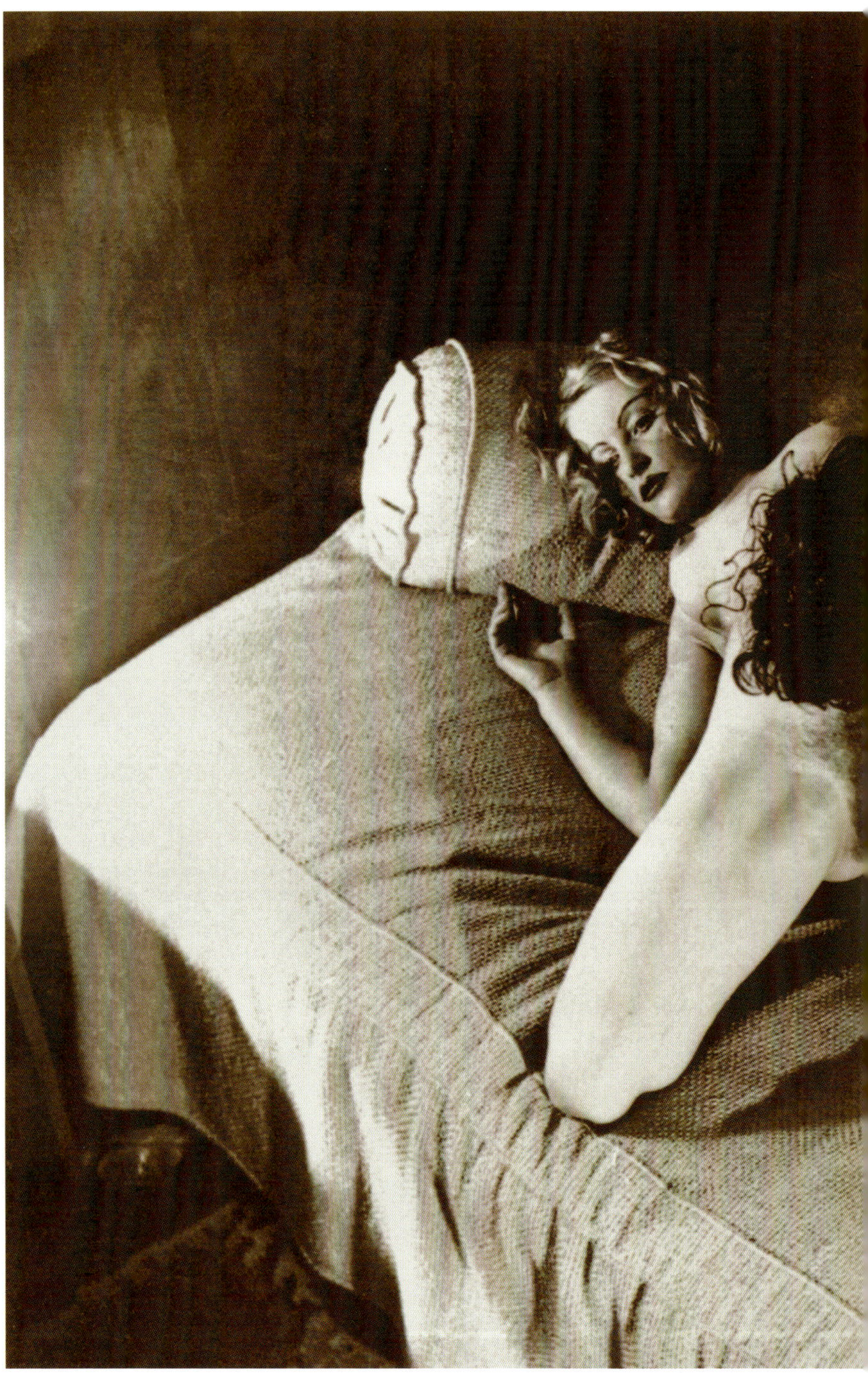

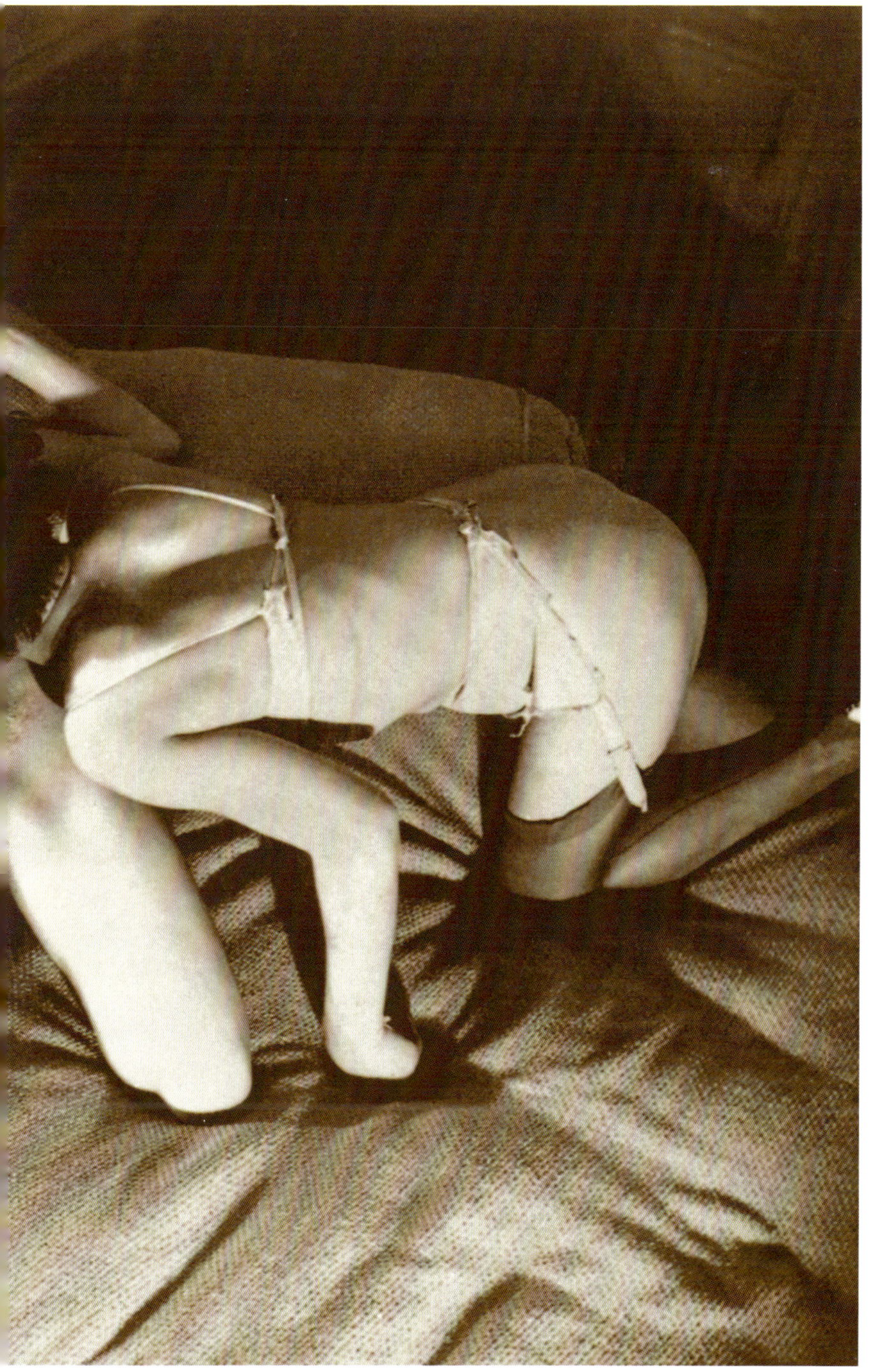

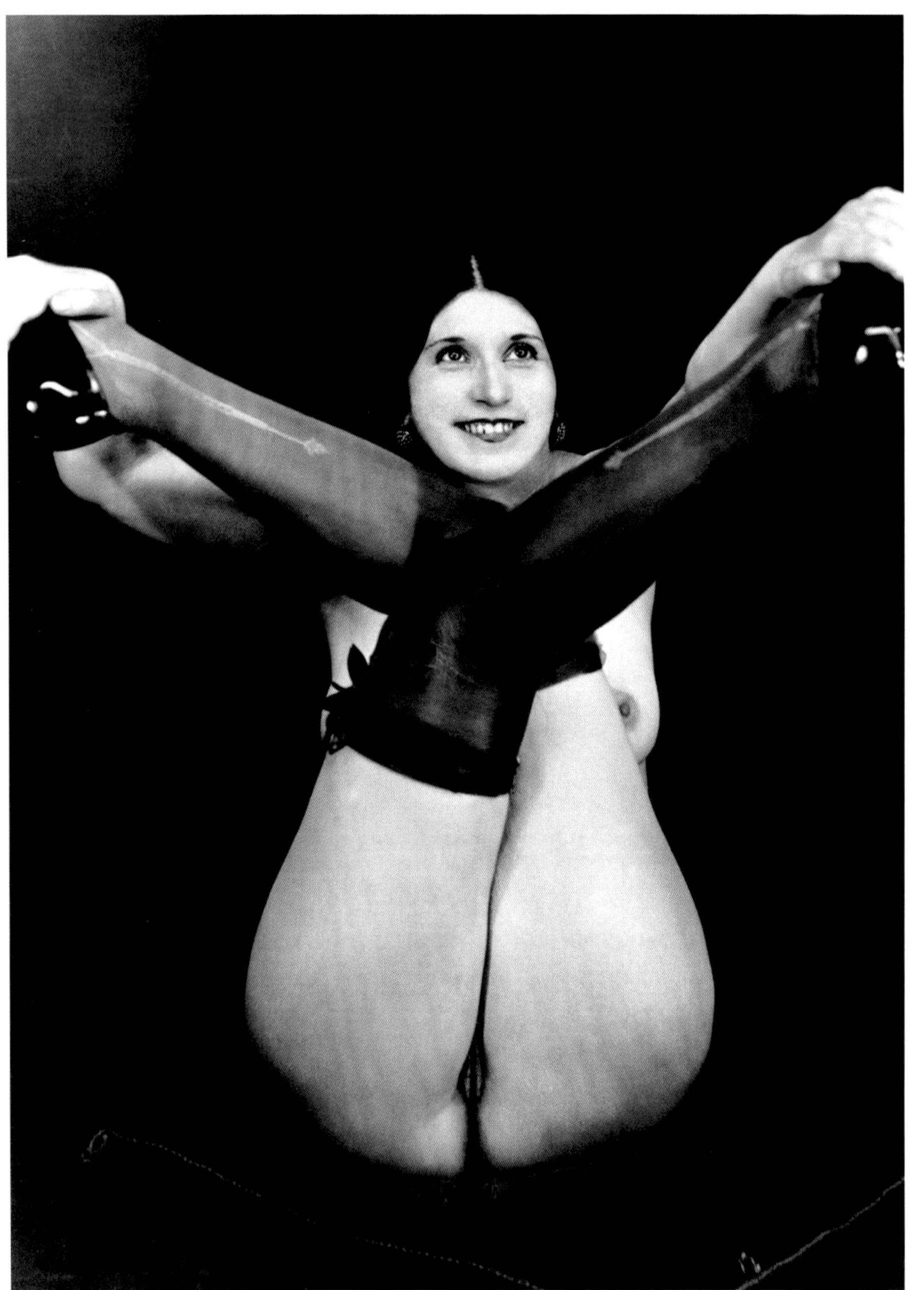

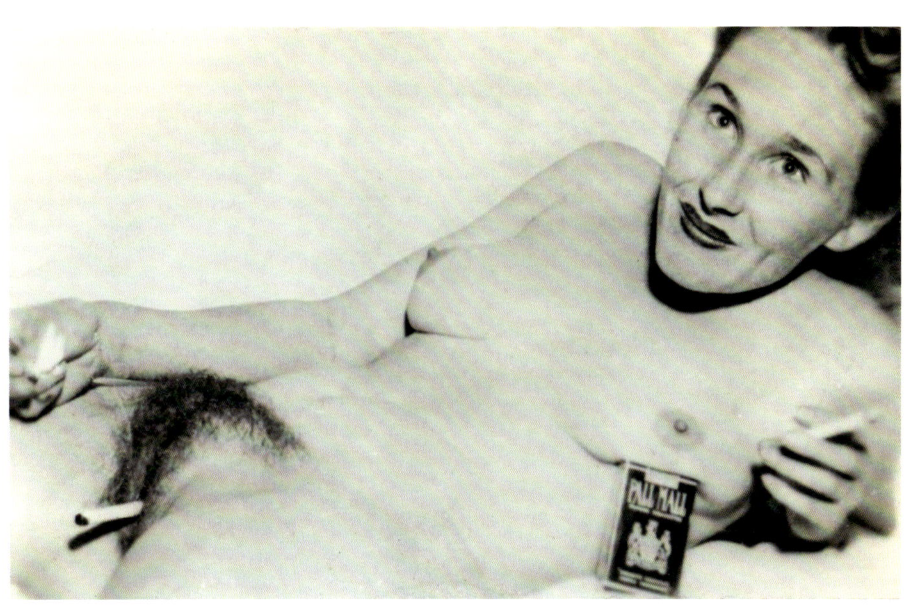

PAGES 32-33 AND OPPOSITE **Unknown**
ABOVE **The "smoking pussy" was a common pornography trope throughout the 20th century. This model, posing with Pall Mall "Famous Cigarettes," dates to the 1940s.**
PAGES 36-37 **Unknown**, MONSIEUR X, C. 1925, STEVEN KASHER GALLERY, NEW YORK

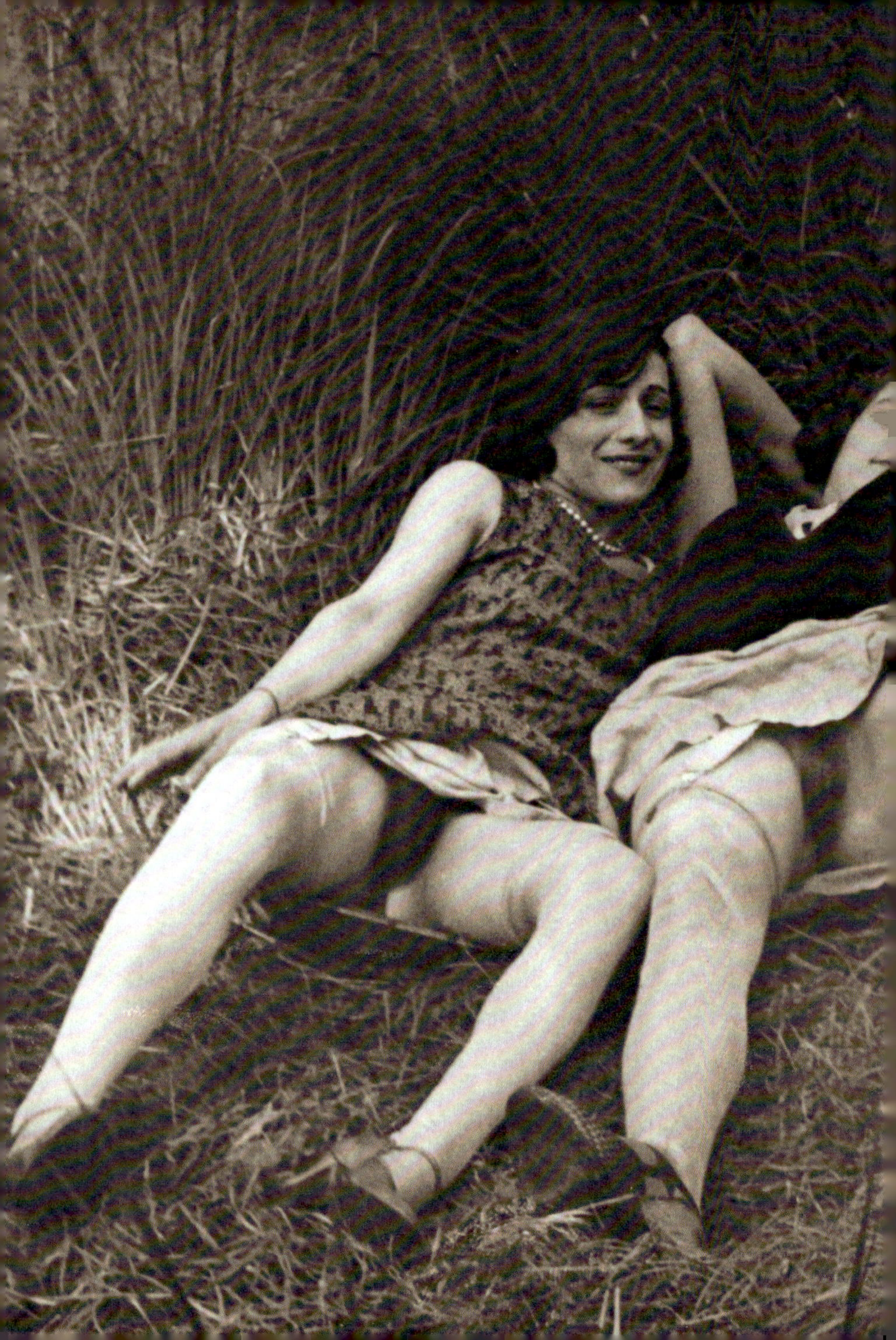

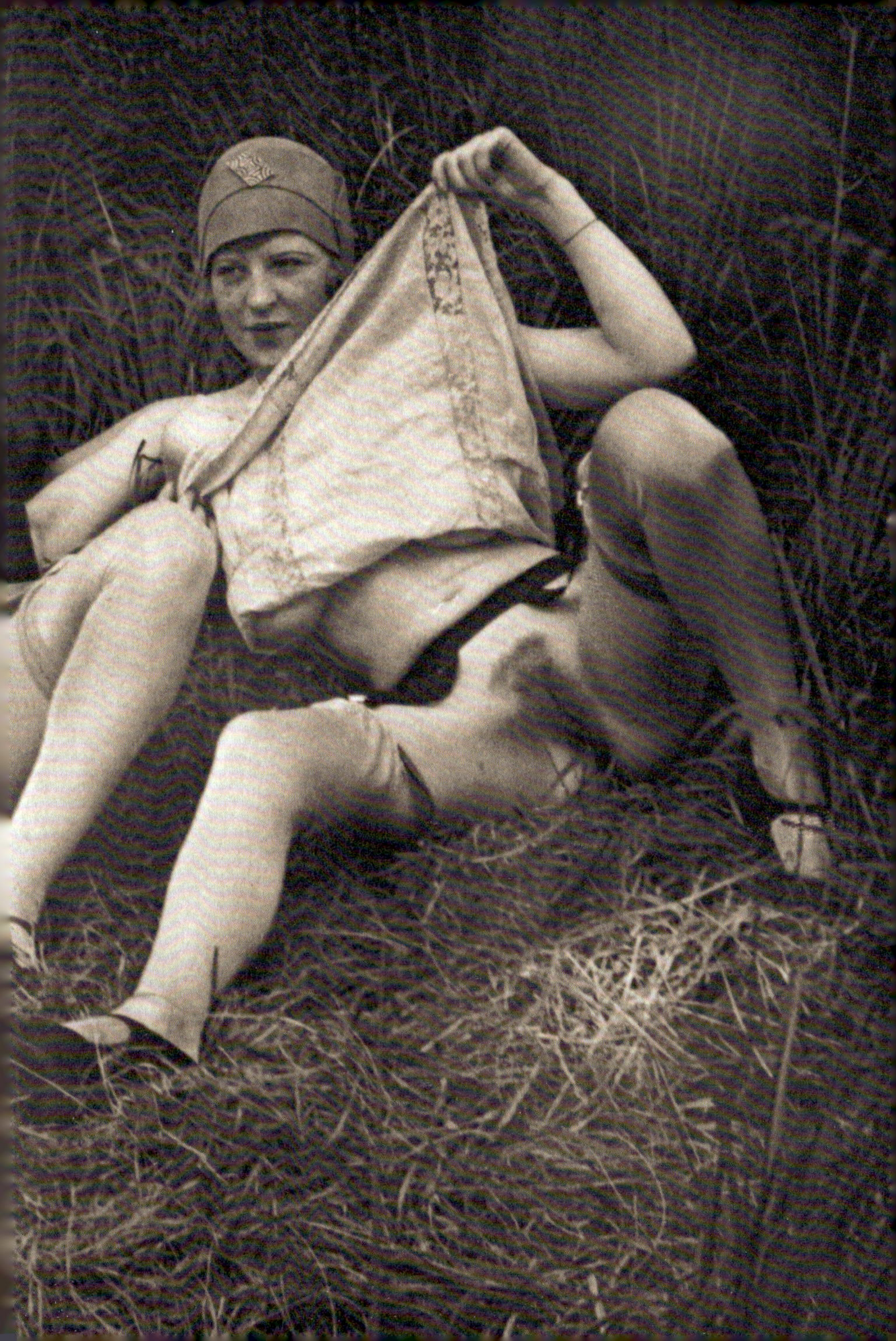

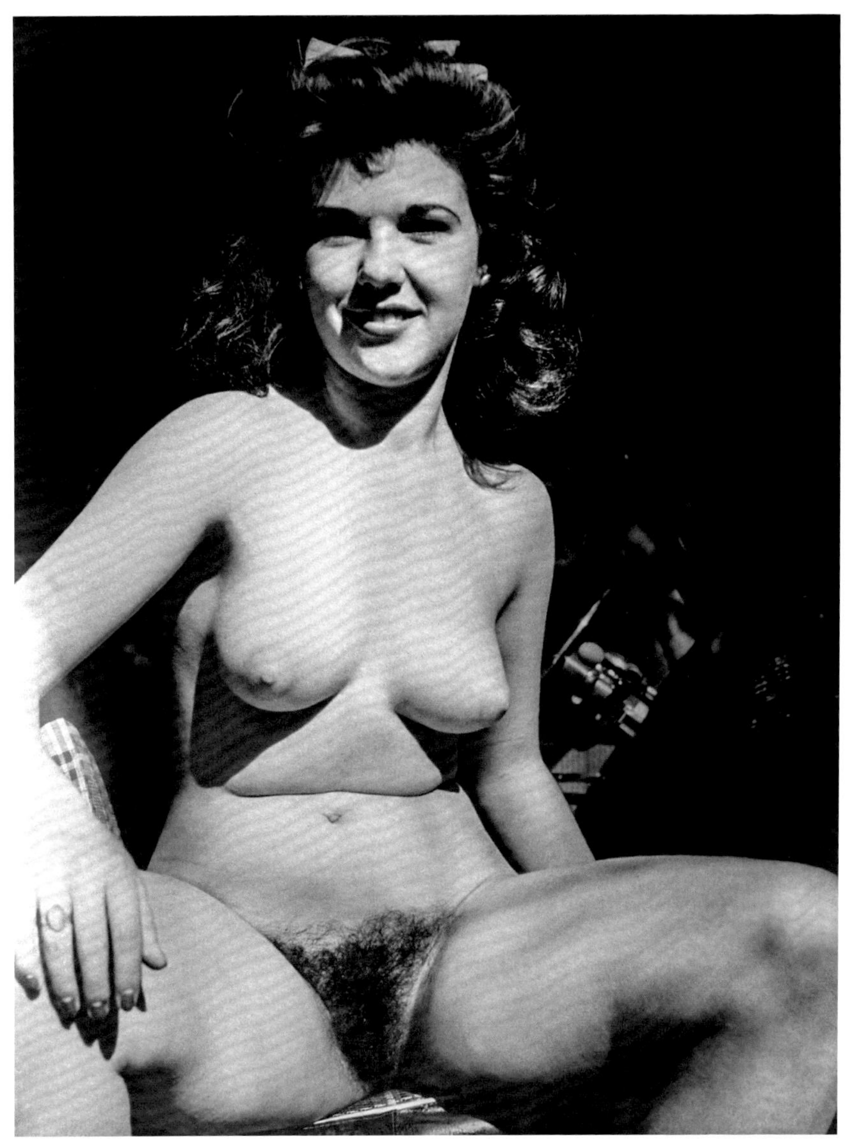

Unknown

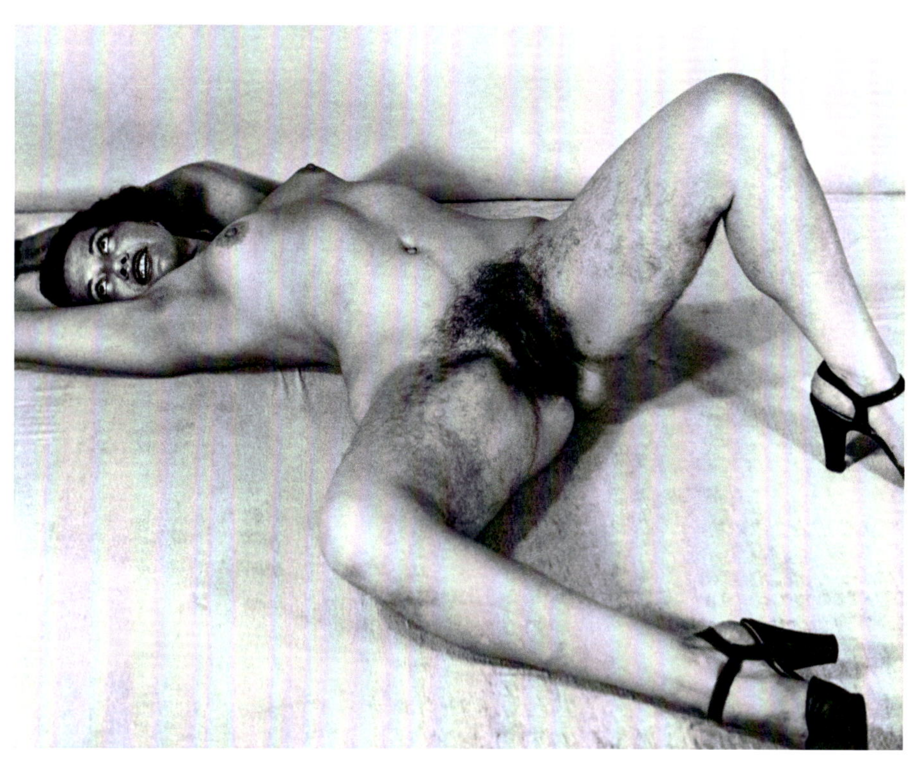

ABOVE **Most American women did not shave their legs until 1945.**
Unknown, circa 1940.
PAGES 40-41 **Unknown**

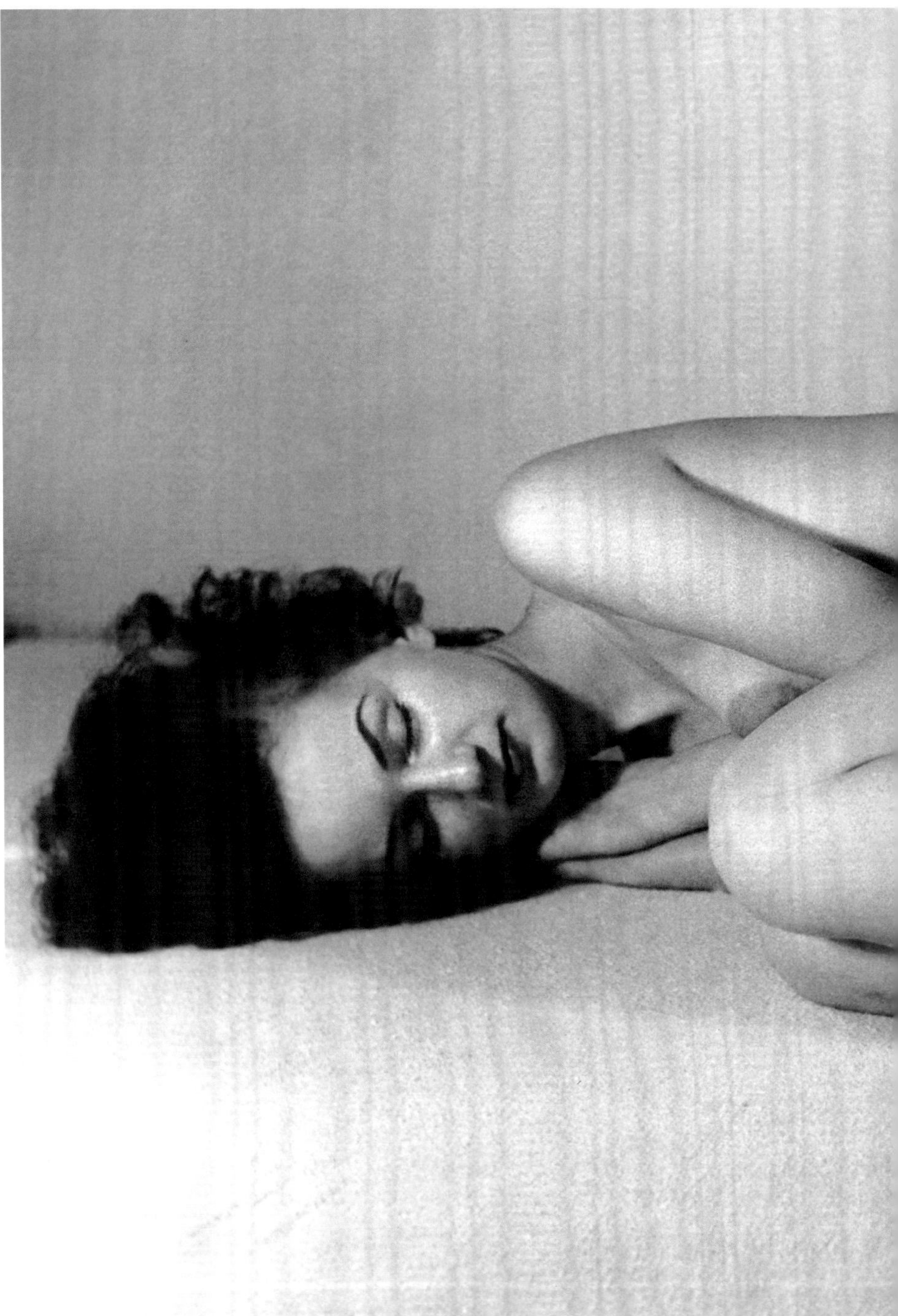

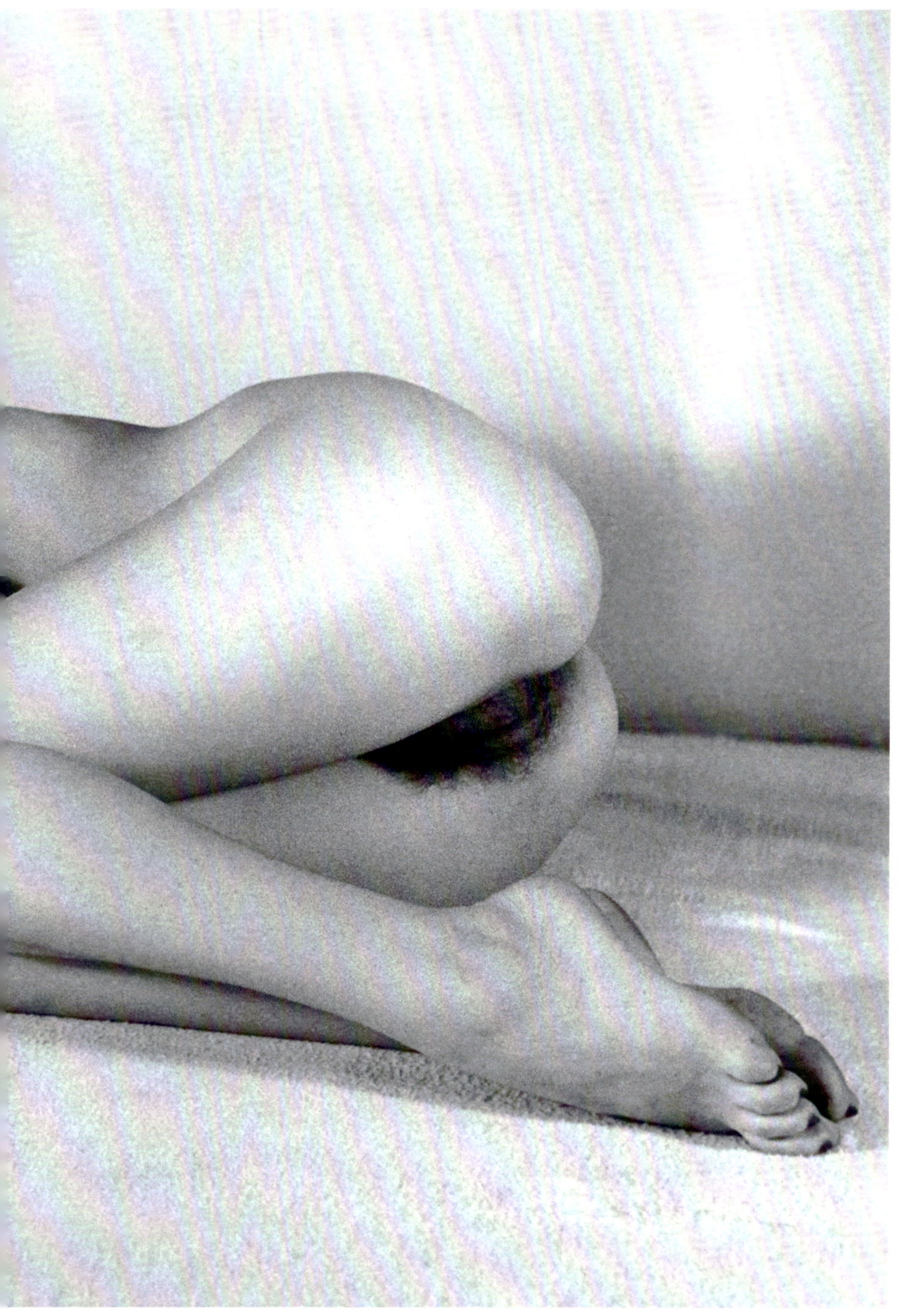

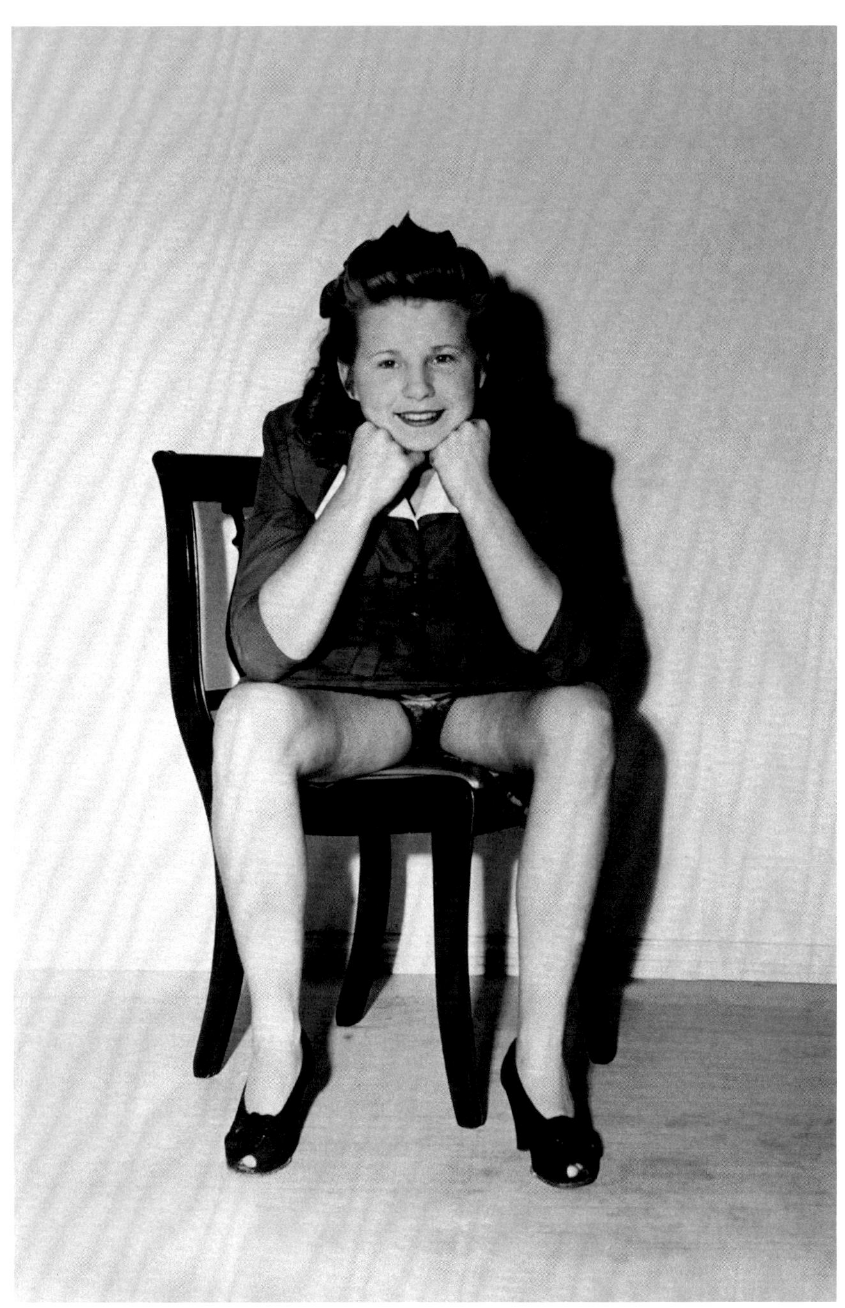

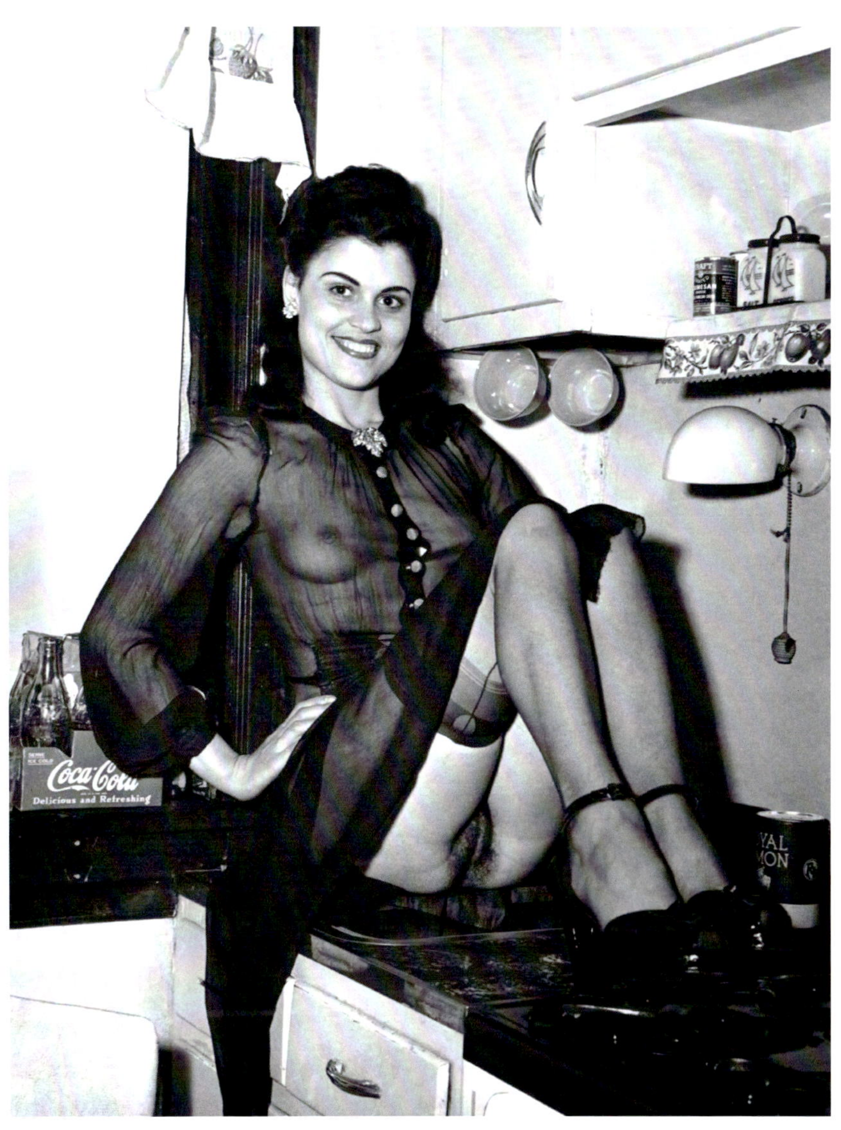

OPPOSITE AND ABOVE **Unknown**

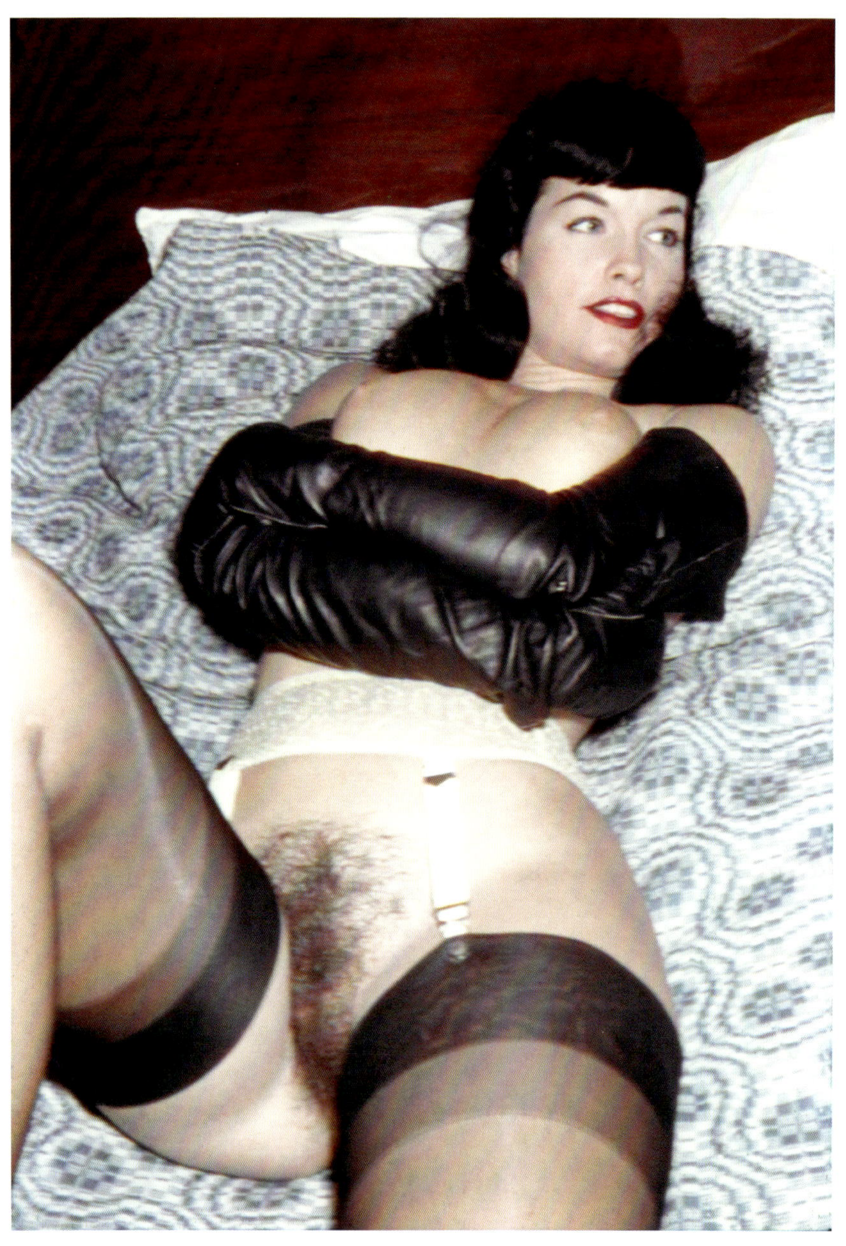

ABOVE AND OPPOSITE **Bettie Page**, CHARLES WEST   PAGES 46-47 **Julie**, CHARLES WEST

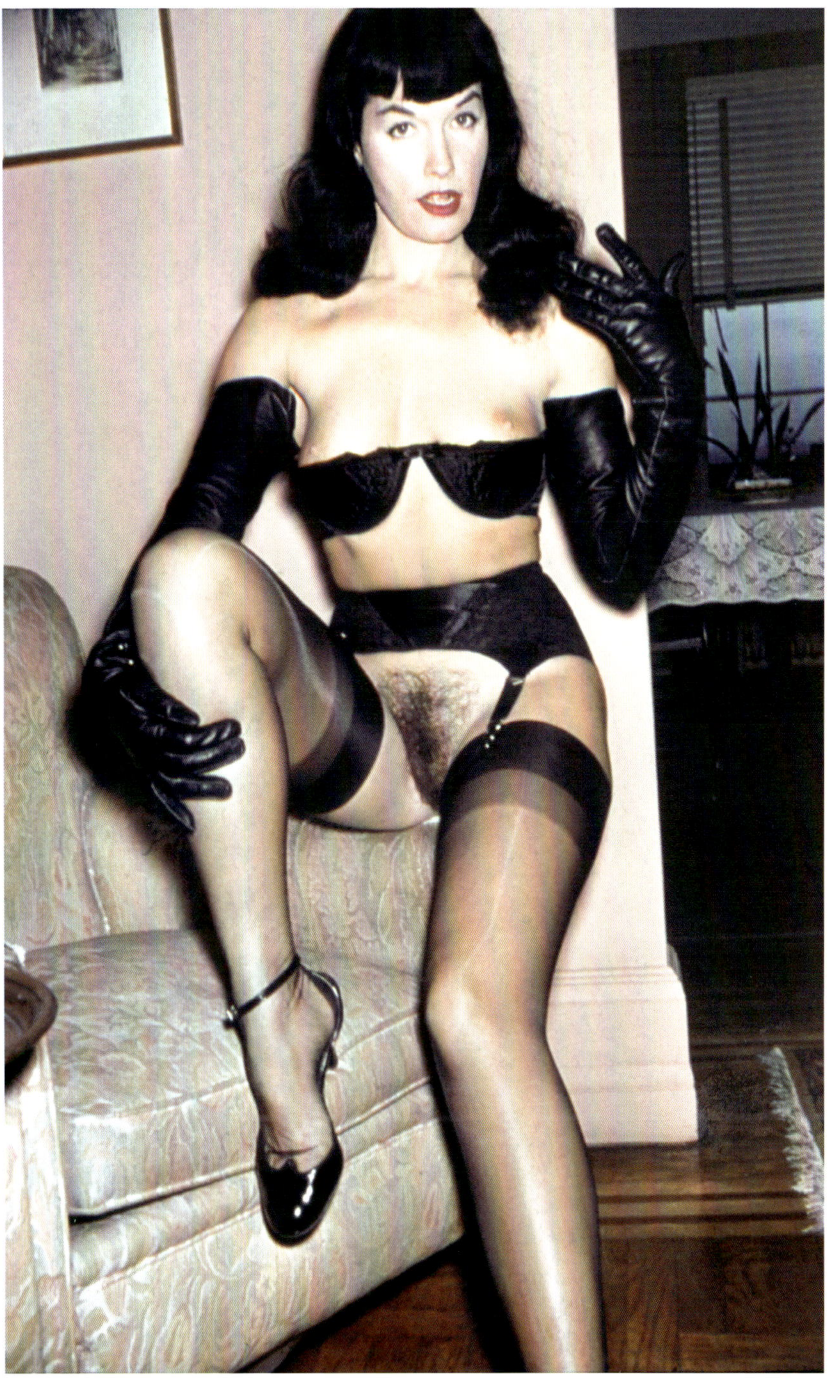

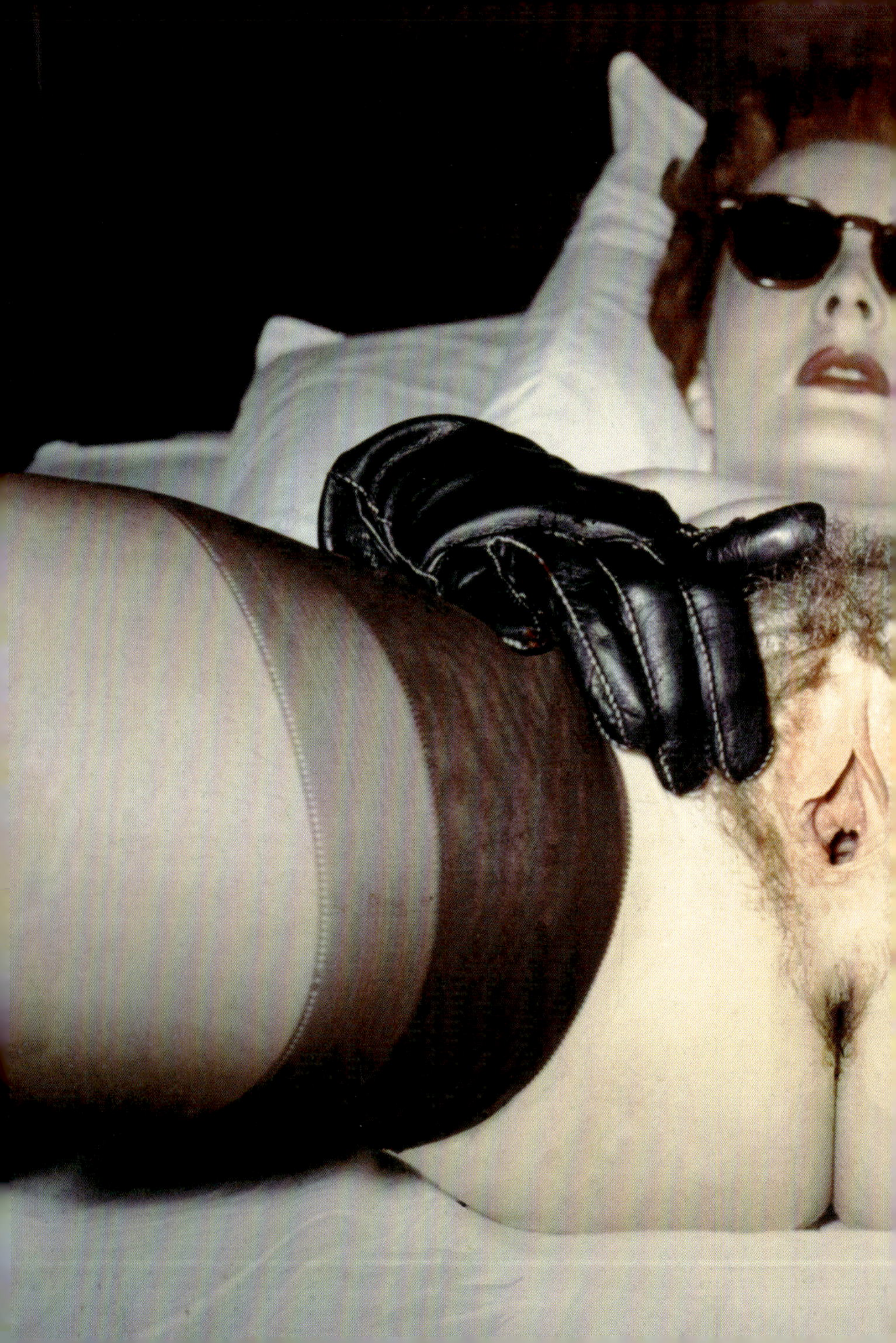

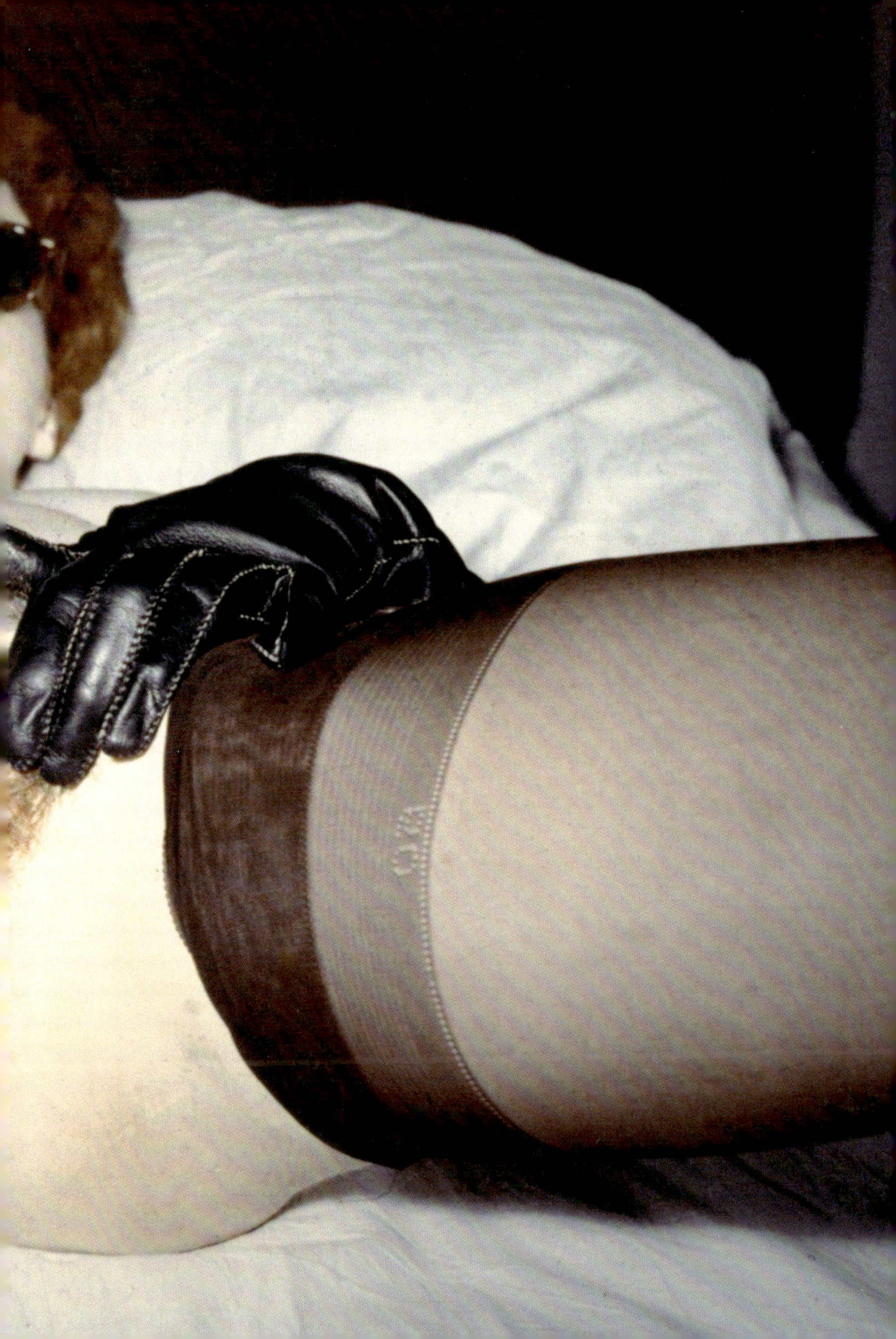

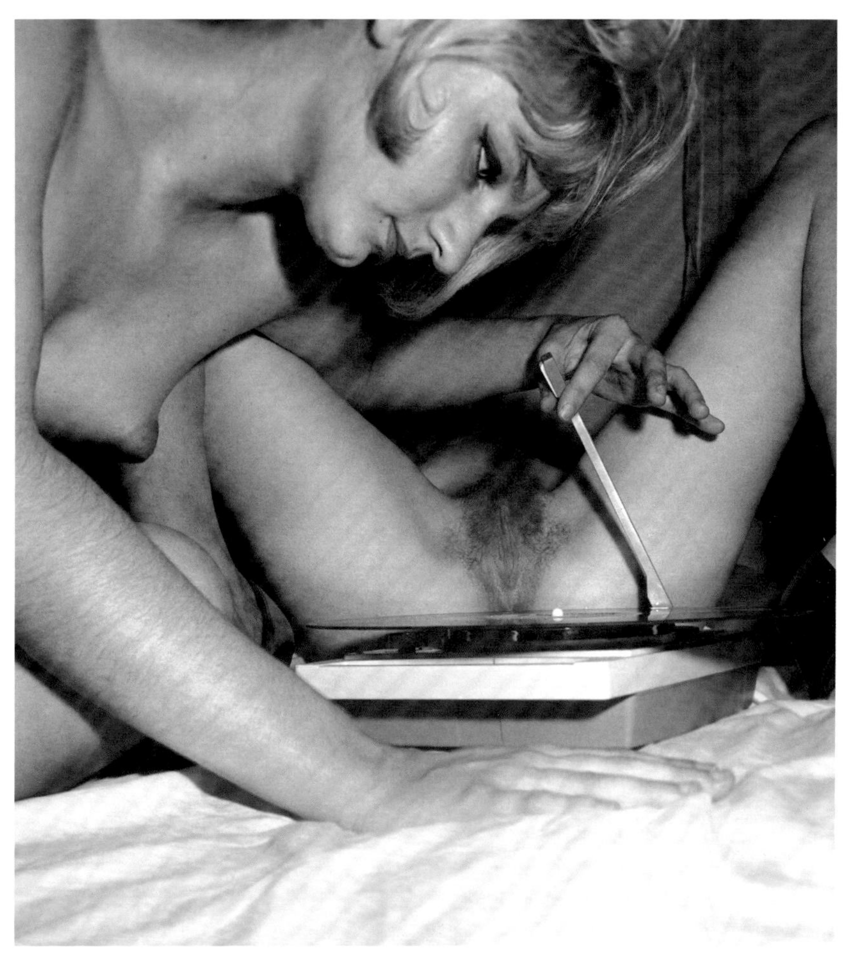

Unknown

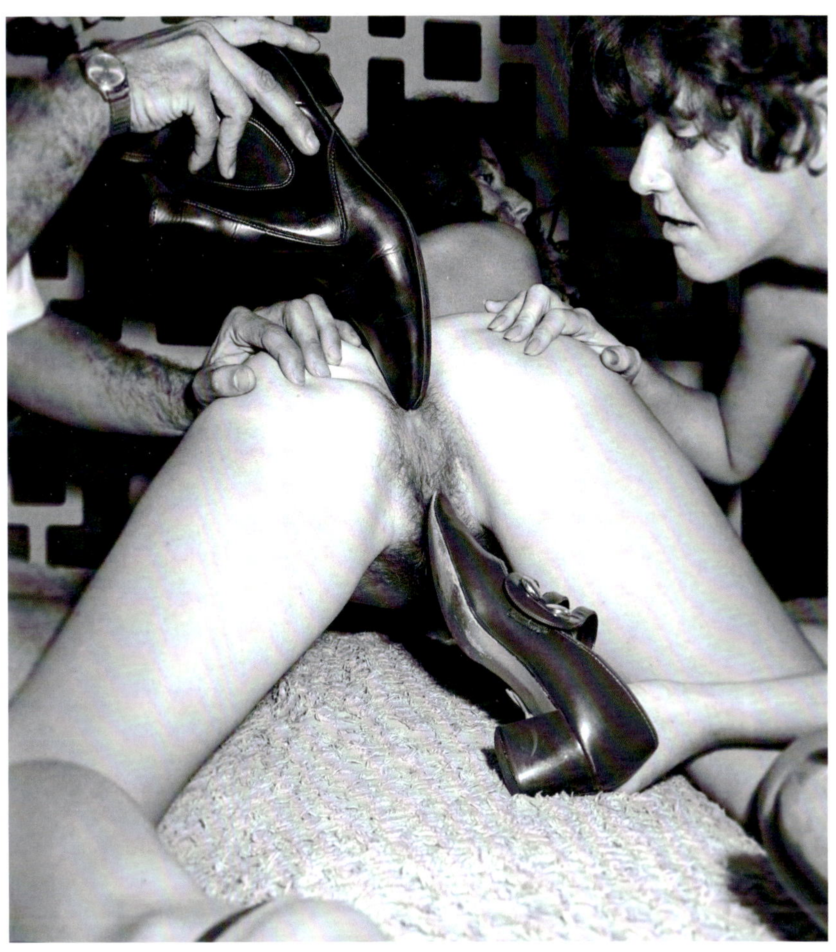

Unknown

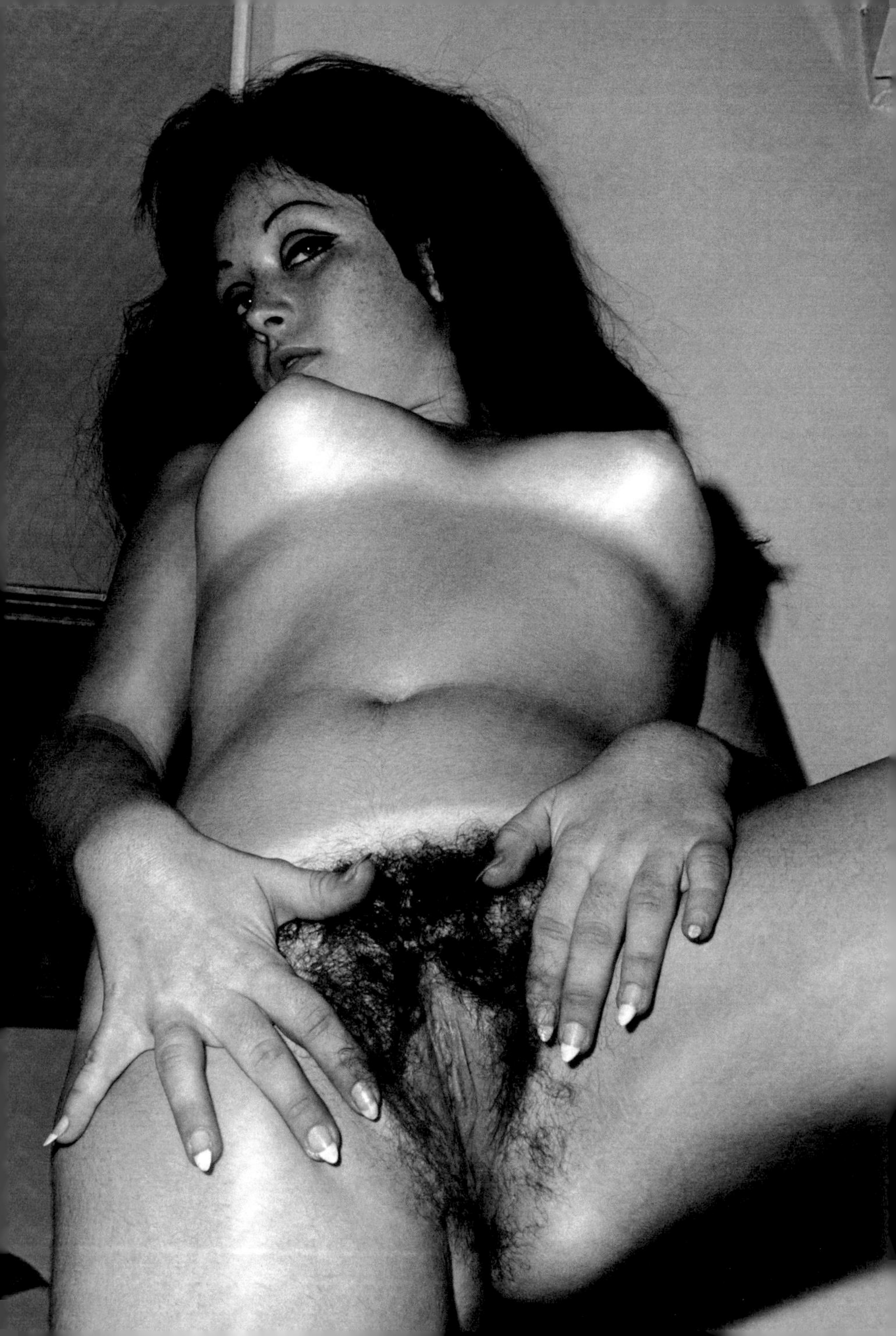

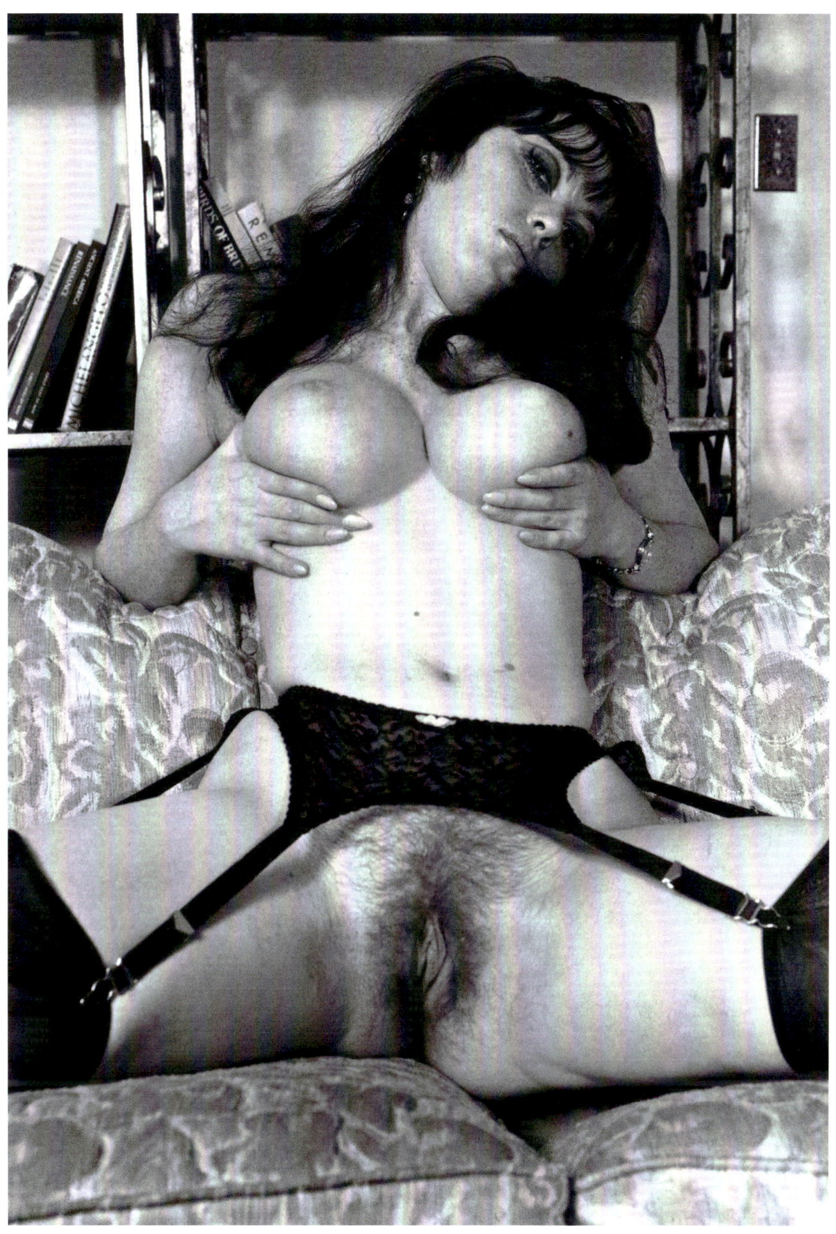

OPPOSITE AND ABOVE **Unknown**

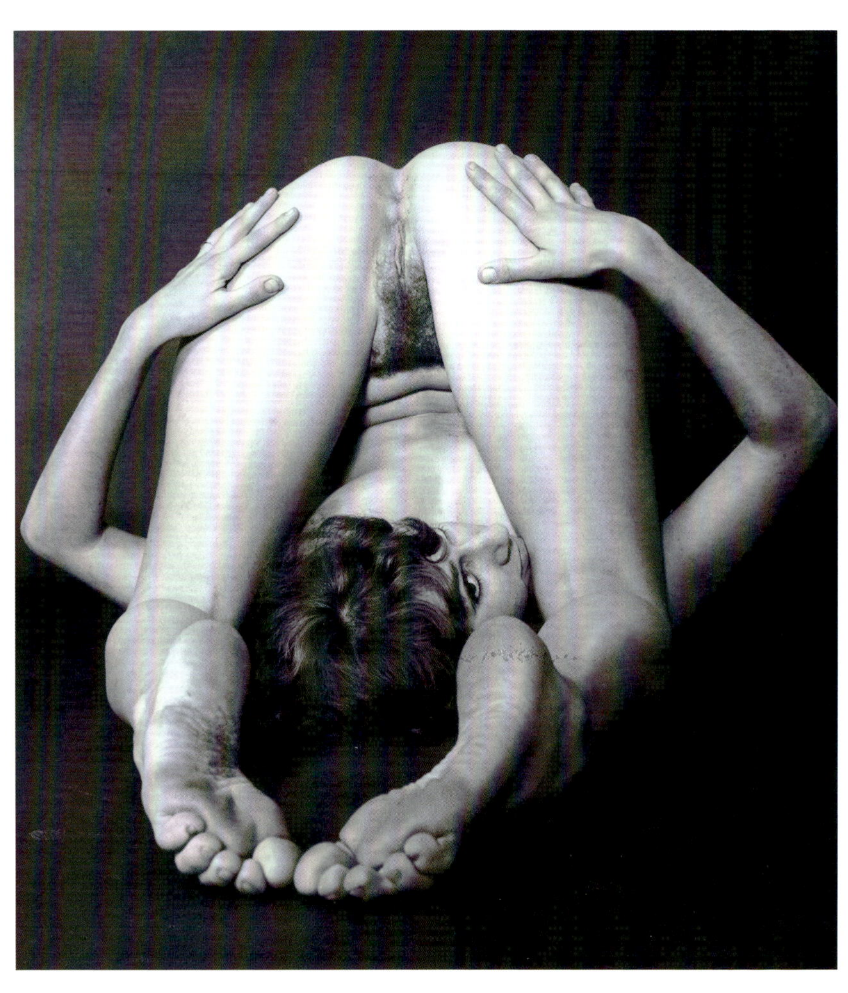

ABOVE **Unknown**   OPPOSITE **Rebecca Perlman**

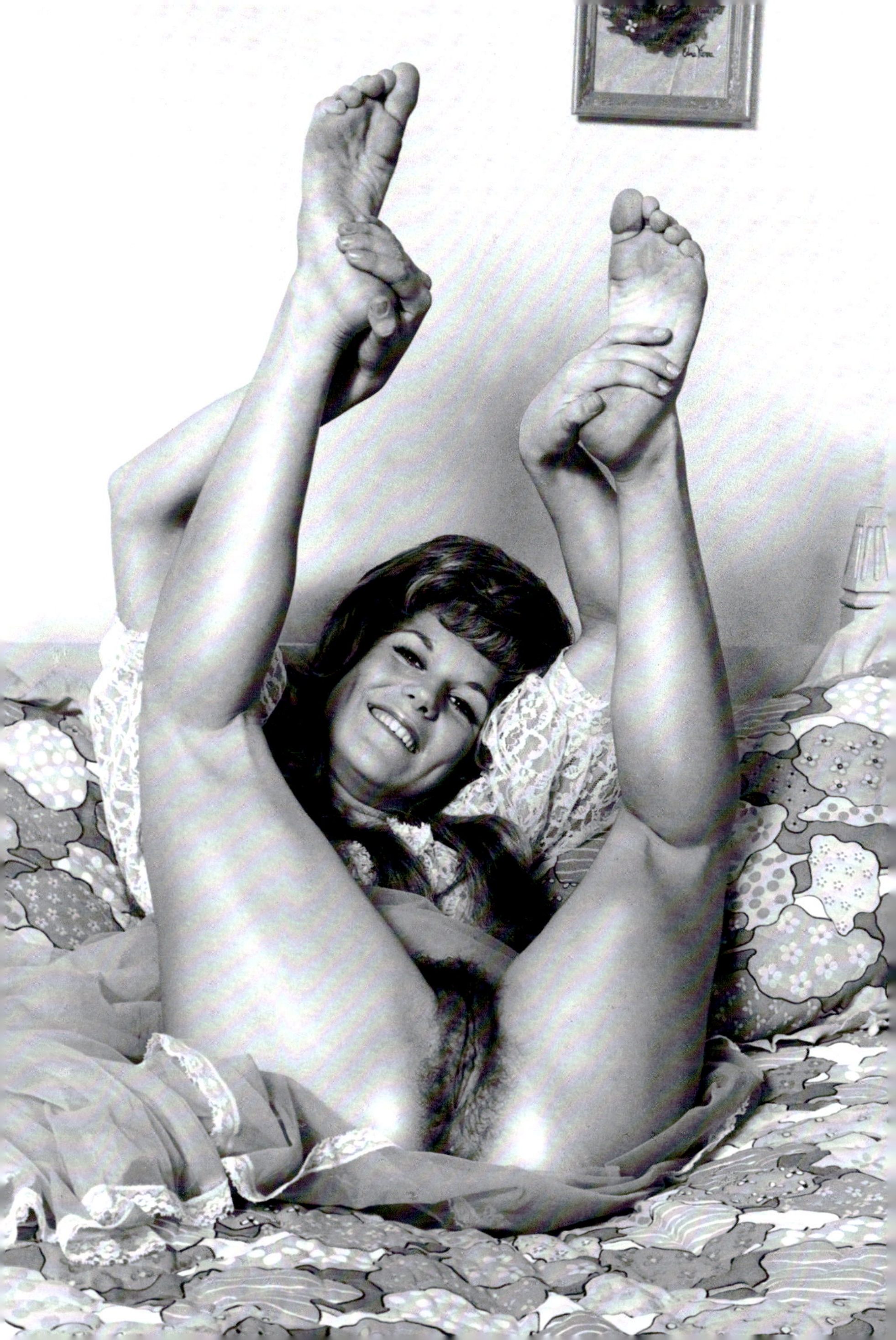

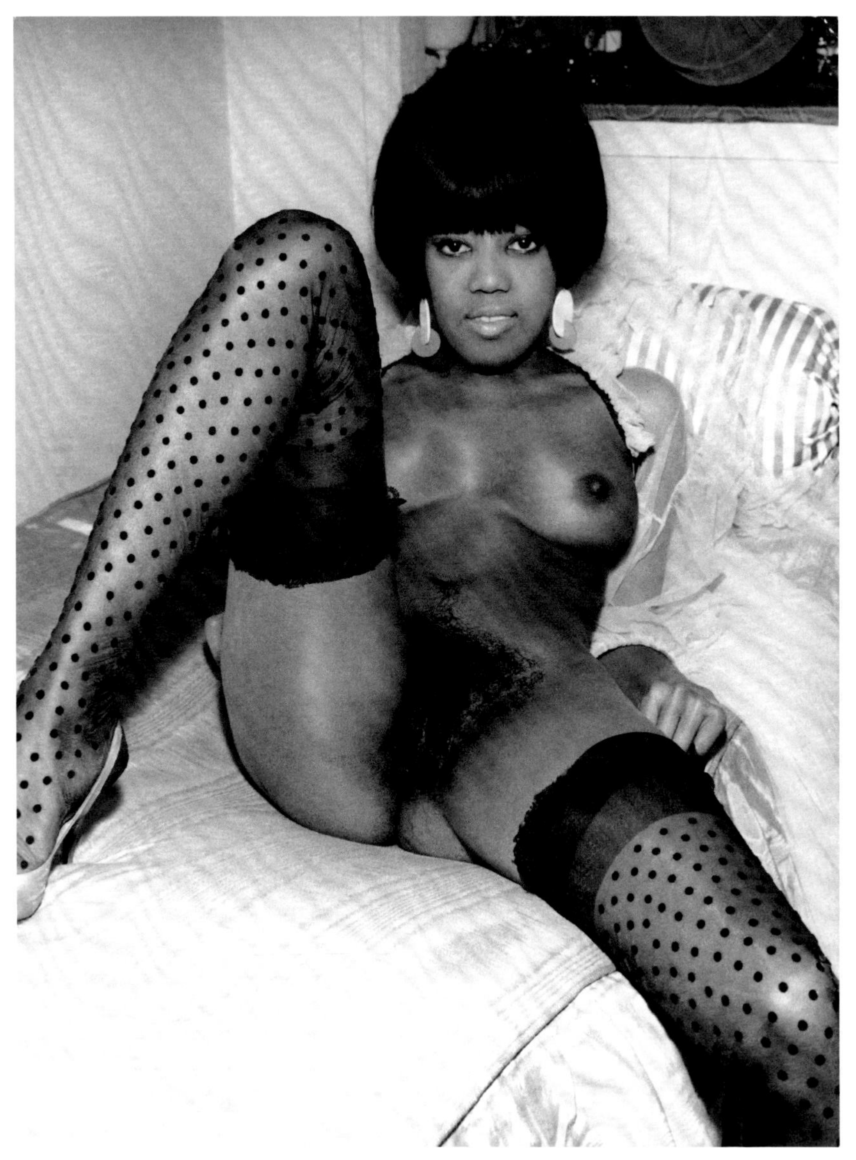

Unknown

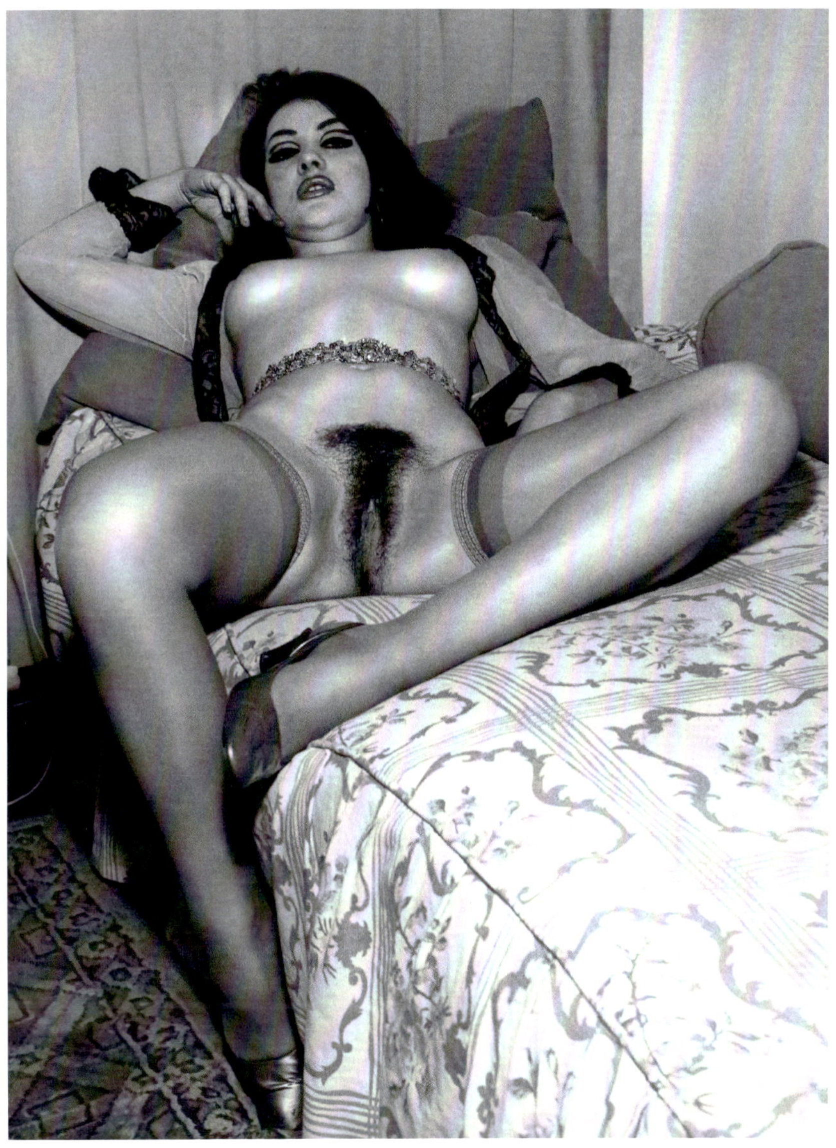

Unknown

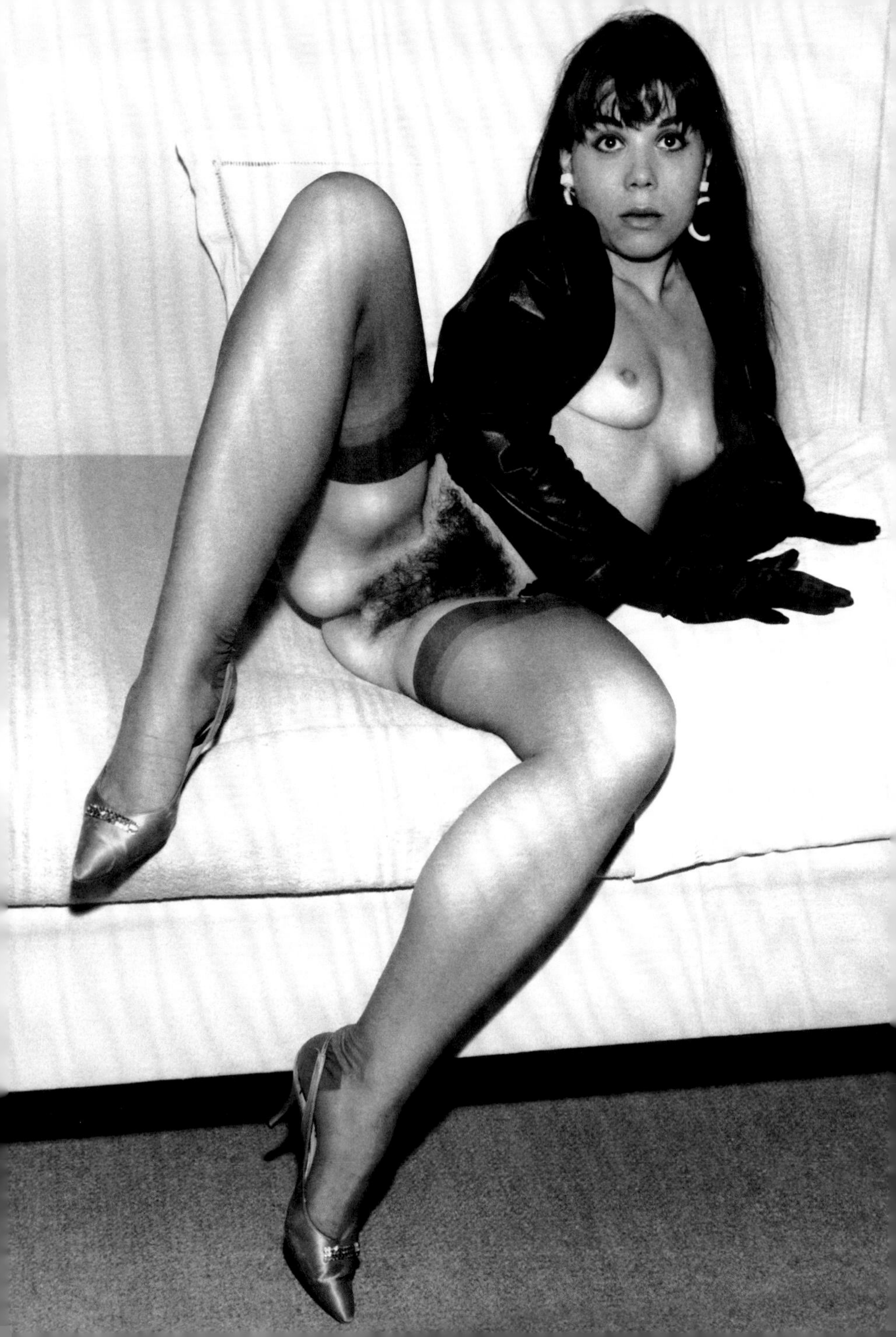

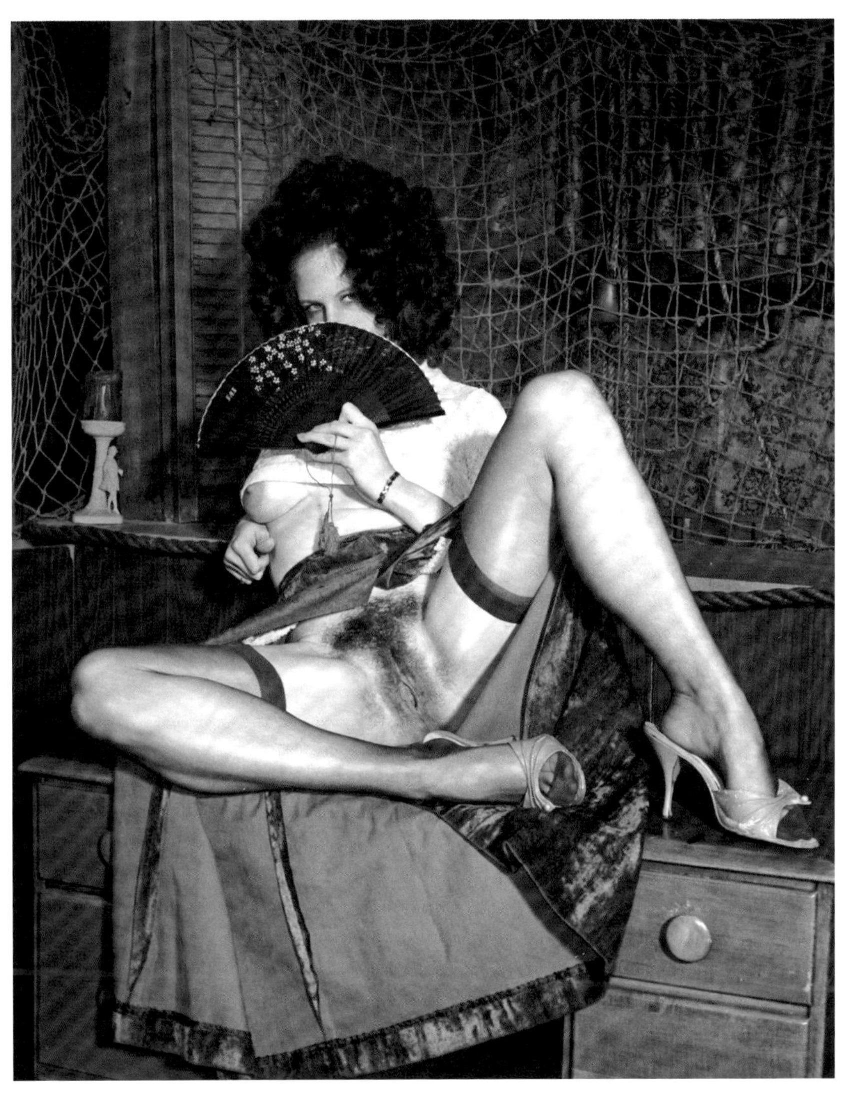

OPPOSITE **Cendrine Bellon**   ABOVE **Marilyn Vari**

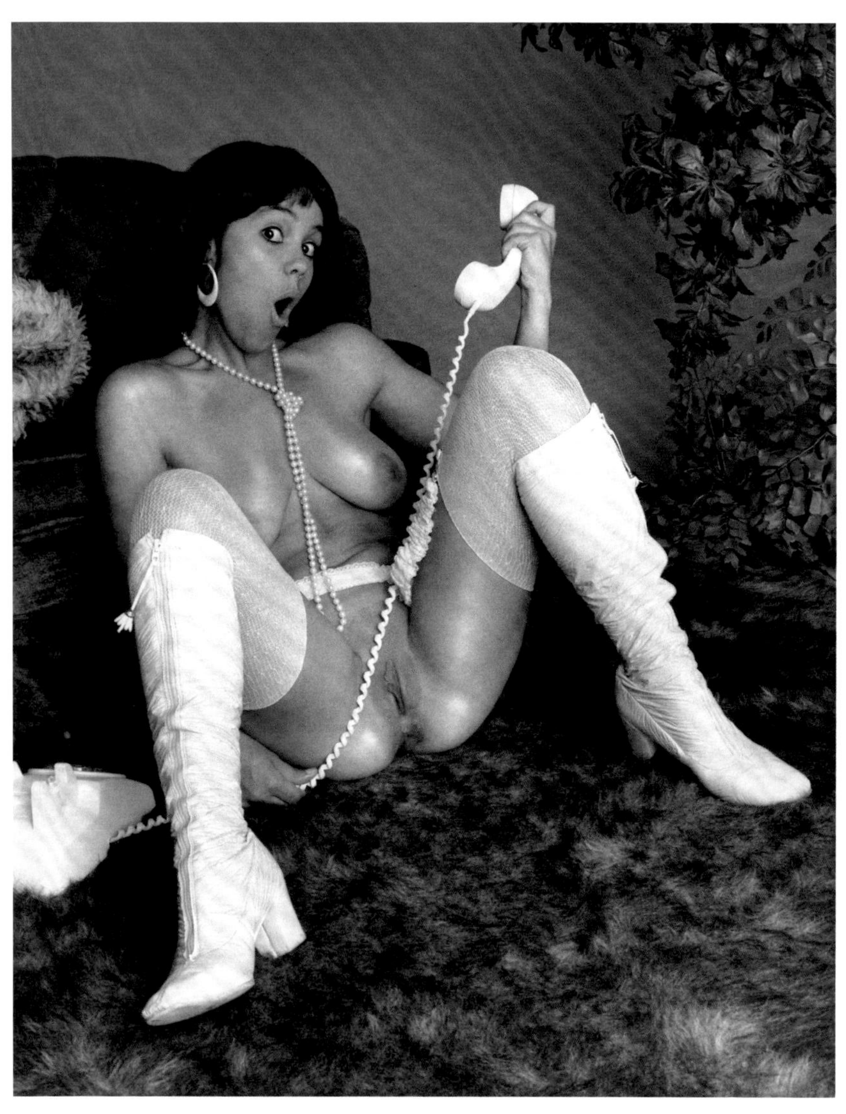

Kacey Quinn

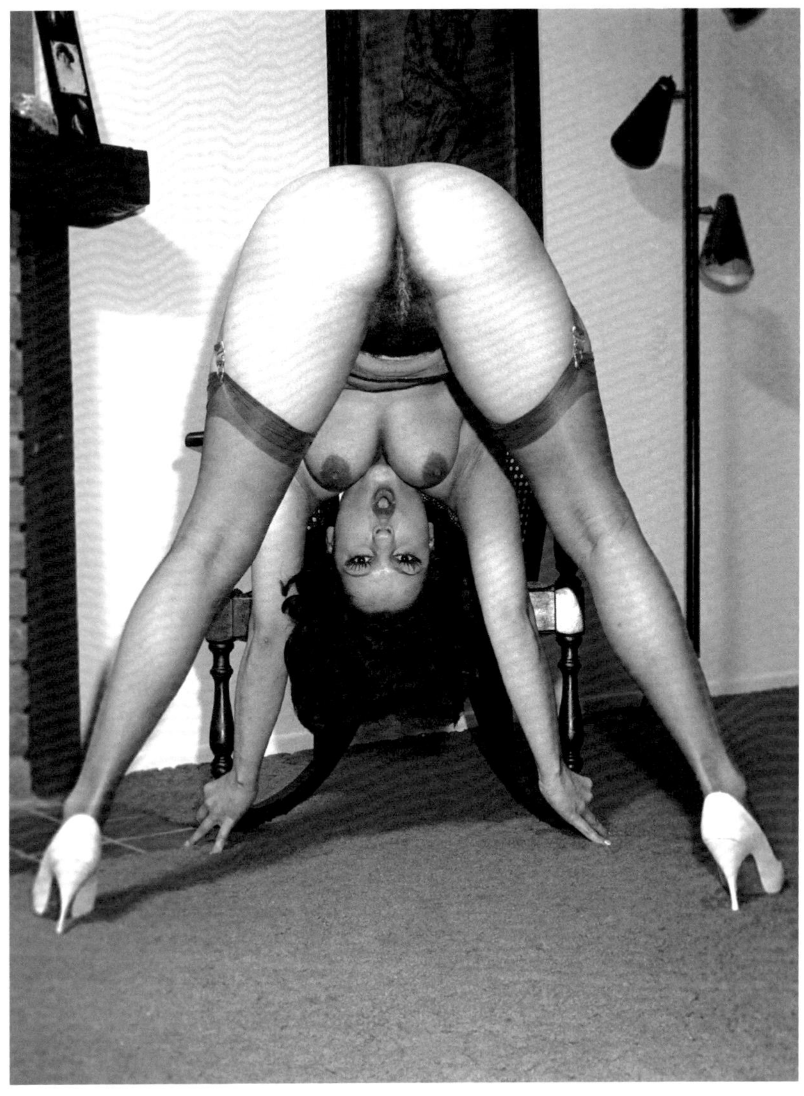

Unknown

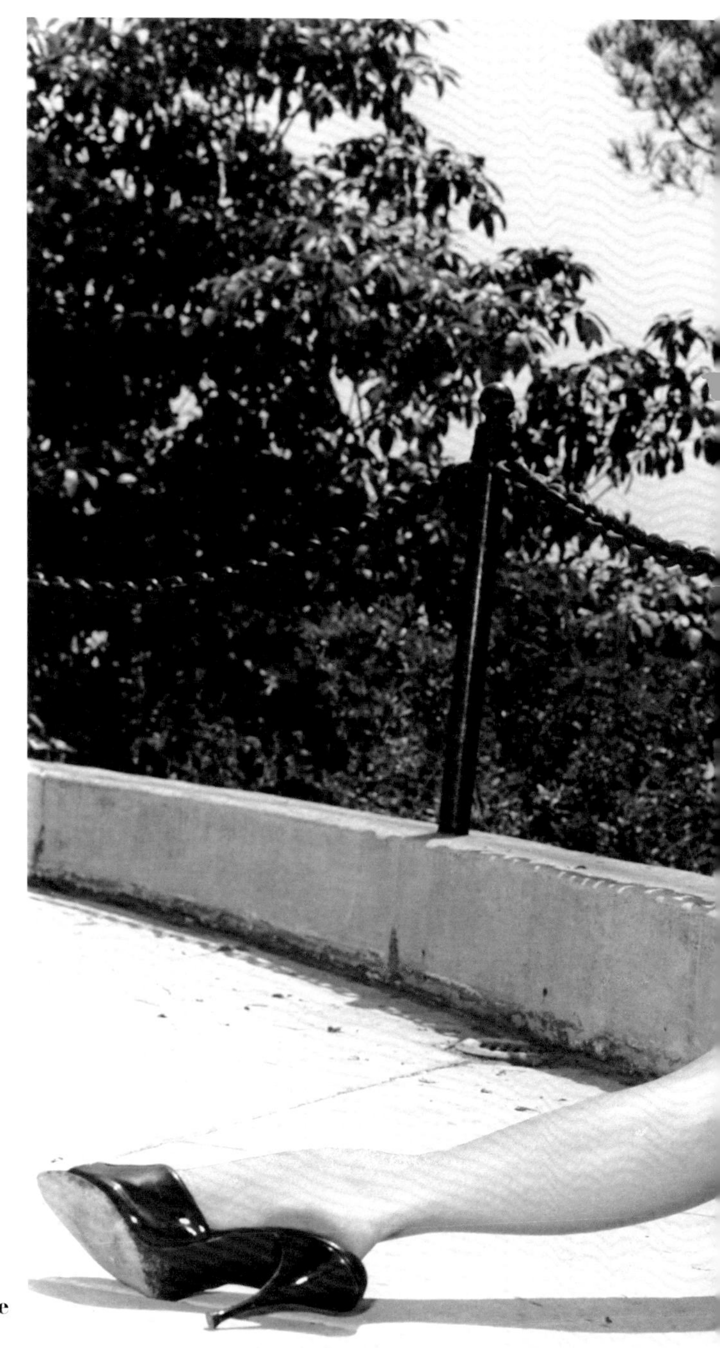

Debbie Osborne

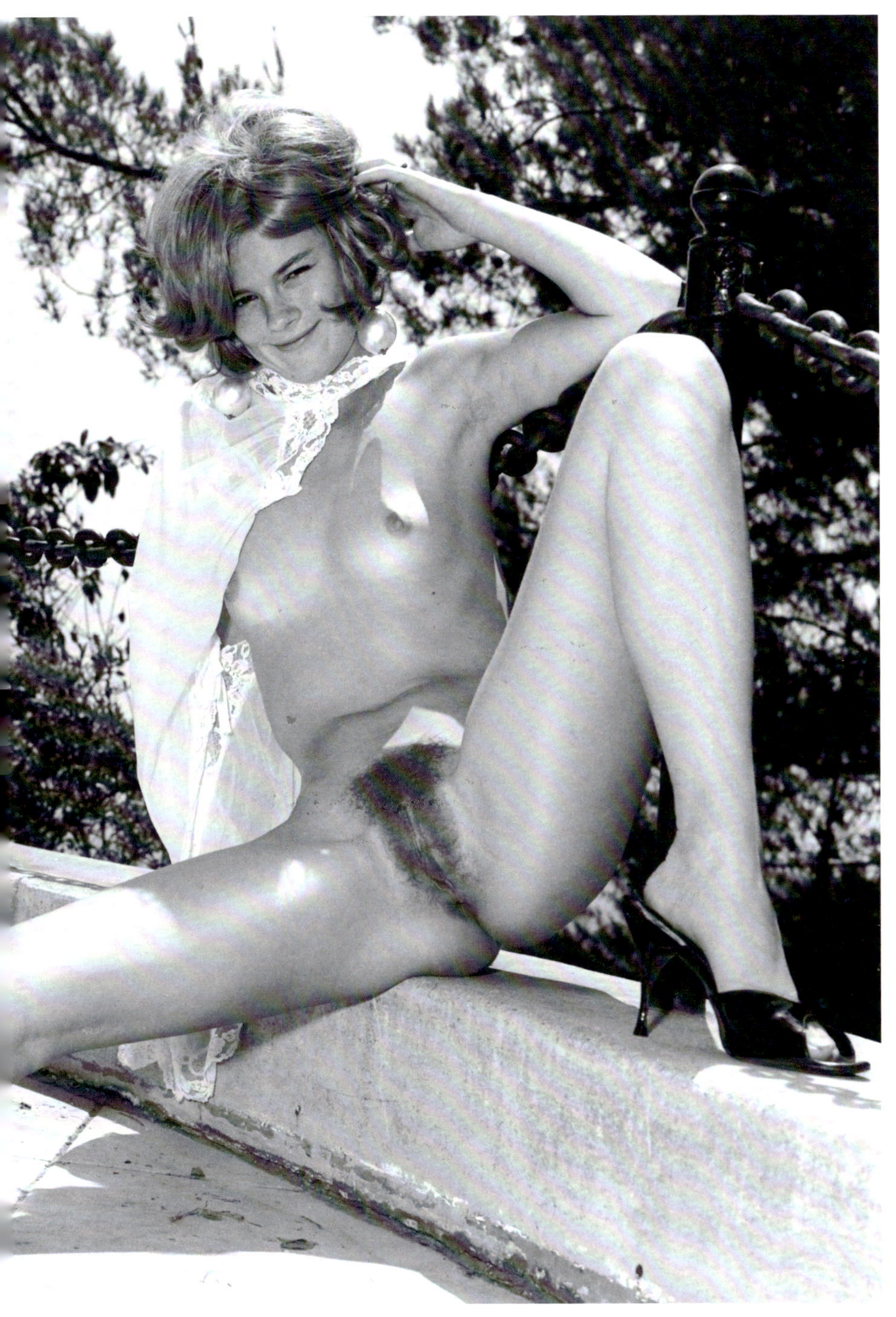

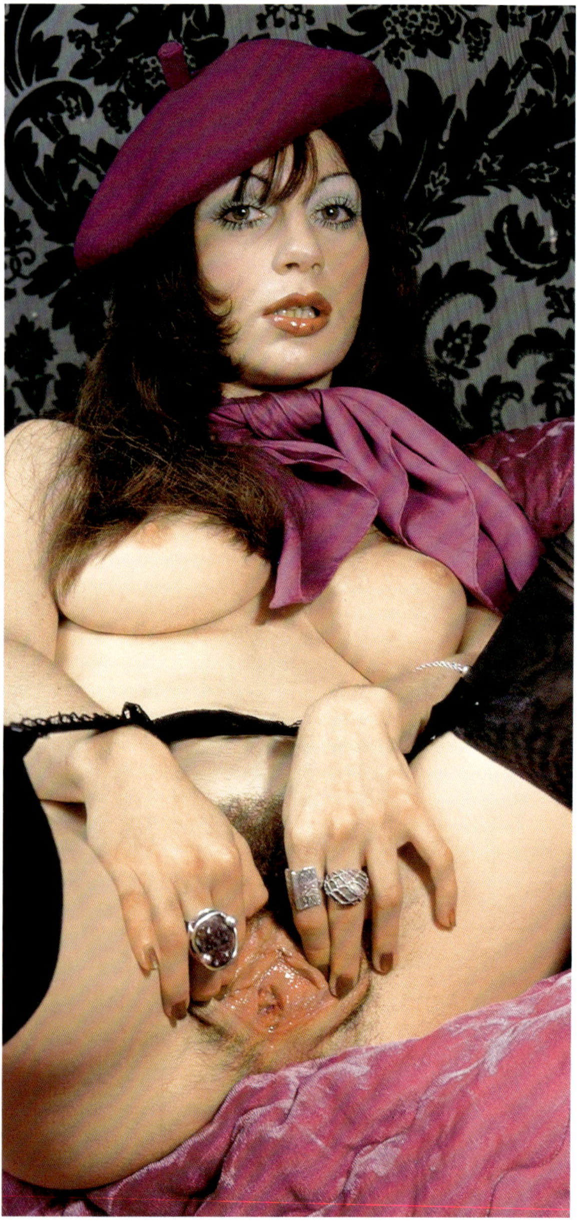

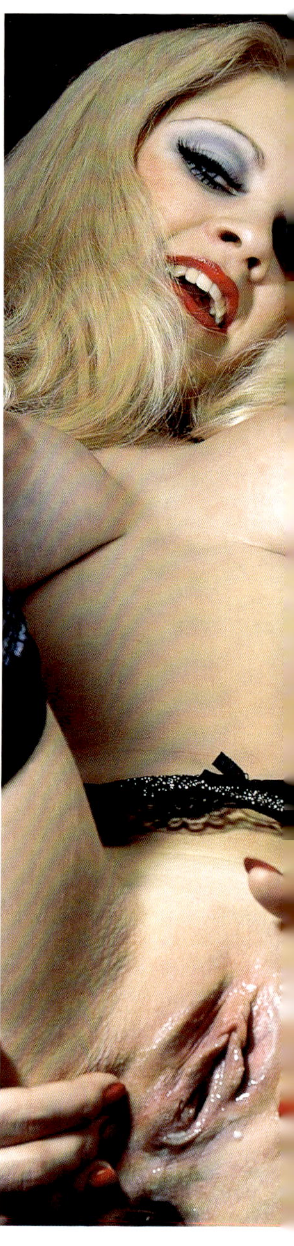

ABOVE LEFT **Lollo**   ABOVE RIGHT **Stacy**   OPPOSITE **Anita**

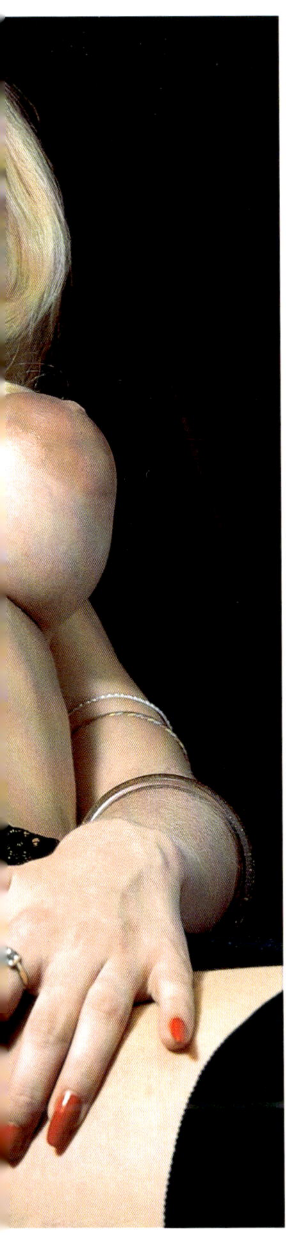

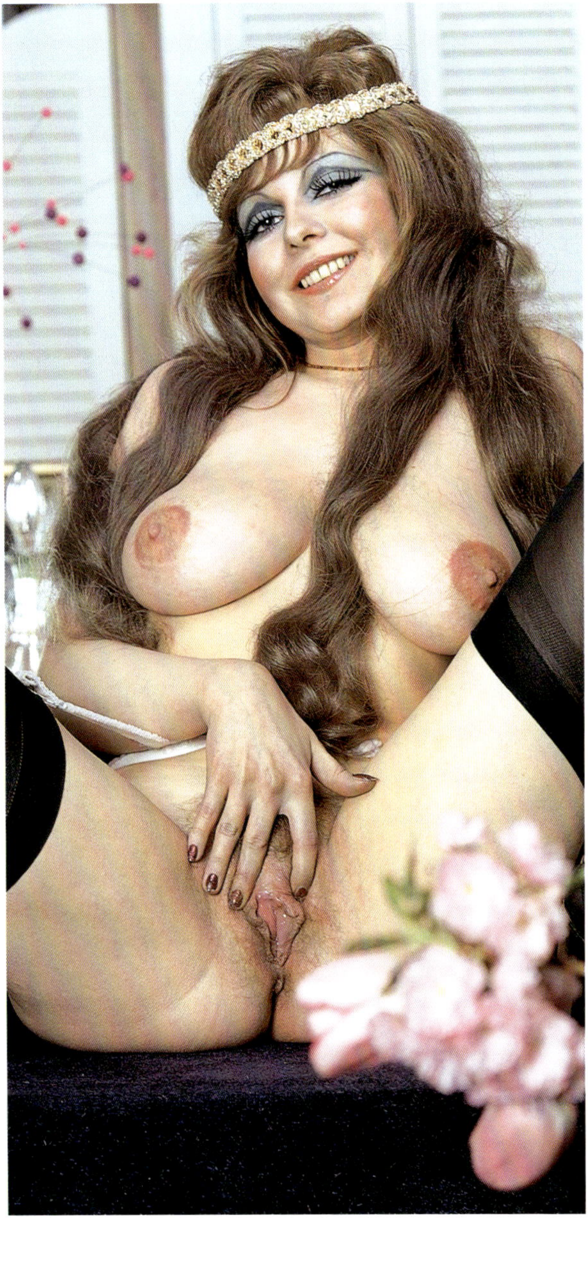

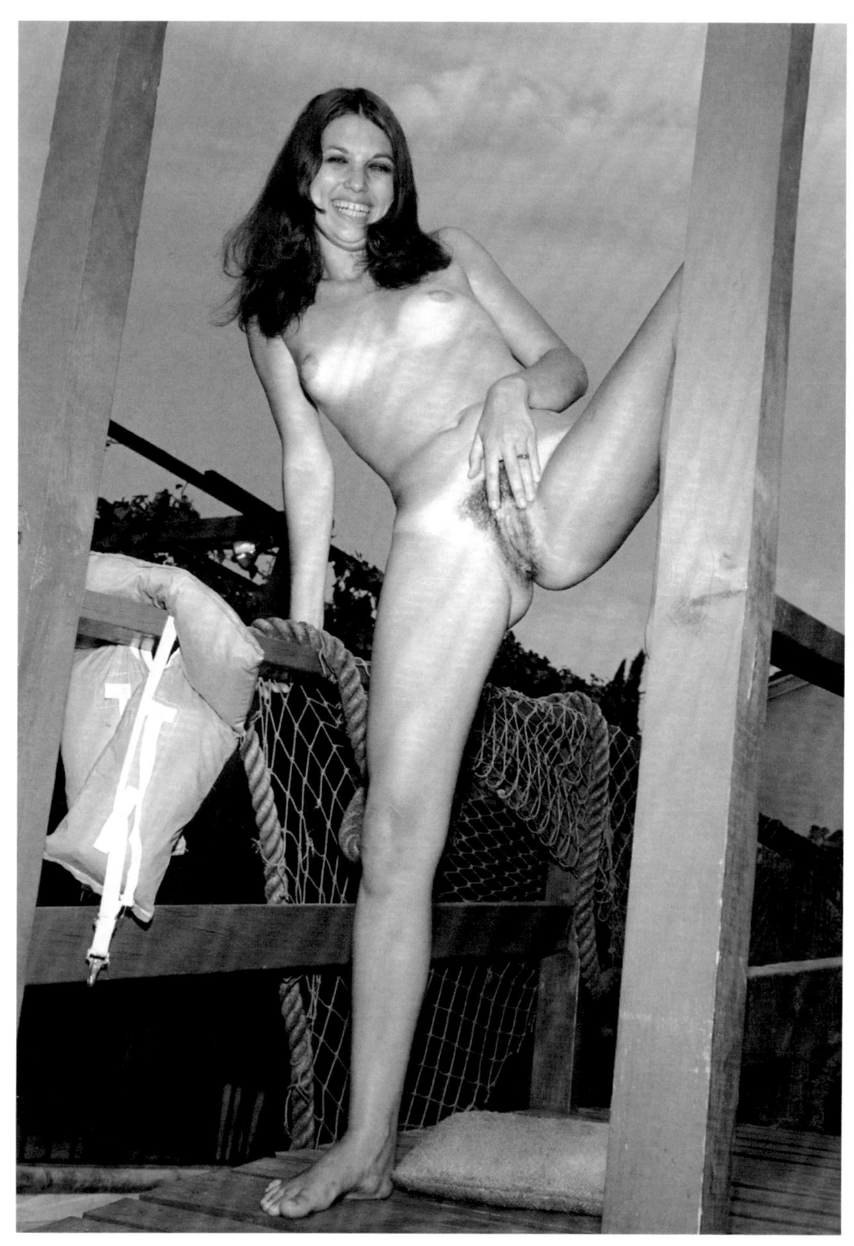

ABOVE **Kathy McIntosh** OPPOSITE **Unknown**

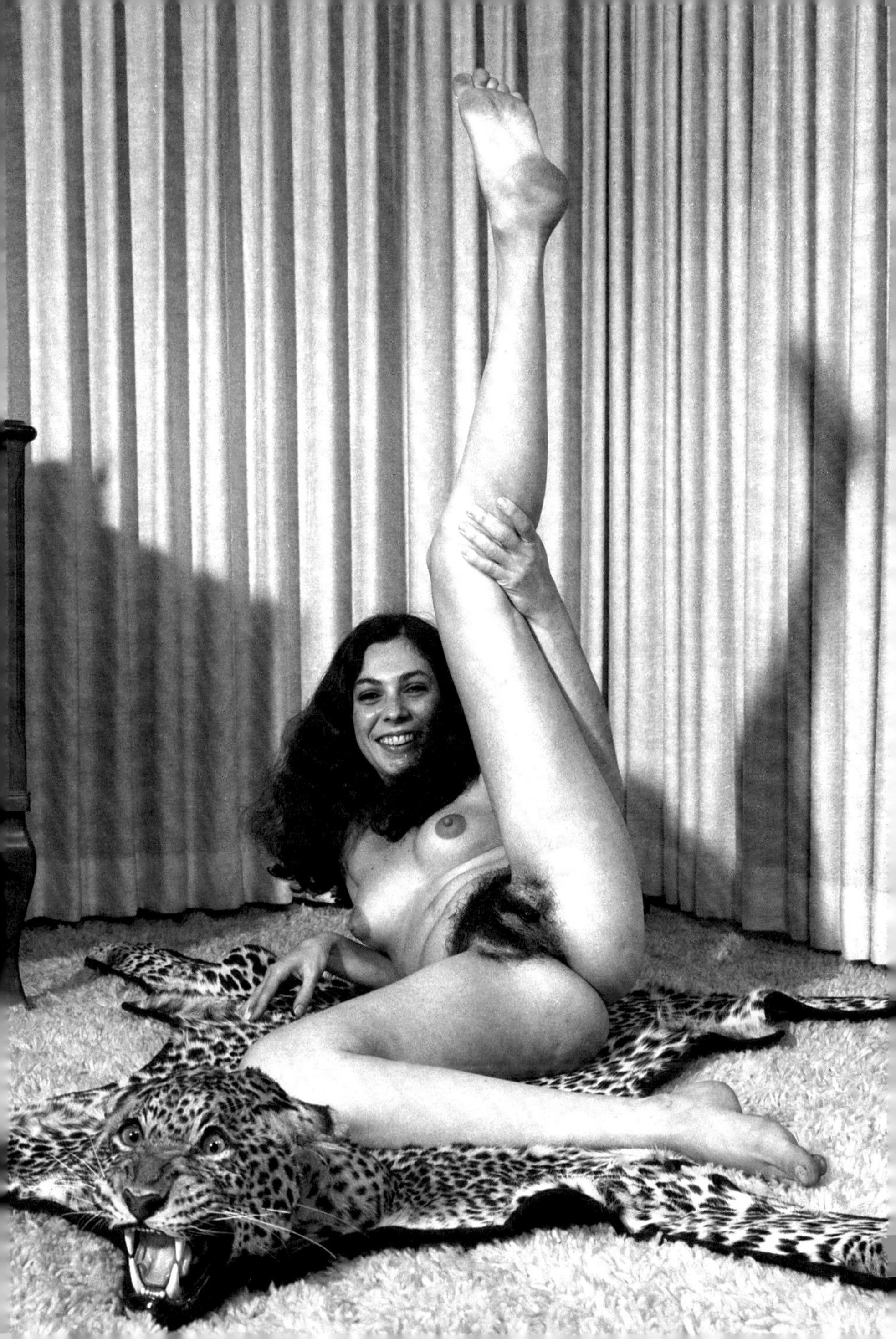

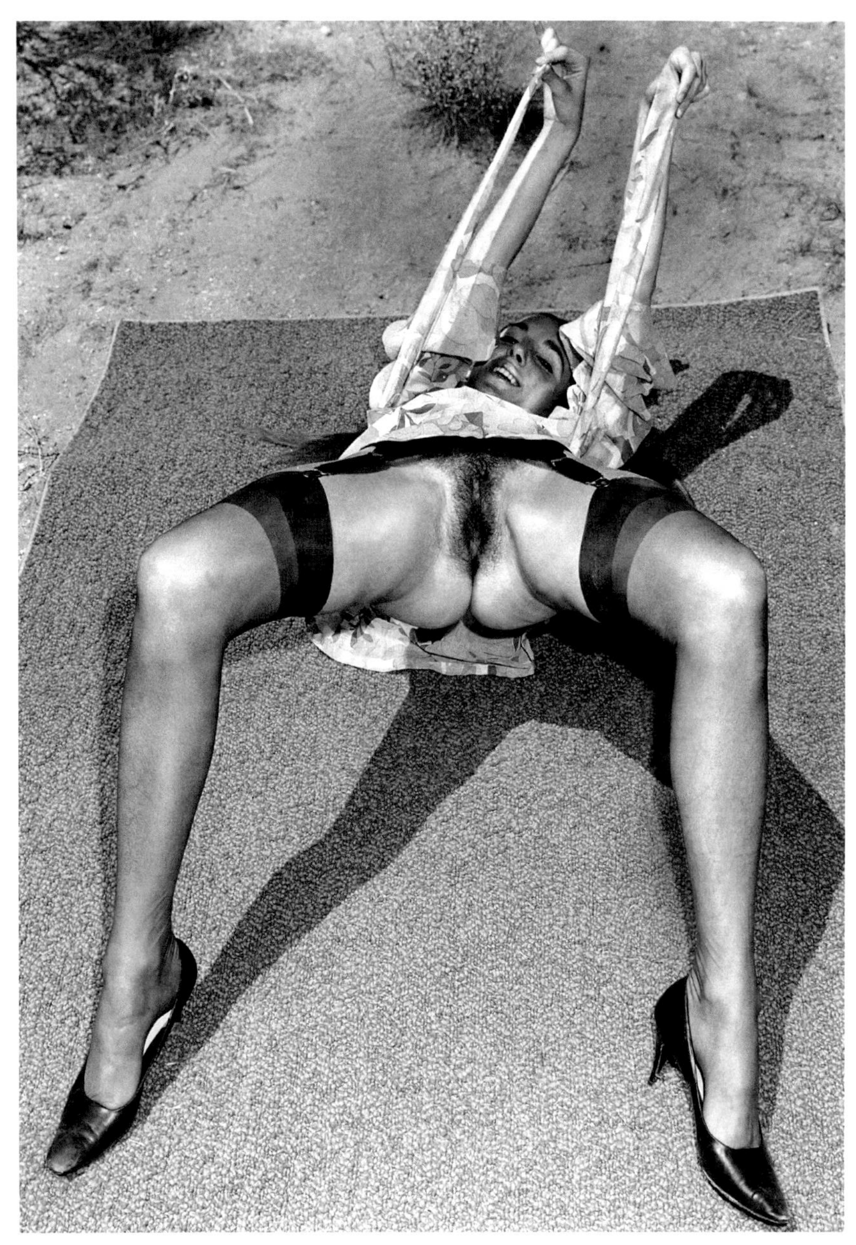

ABOVE **Unknown**   OPPOSITE **Nicole Bertin**

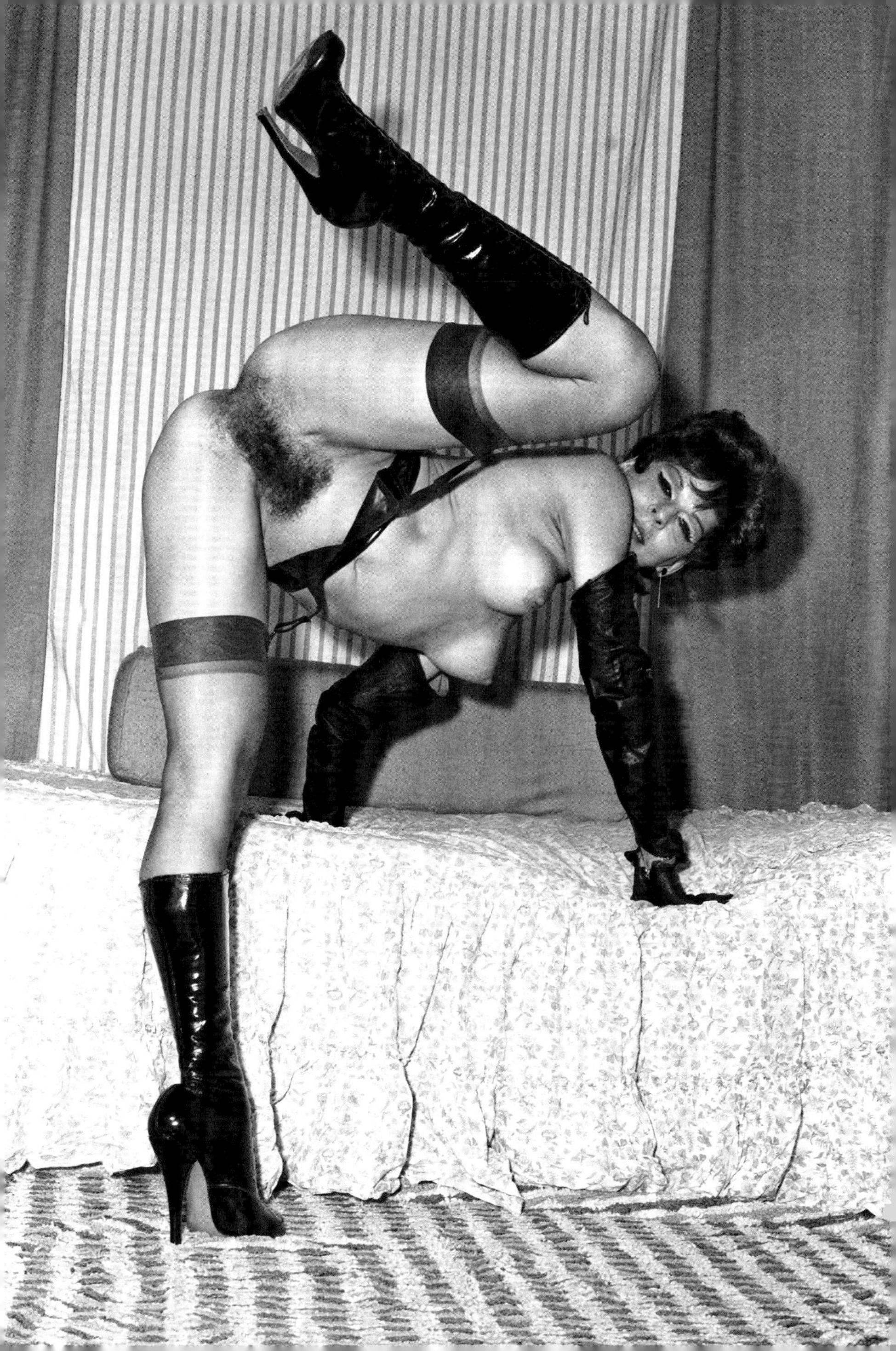

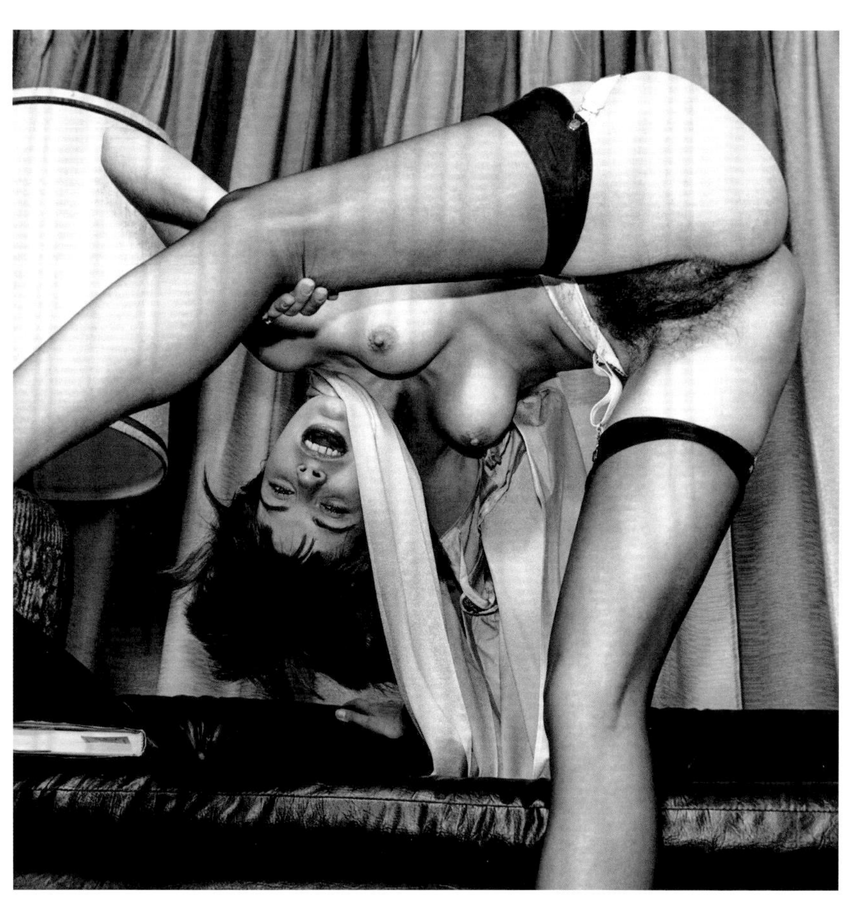

ABOVE **Sandy Dempsey** OPPOSITE **Unknown** PAGES 70-71 **Kathi Greene**

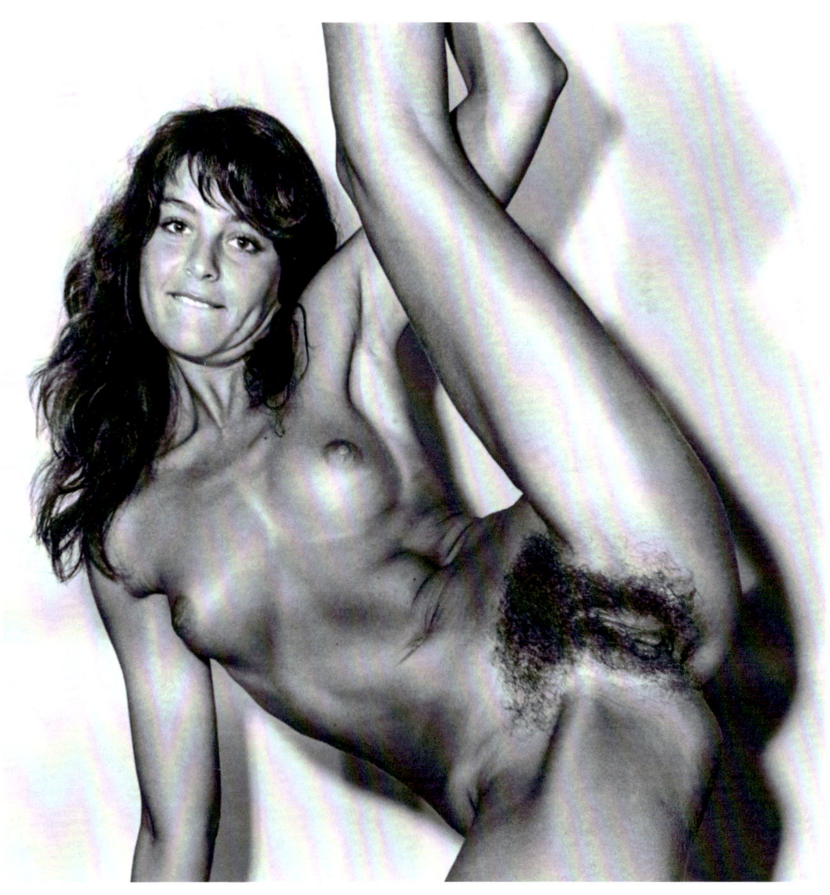

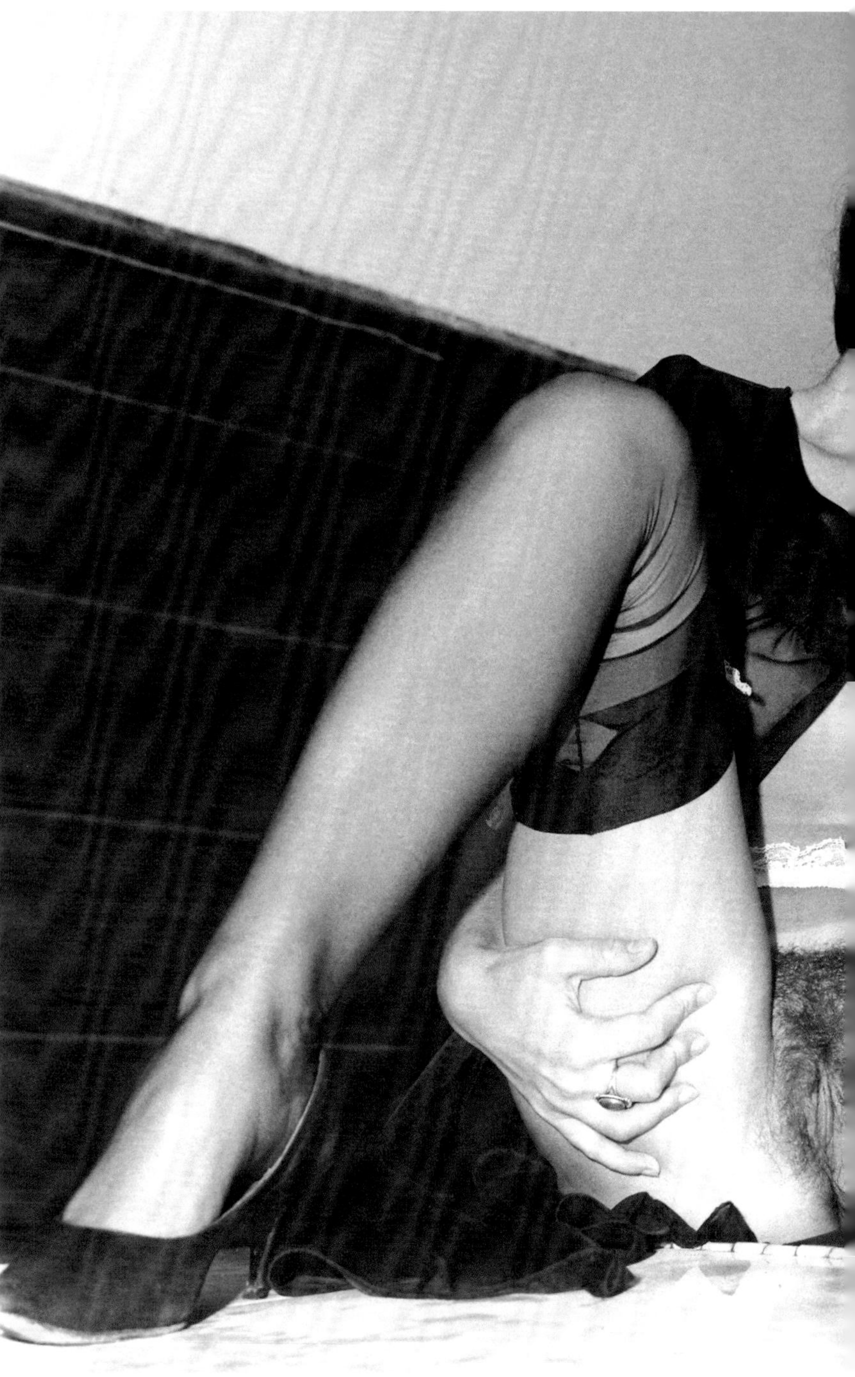

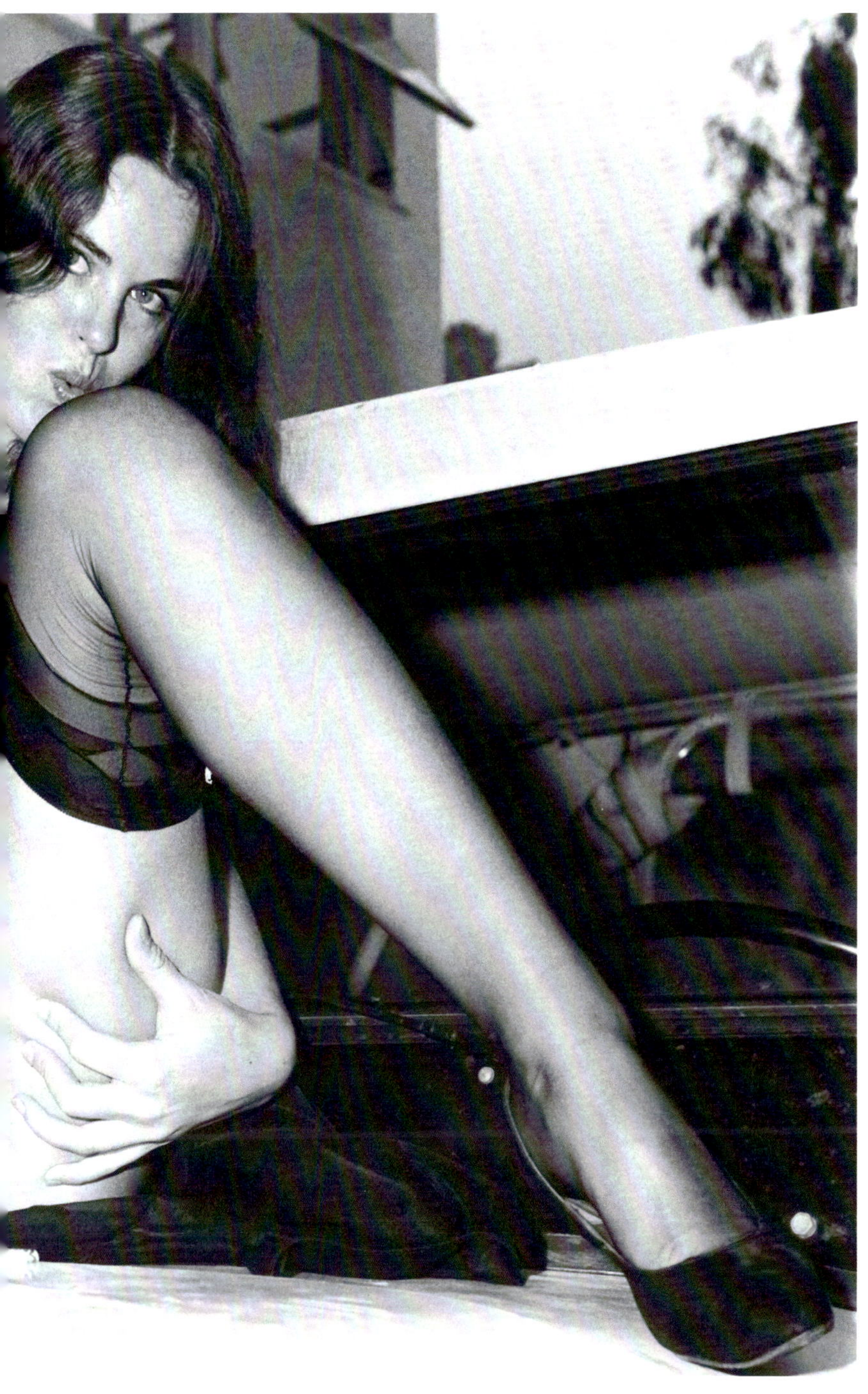

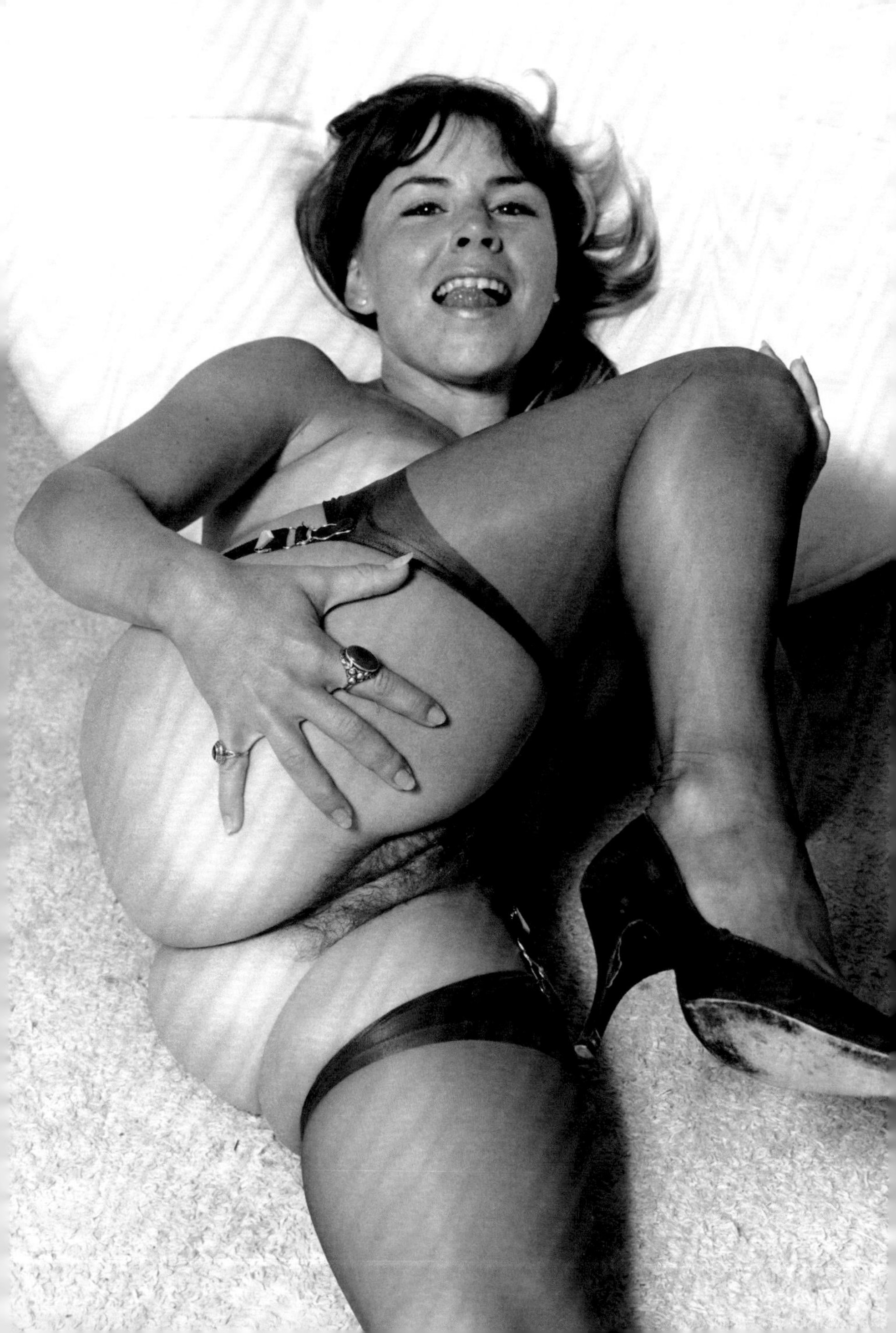

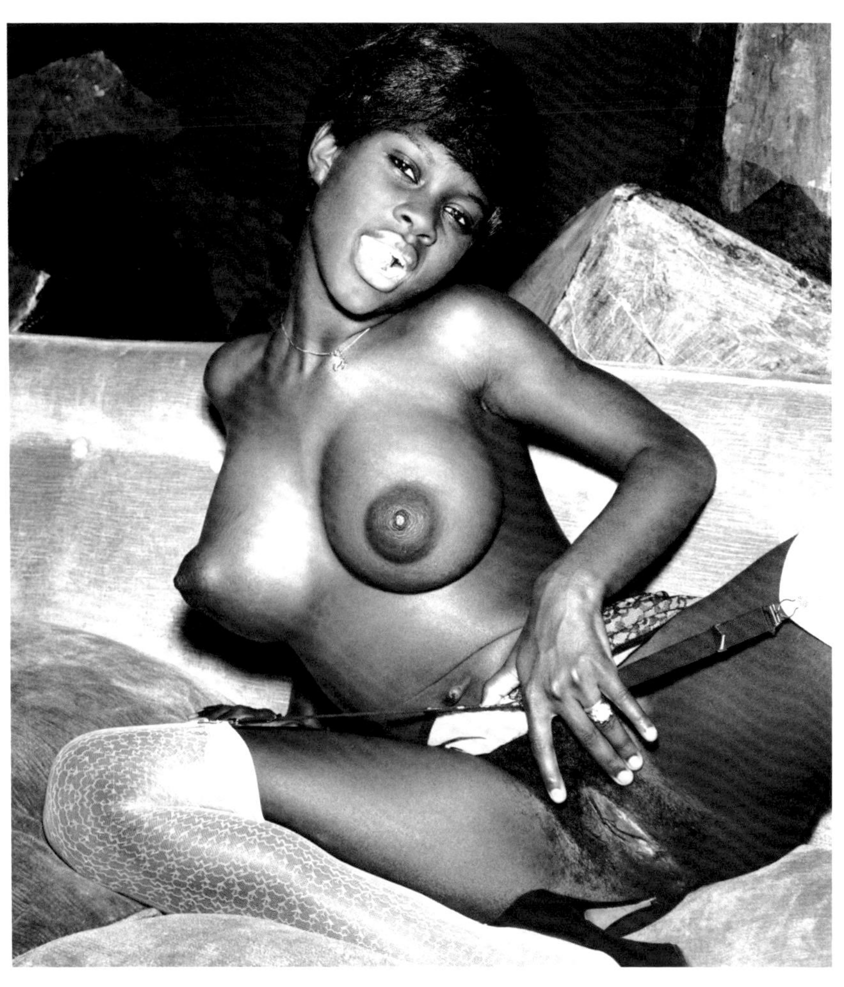

OPPOSITE **Michelle Hanson**   ABOVE **Regina Christian**

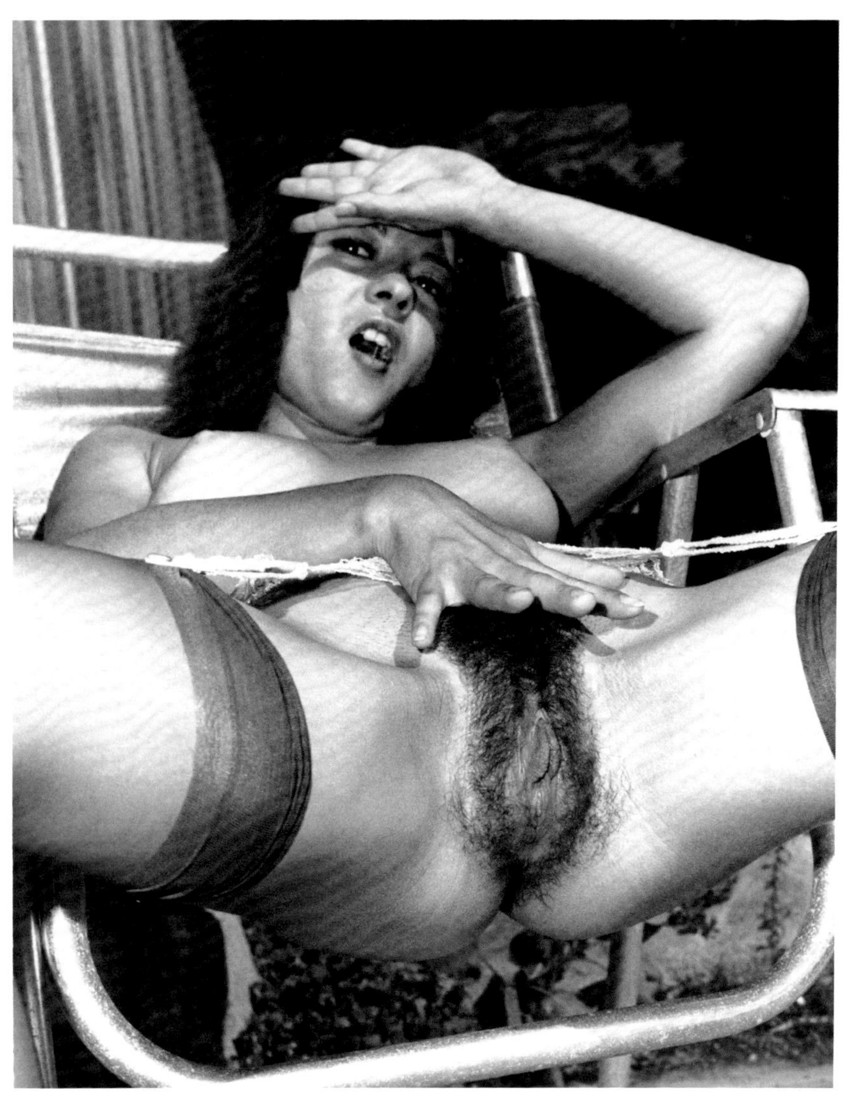

Norma McGhee

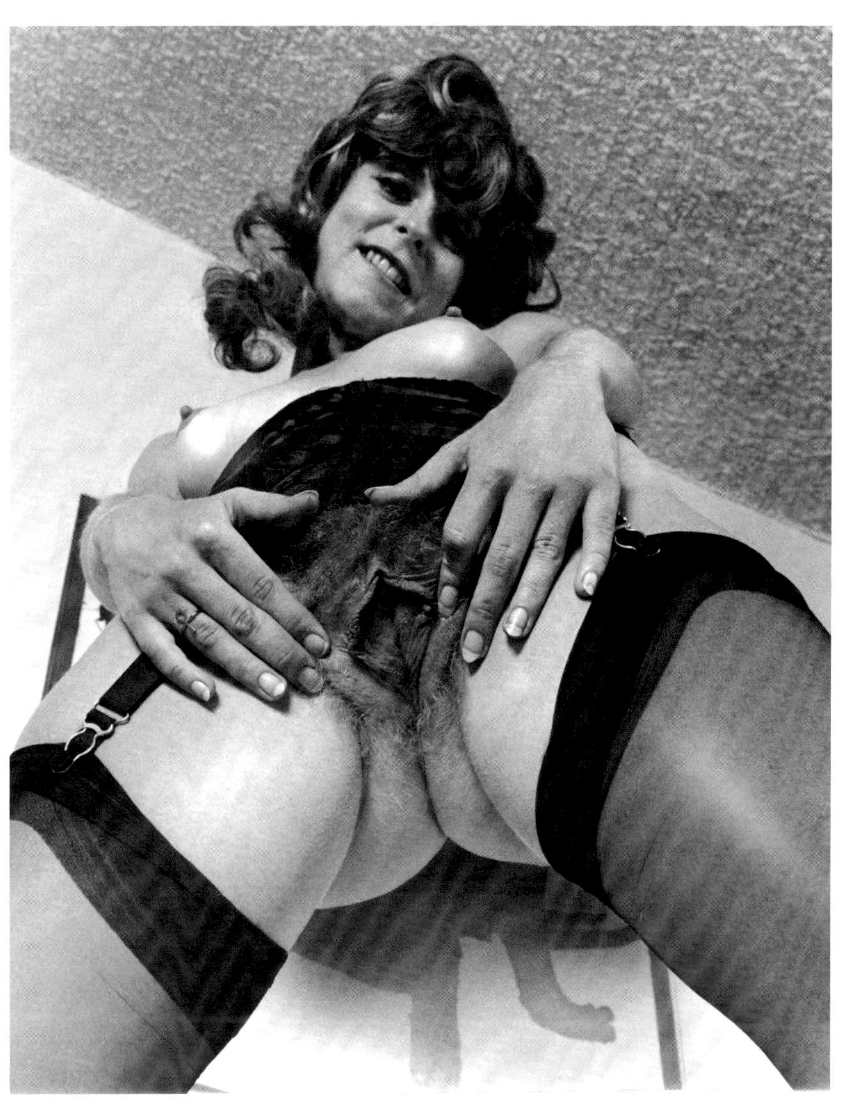

Shelly McClelland

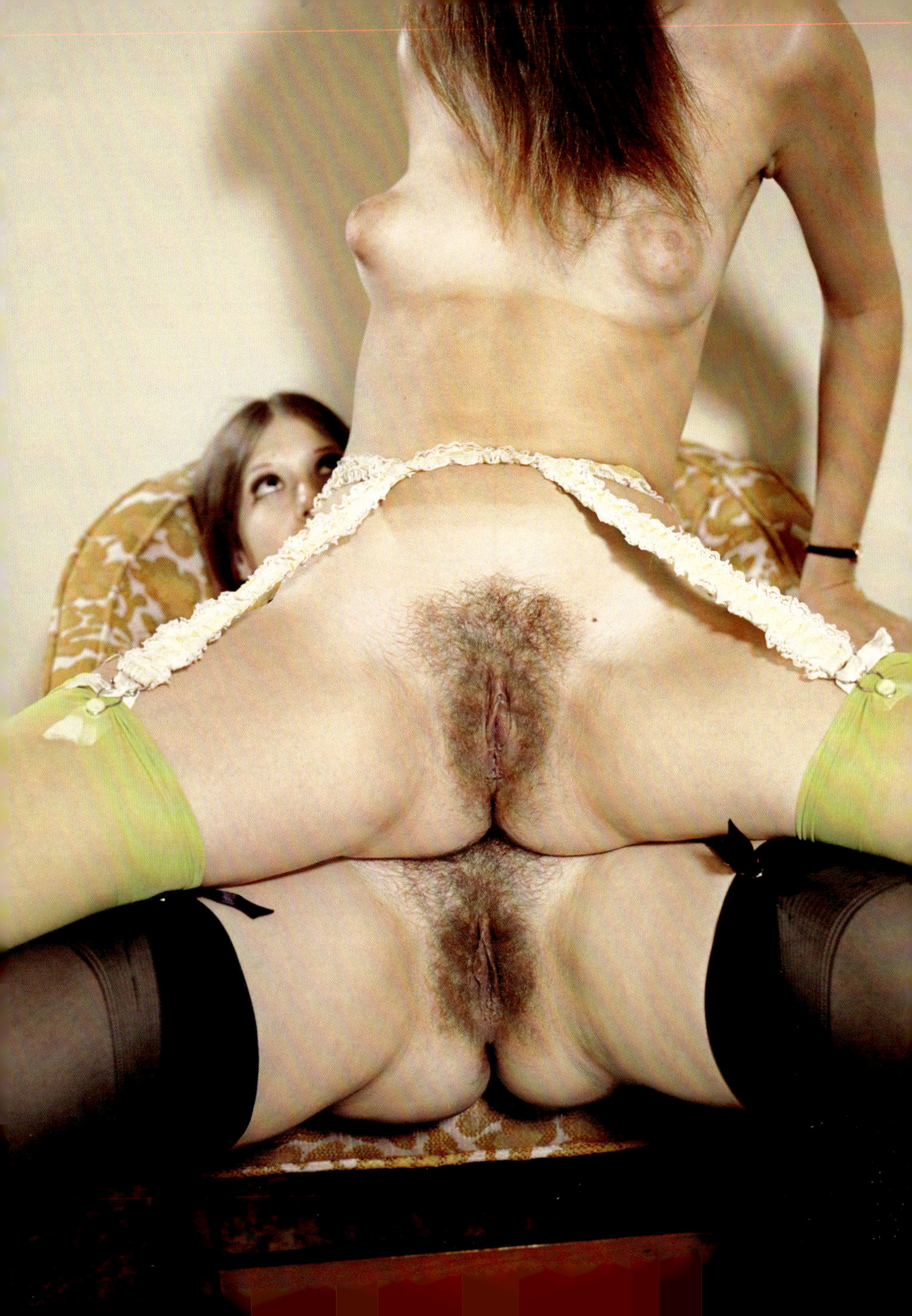

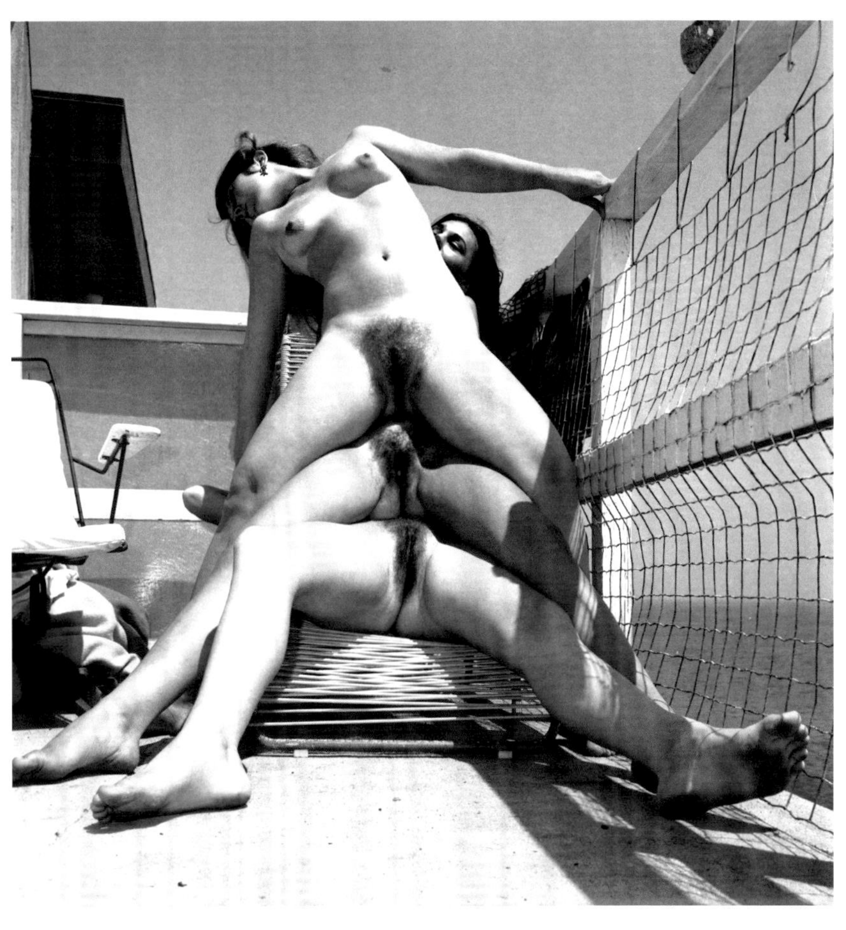

OPPOSITE **Janine & Laurie Lewis**   ABOVE AND PAGES 78-79 **Unknown**

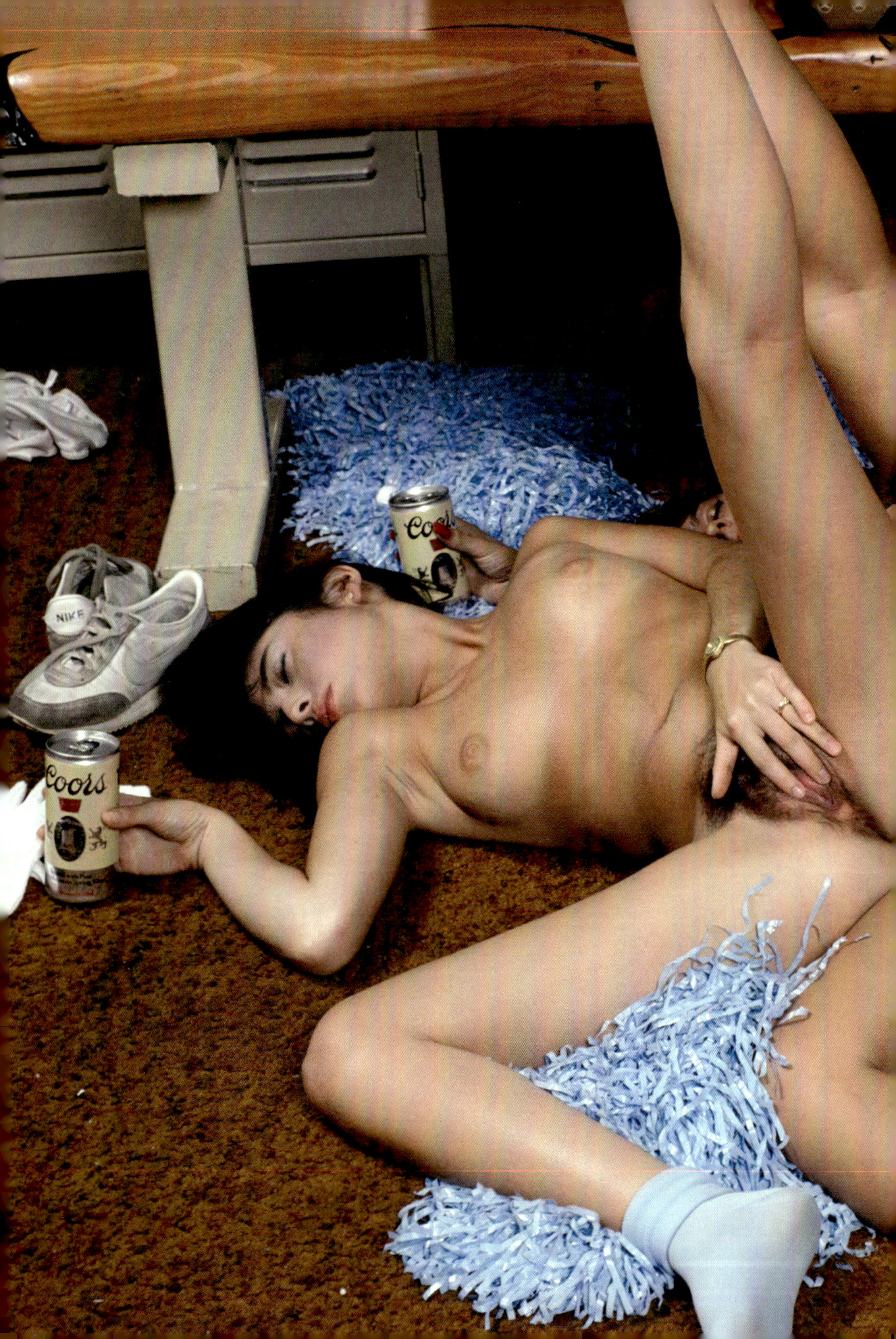

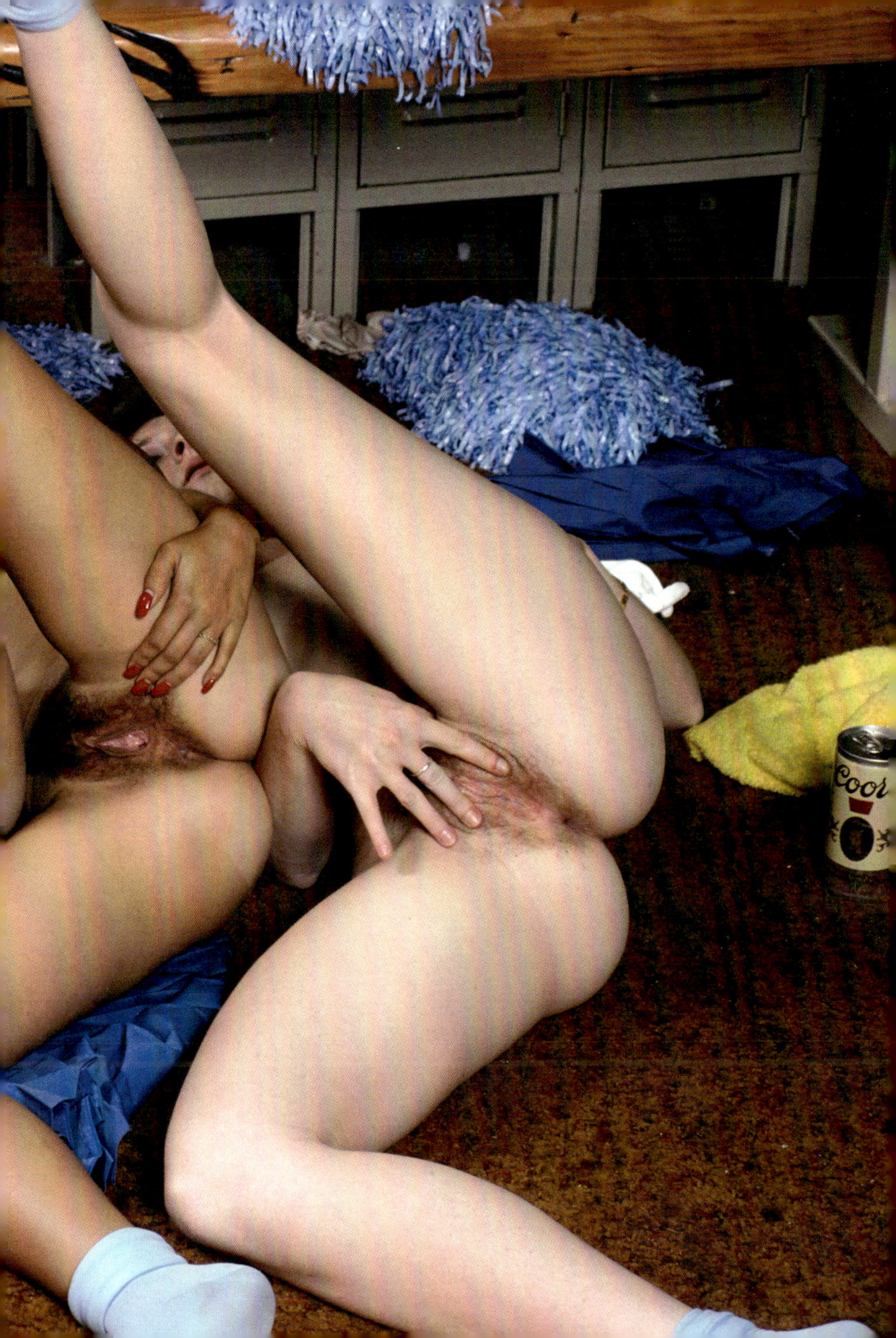

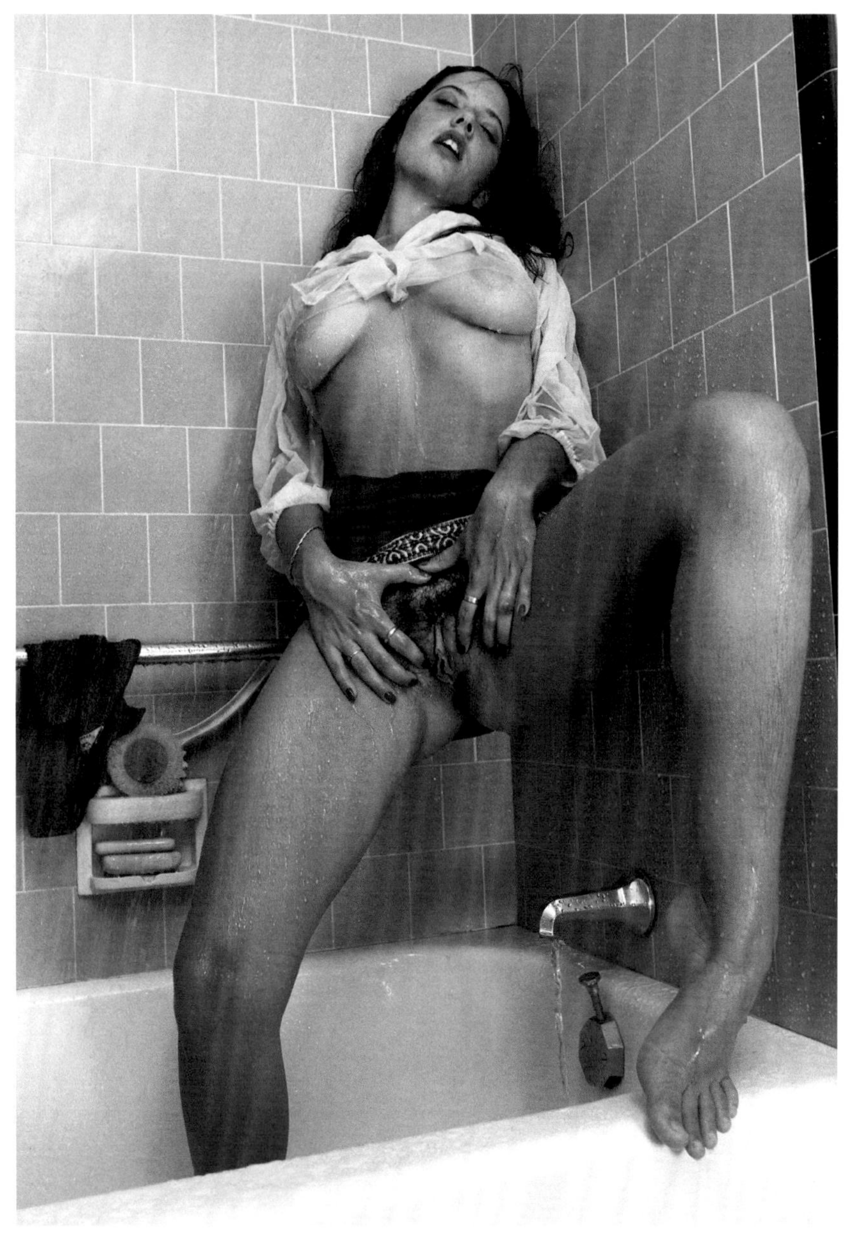

Unknown

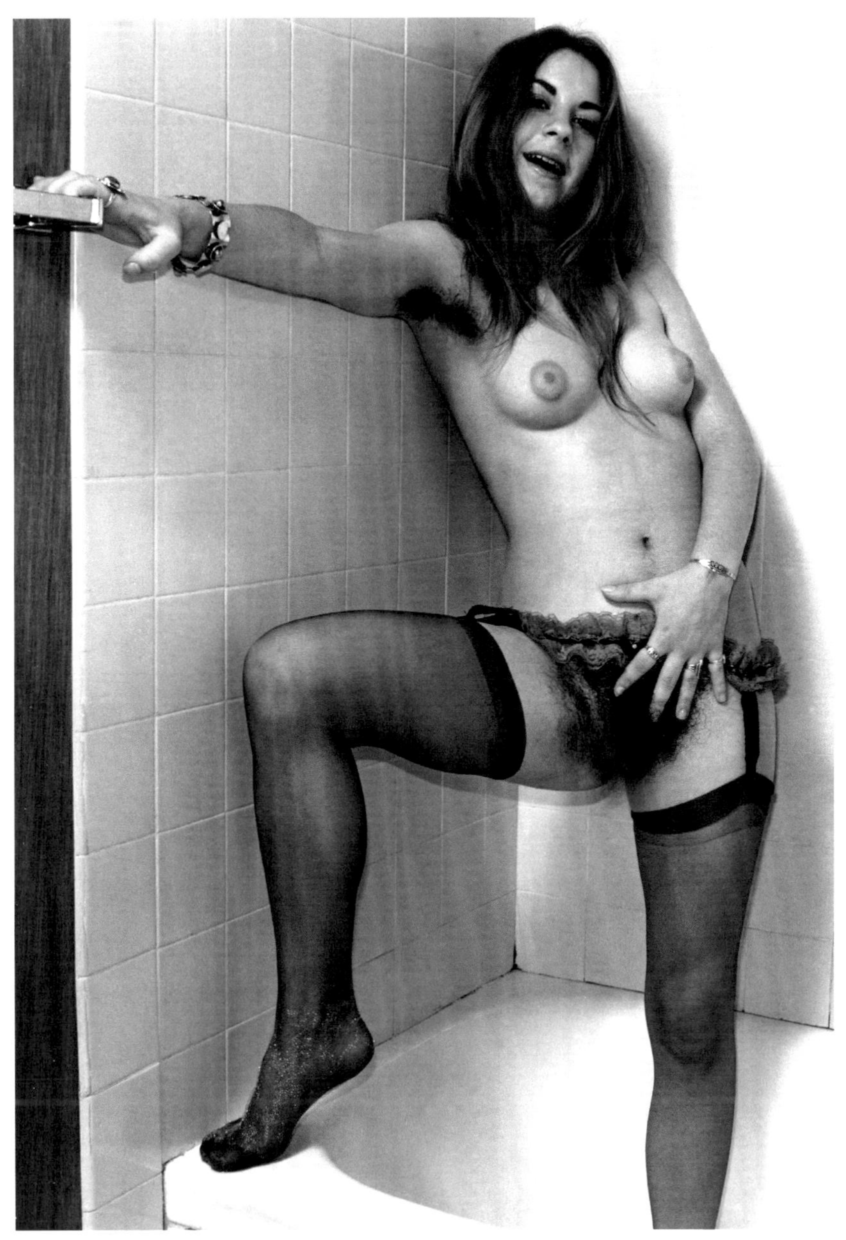

Lisa Collara

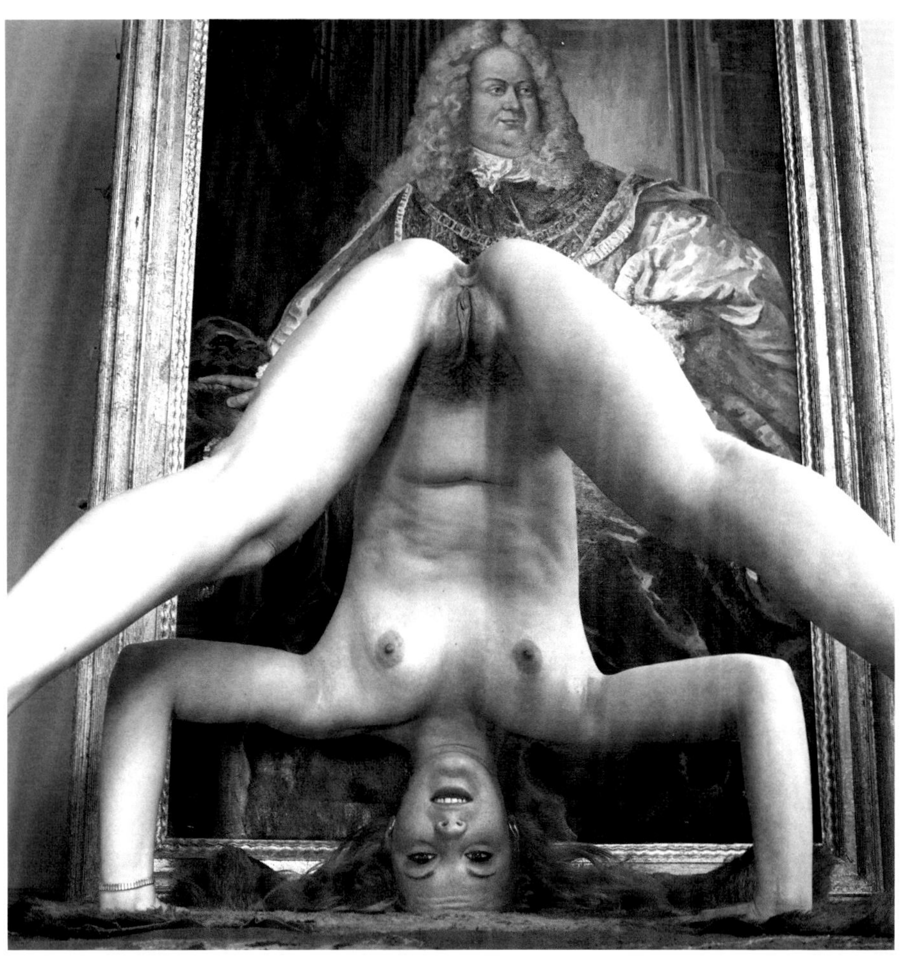

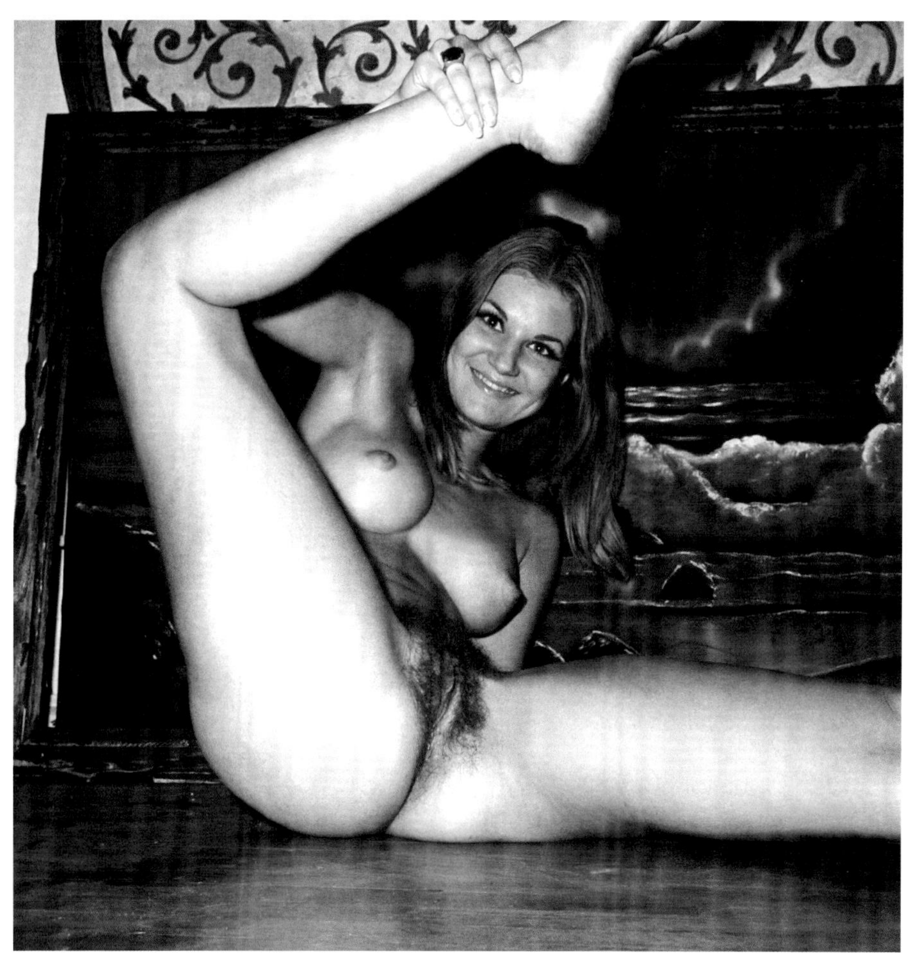

OPPOSITE AND ABOVE **Unknown**

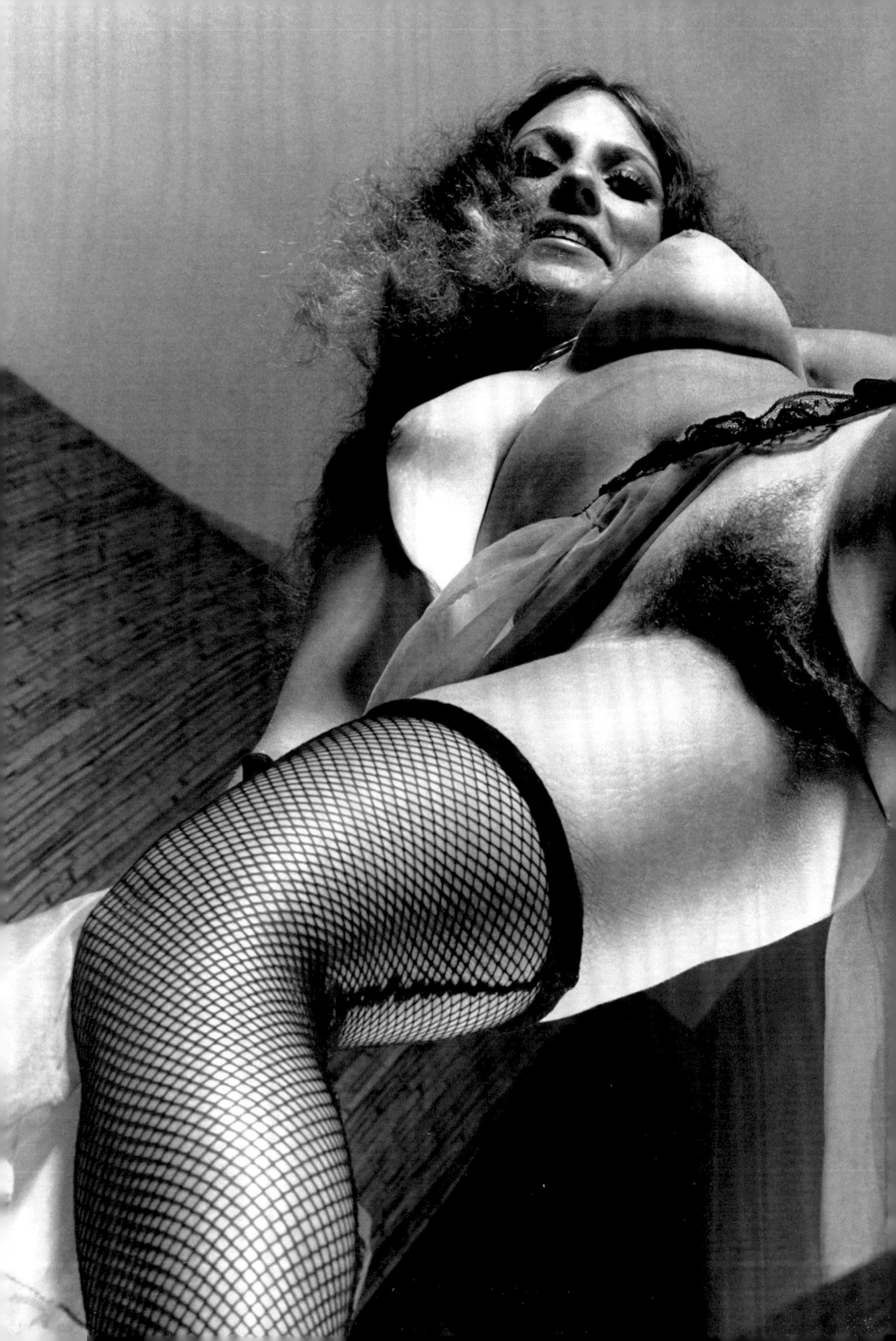

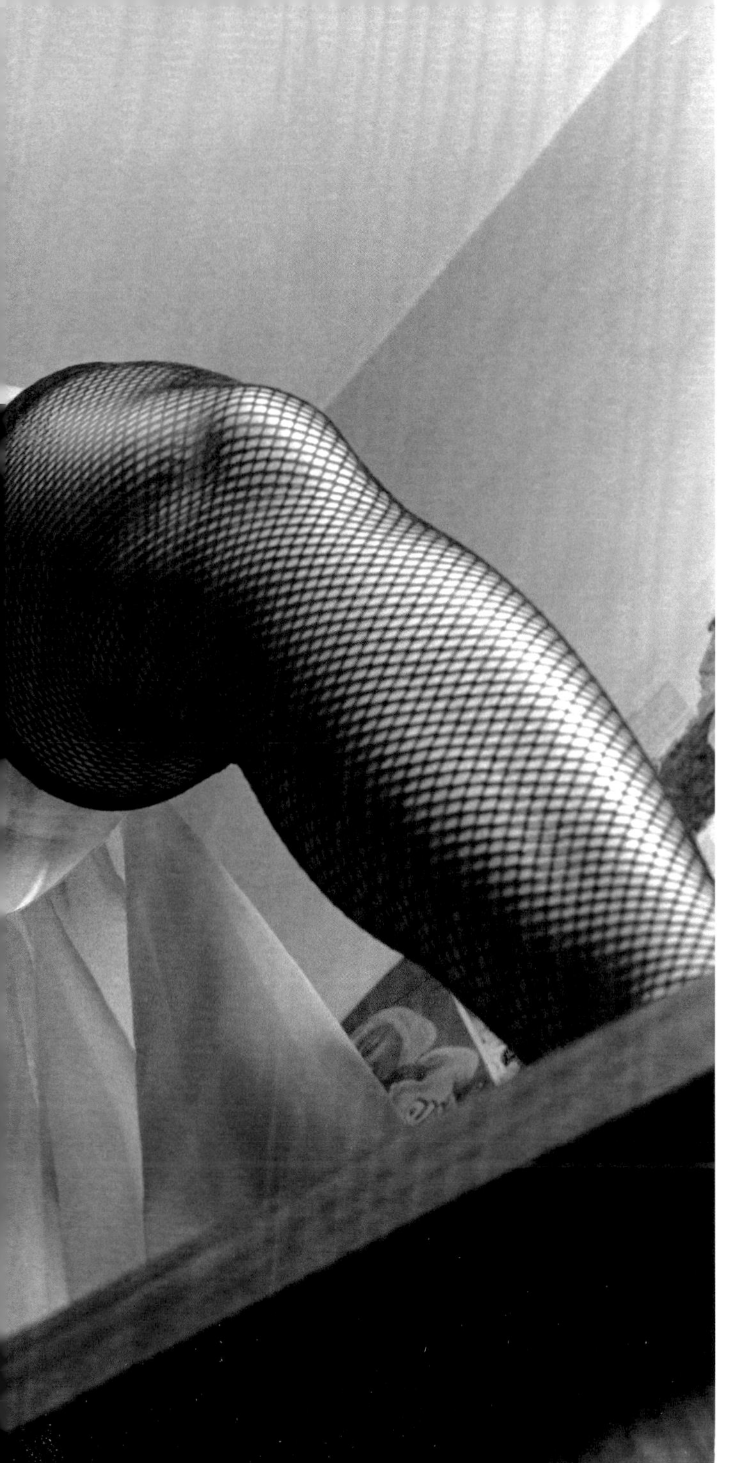

Marie Arnold

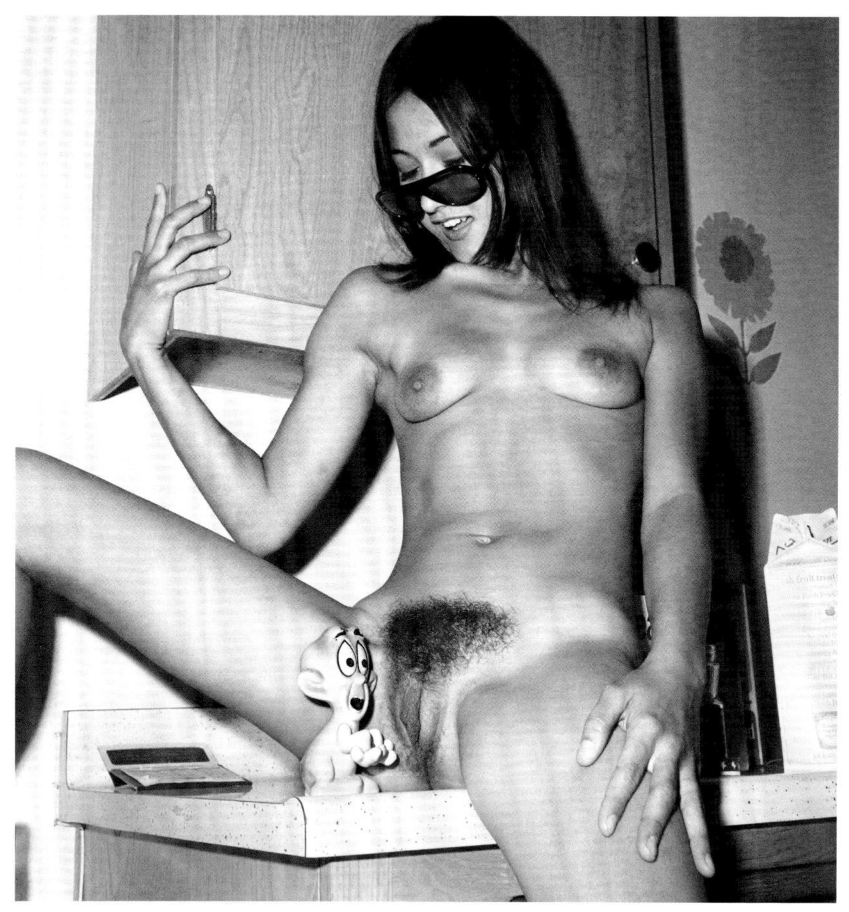

Unknown

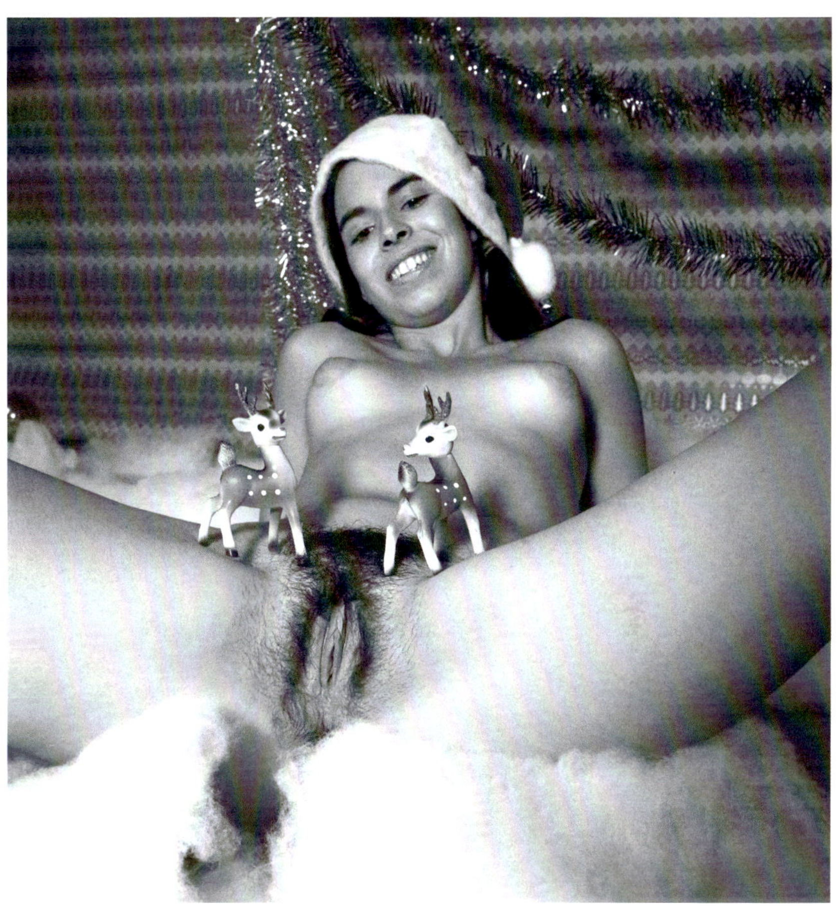

Unknown

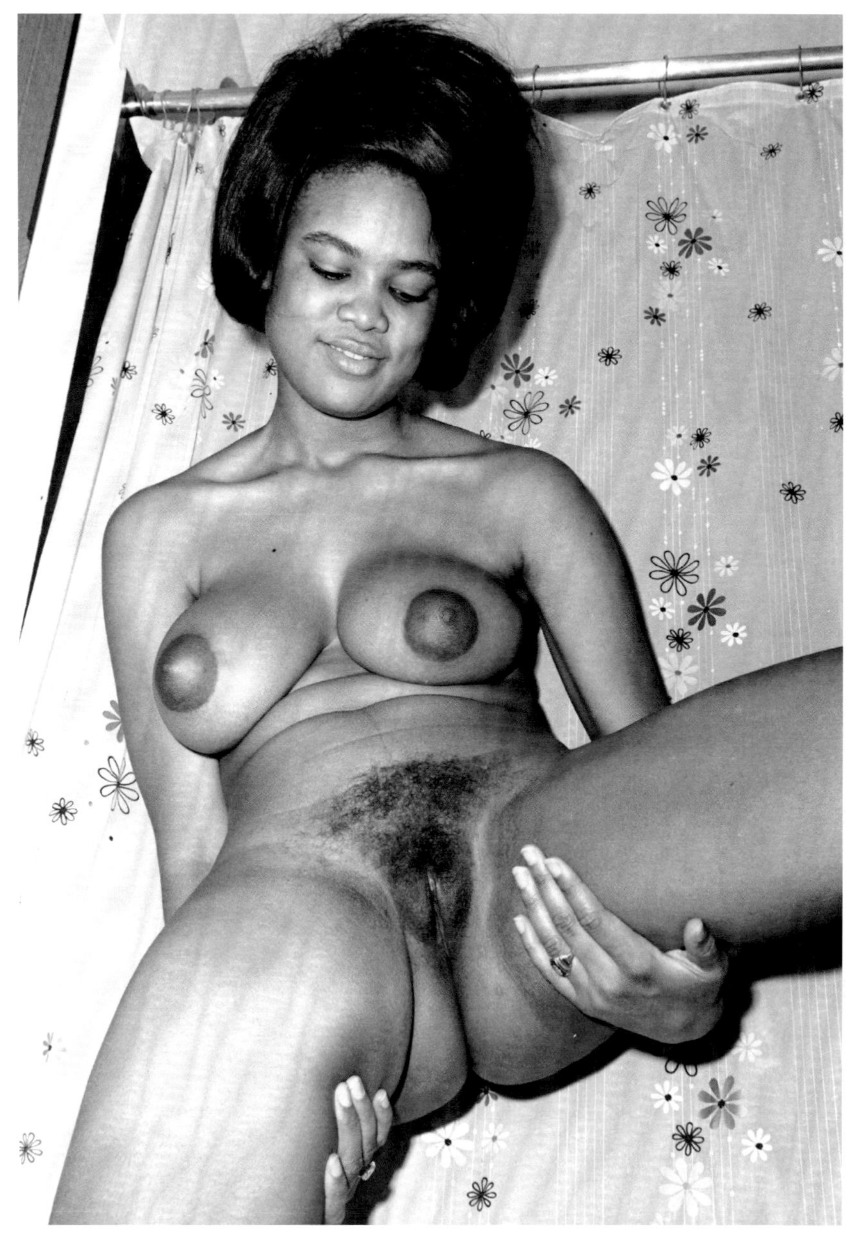

Mia Coco

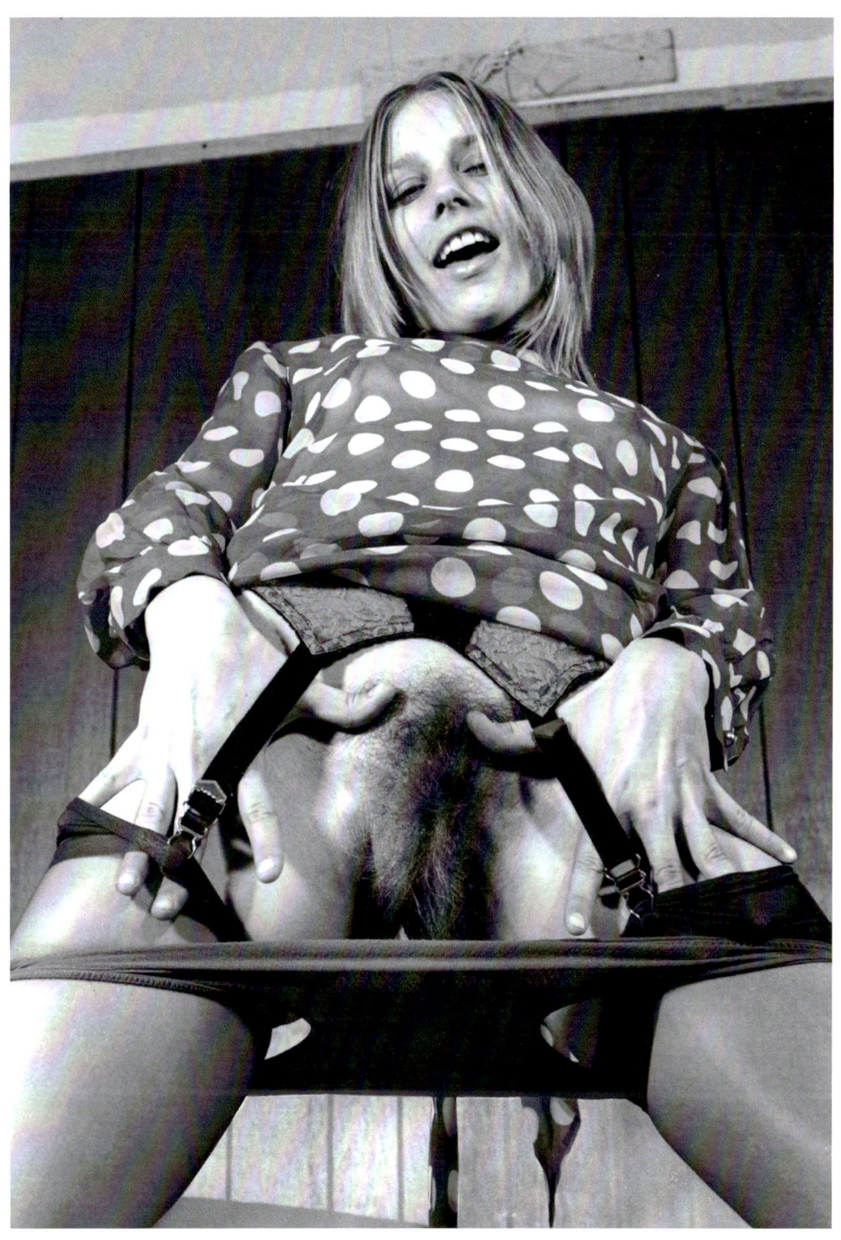

ABOVE **Jane Peters**   PAGES 90-91 **Unknown**

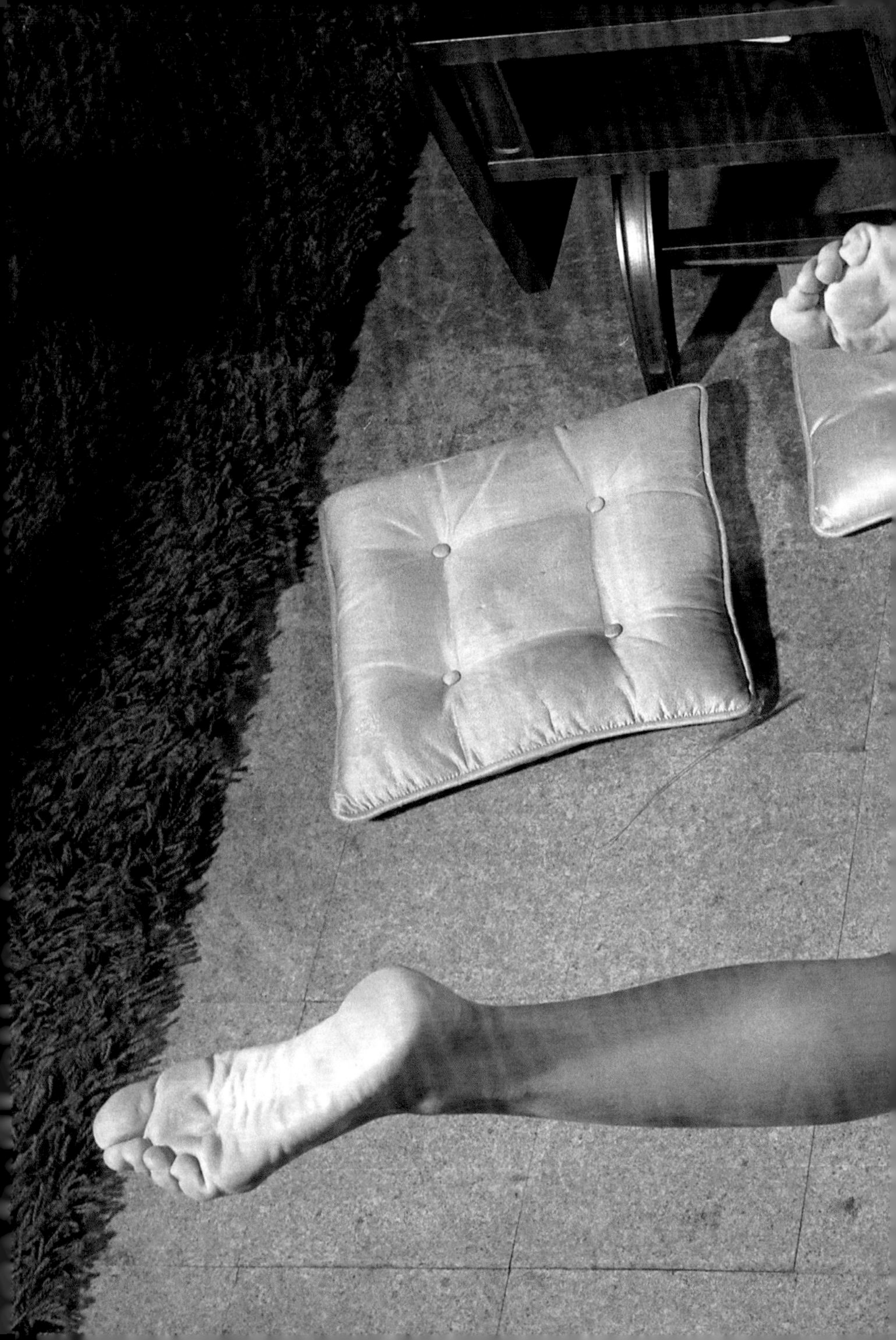

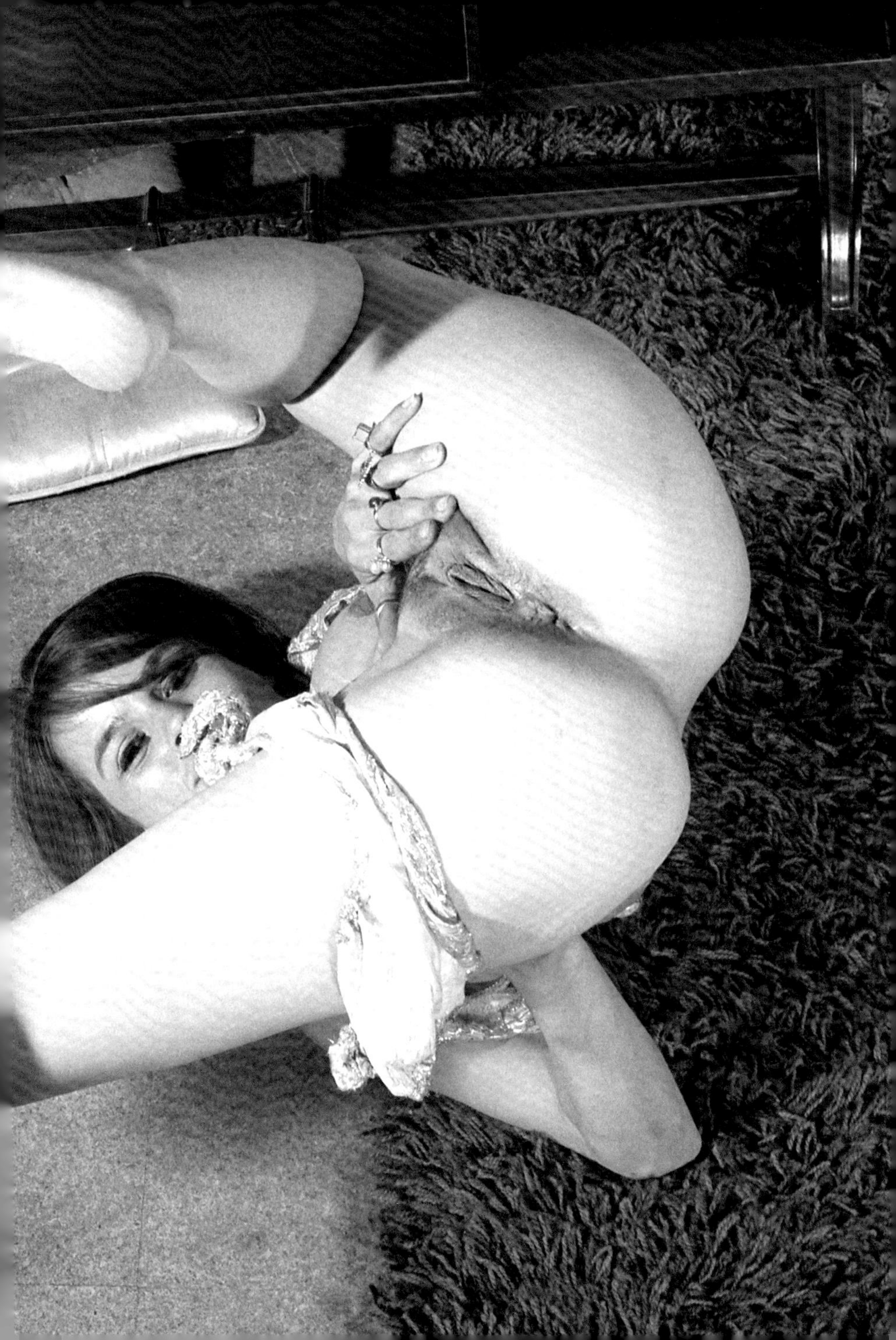

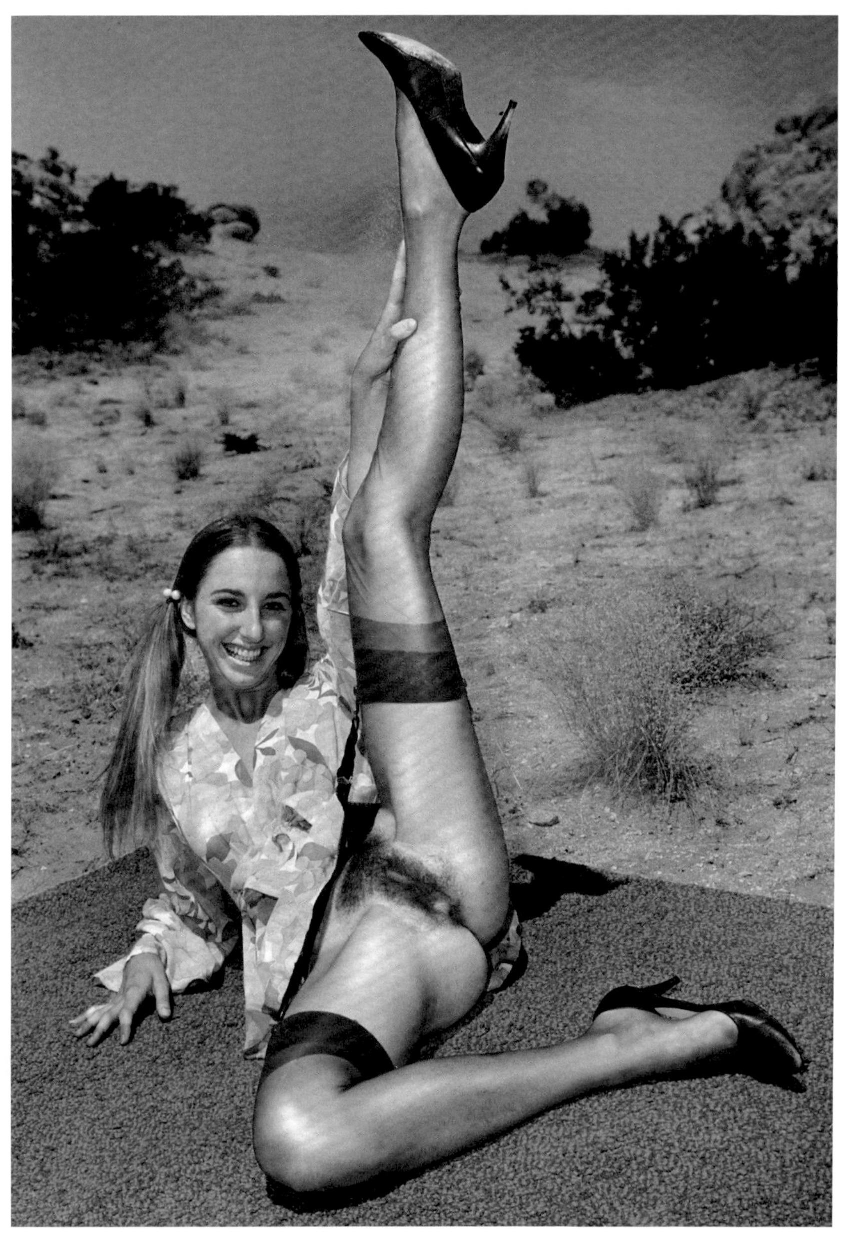

Robin Dragge

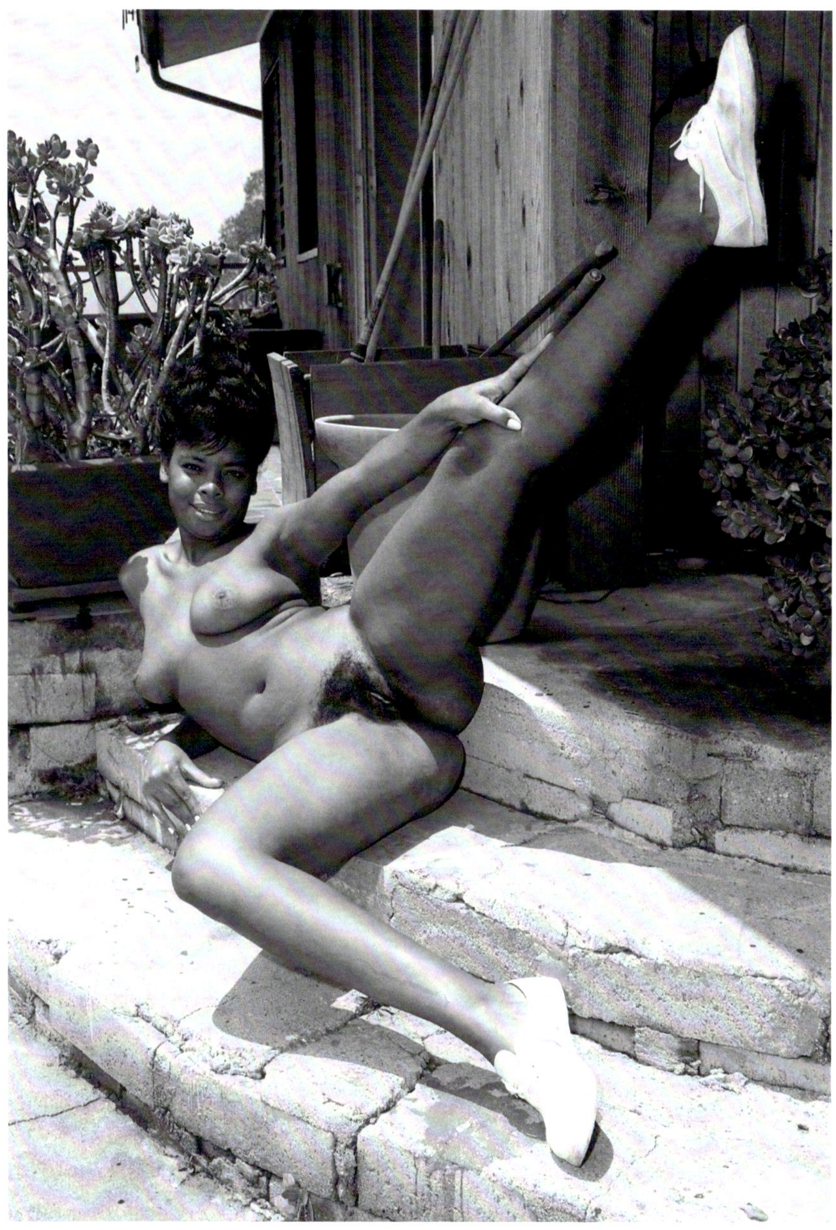

Unknown

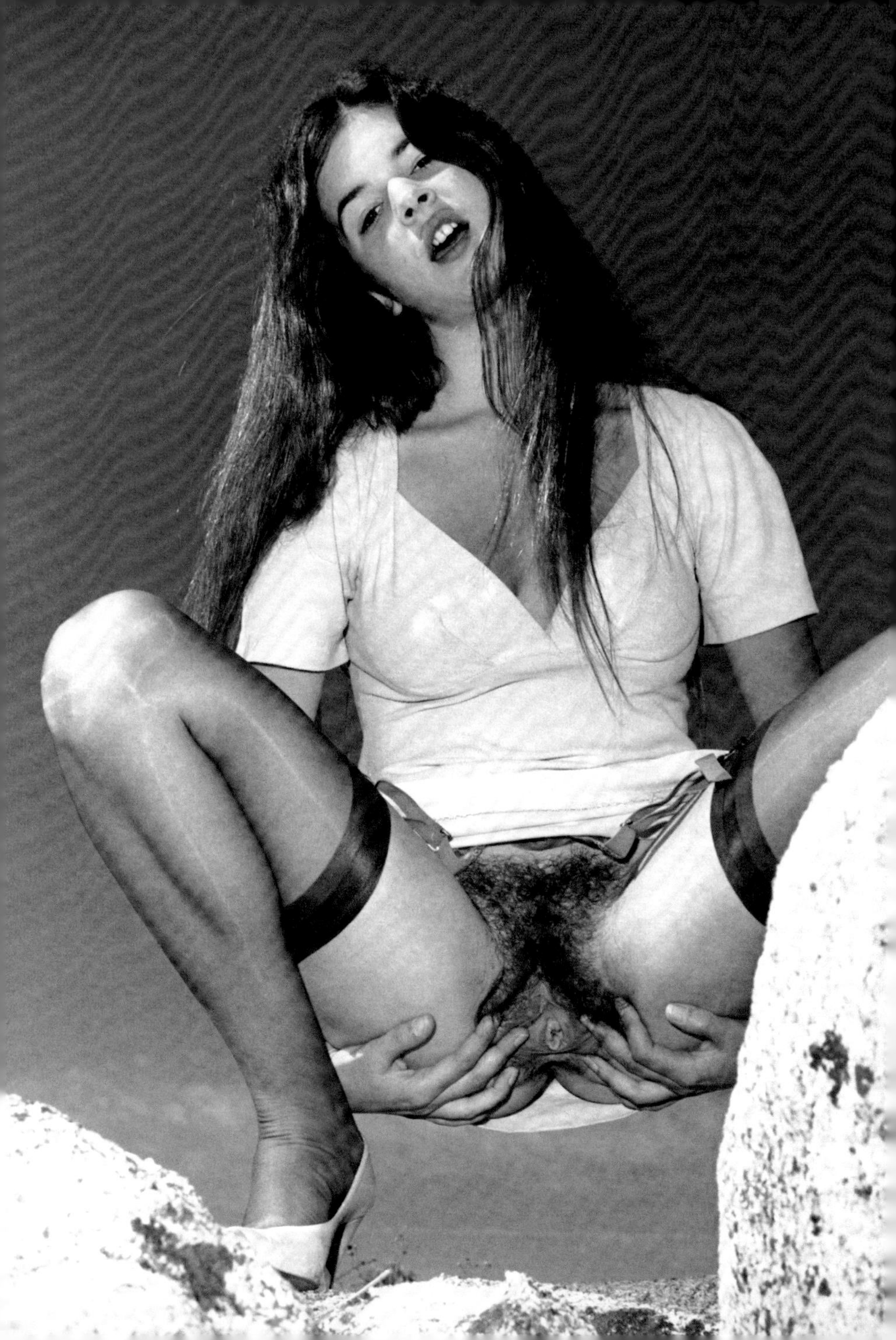

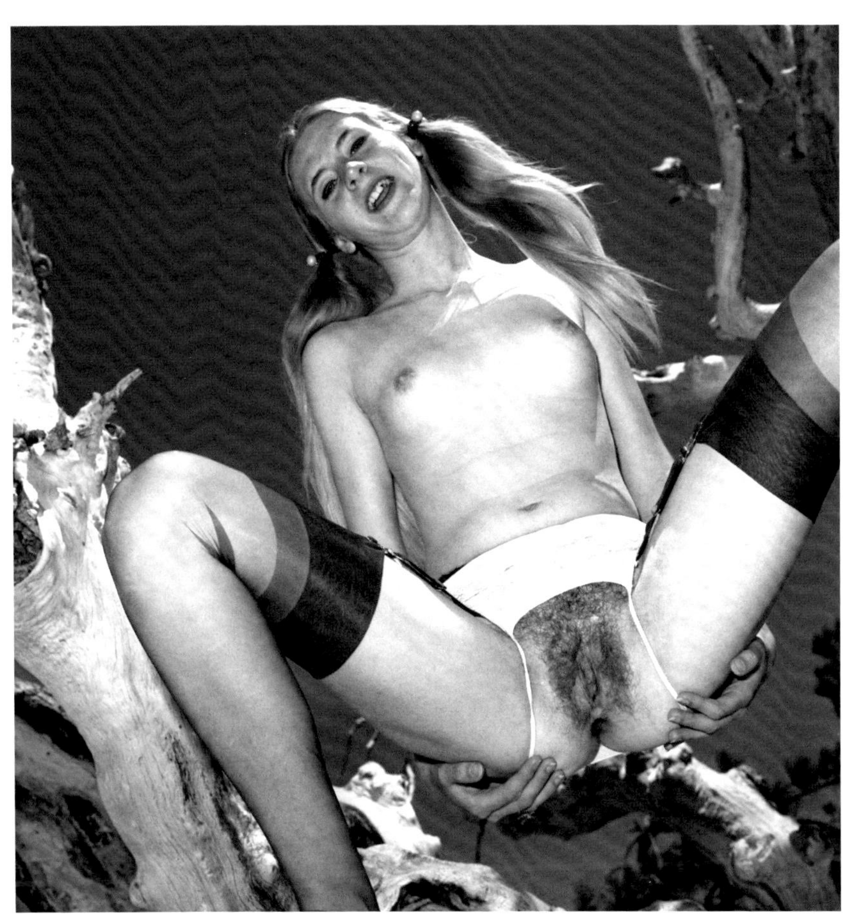

OPPOSITE **Sarah Holloway**   ABOVE **Unknown**

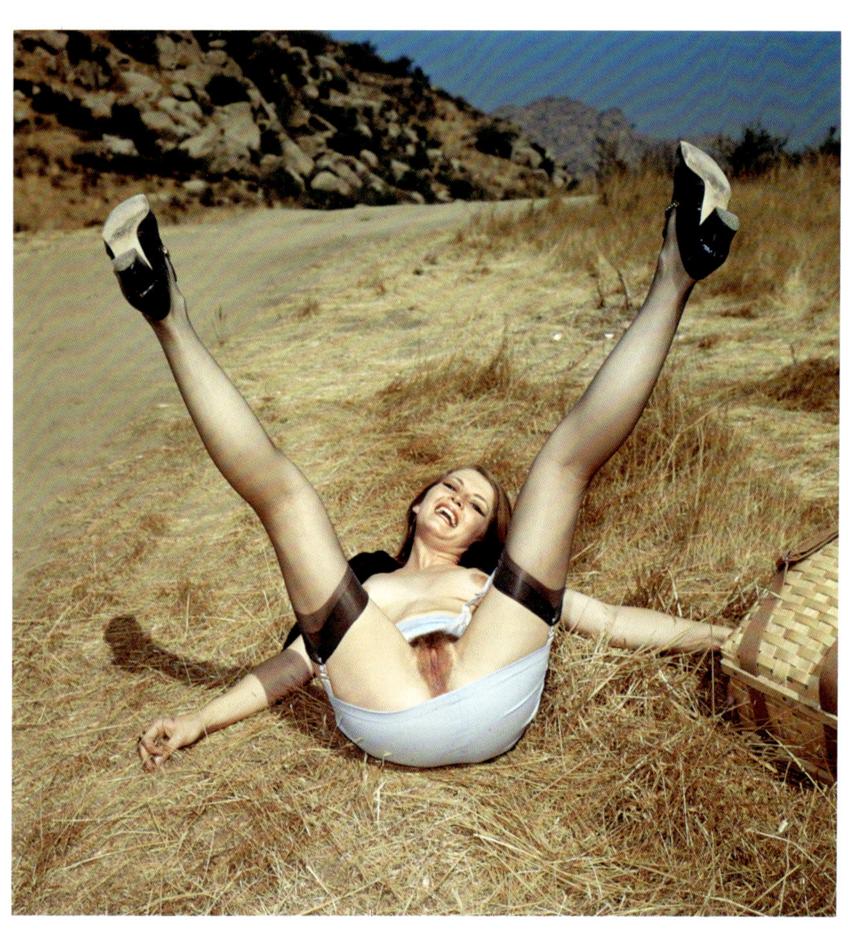

ABOVE **Unknown** OPPOSITE **Carol Habberley**

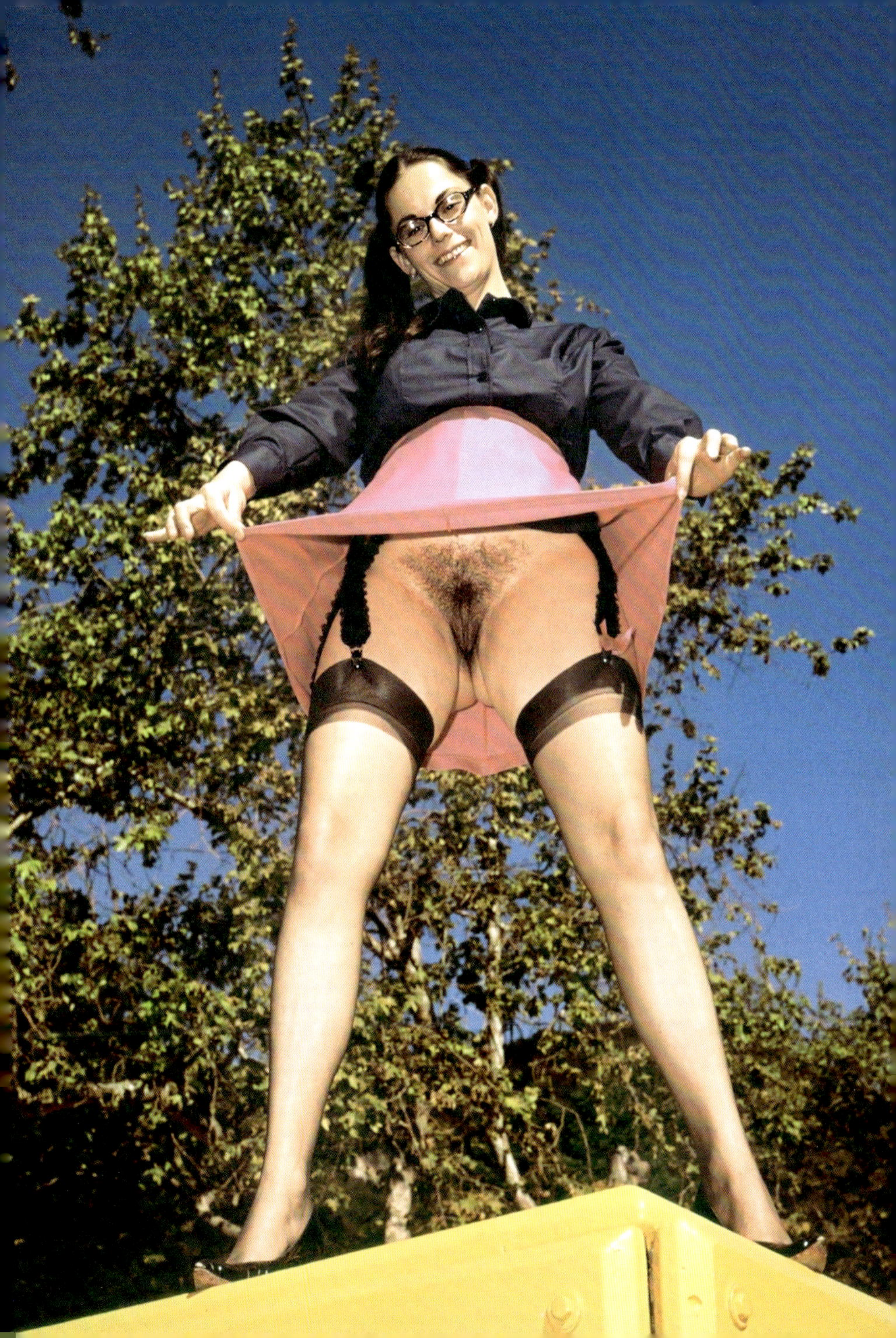

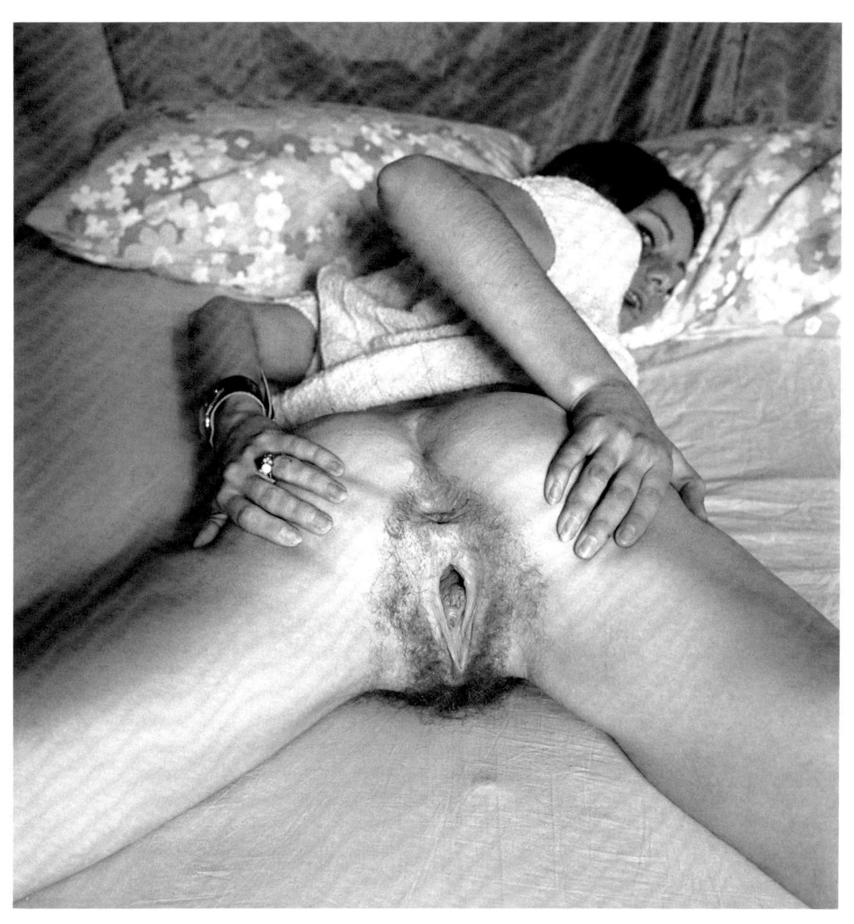

Unknown

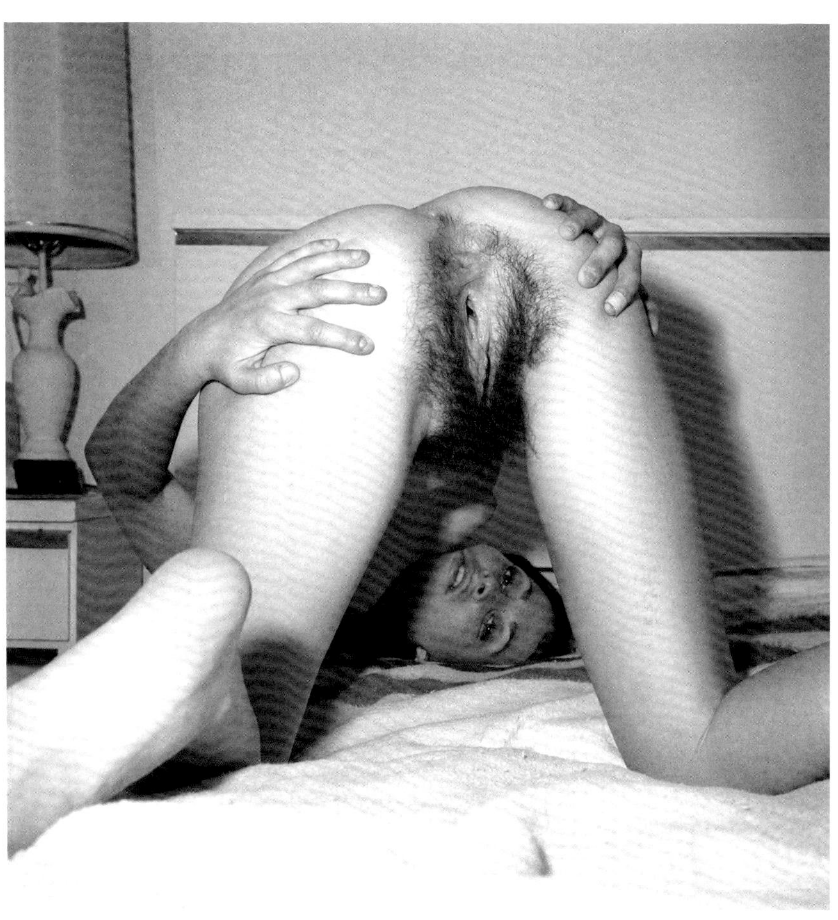

Unknown

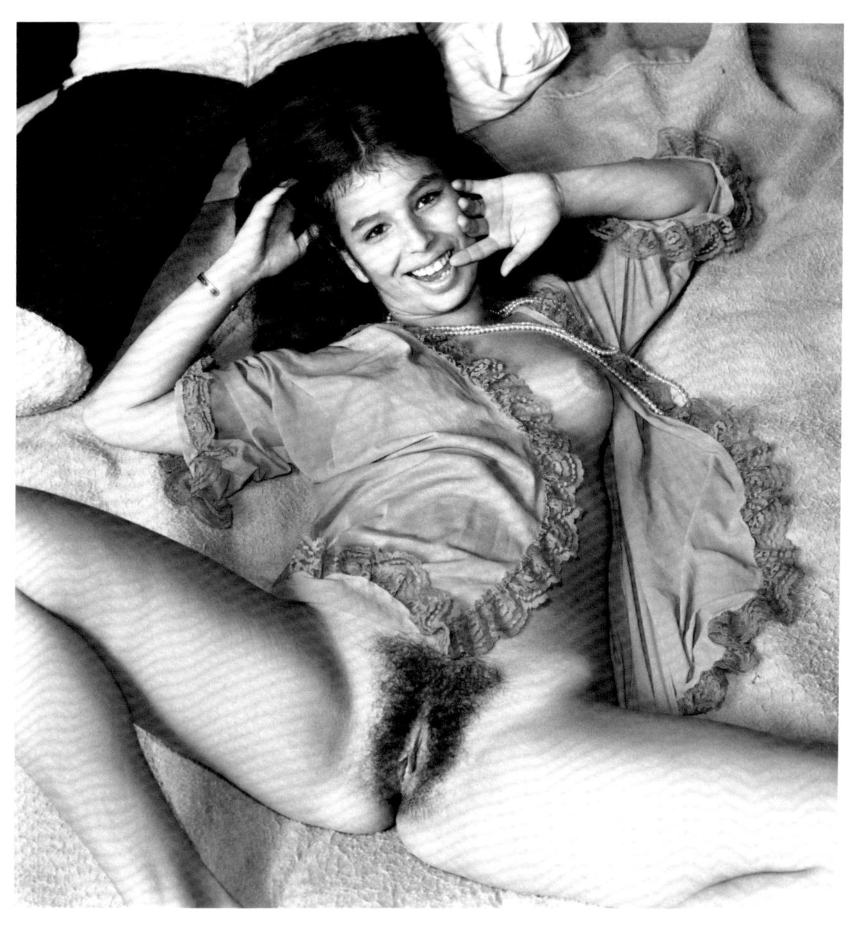

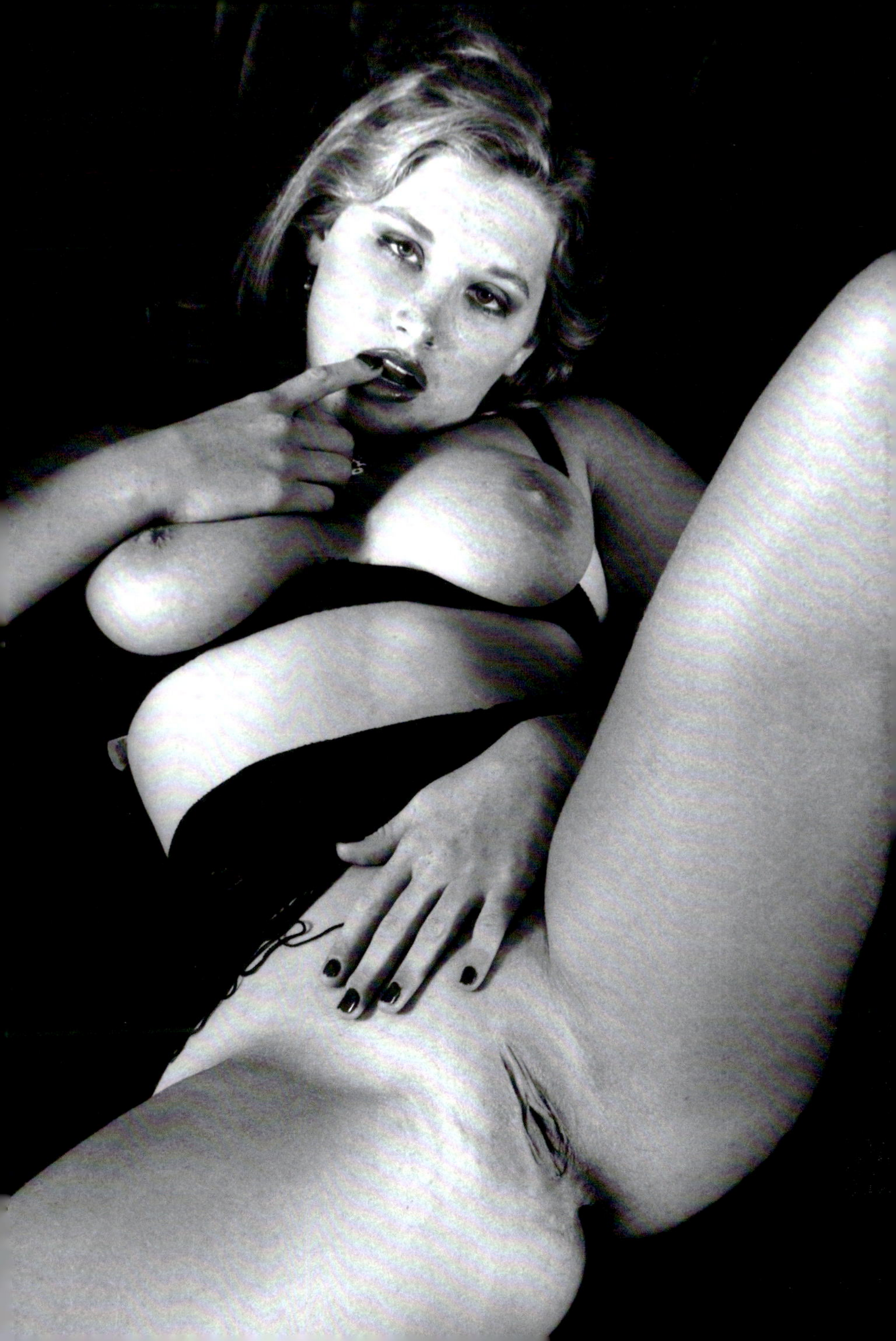

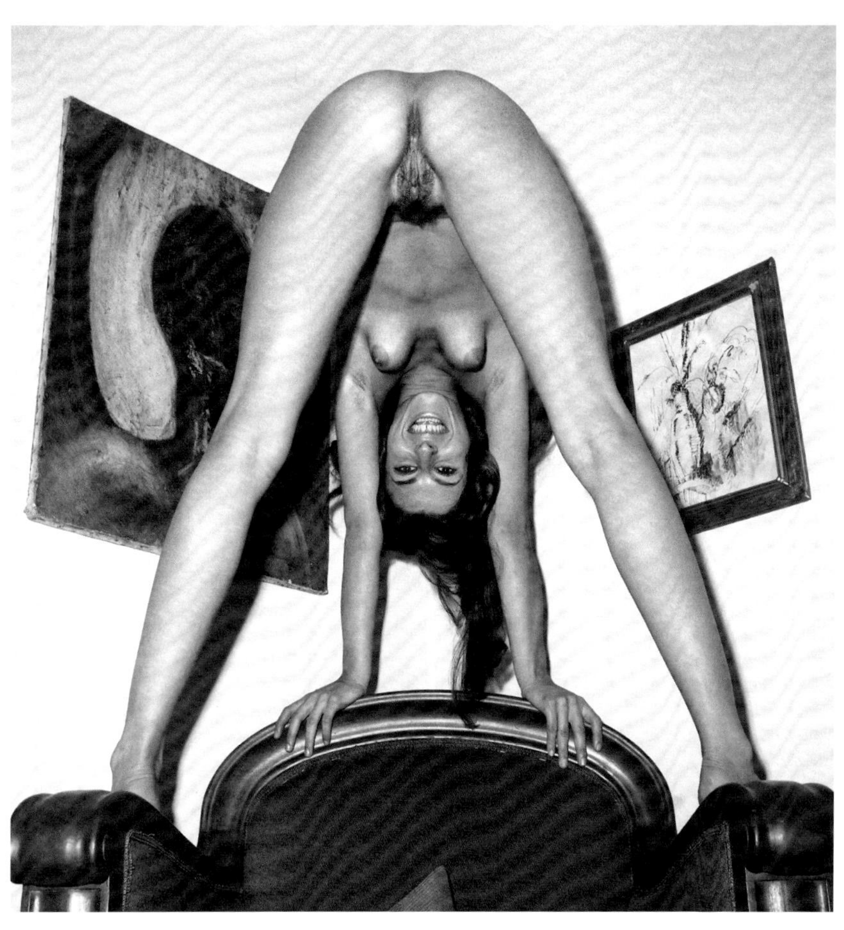

ABOVE AND OPPOSITE **Unknown**

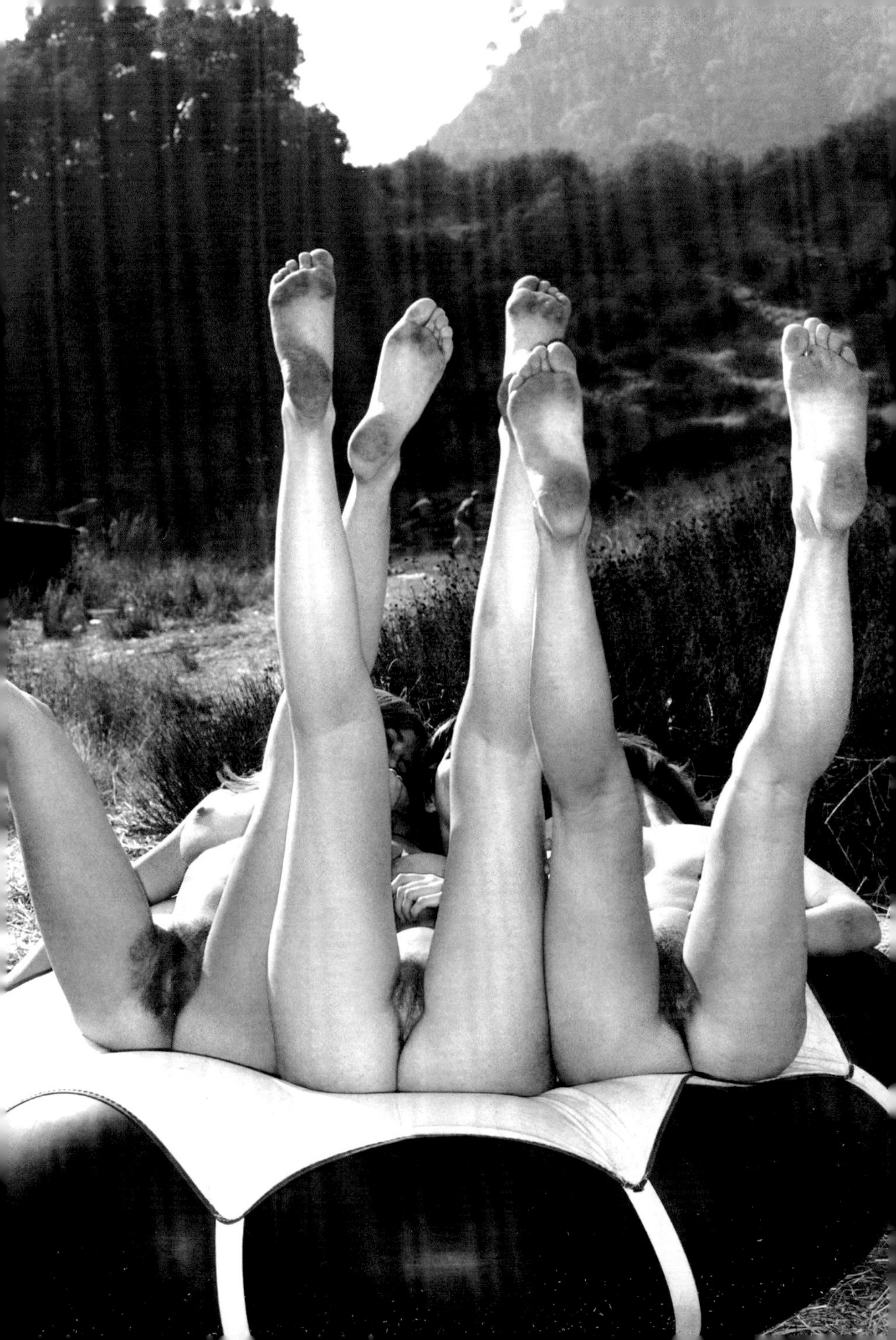

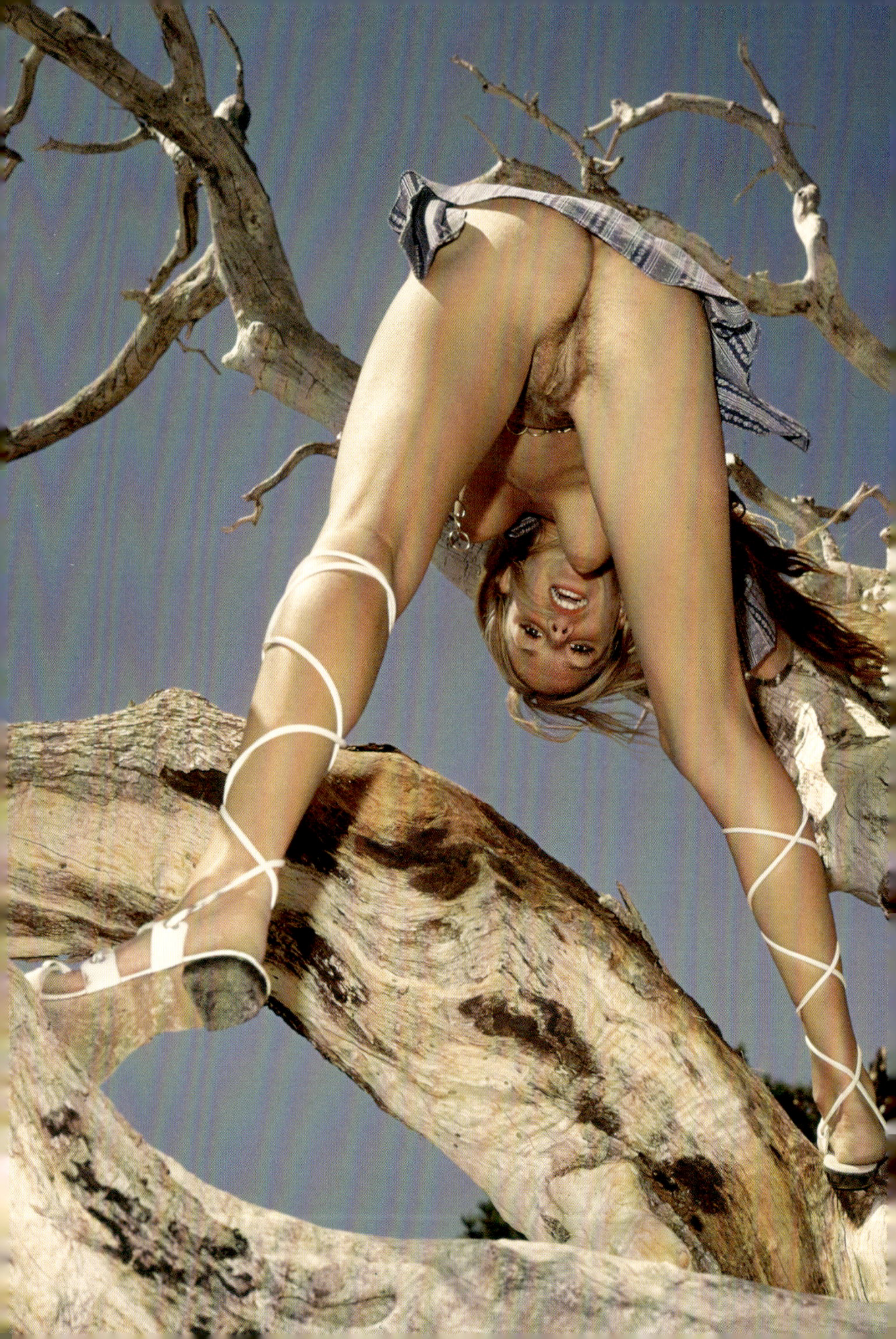

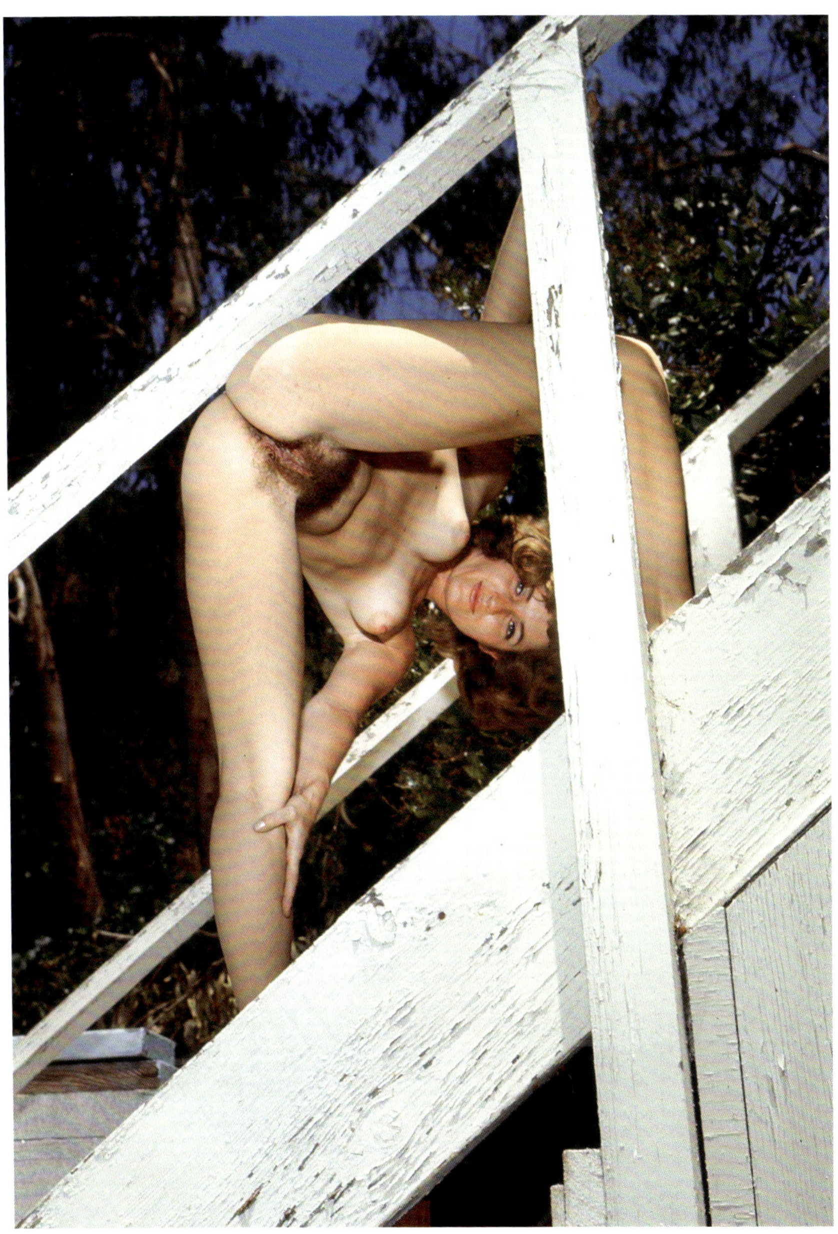

OPPOSITE AND ABOVE **Unknown**

Wednesday- Track meet Fairfield High
Thursday- Math Exam
Friday- Date with
Saturday-Date wi
Sunday -Tri

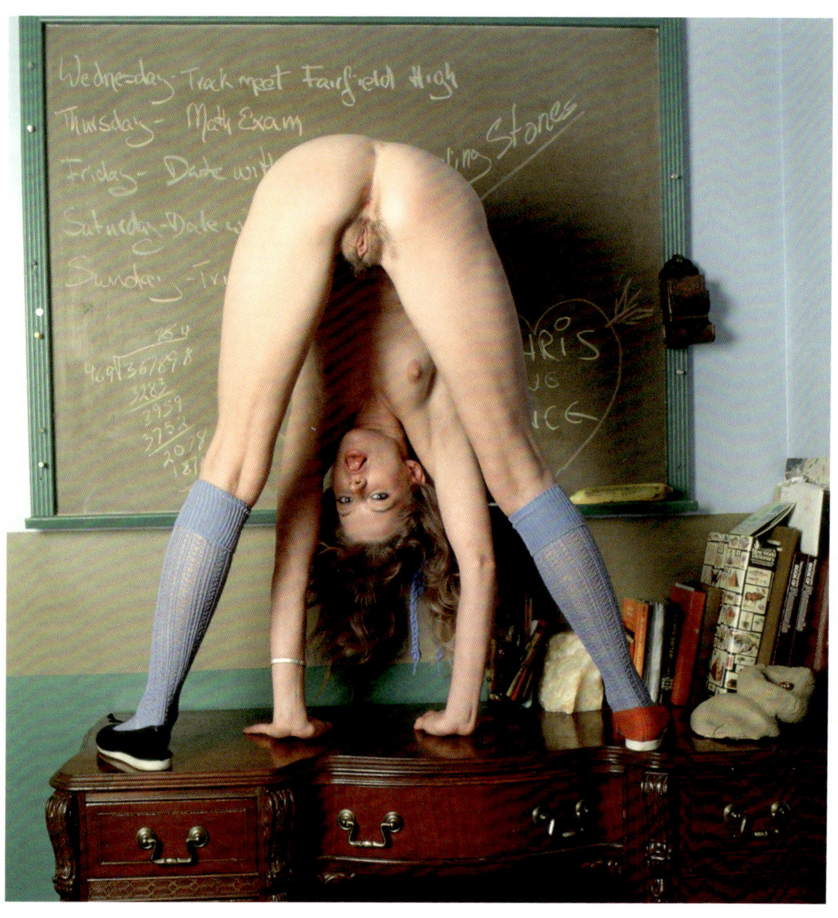

Unknown

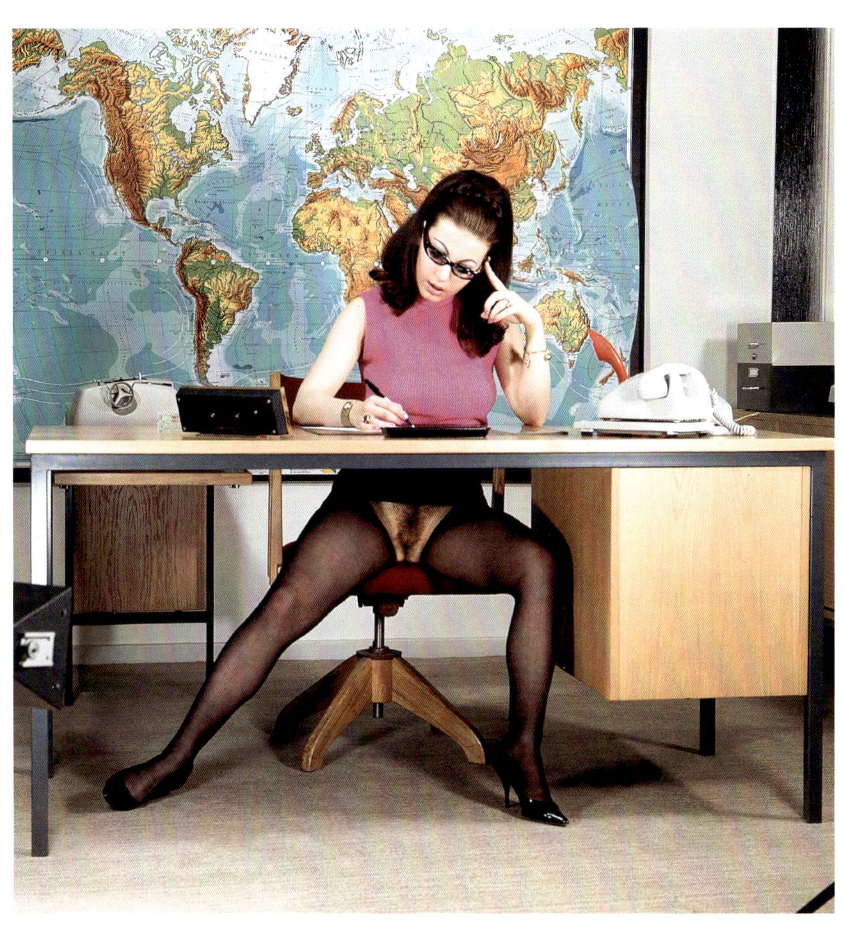

ABOVE **Veronica**   PAGES 108-109 **Unknown**

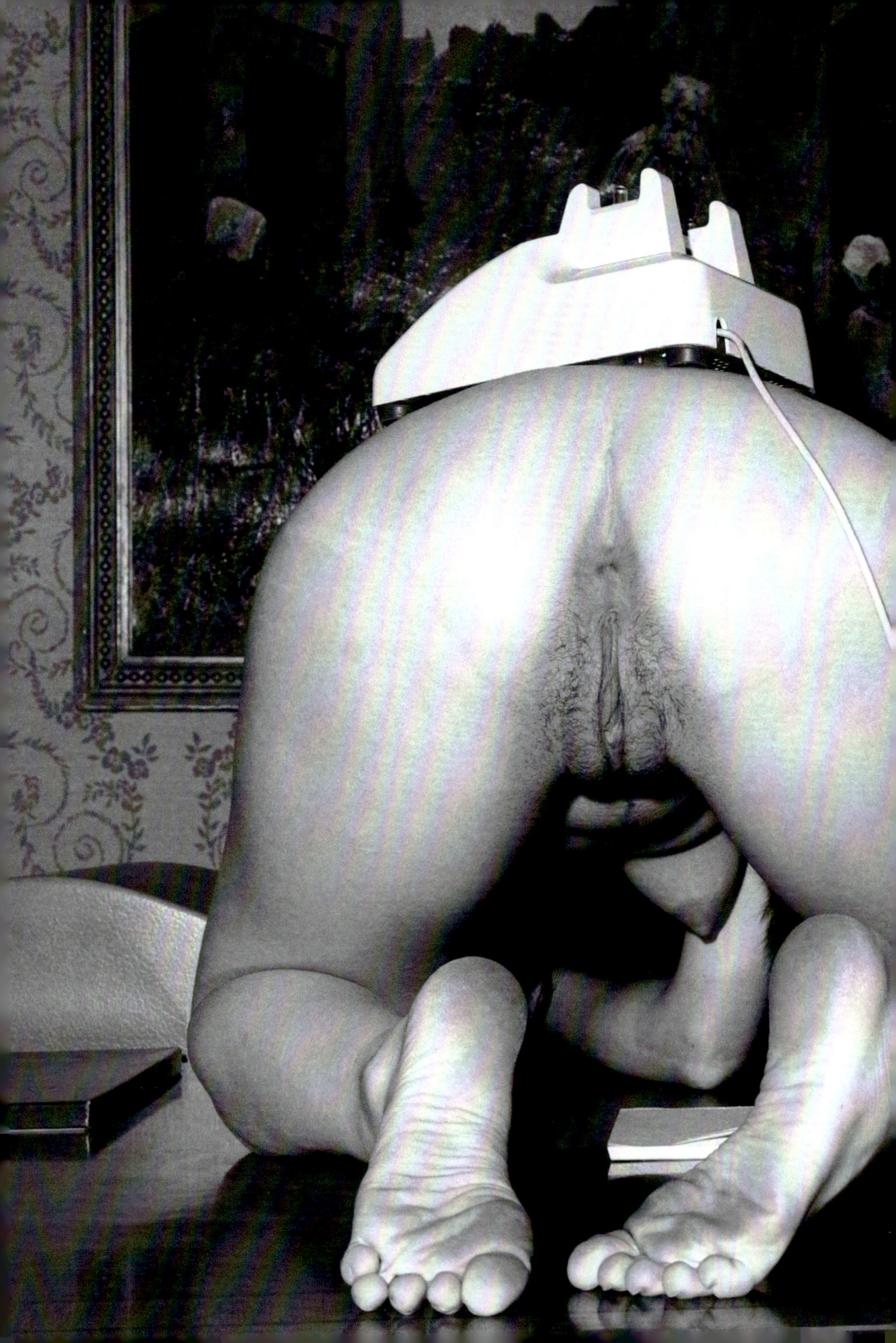

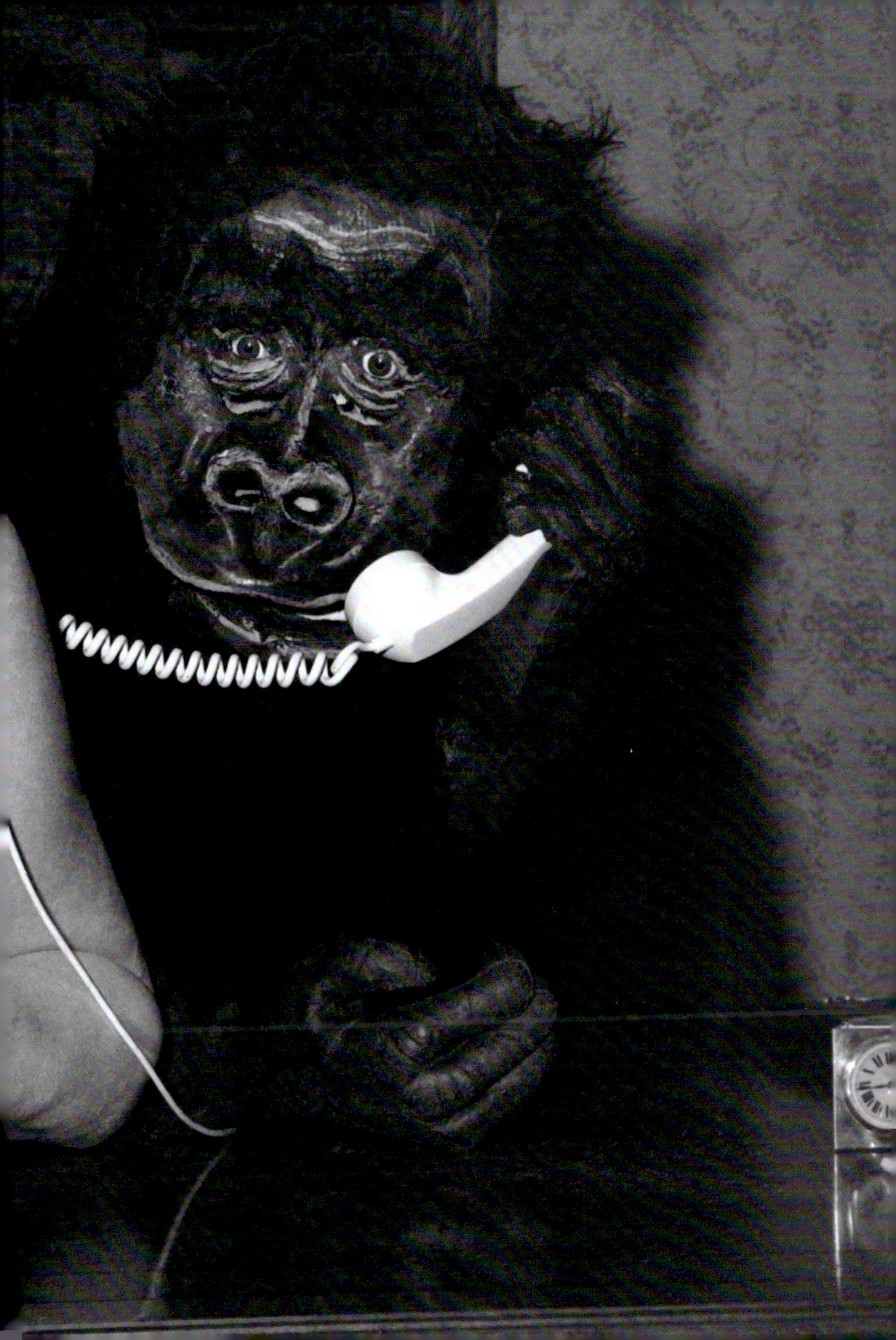

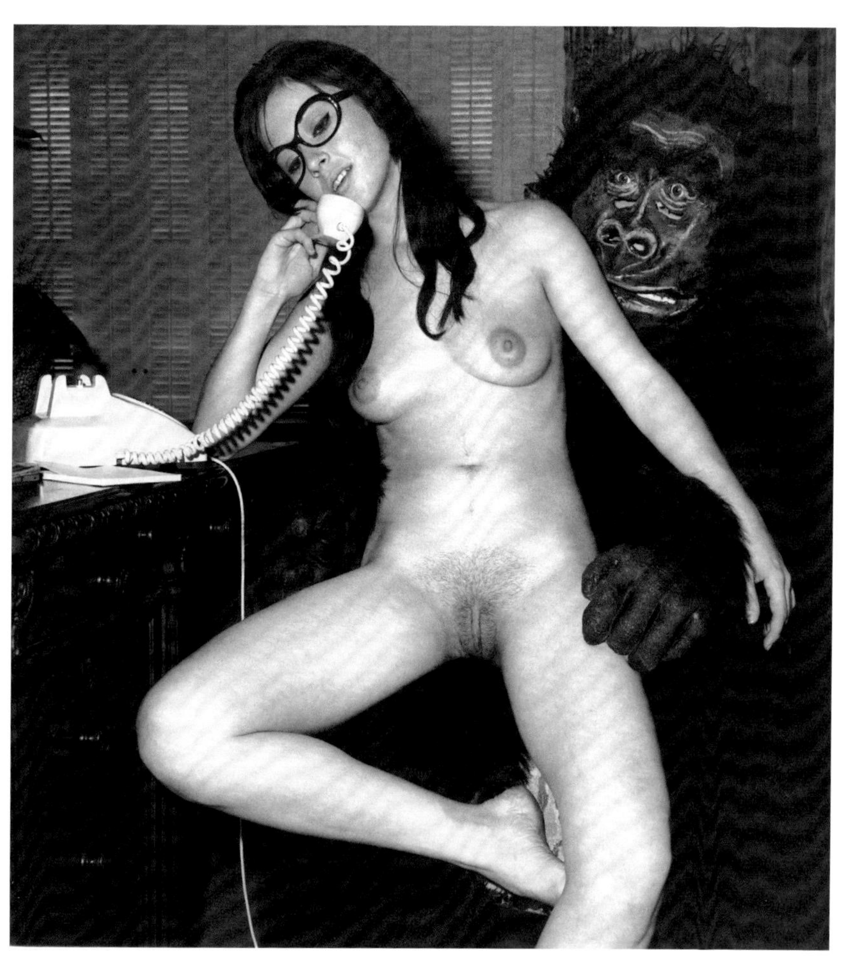

ABOVE AND OPPOSITE **Unknown**

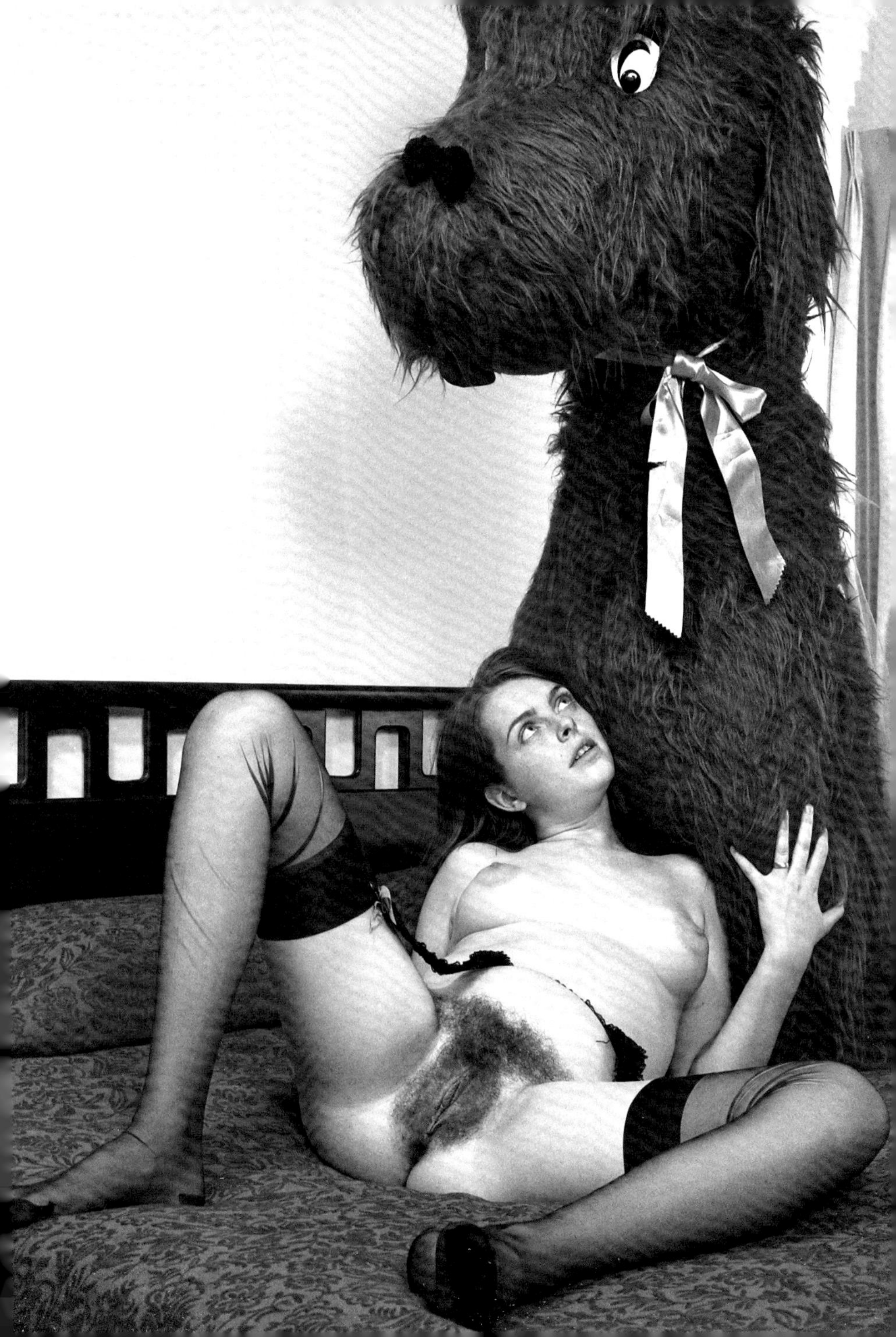

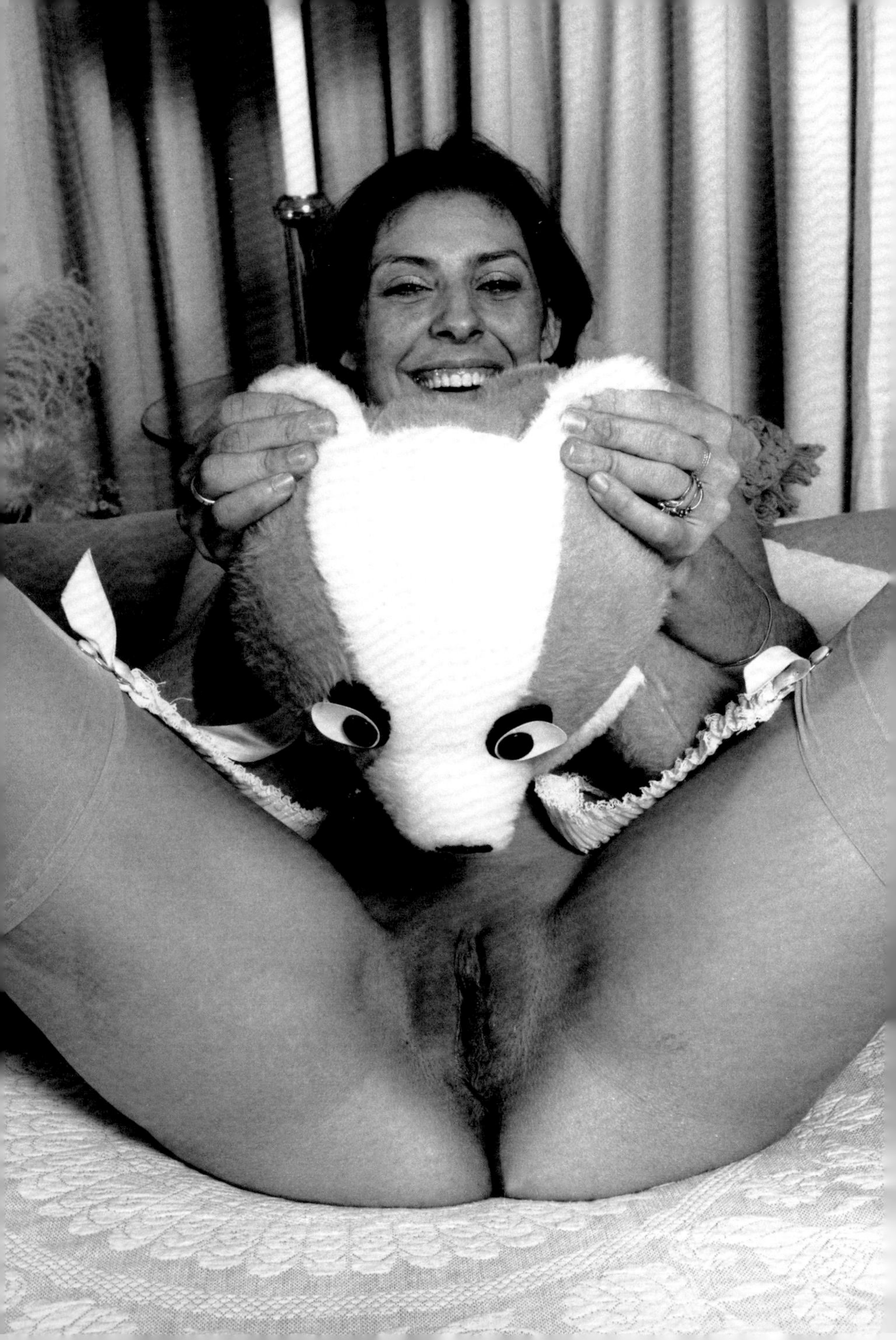

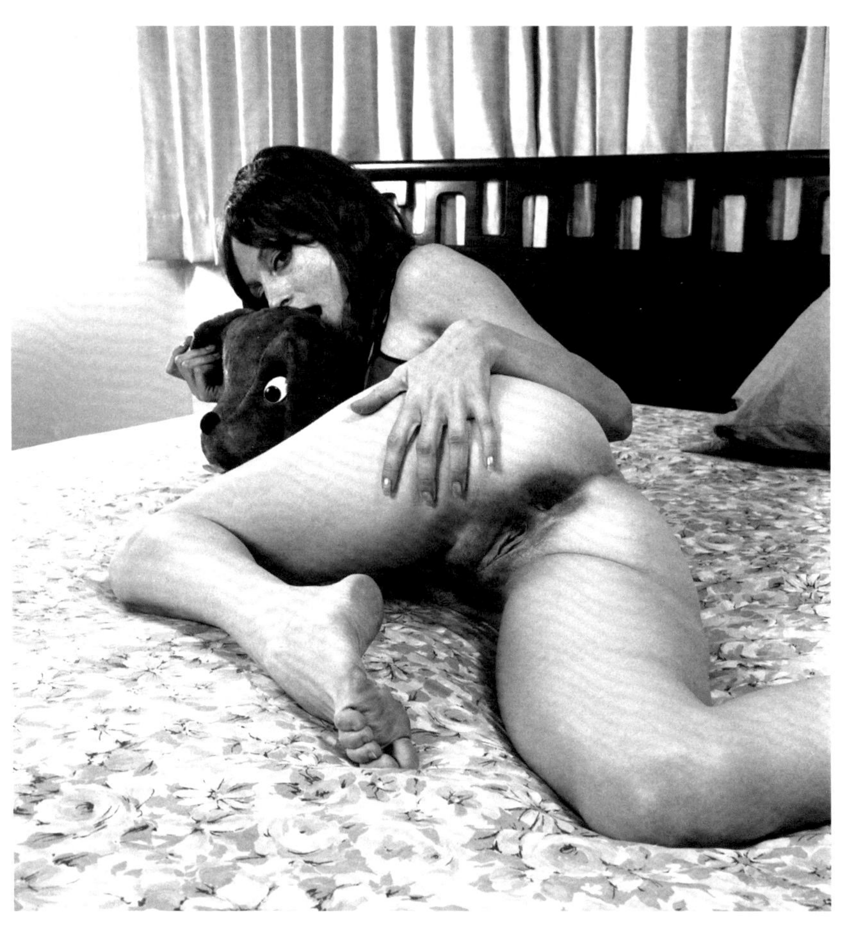

OPPOSITE **Linda Moore**   ABOVE **Nancy Young**   PAGES 114-115 **Unknown**

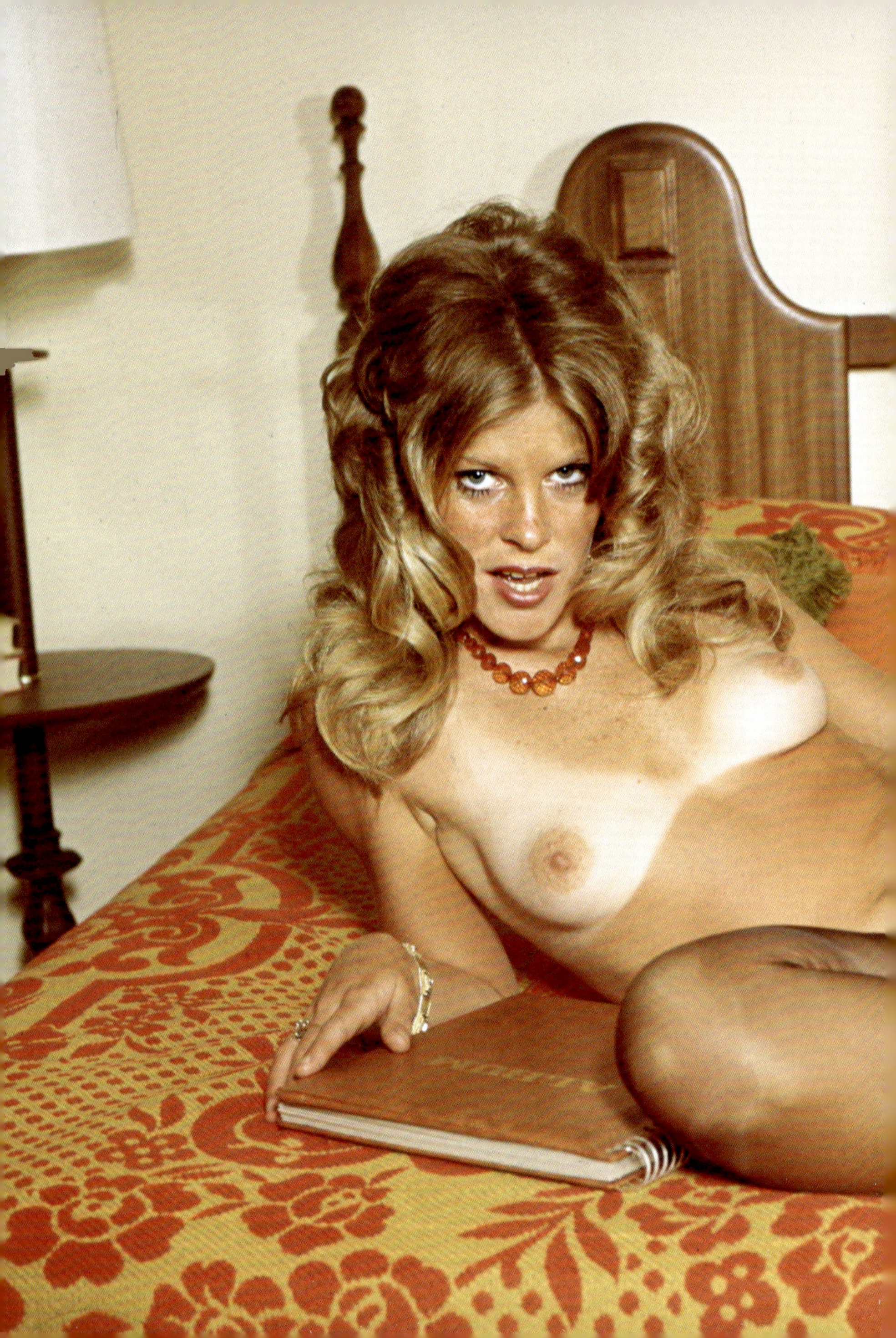

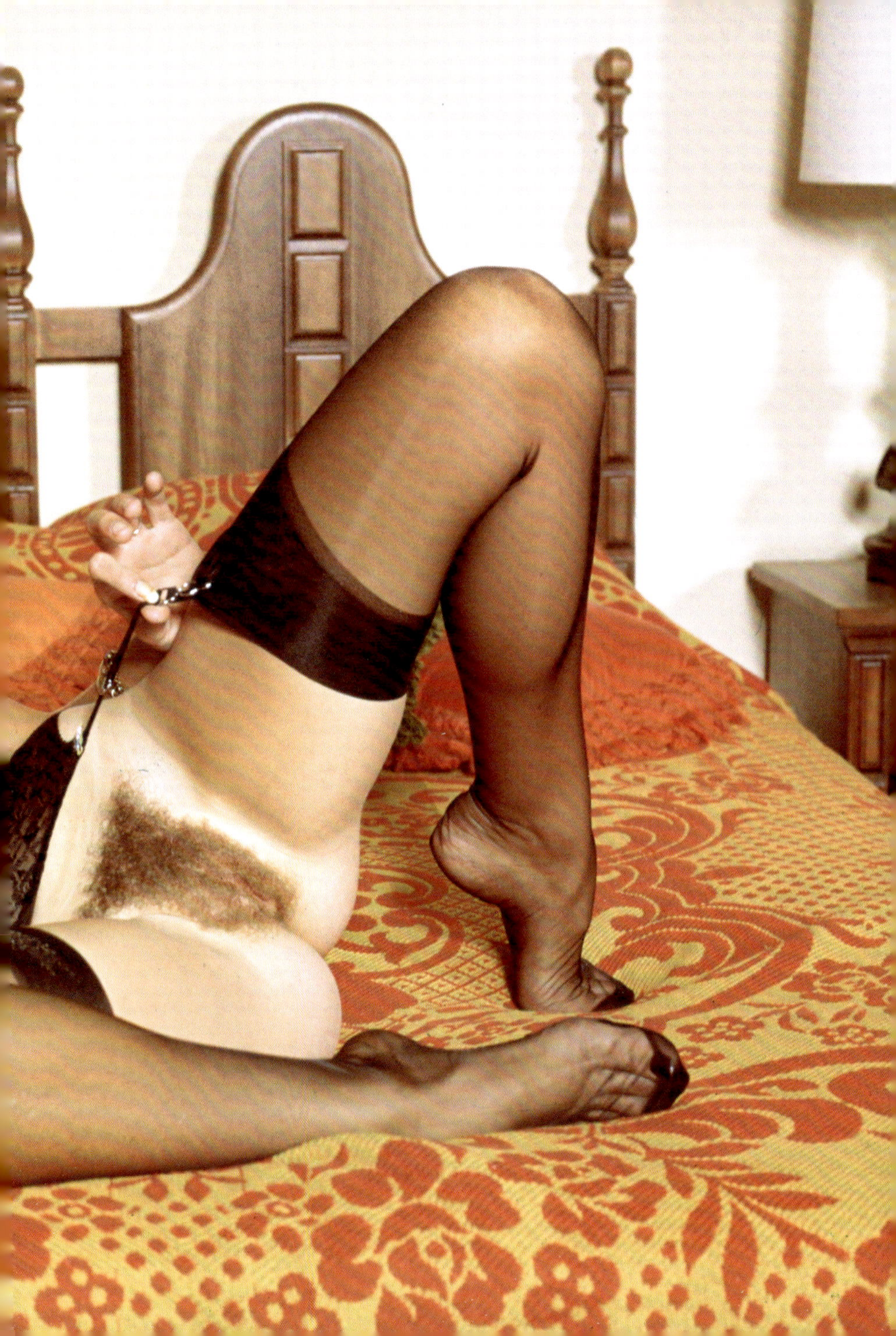

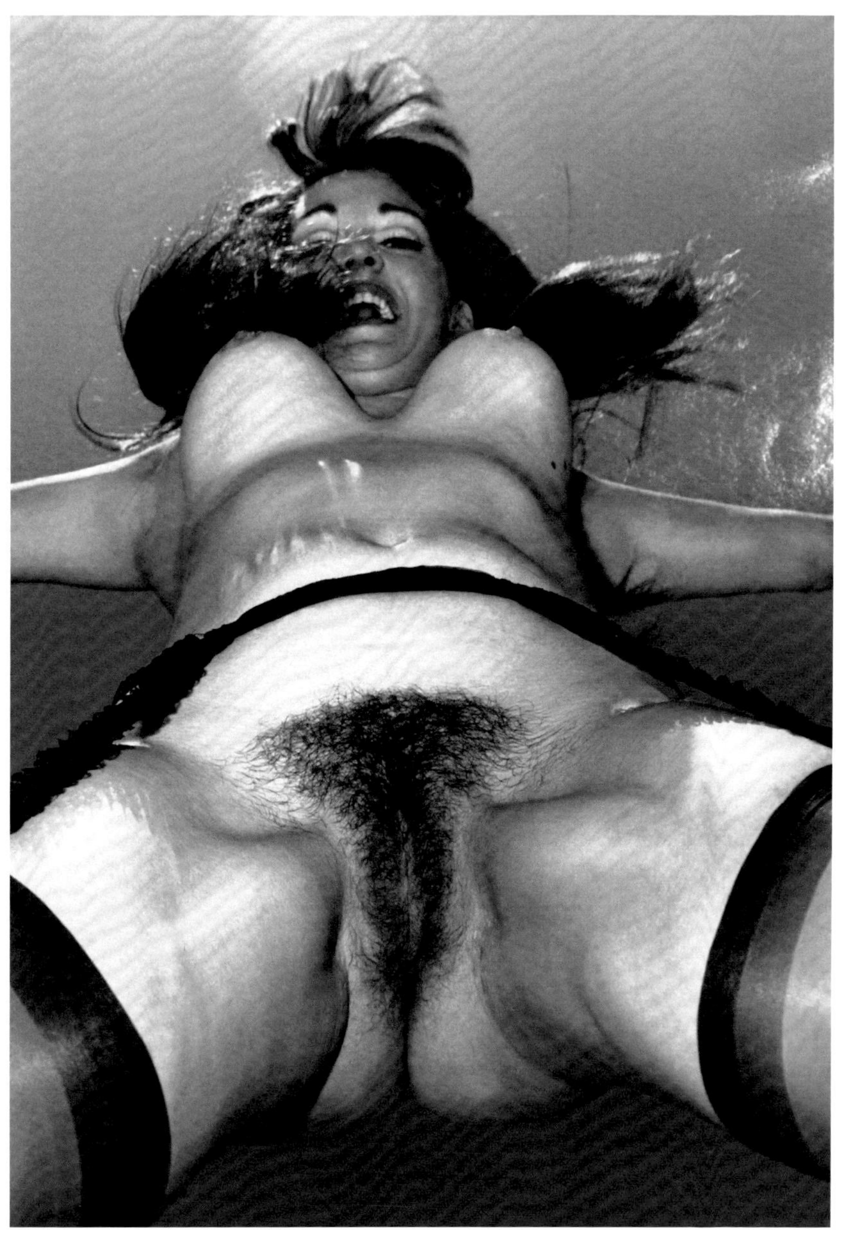

Vicky Warner

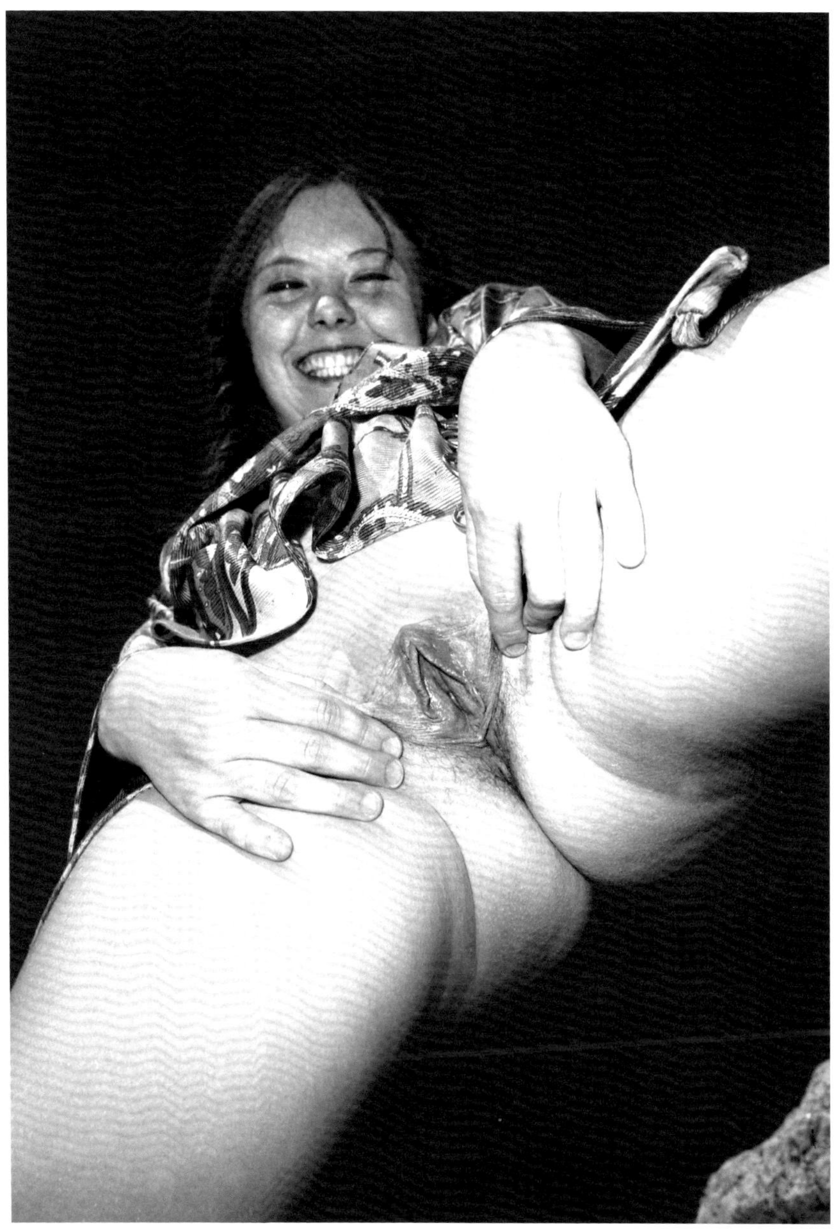

Unknown

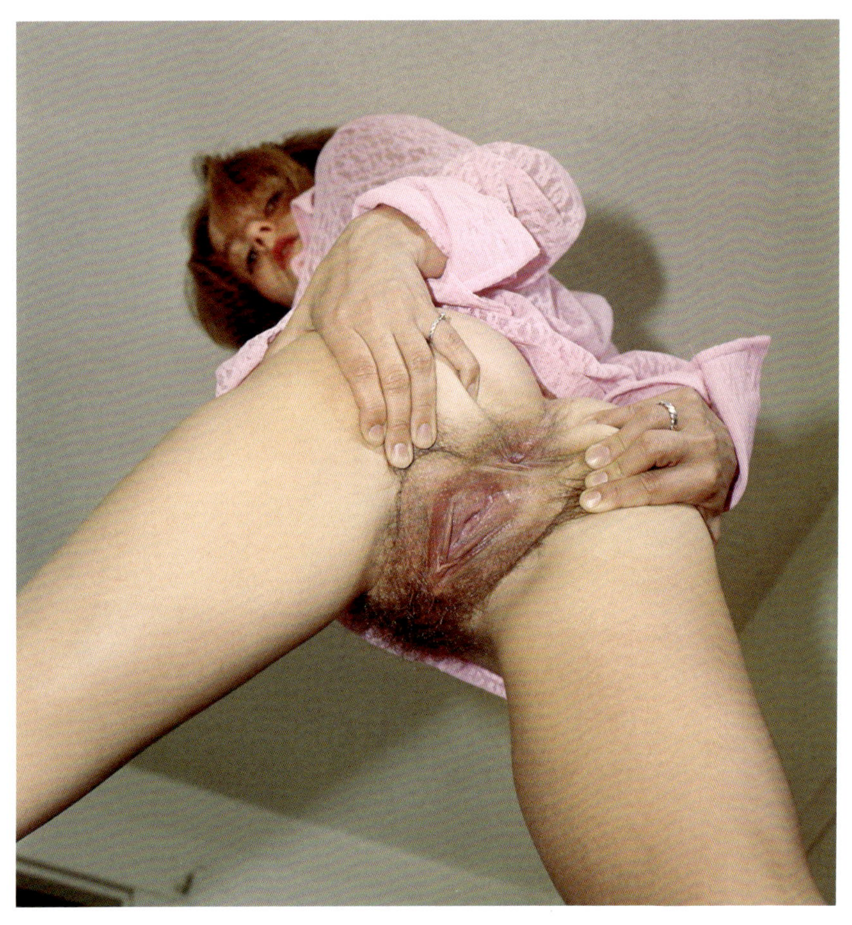

Unknown

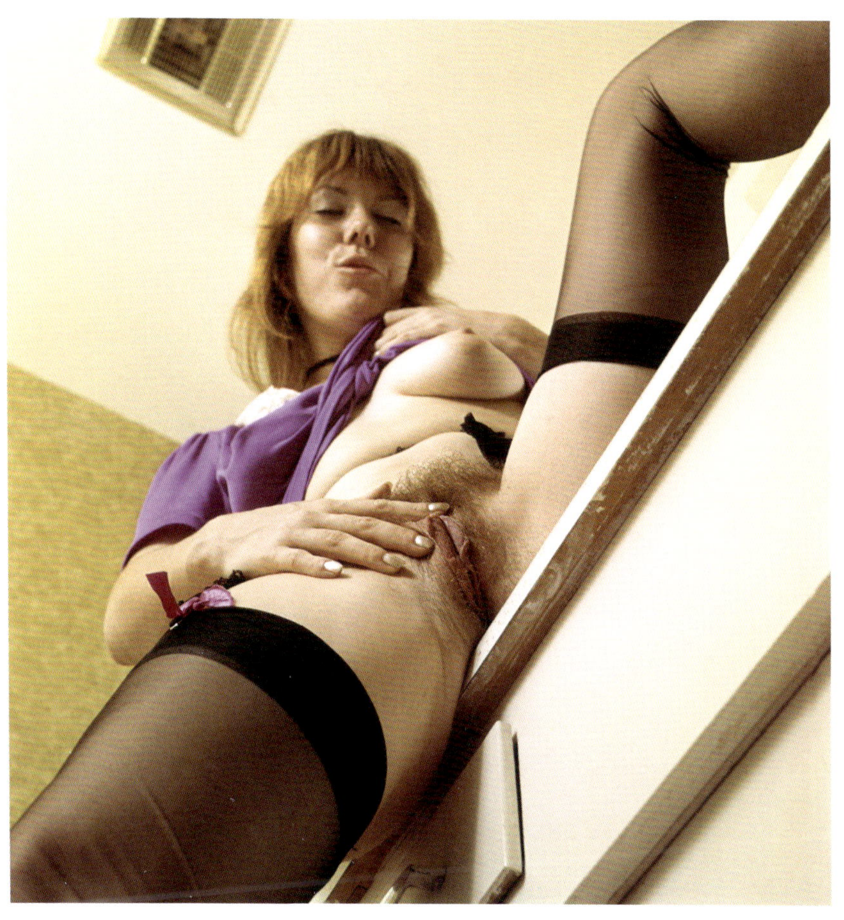

Unknown

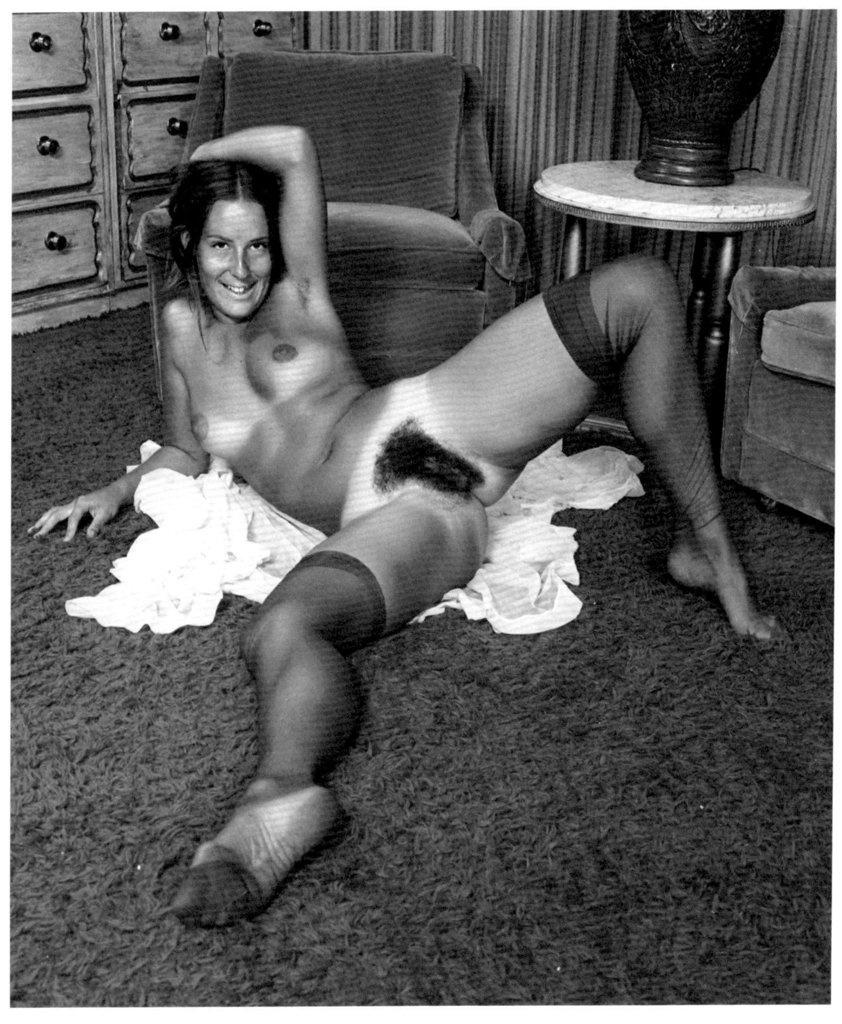

Unknown

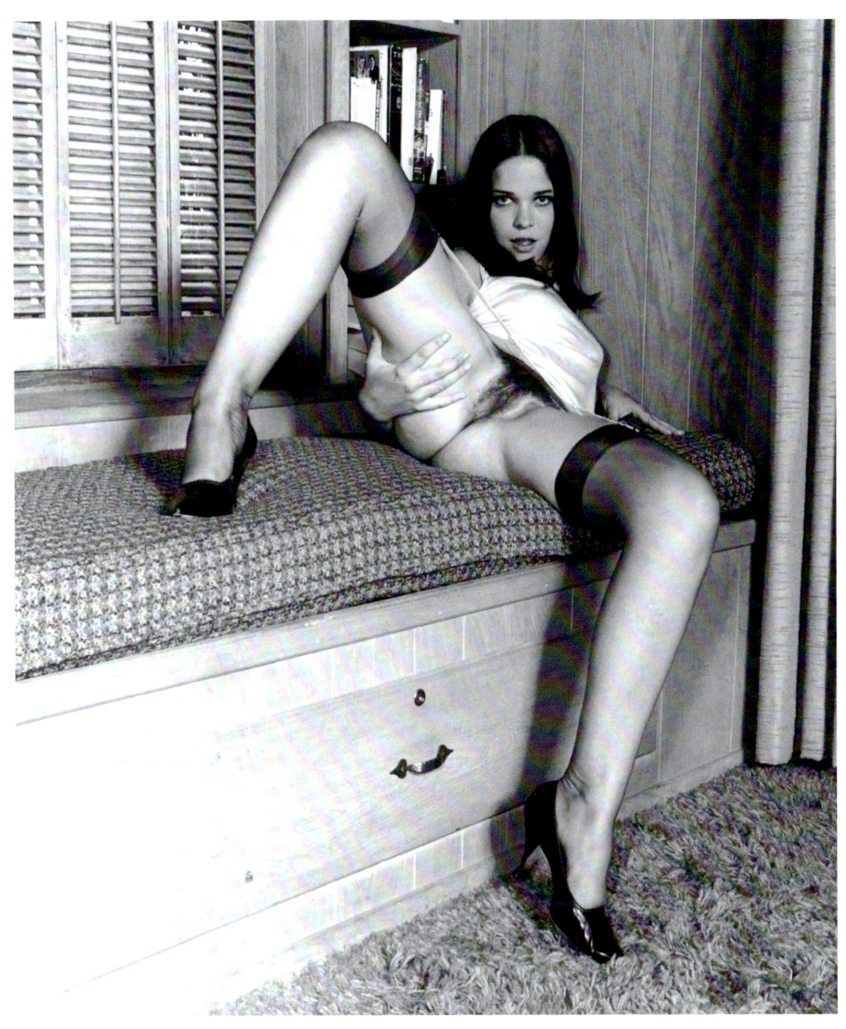

Debbie Stewart

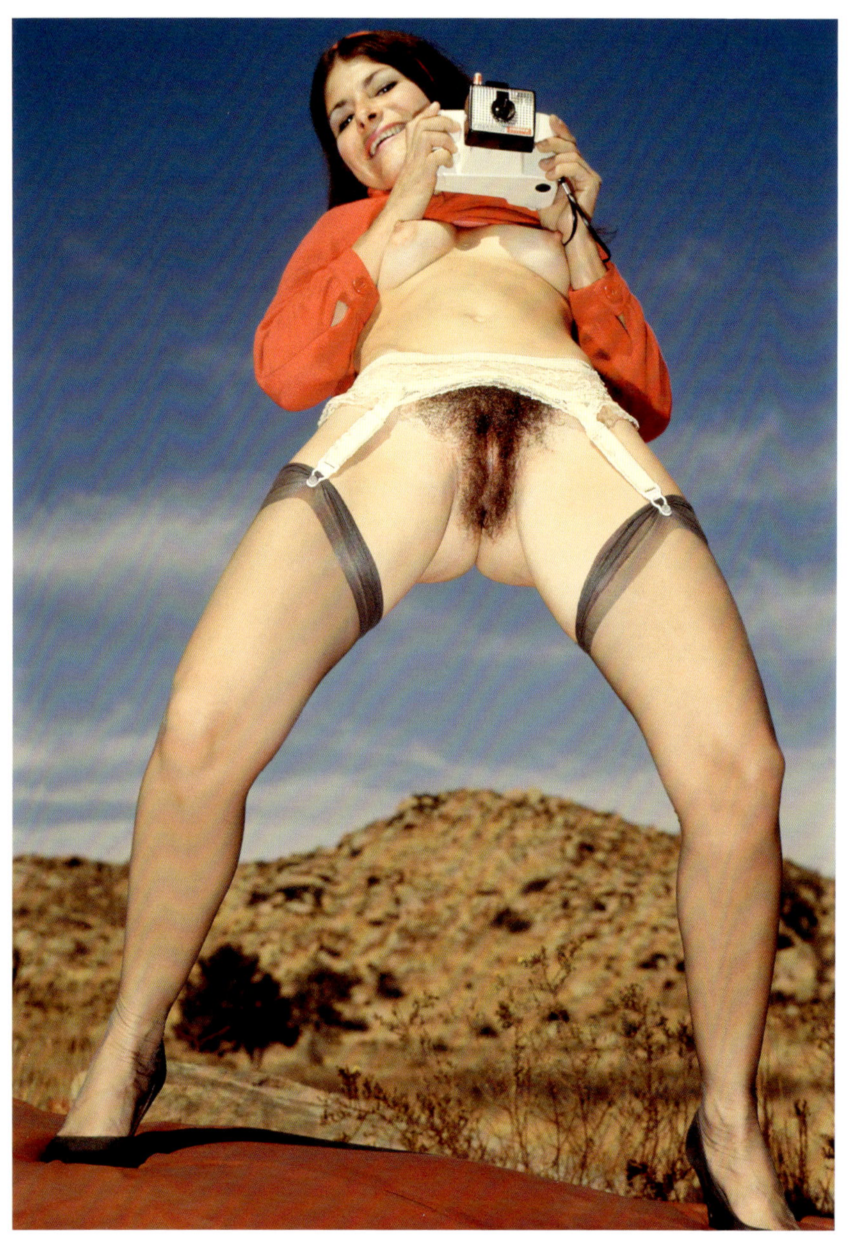

ABOVE AND OPPOSITE **Unknown**

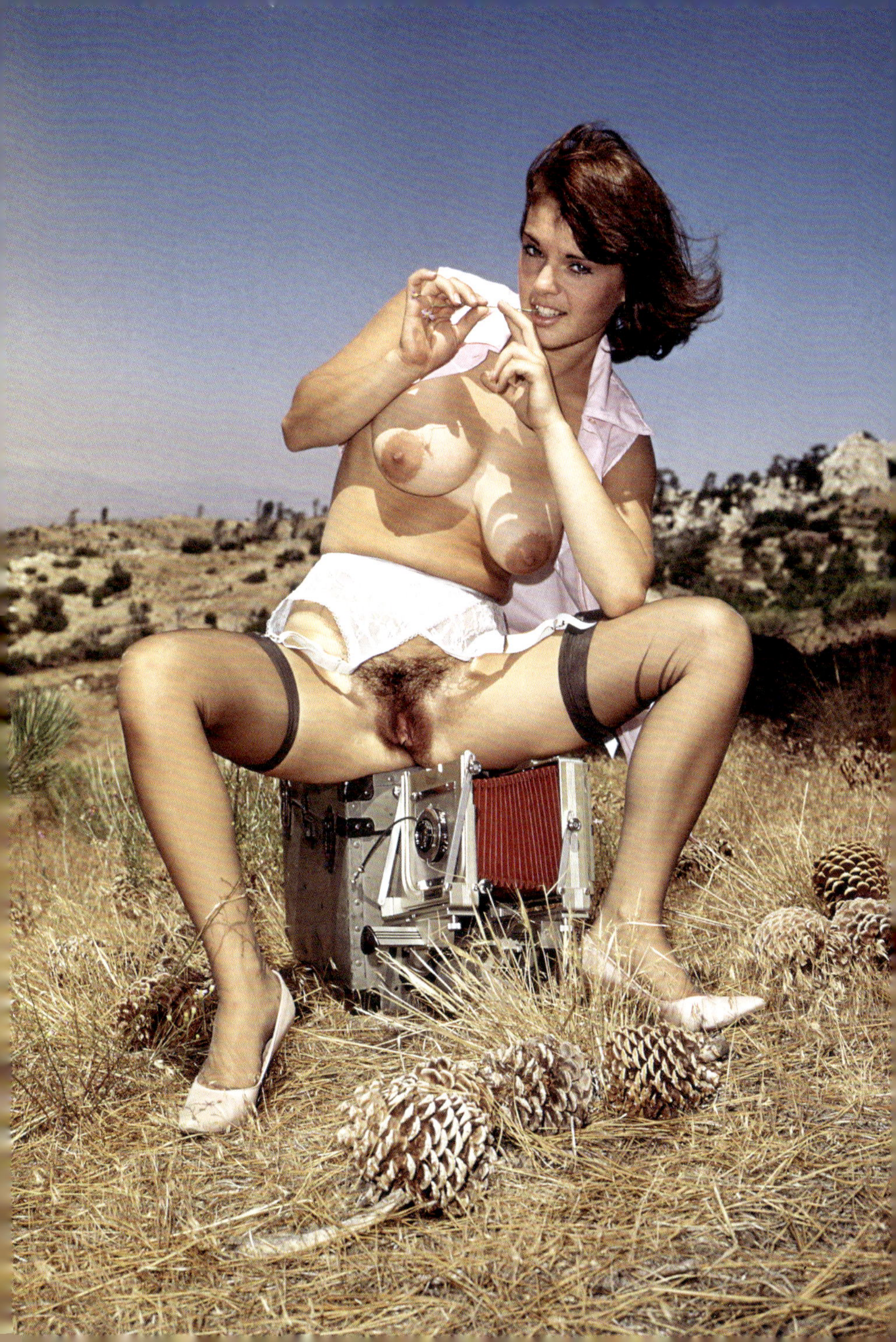

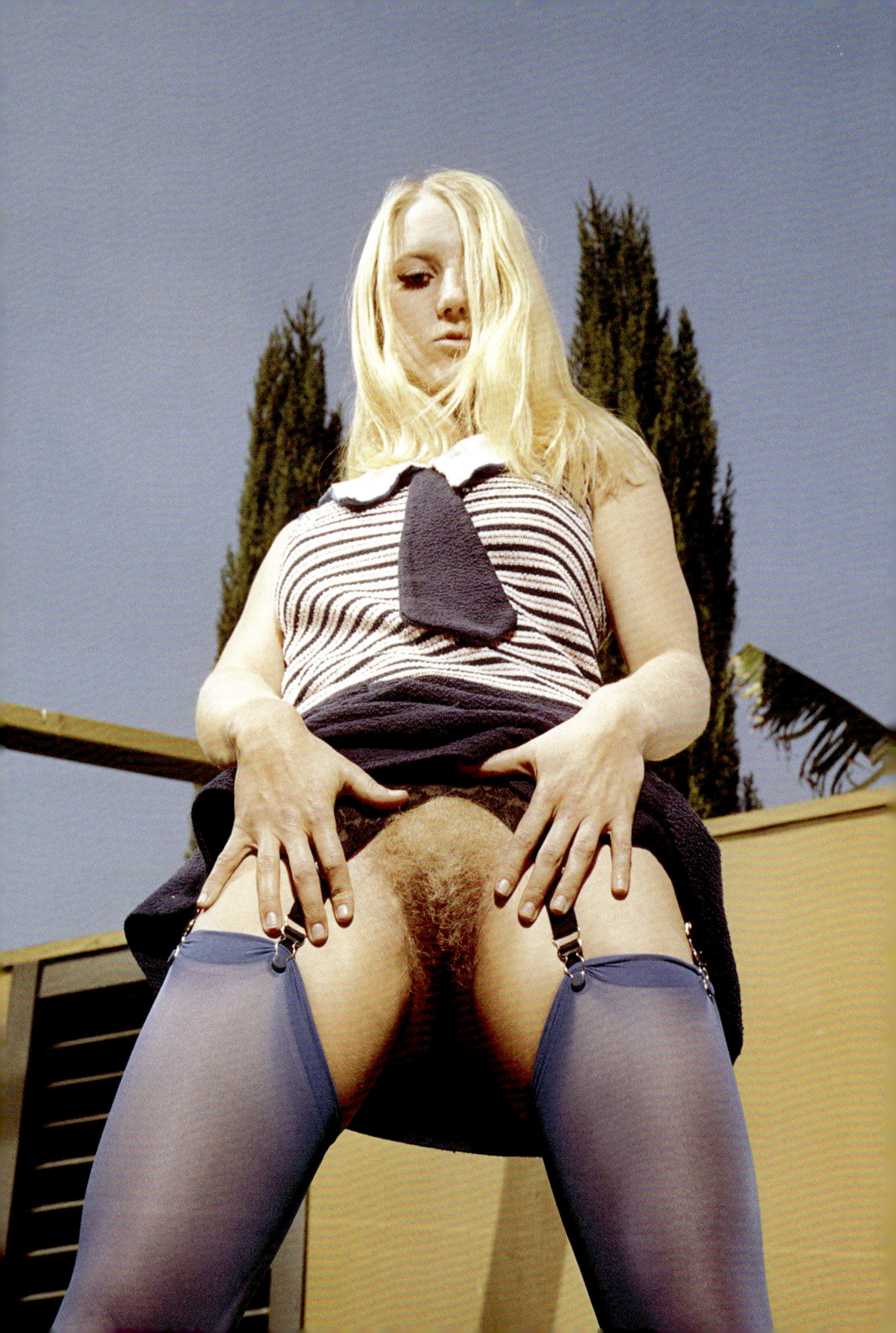

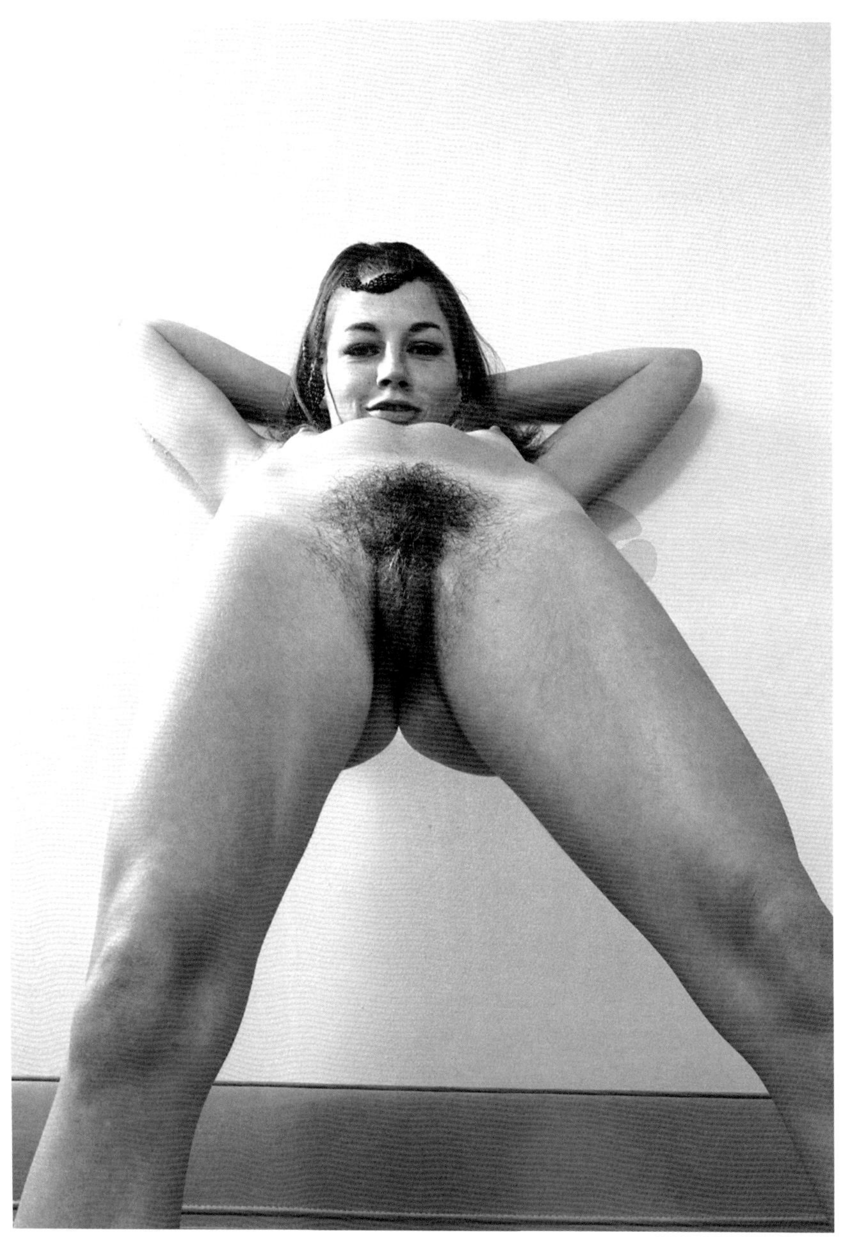

OPPOSITE AND ABOVE **Unknown**   PAGES 126-127 **Billy Joe Fitz**

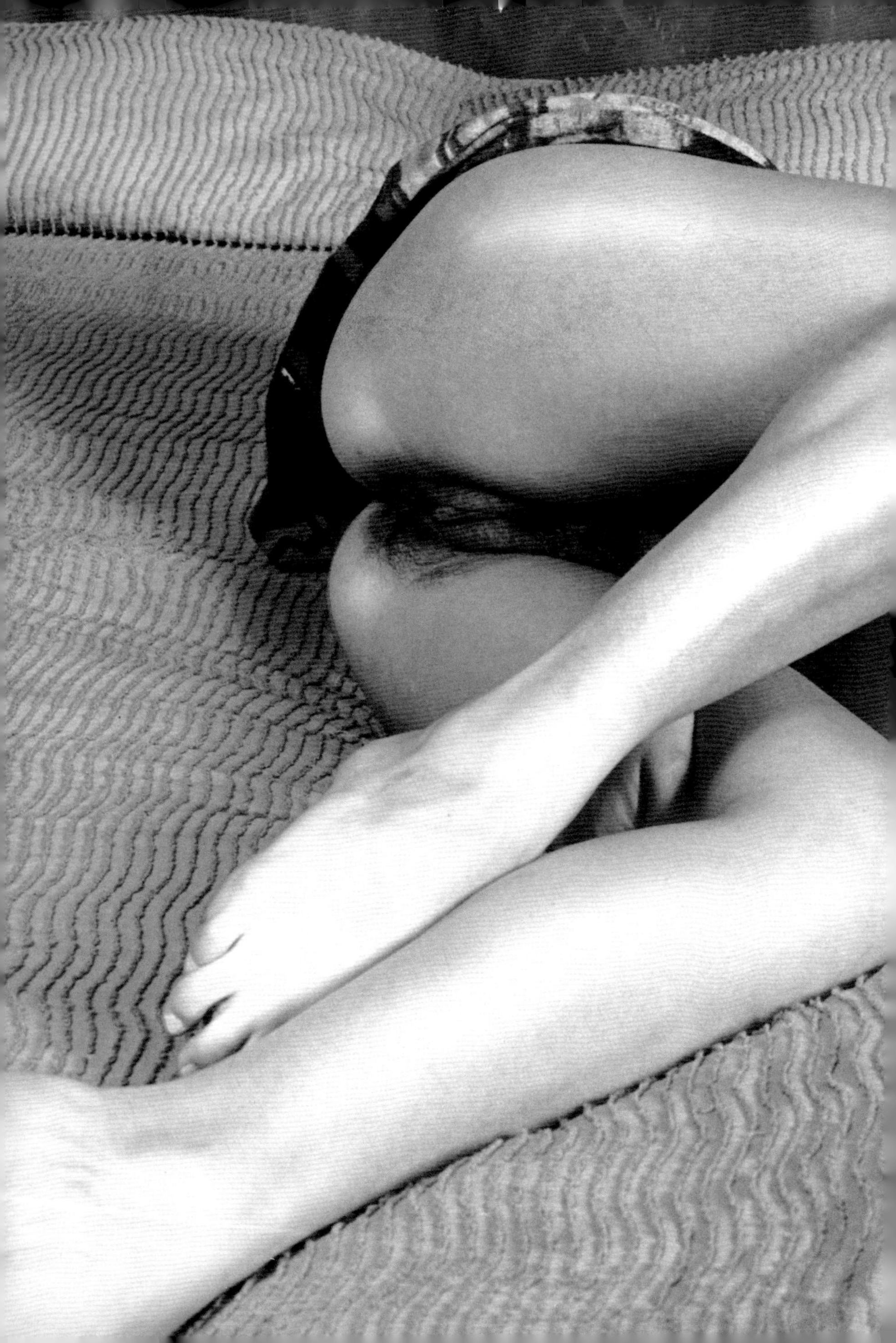

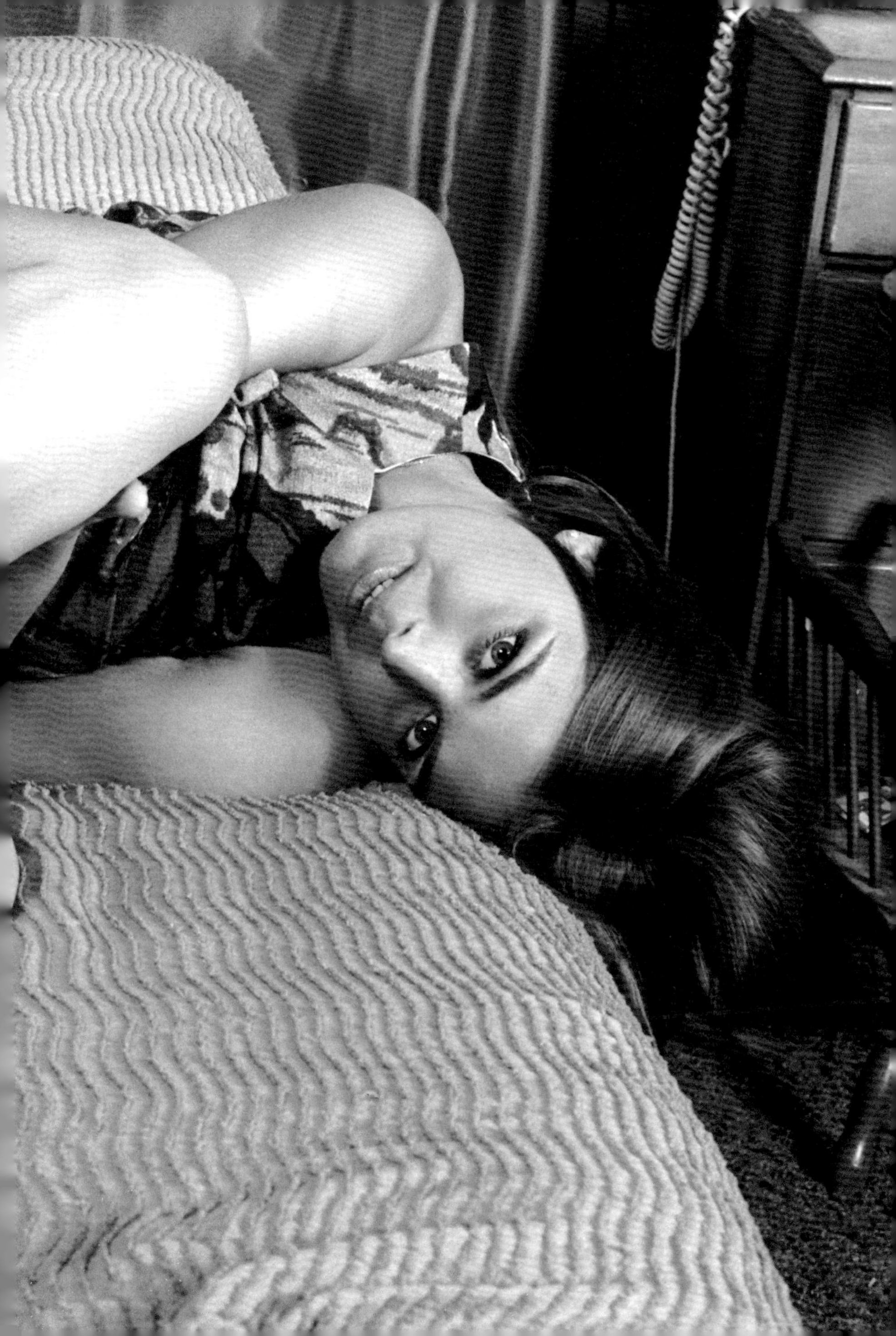

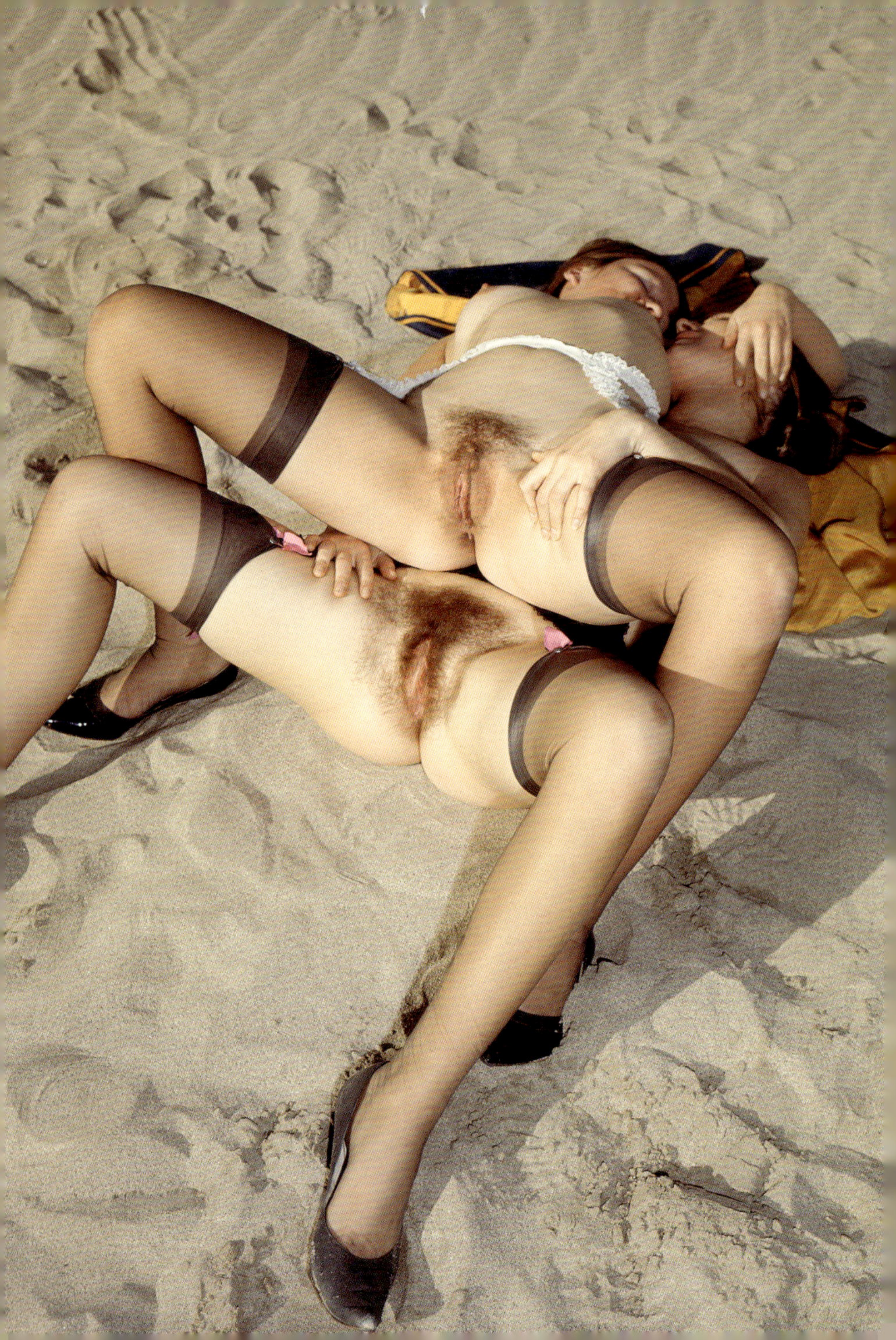

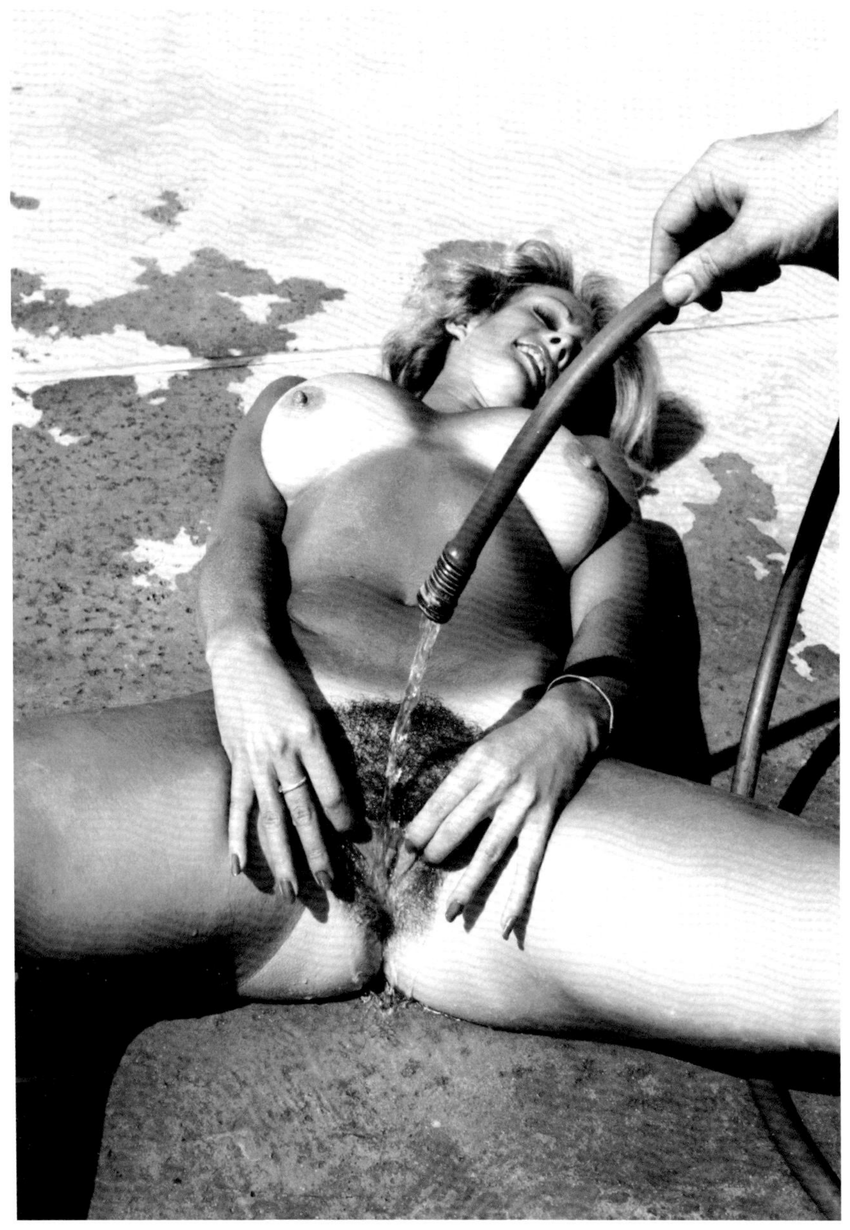

OPPOSITE **Unknown**   ABOVE **Rhonda Jo Petty**

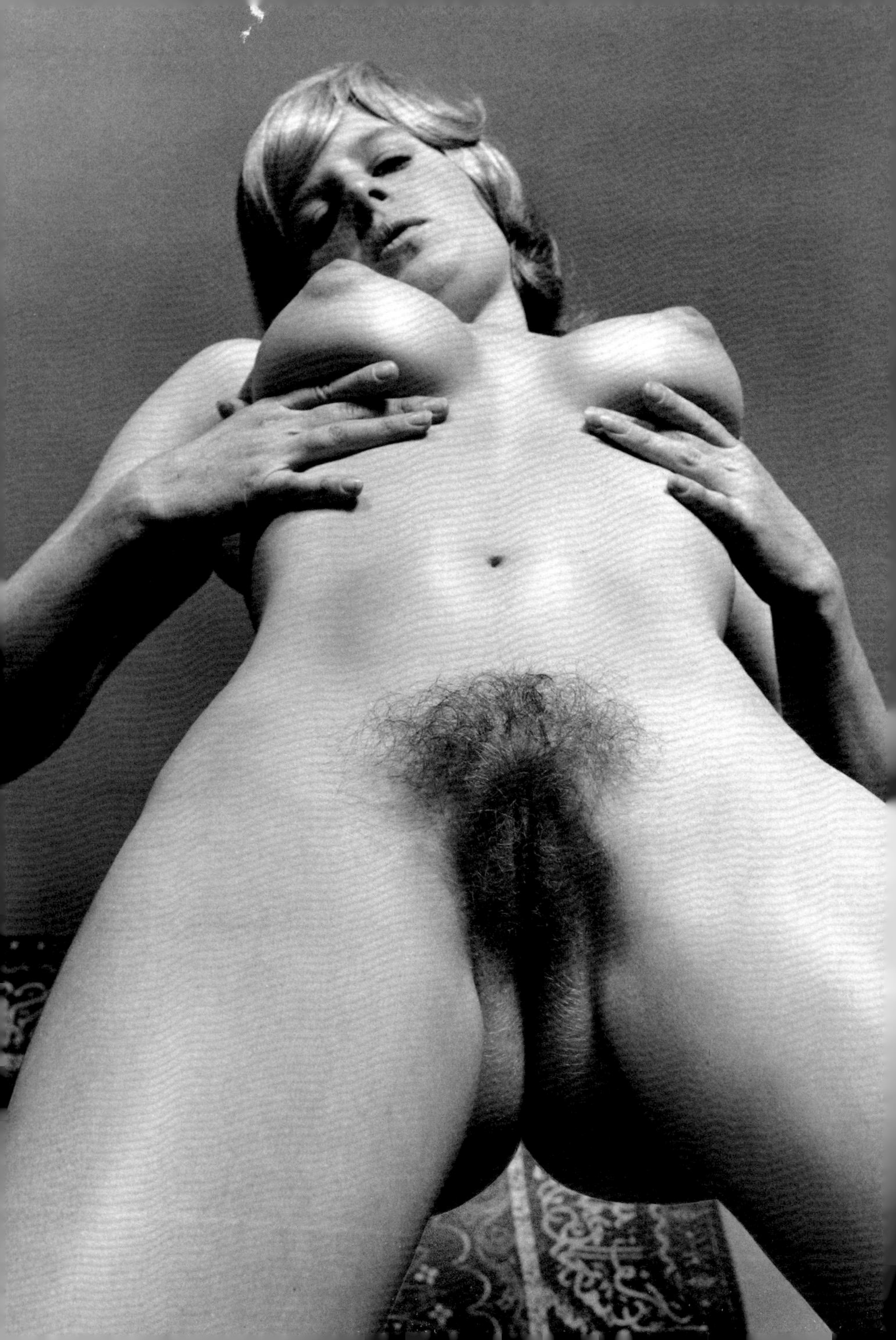

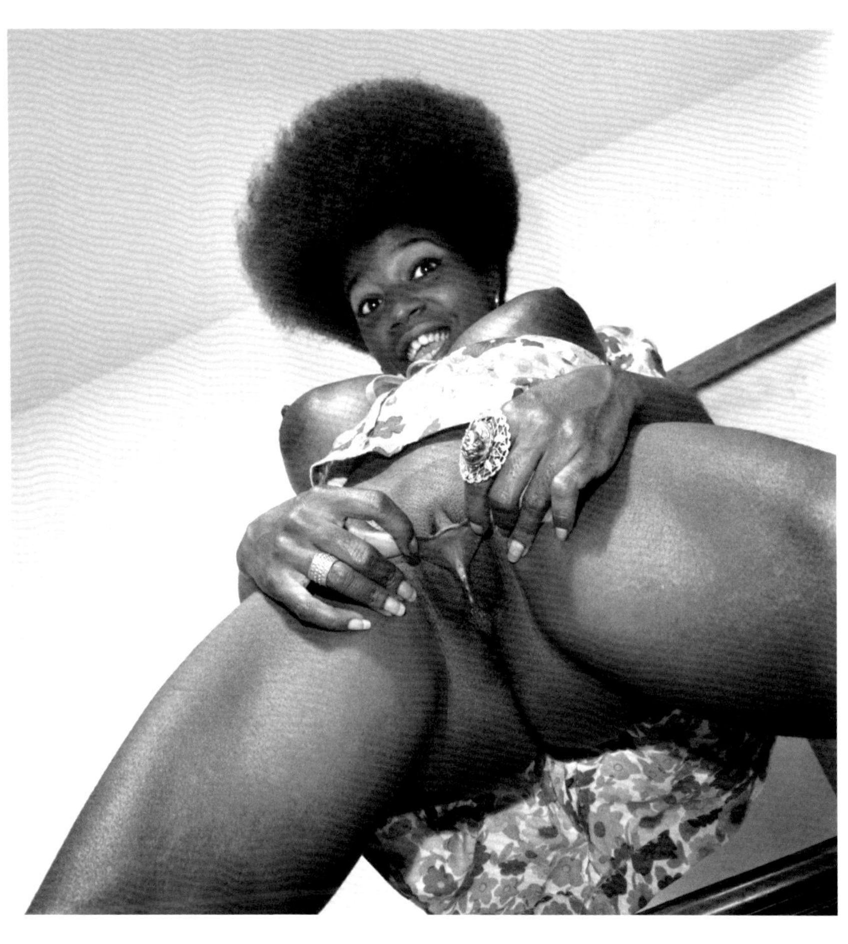

OPPOSITE **Cynthia Stone**   ABOVE **Unknown**   PAGES 132-133 **Linda Lanear**

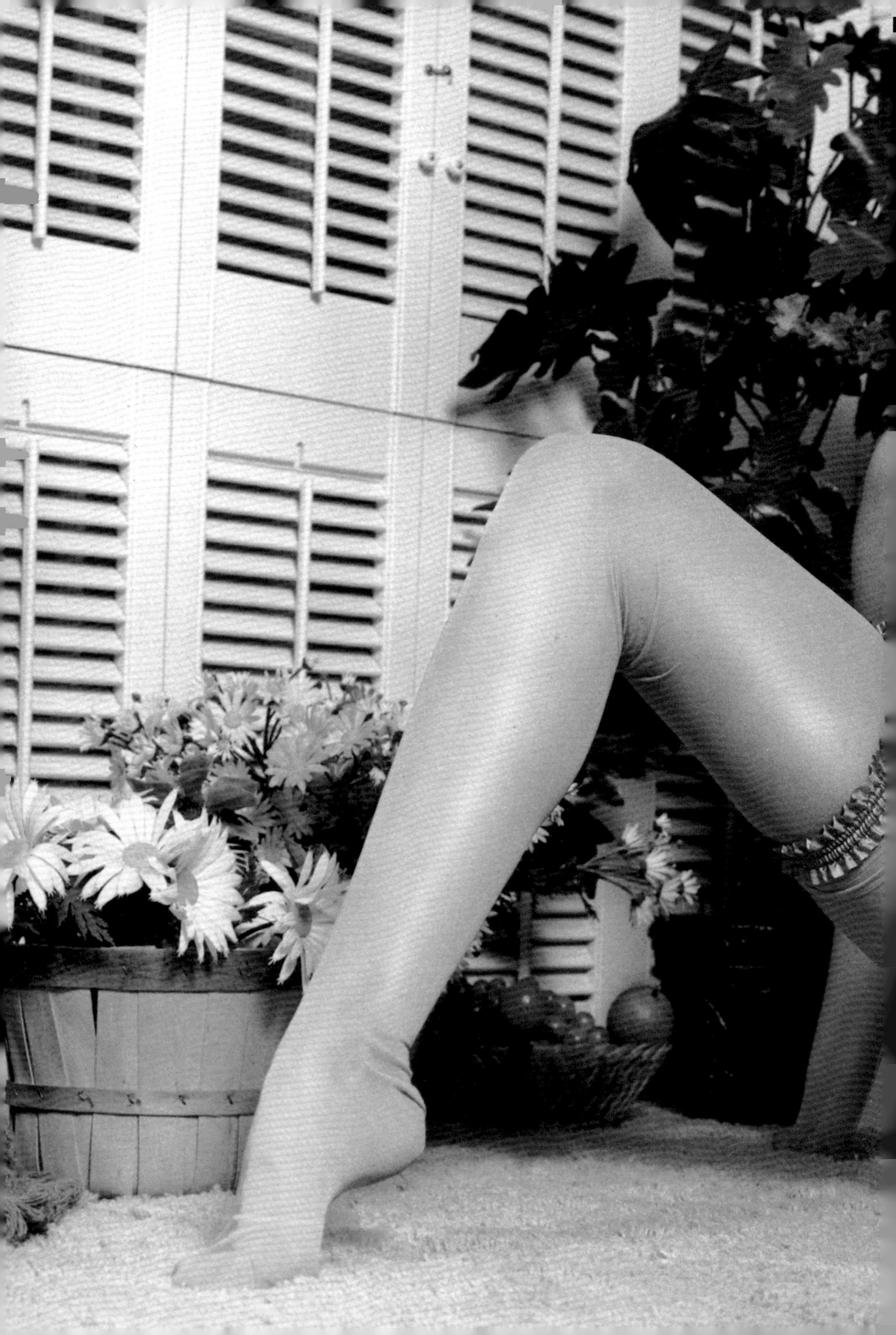

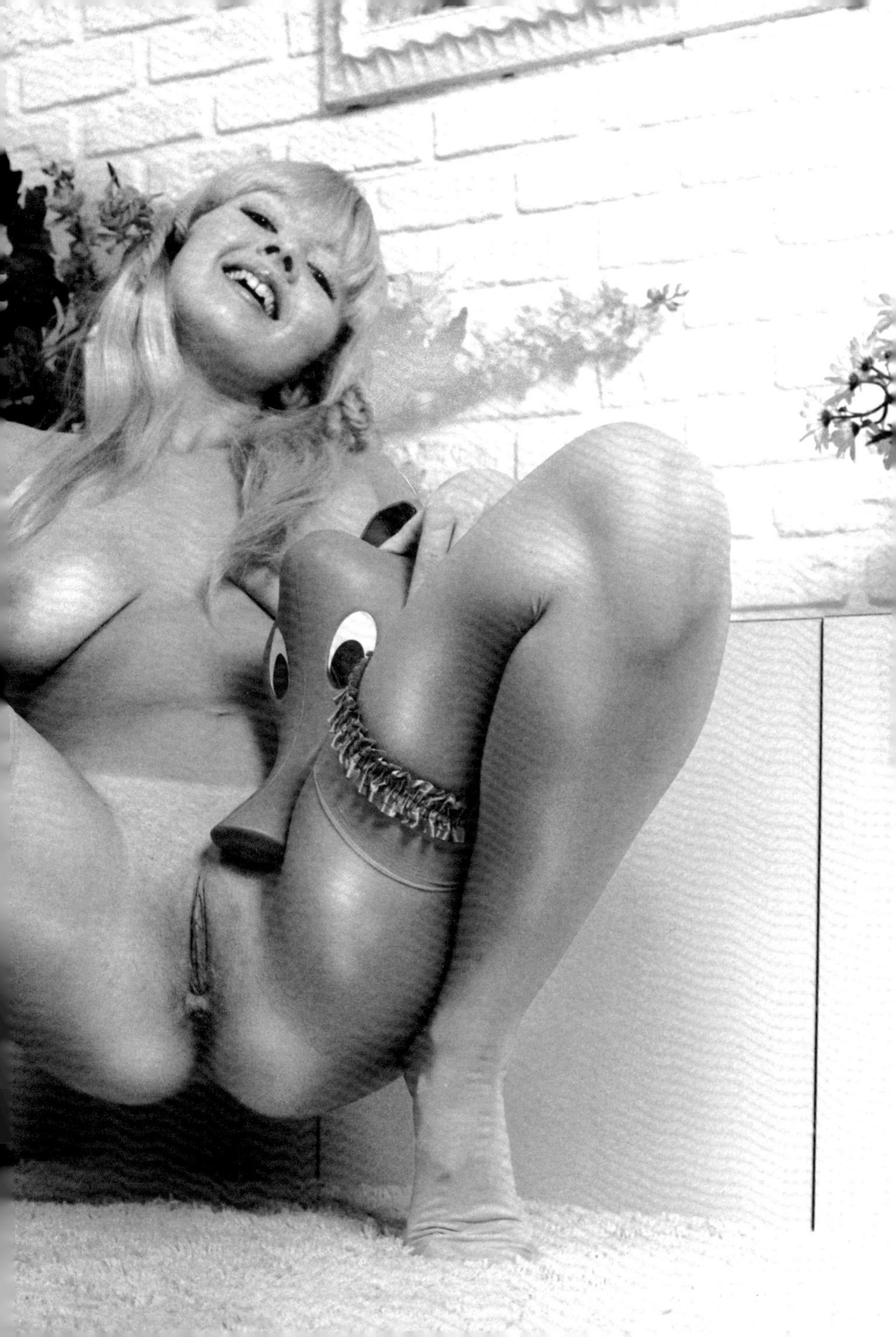

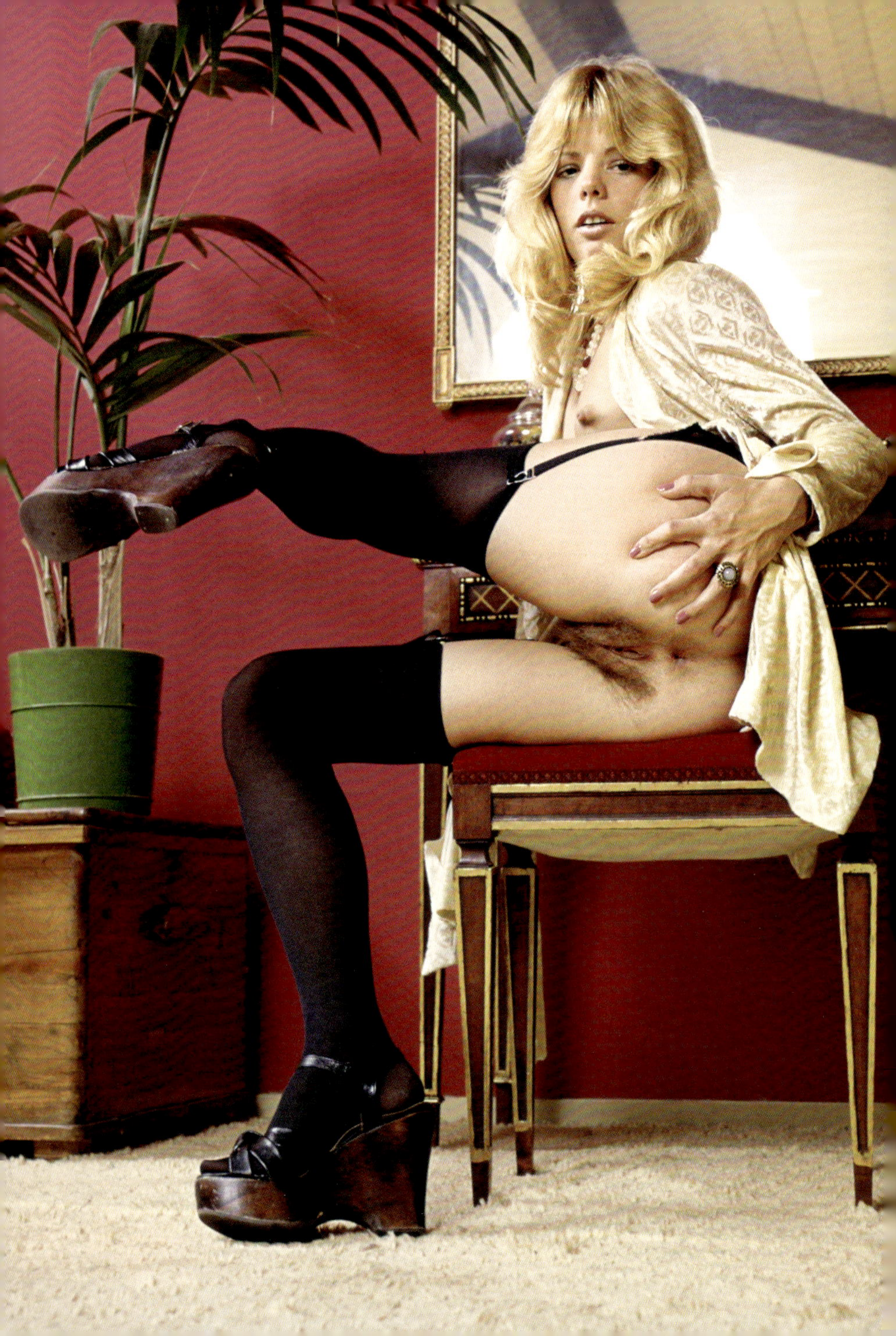

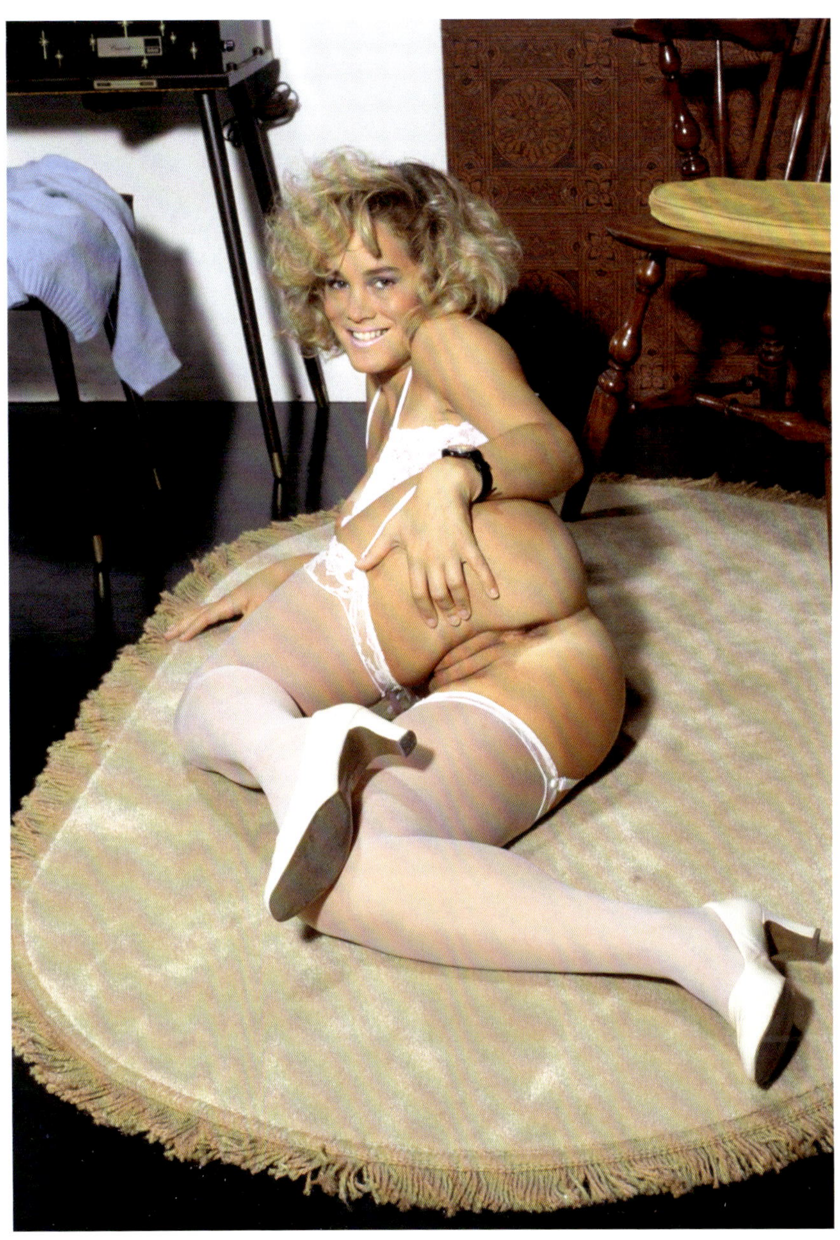

OPPOSITE AND ABOVE **Unknown**

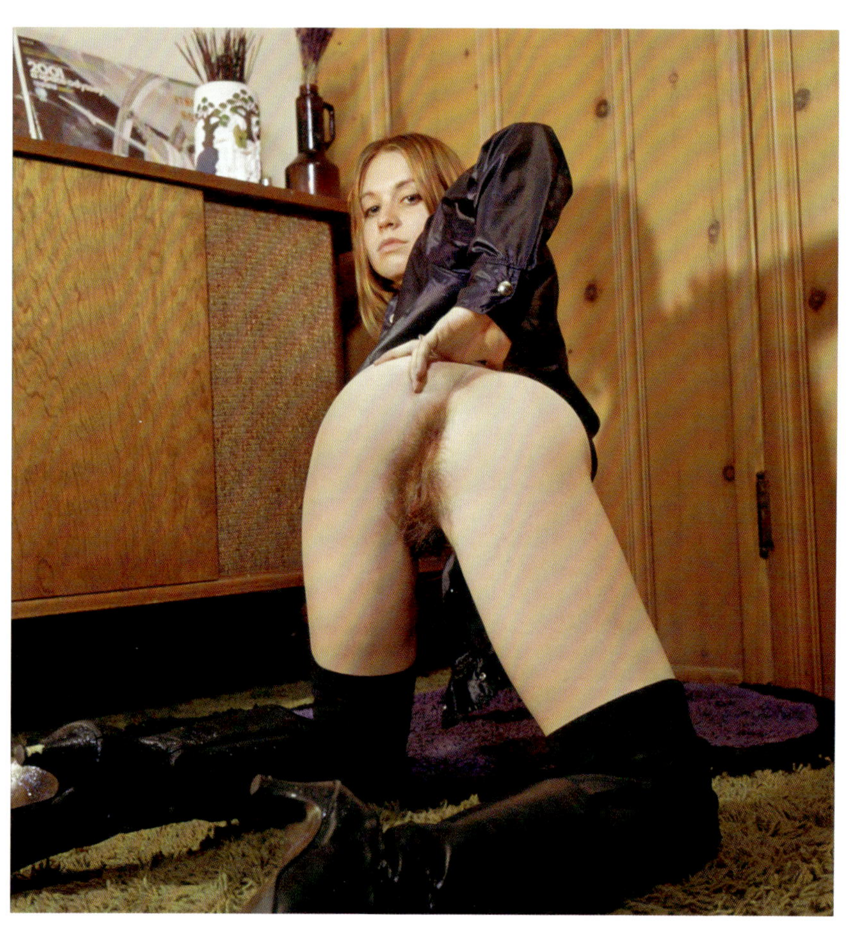

ABOVE AND OPPOSITE **Unknown**

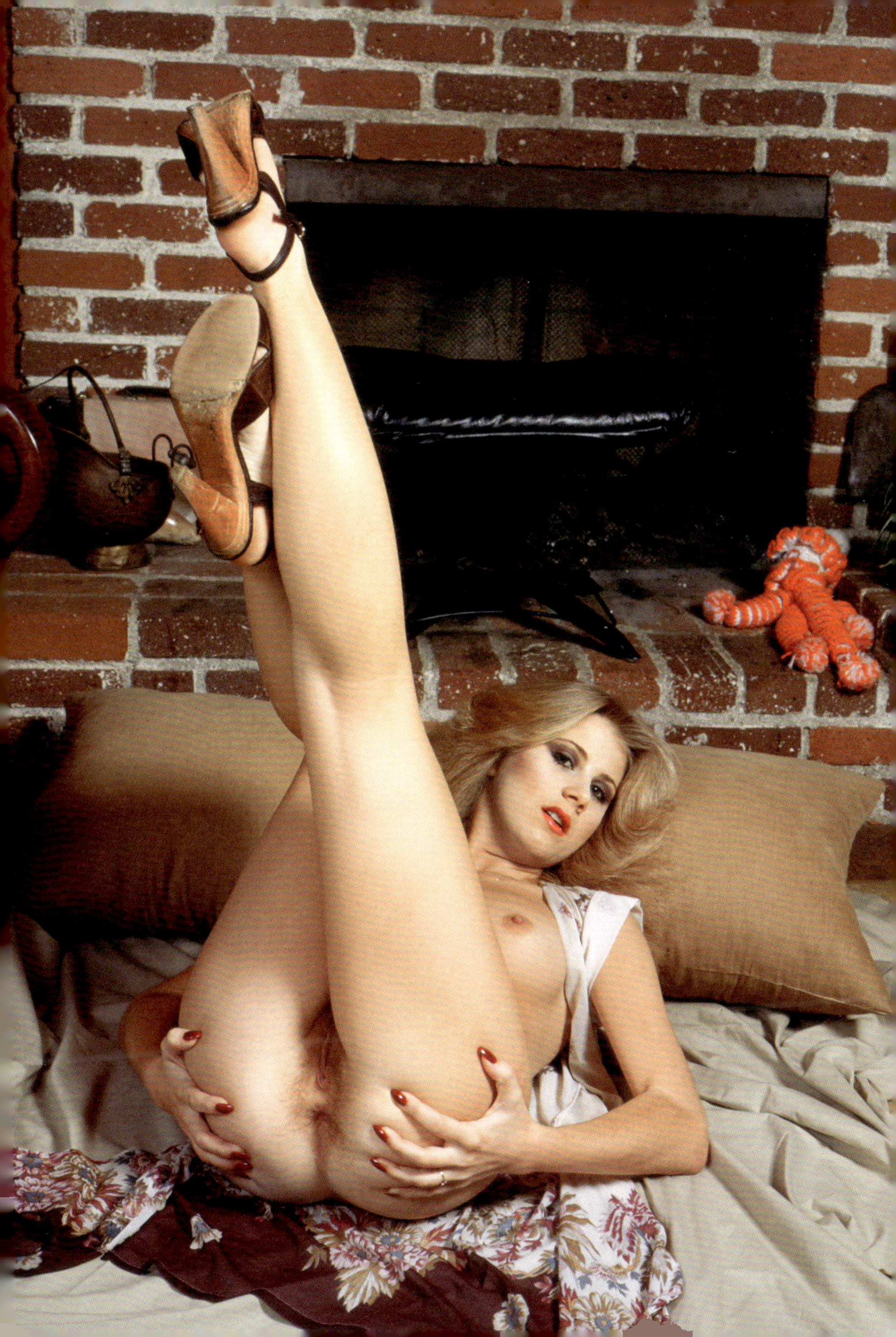

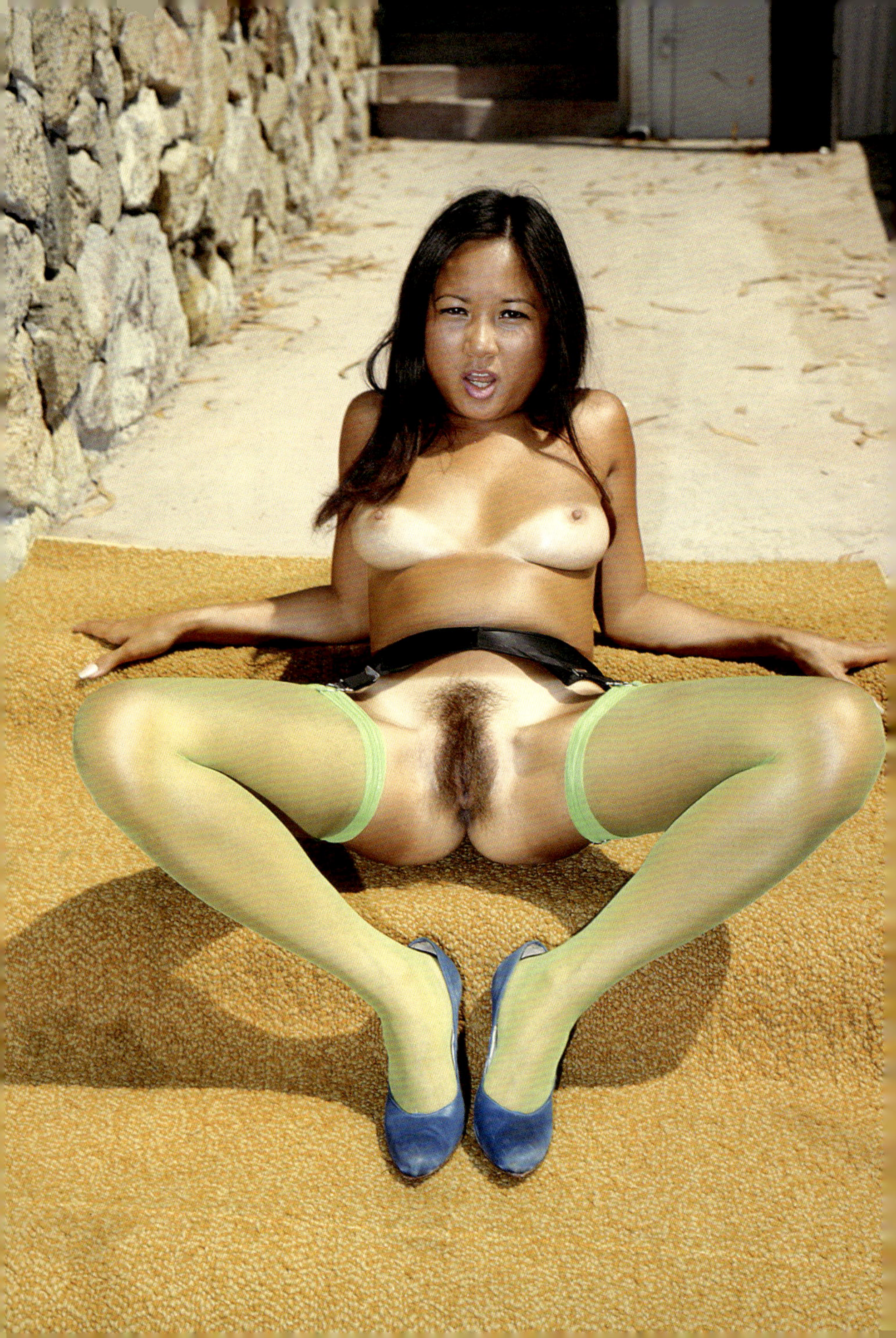

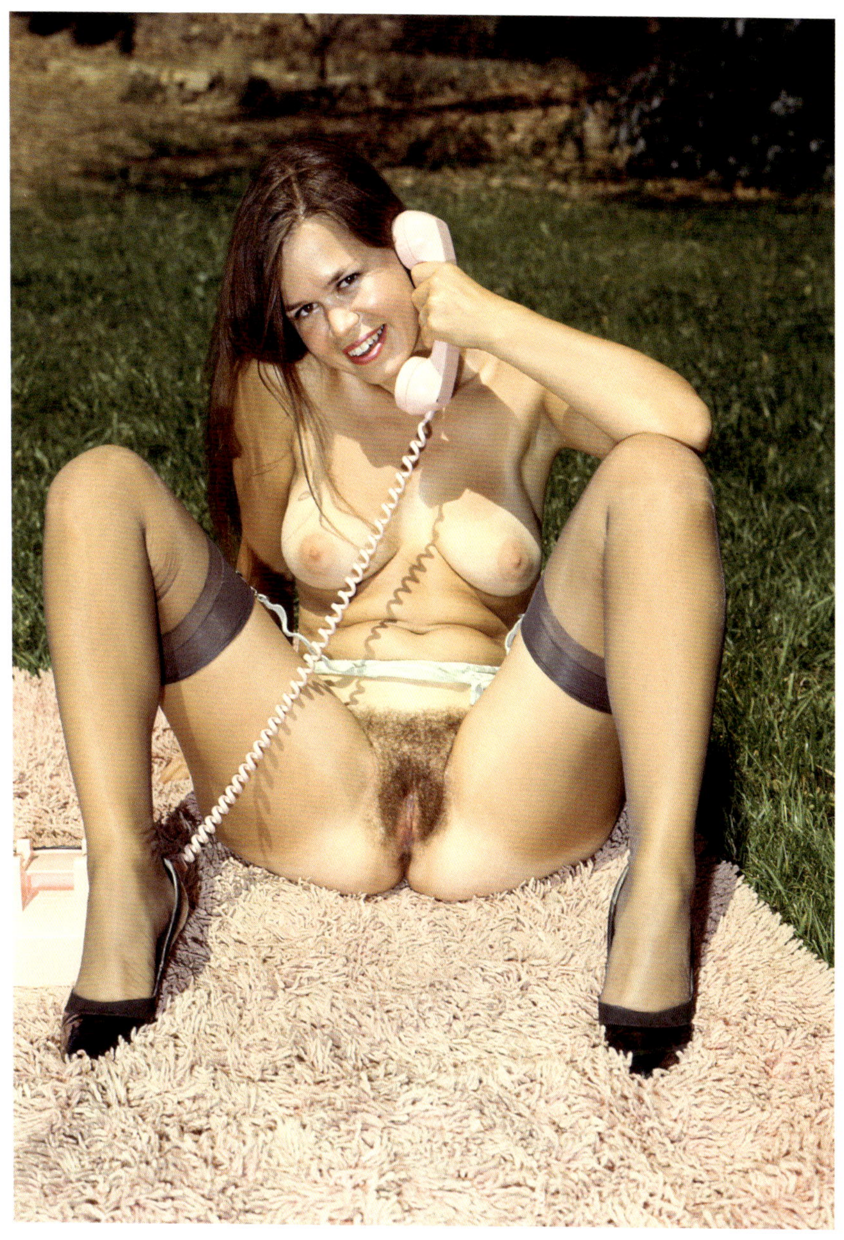

OPPOSITE **Jadi Joe**   ABOVE **Jeanne Machmes**   PAGES 140-141 **Seka**

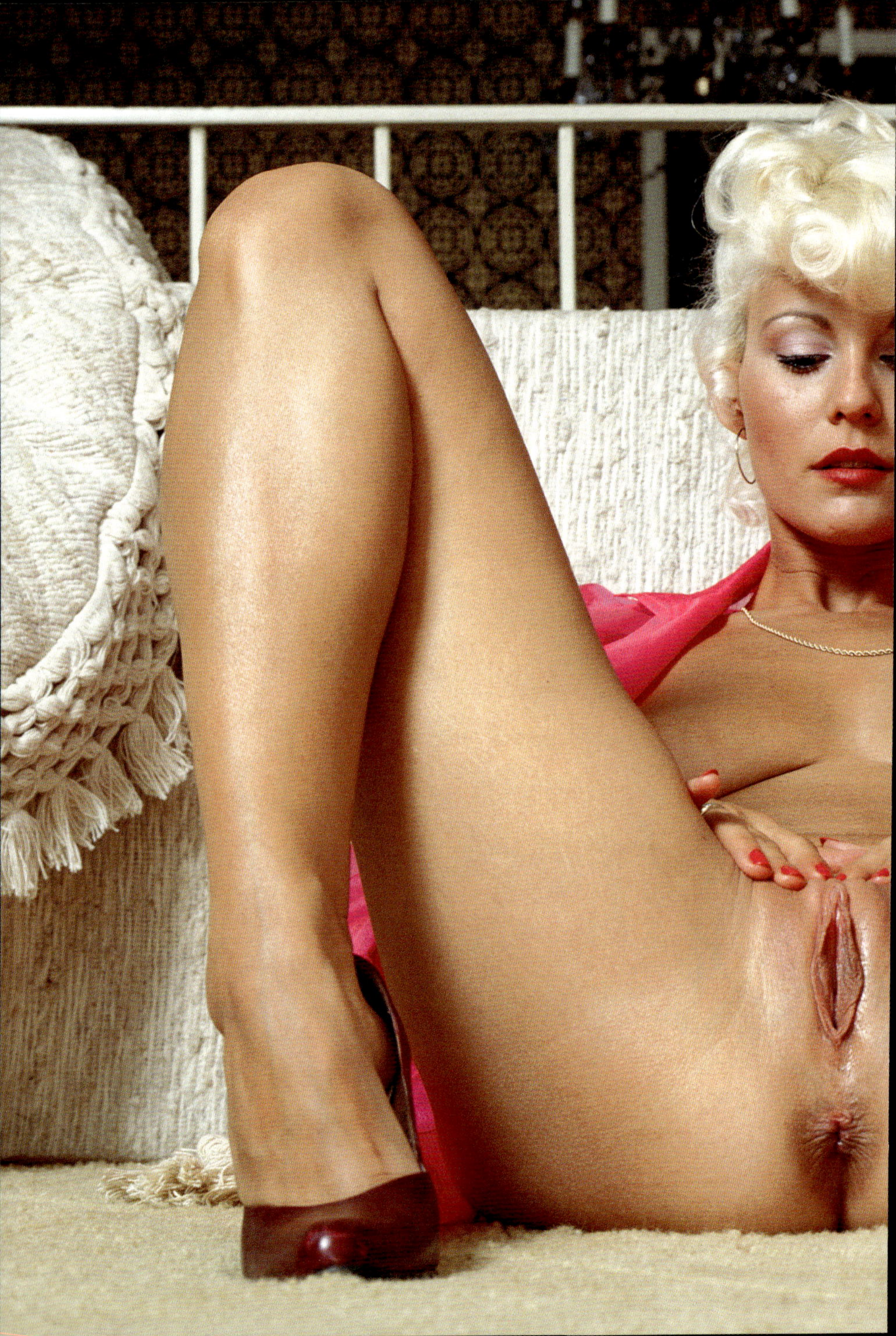

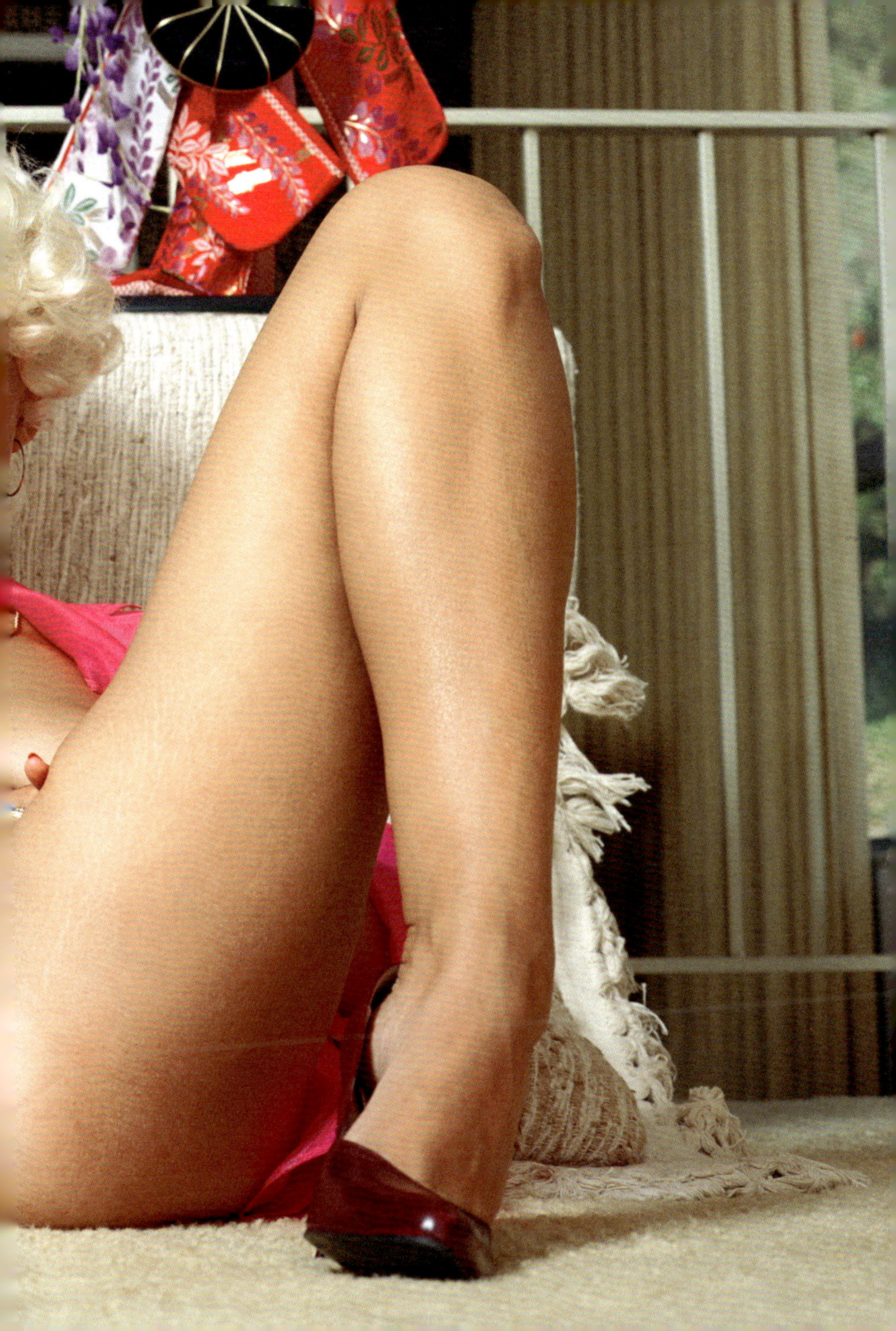

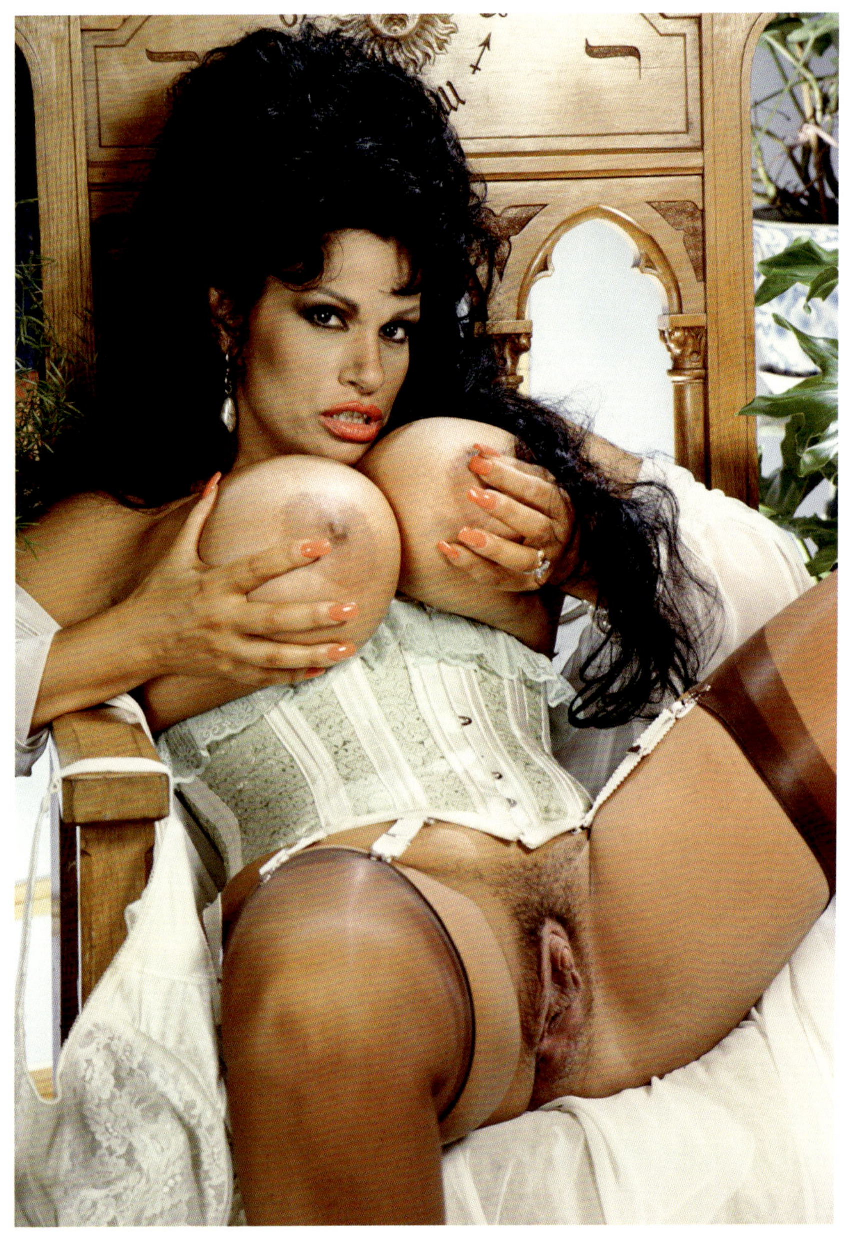

Vanessa del Rio

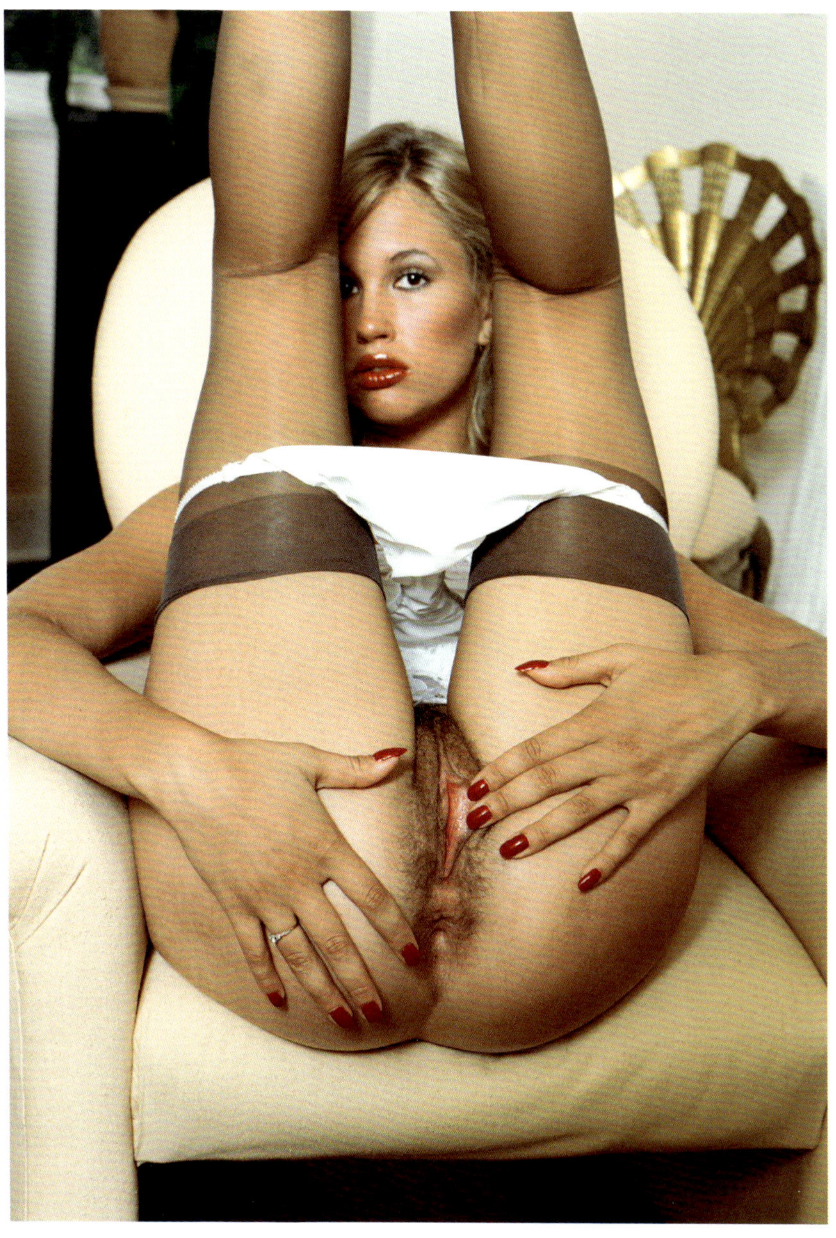

Unknown

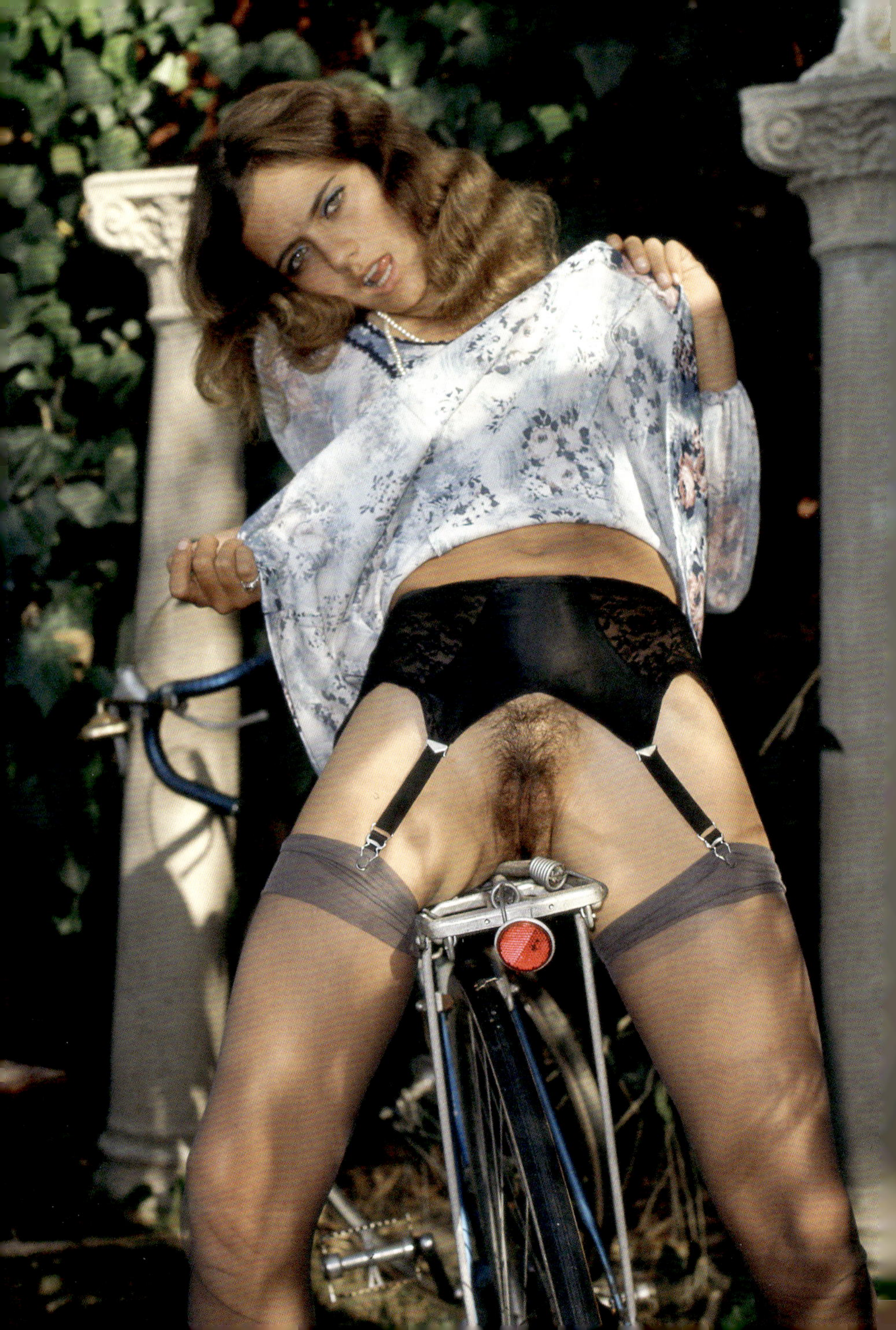

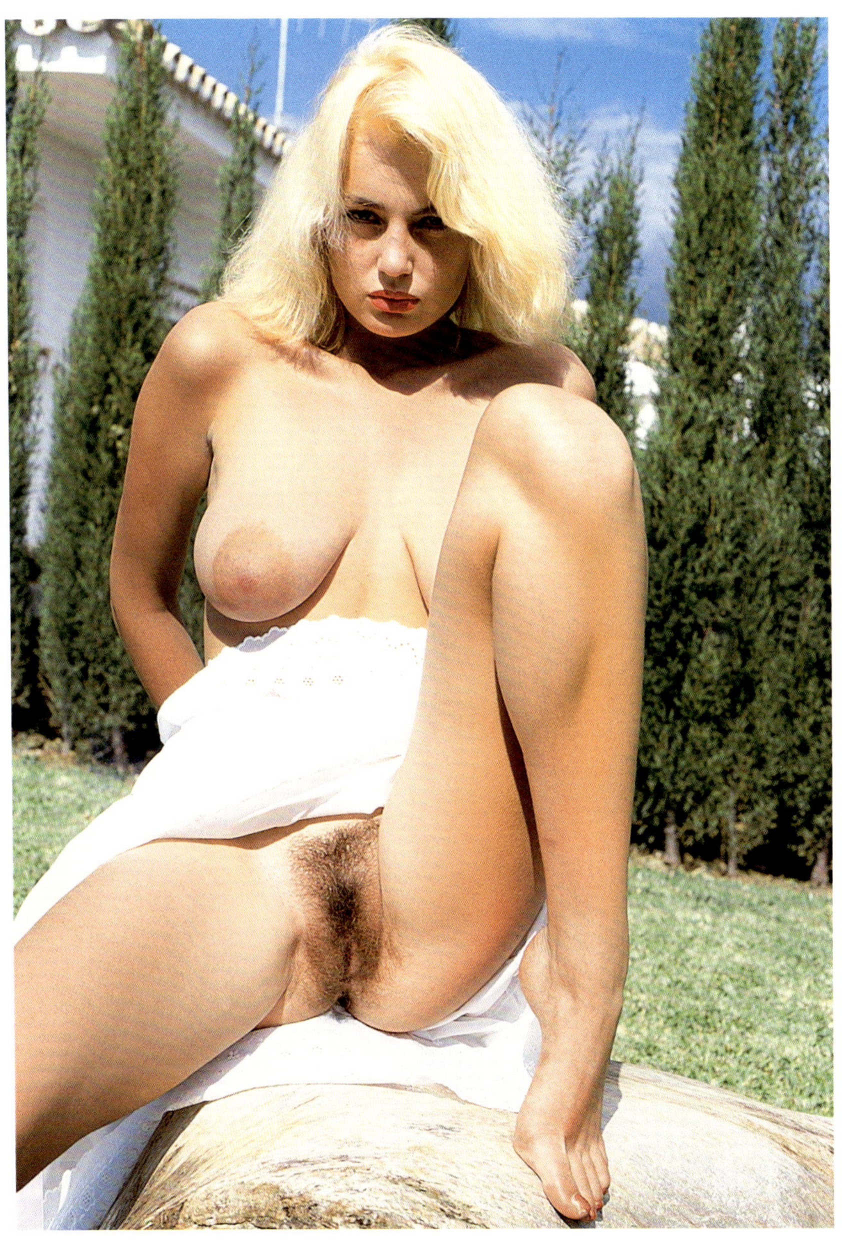

OPPOSITE **Unknown**   ABOVE **Monica**

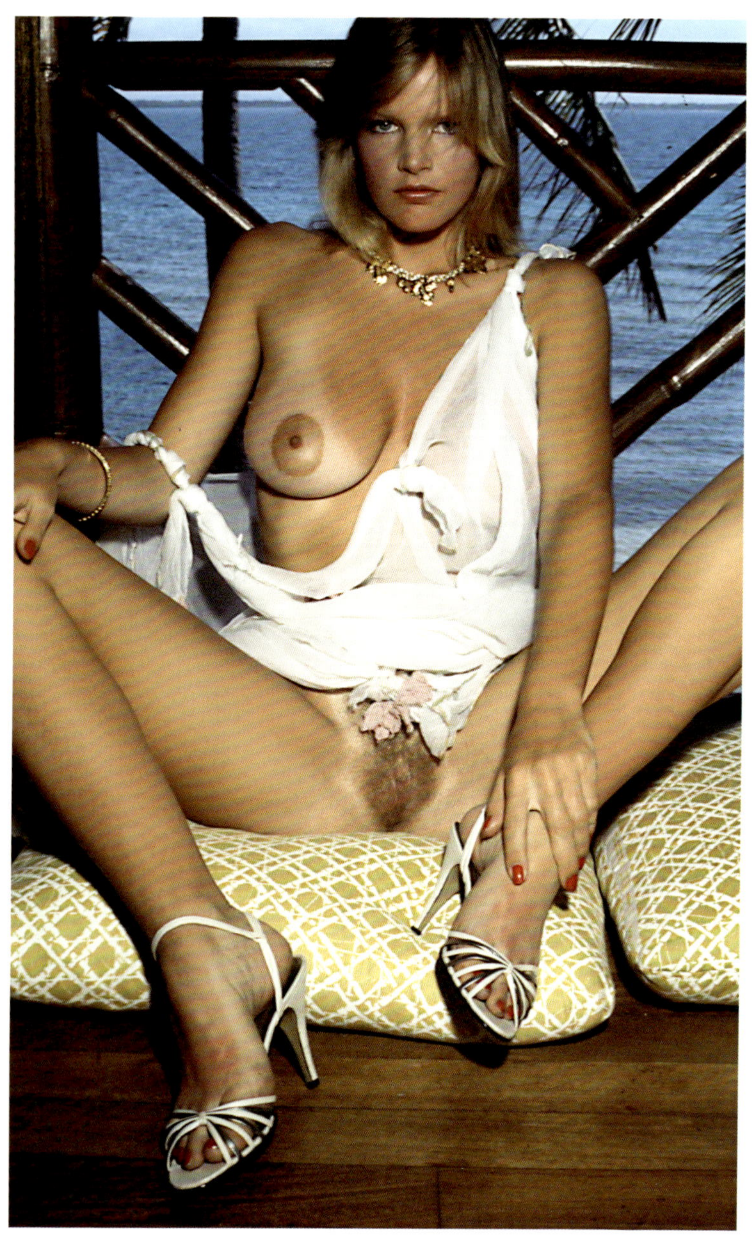

ABOVE **Nadine Greenlaw** OPPOSITE **Terri Lenee Peake**

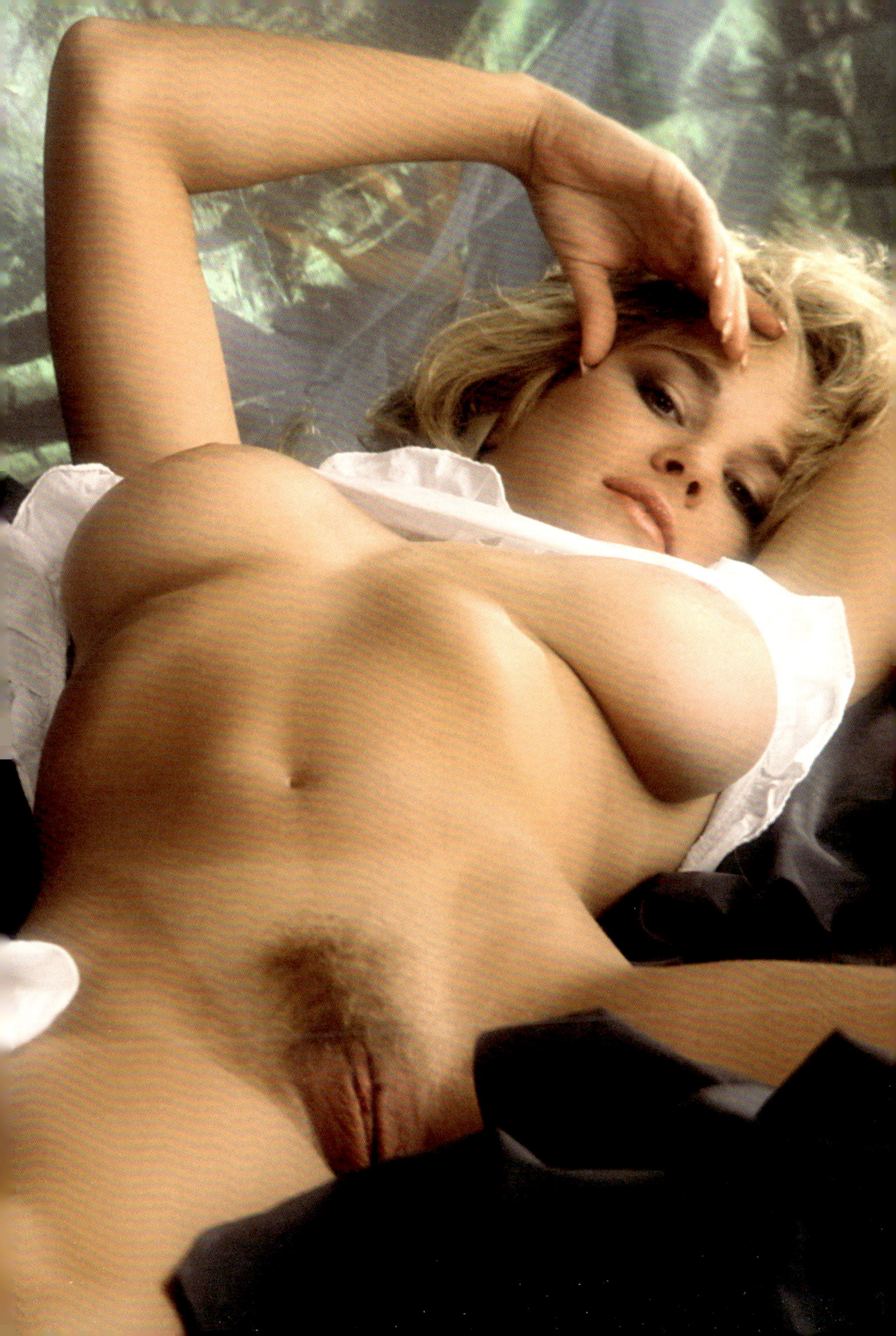

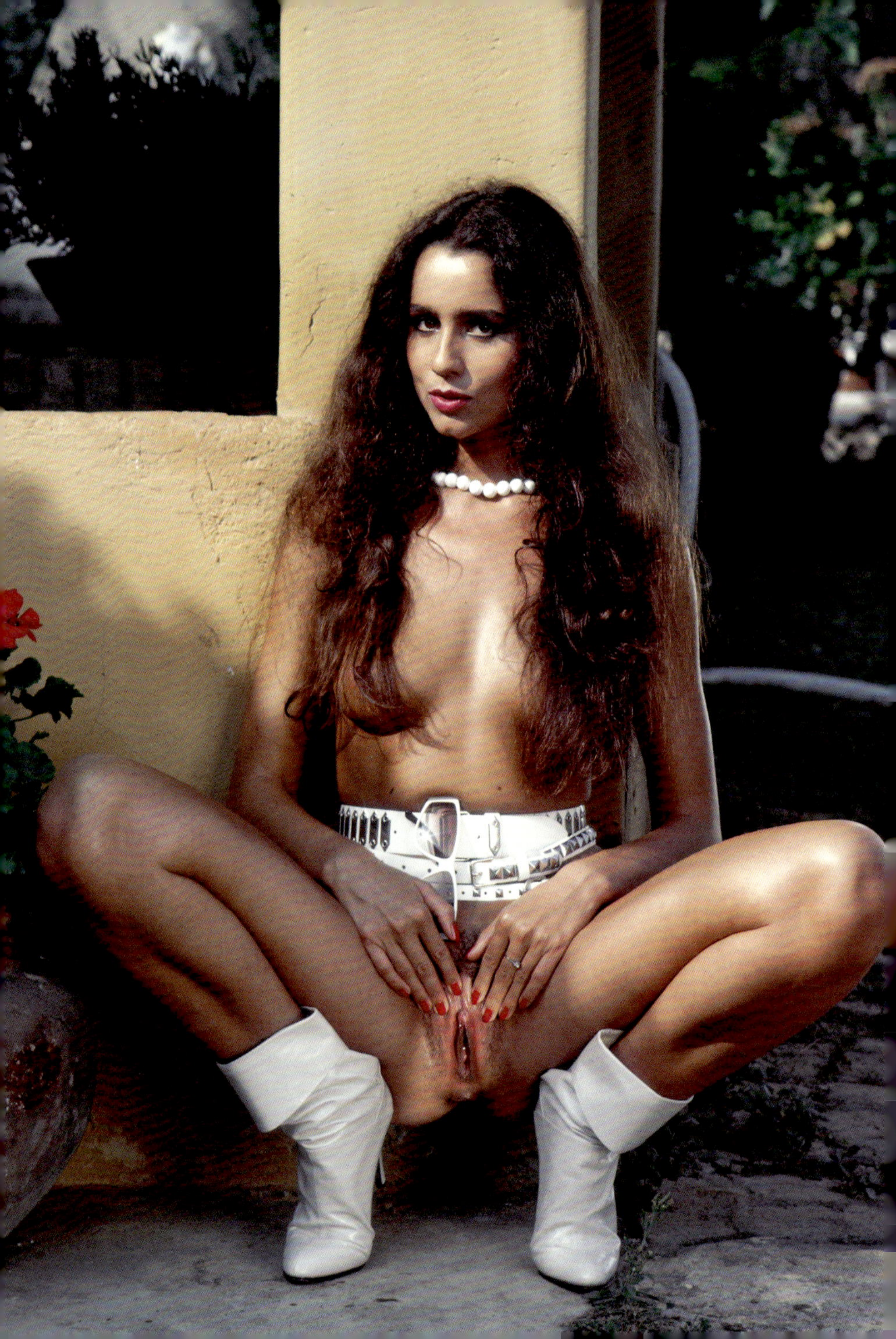

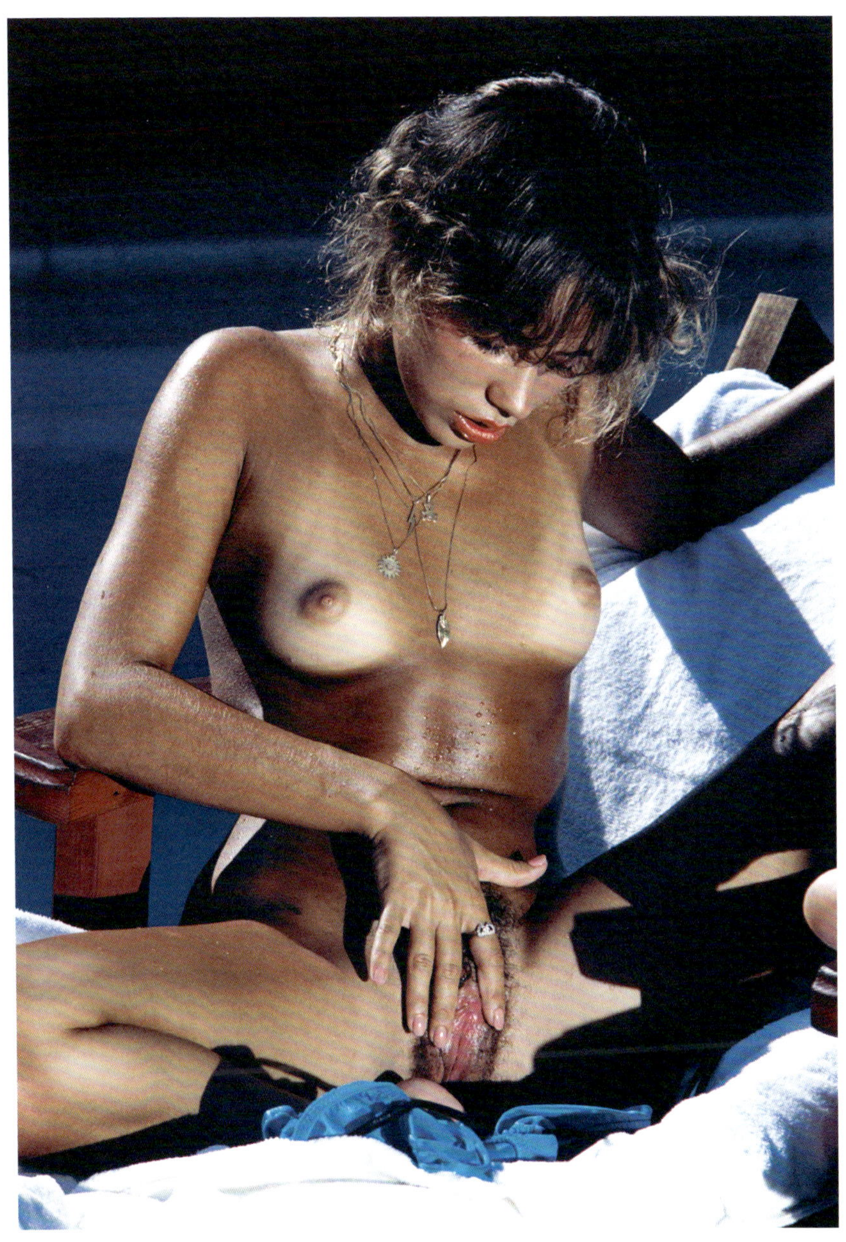

OPPOSITE **Cimmi** ABOVE **Unknown**

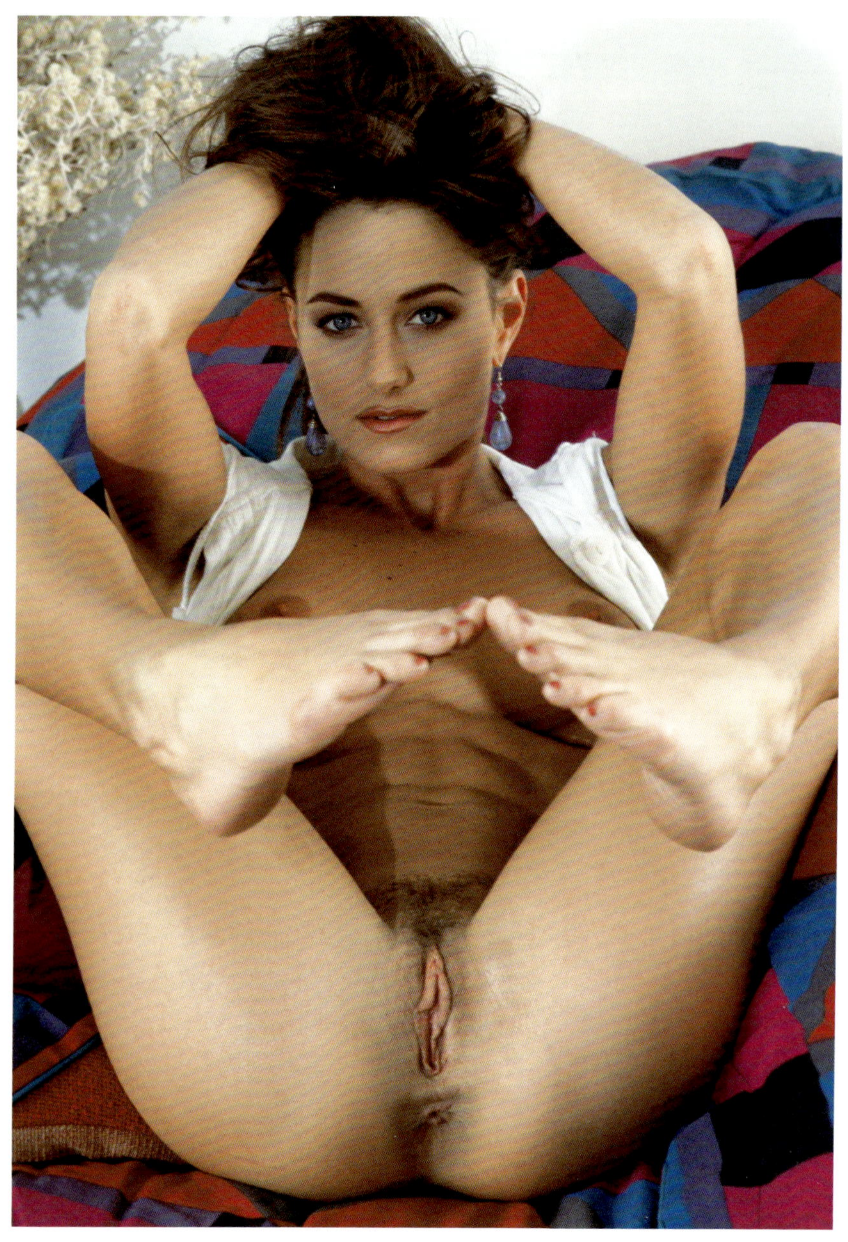

ABOVE **Charlie** OPPOSITE **Unknown**

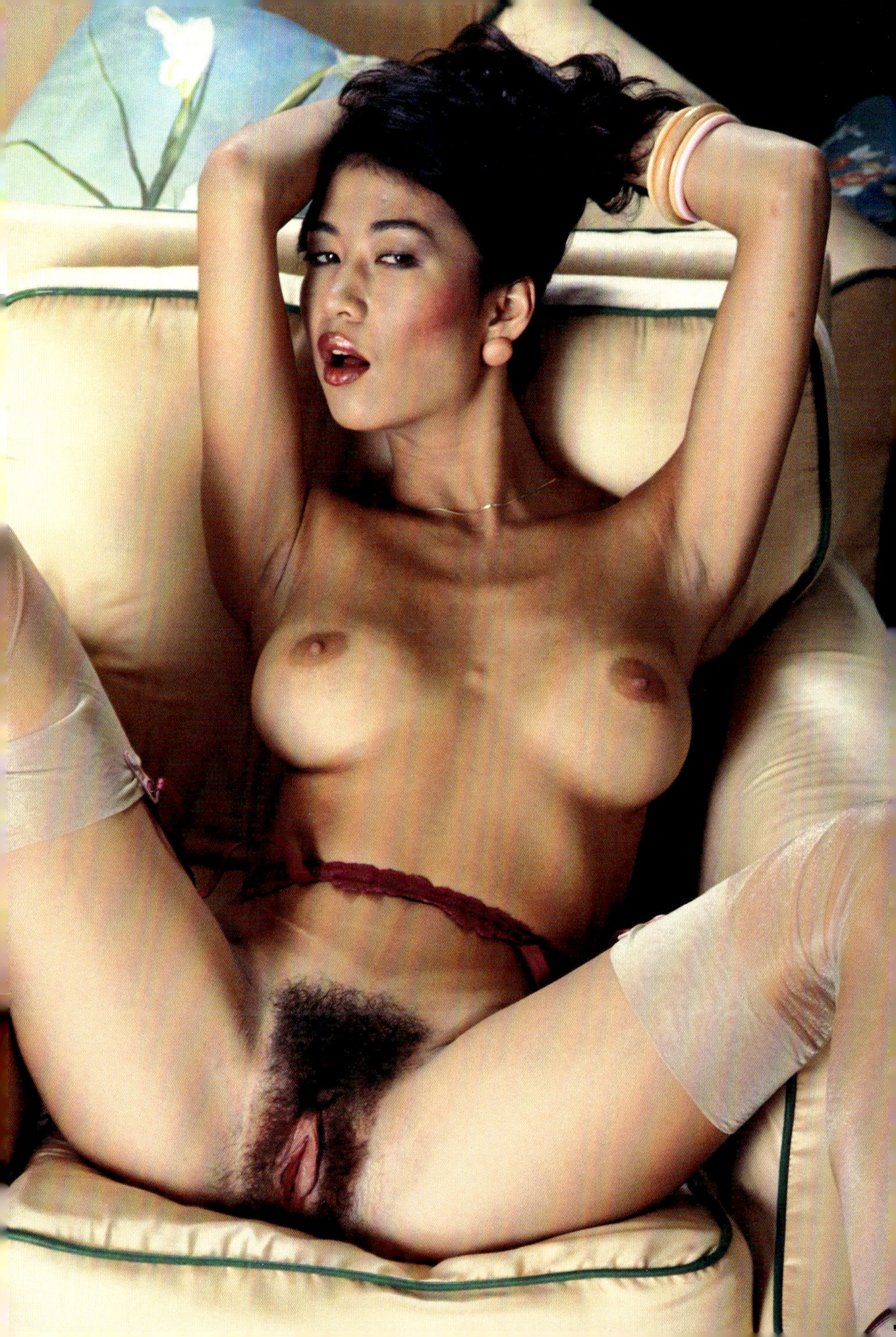

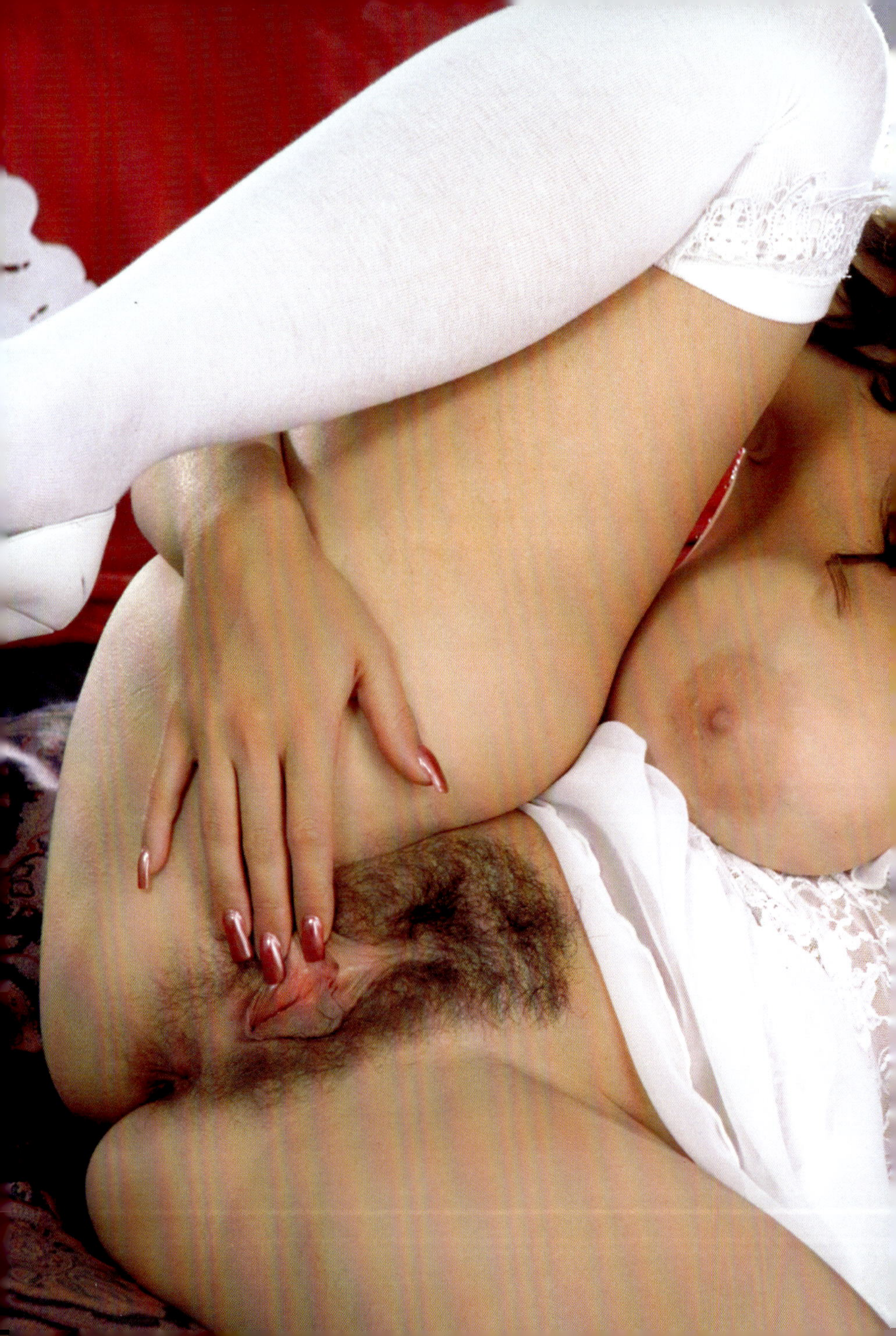

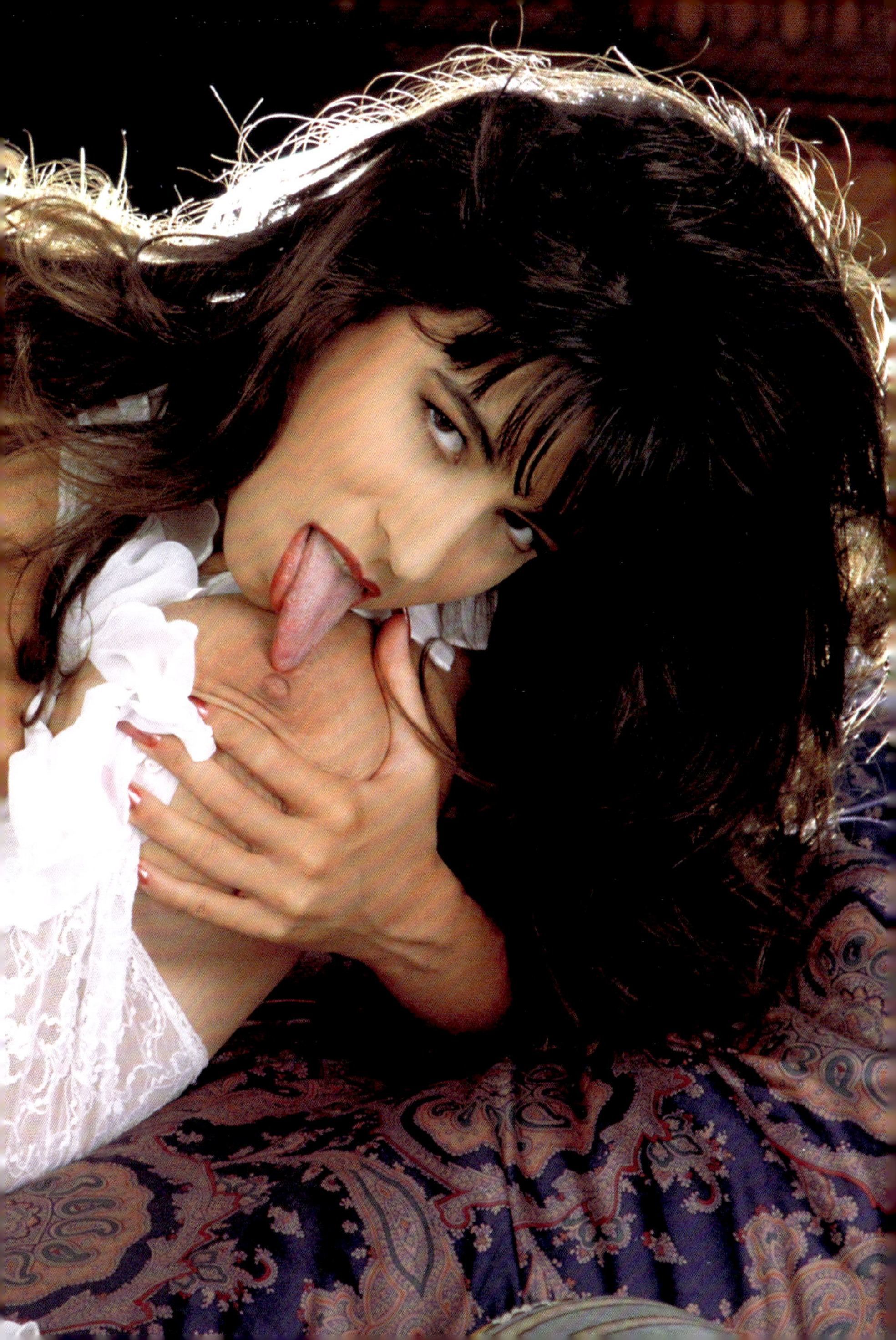

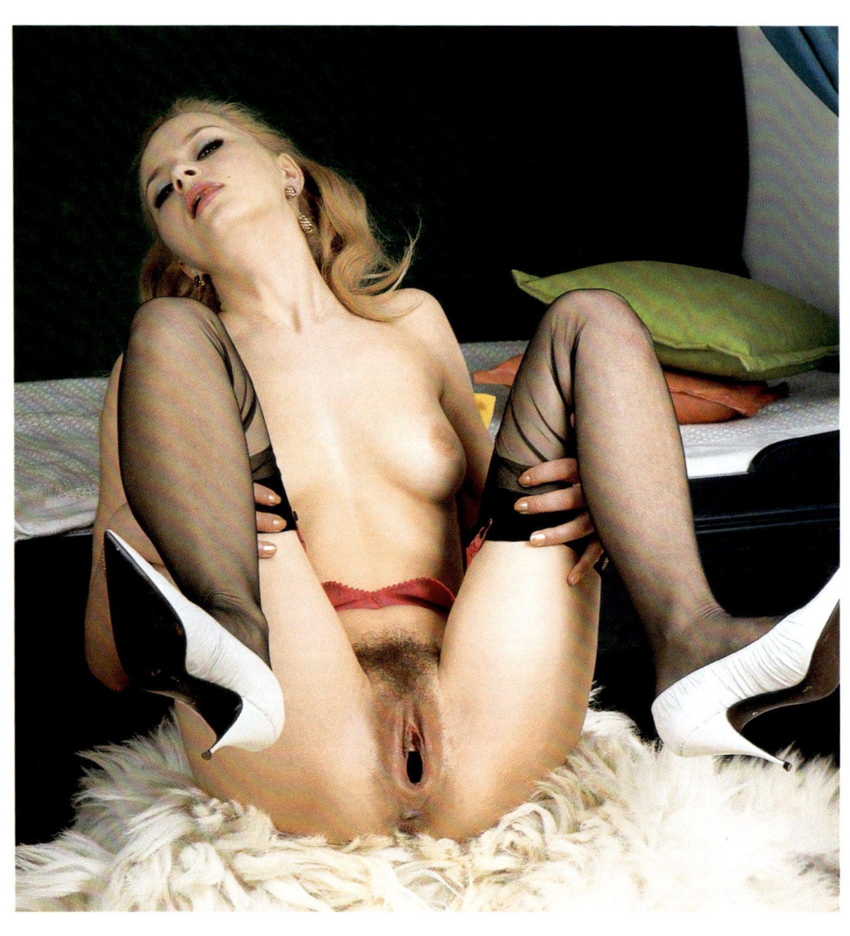

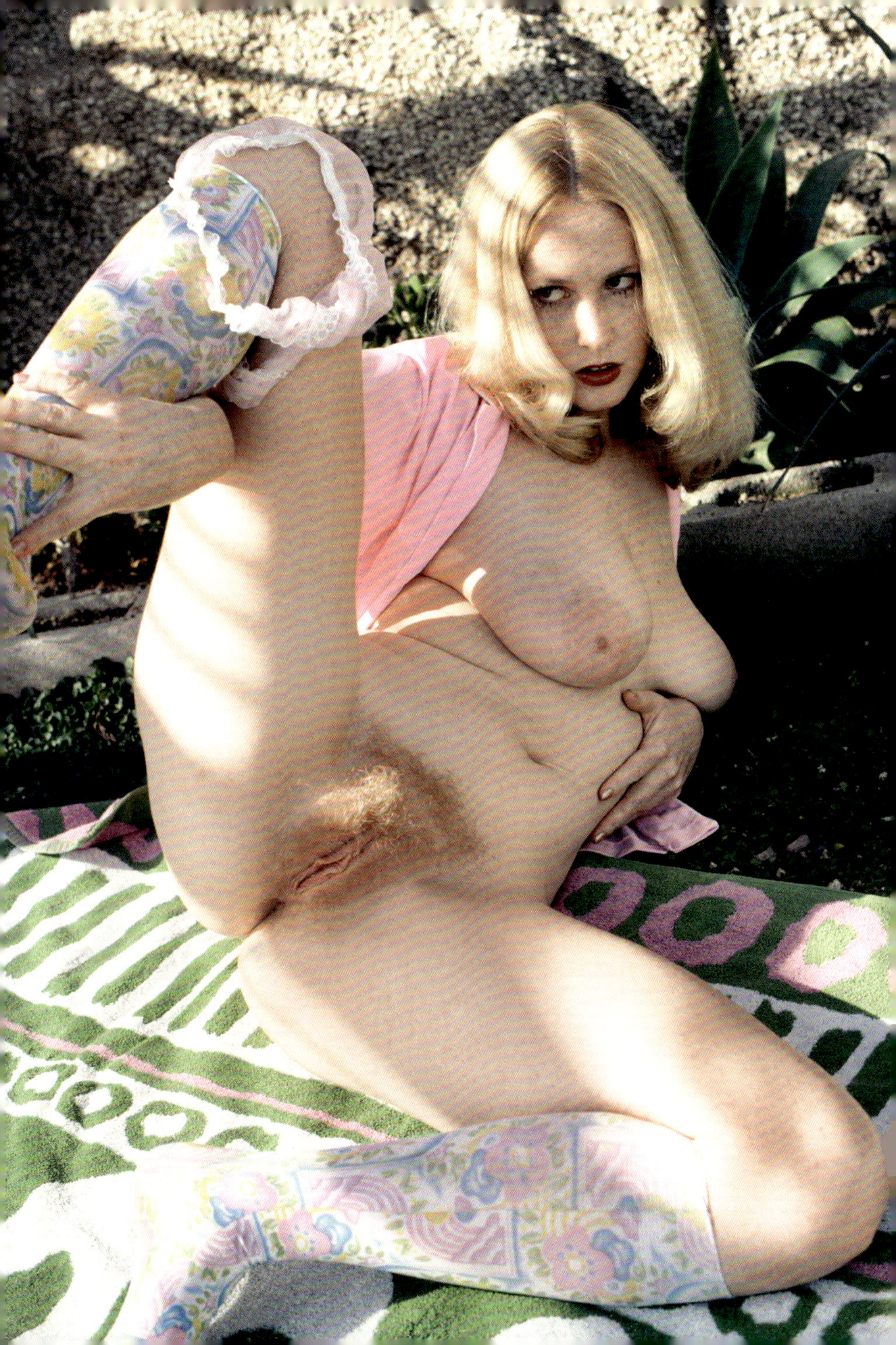

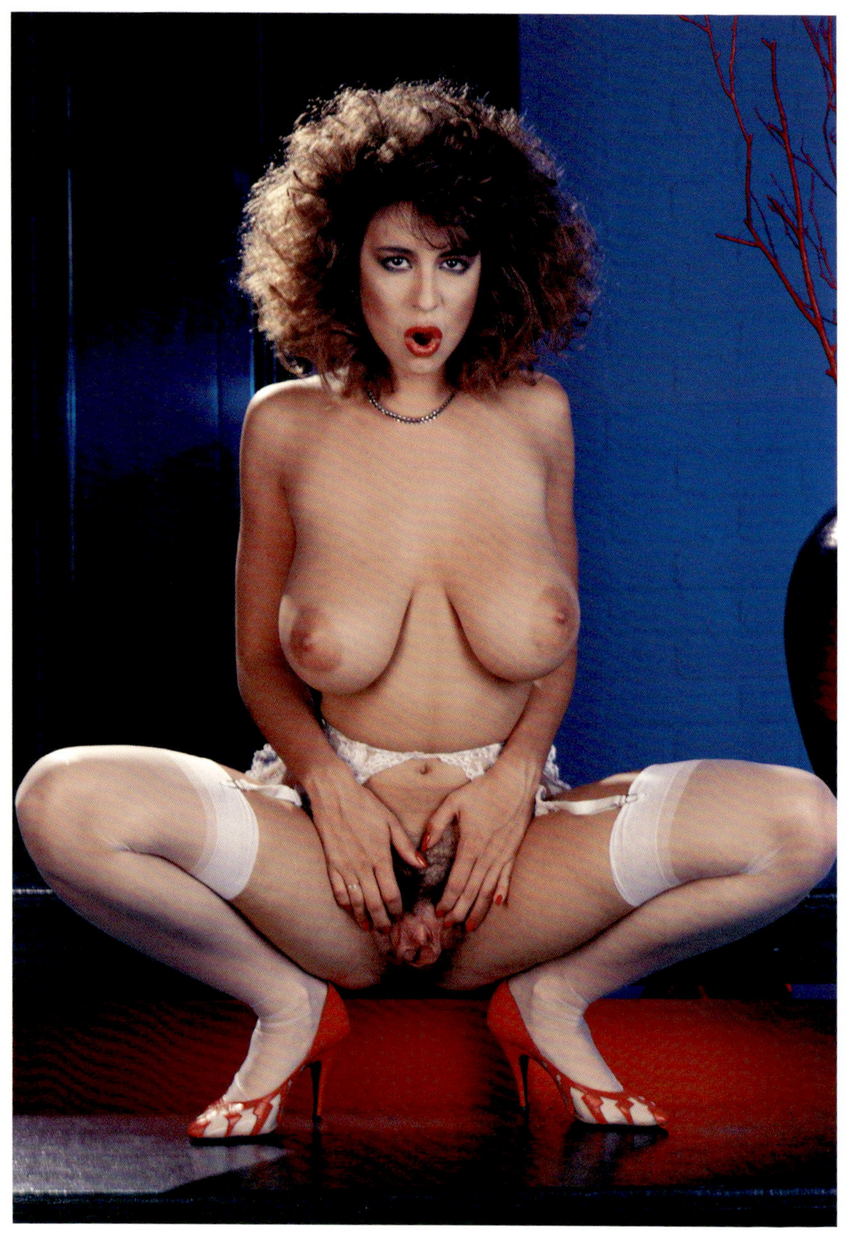

Christy Canyon

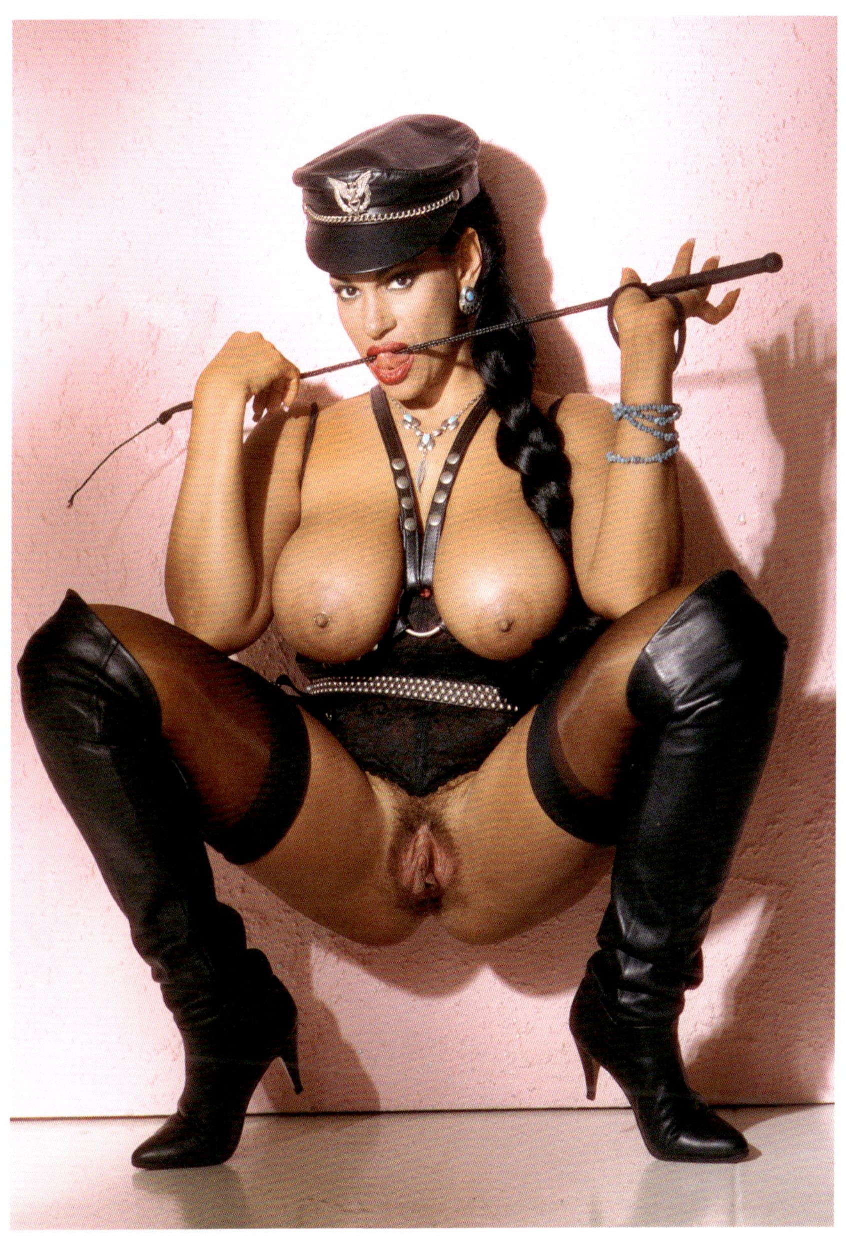

ABOVE **Vanessa del Rio**   PAGES 158-159 **Ginger Lynn**

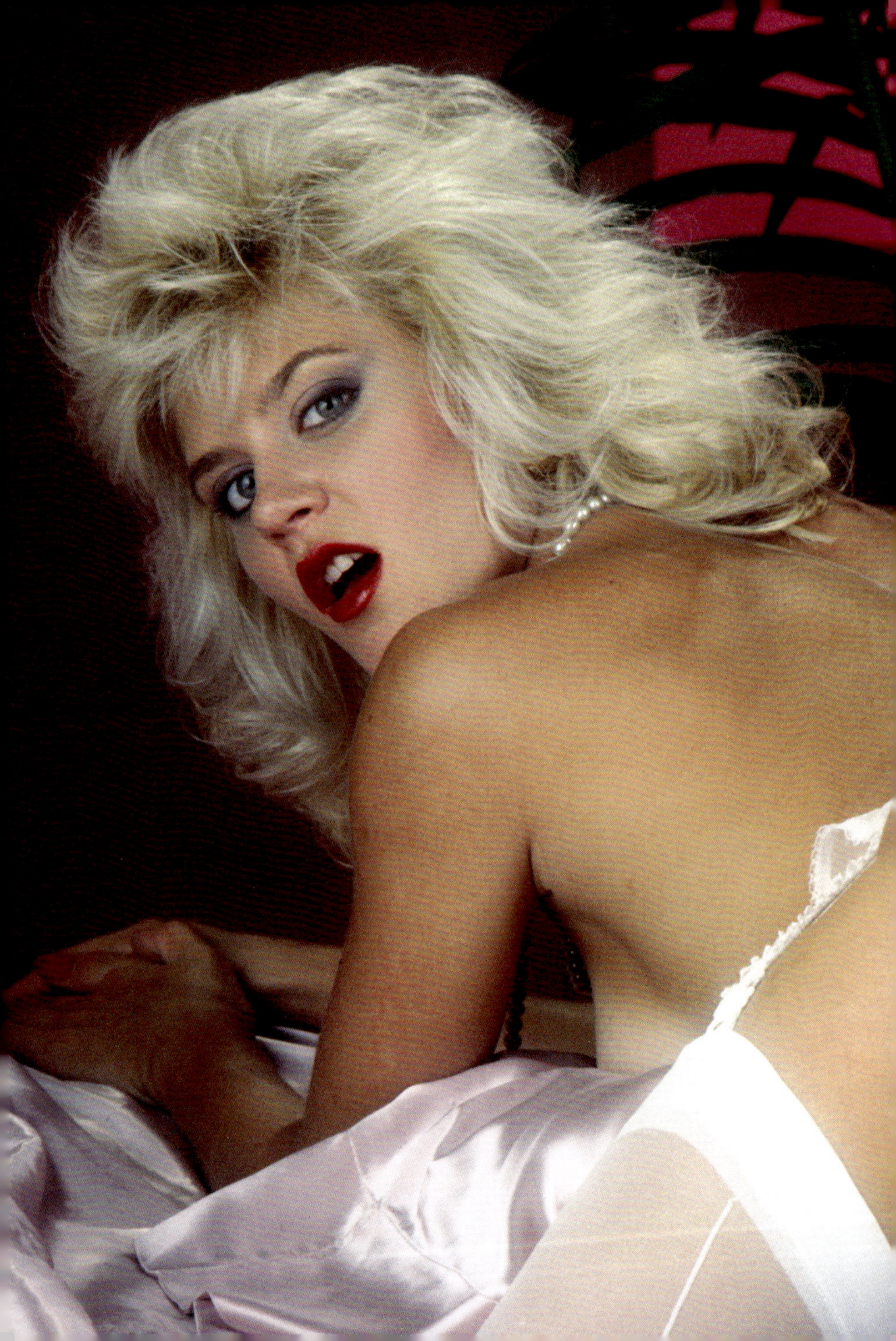

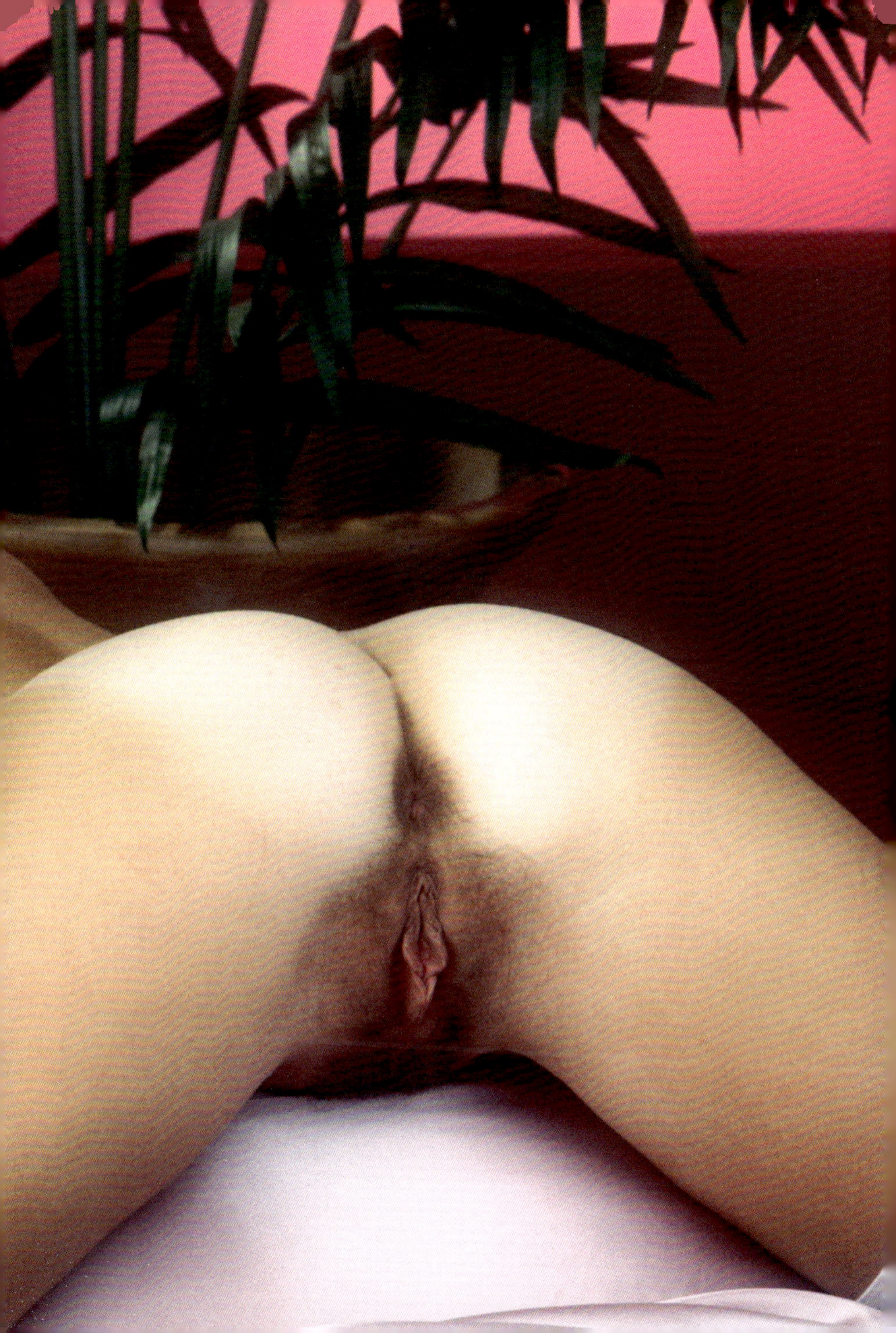

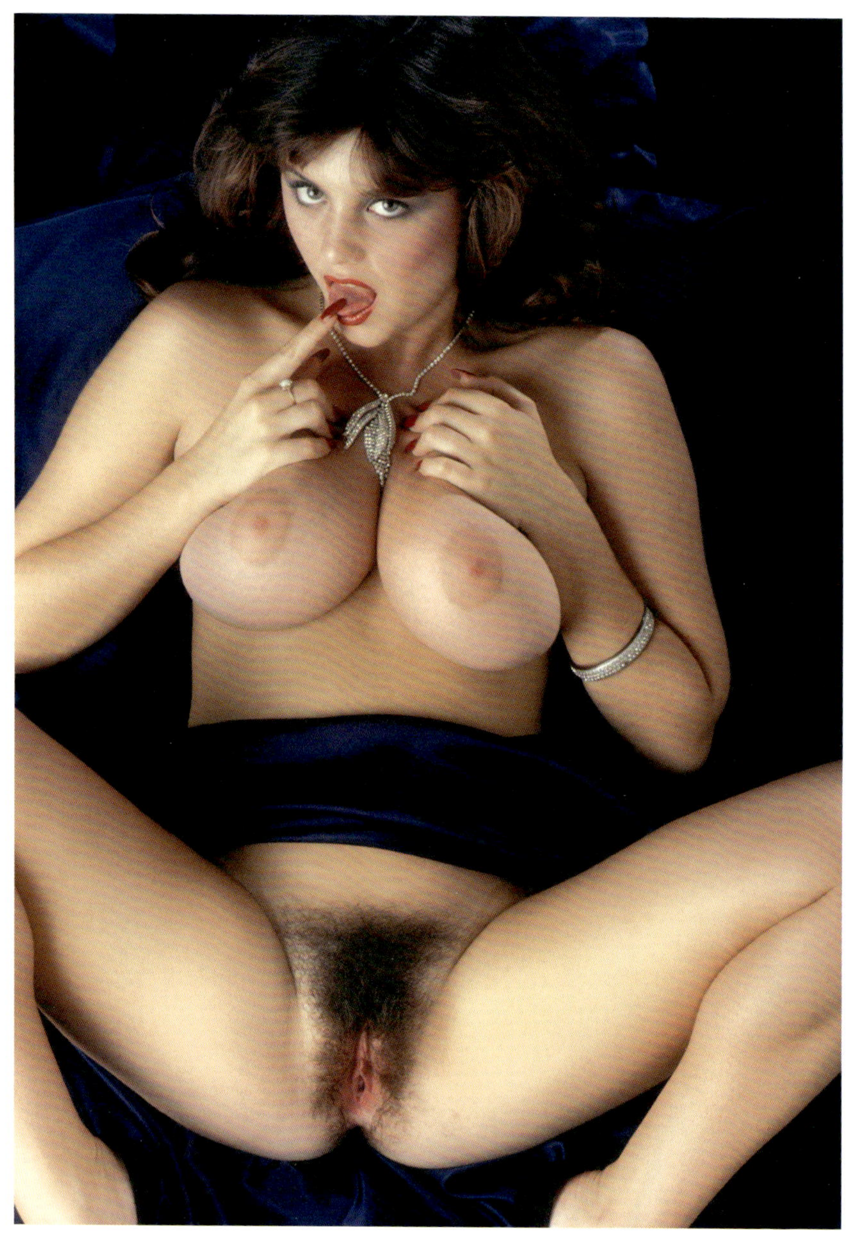

Julie Parton

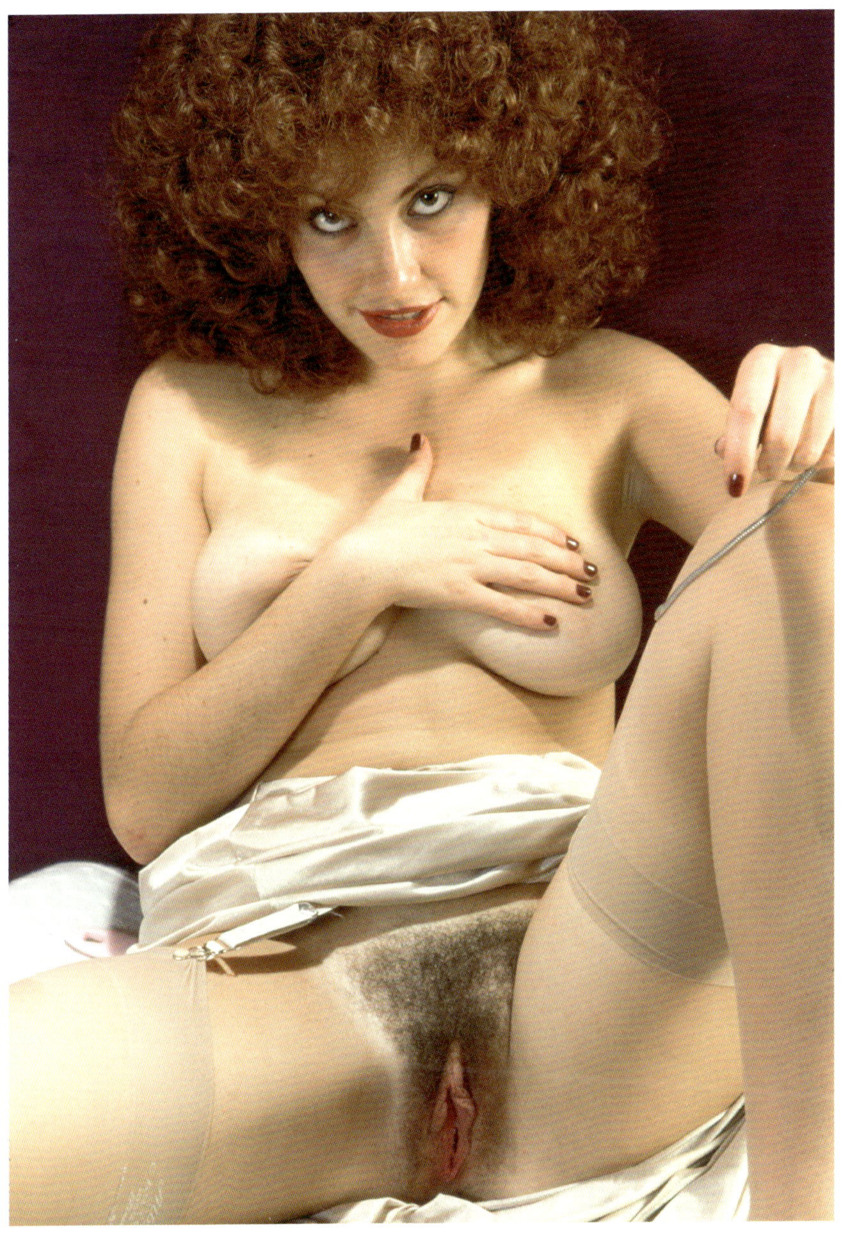

Unknown

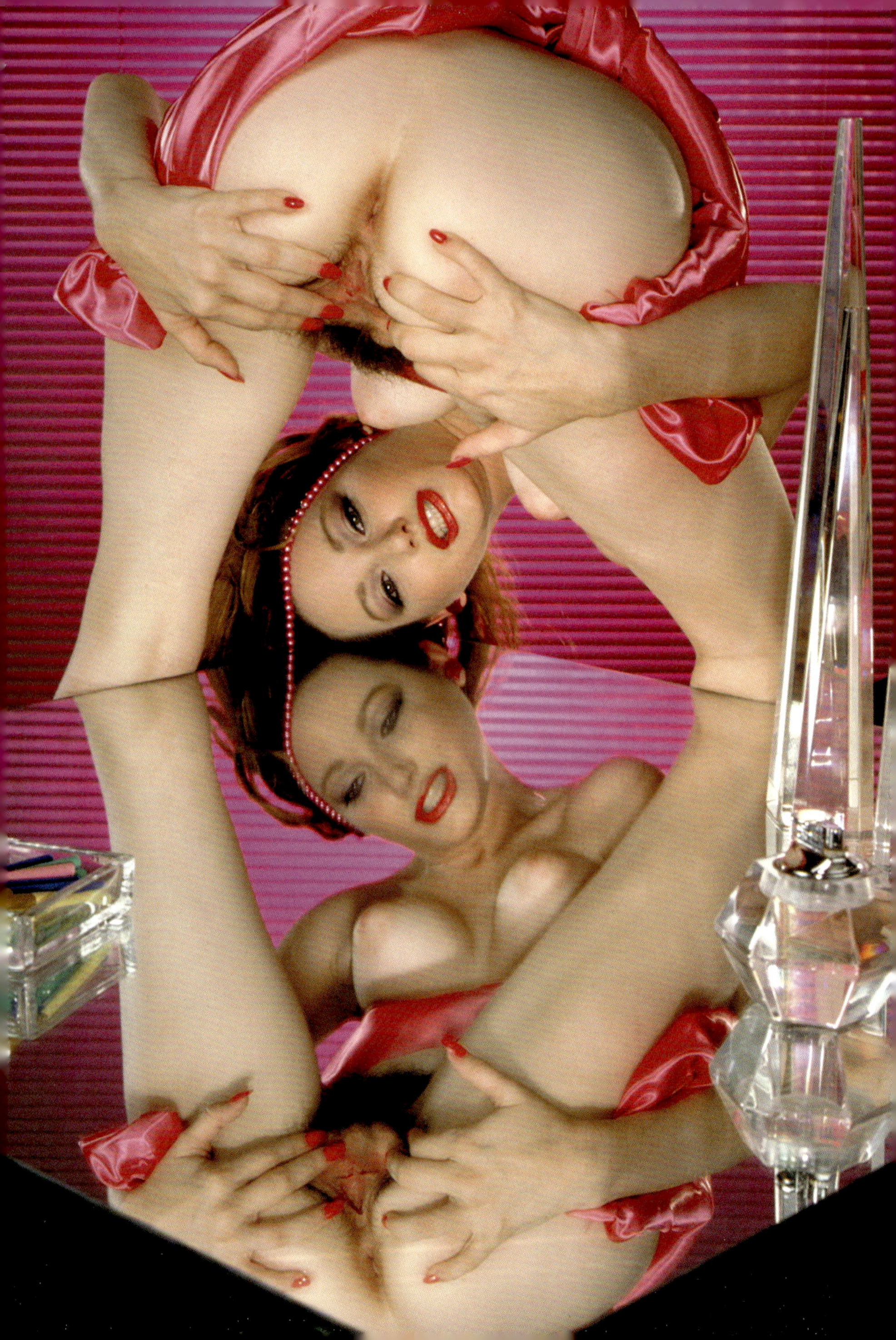

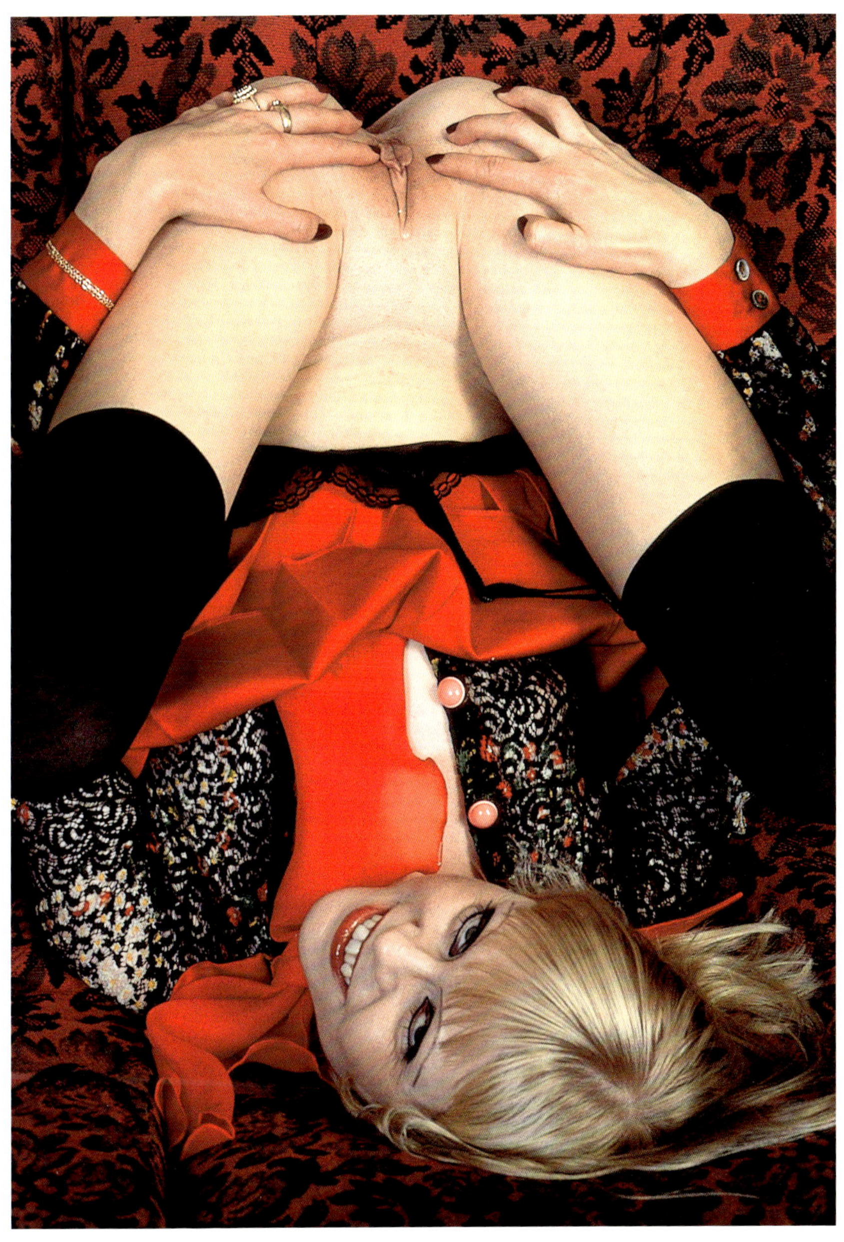

OPPOSITE **Jacqueline Lorians**   ABOVE **Eva**

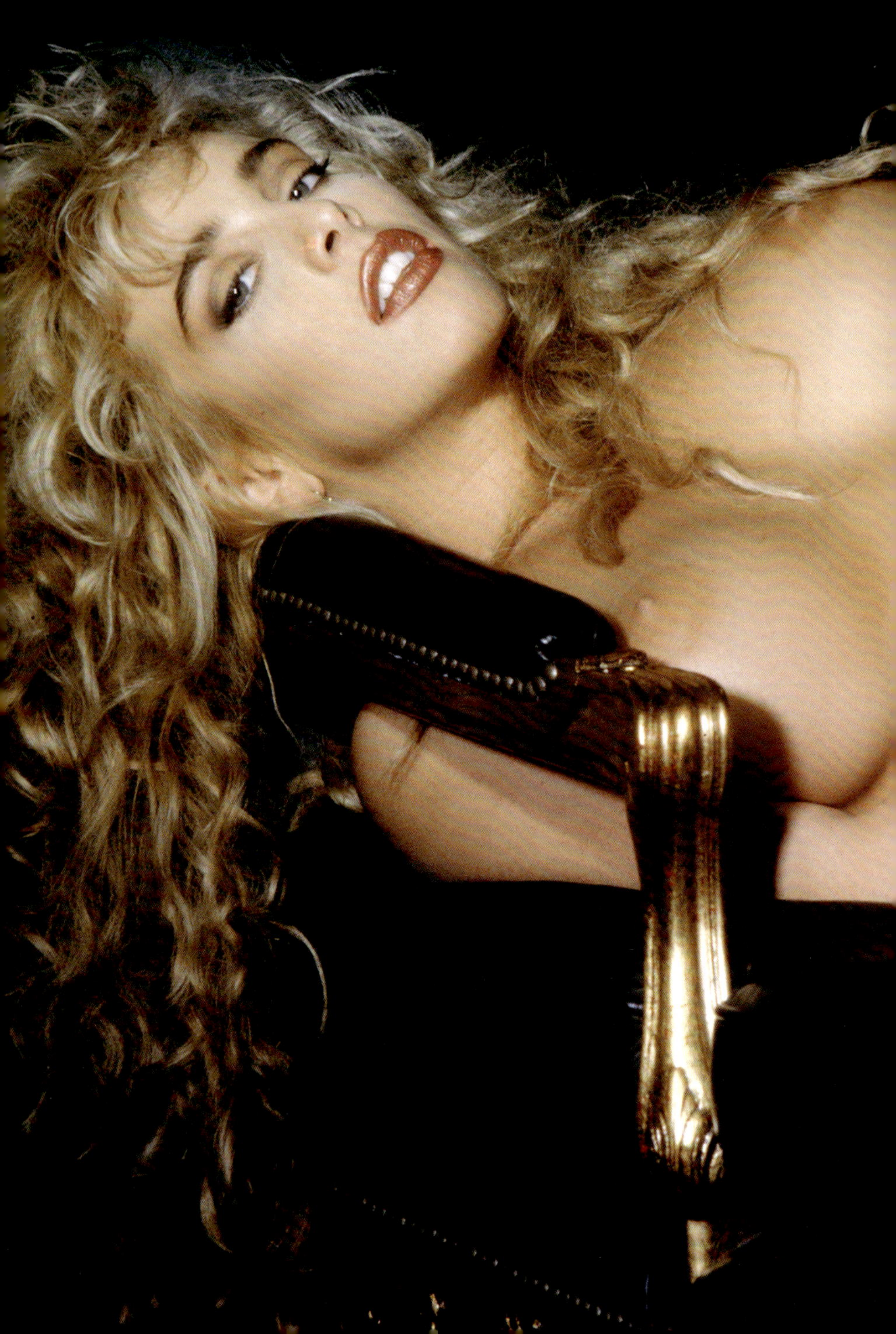

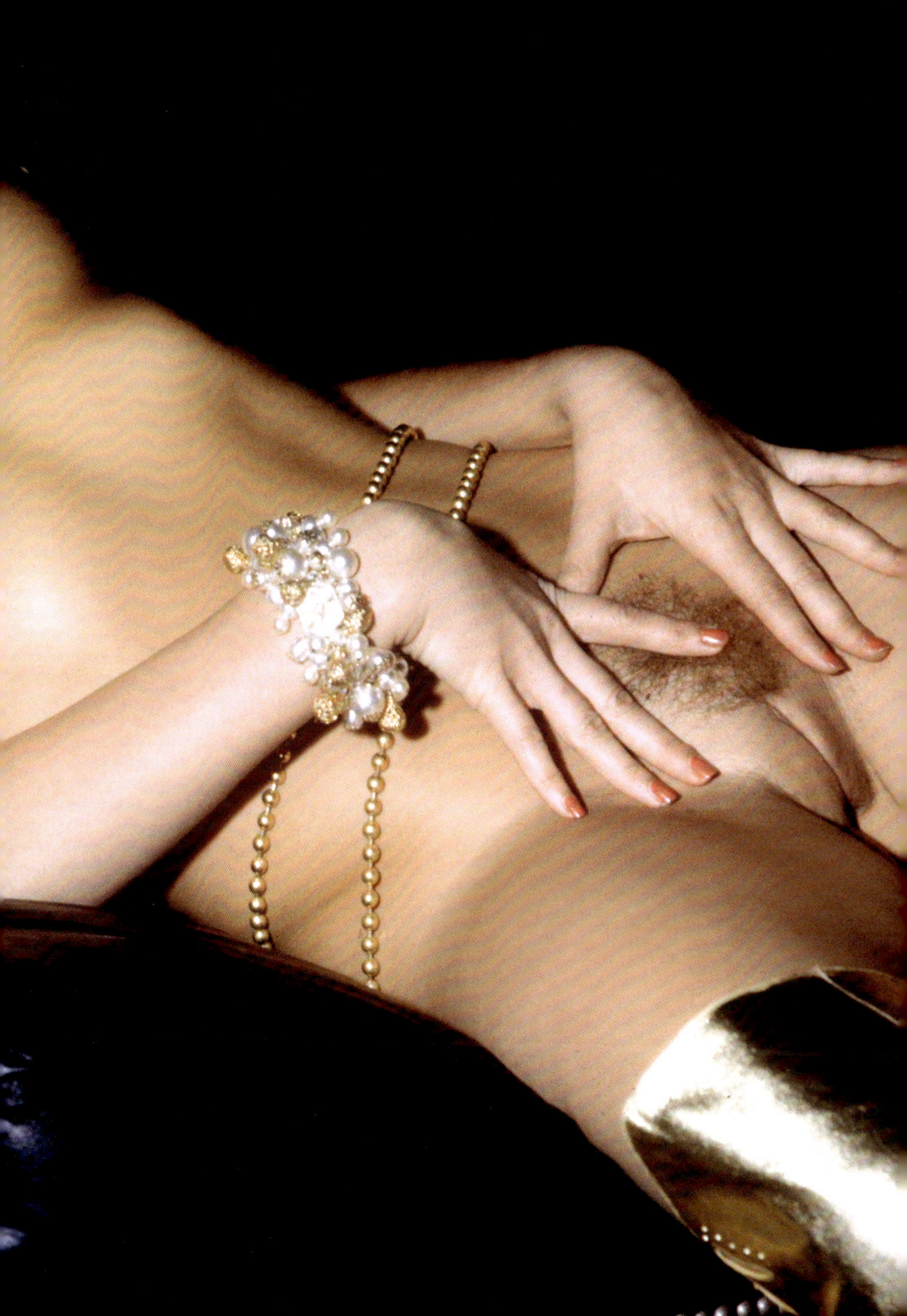

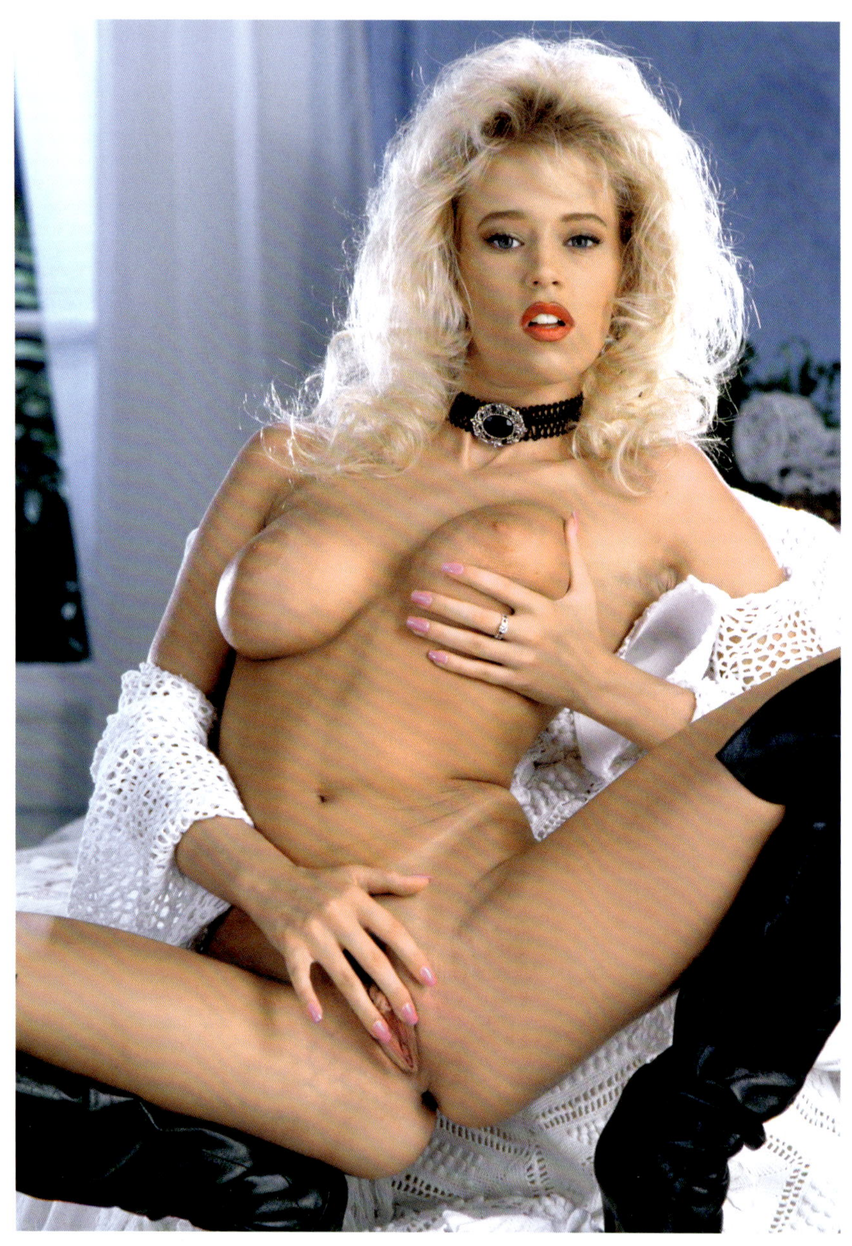

PAGES 164-165 **Sandra Scream**   ABOVE **Jenna Jameson**

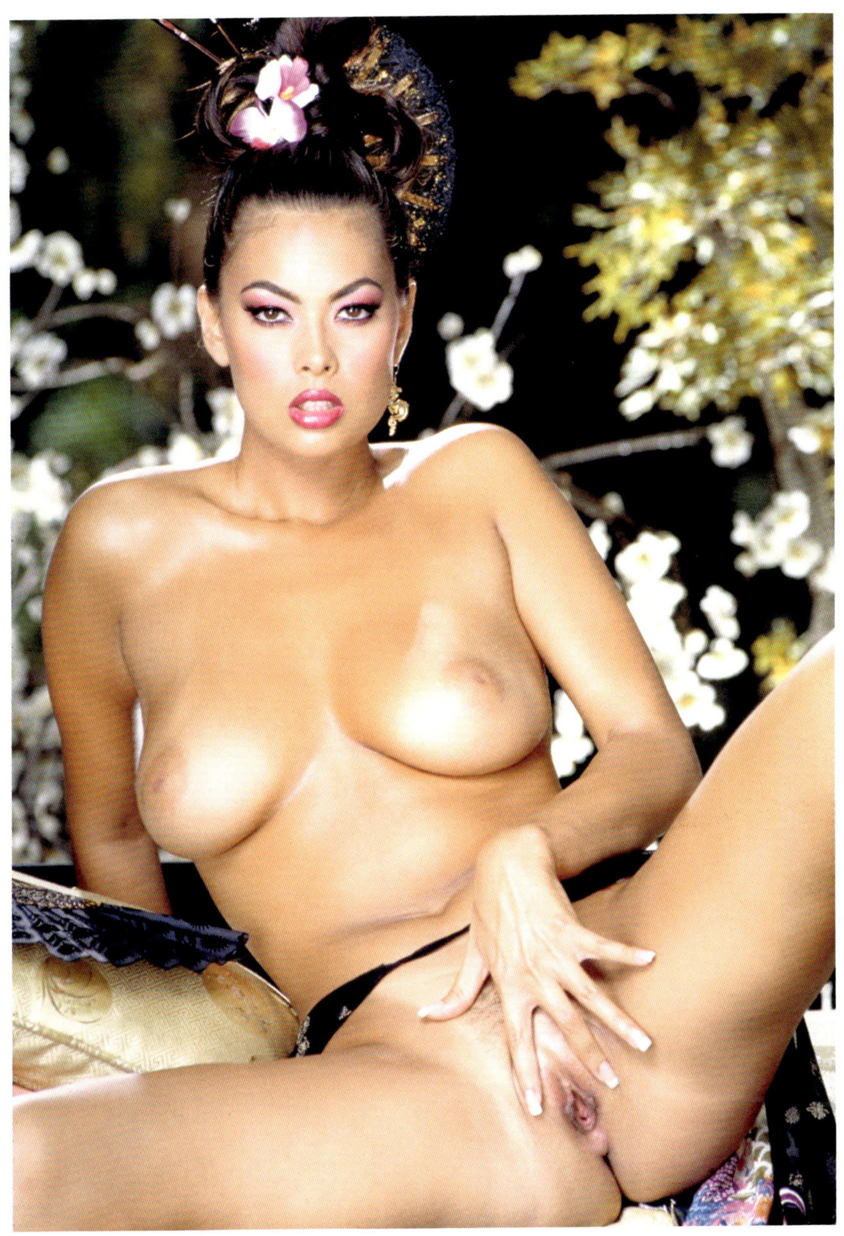

ABOVE **Tera Patrick**   PAGES 168-169 **Kimberly Kane**

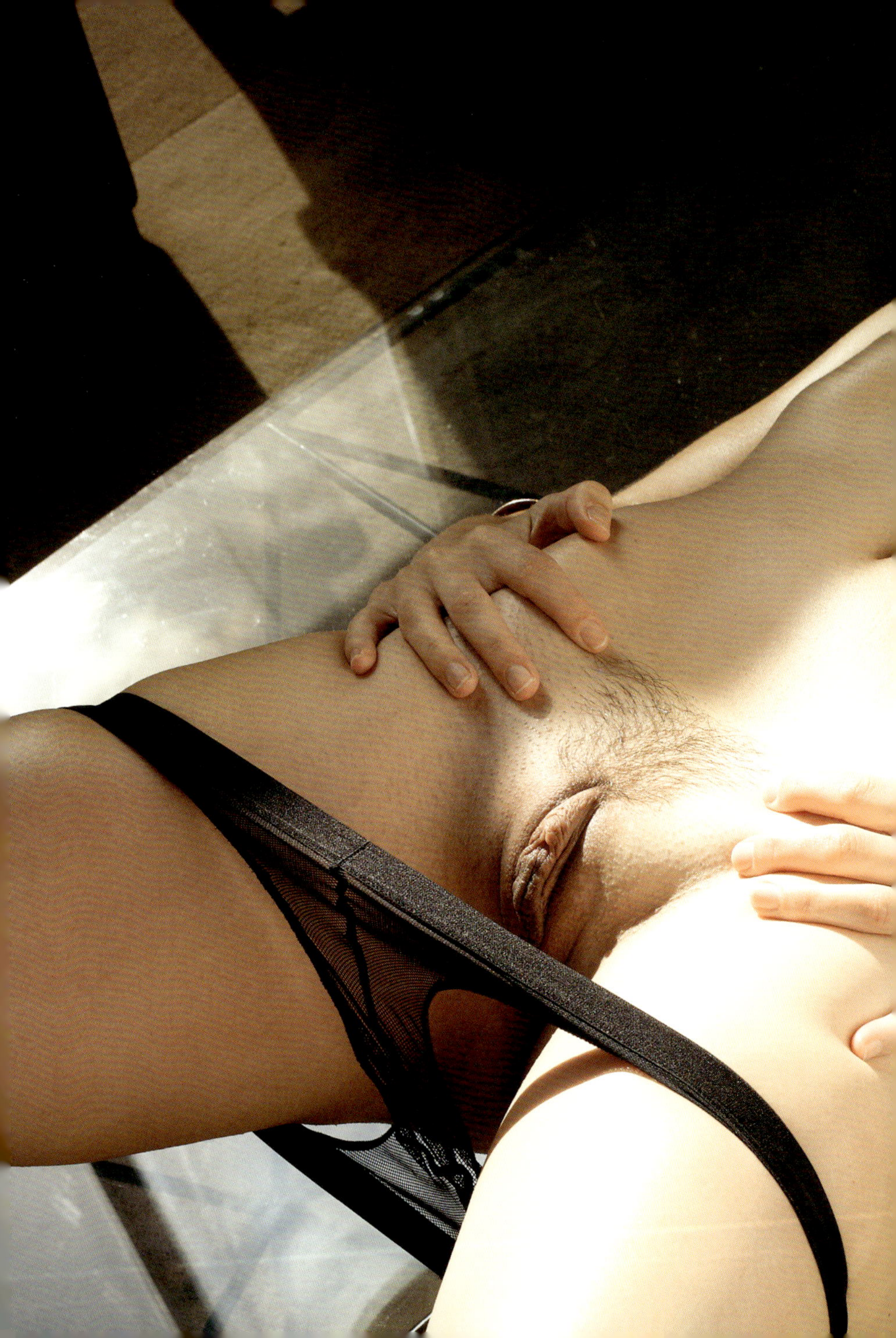

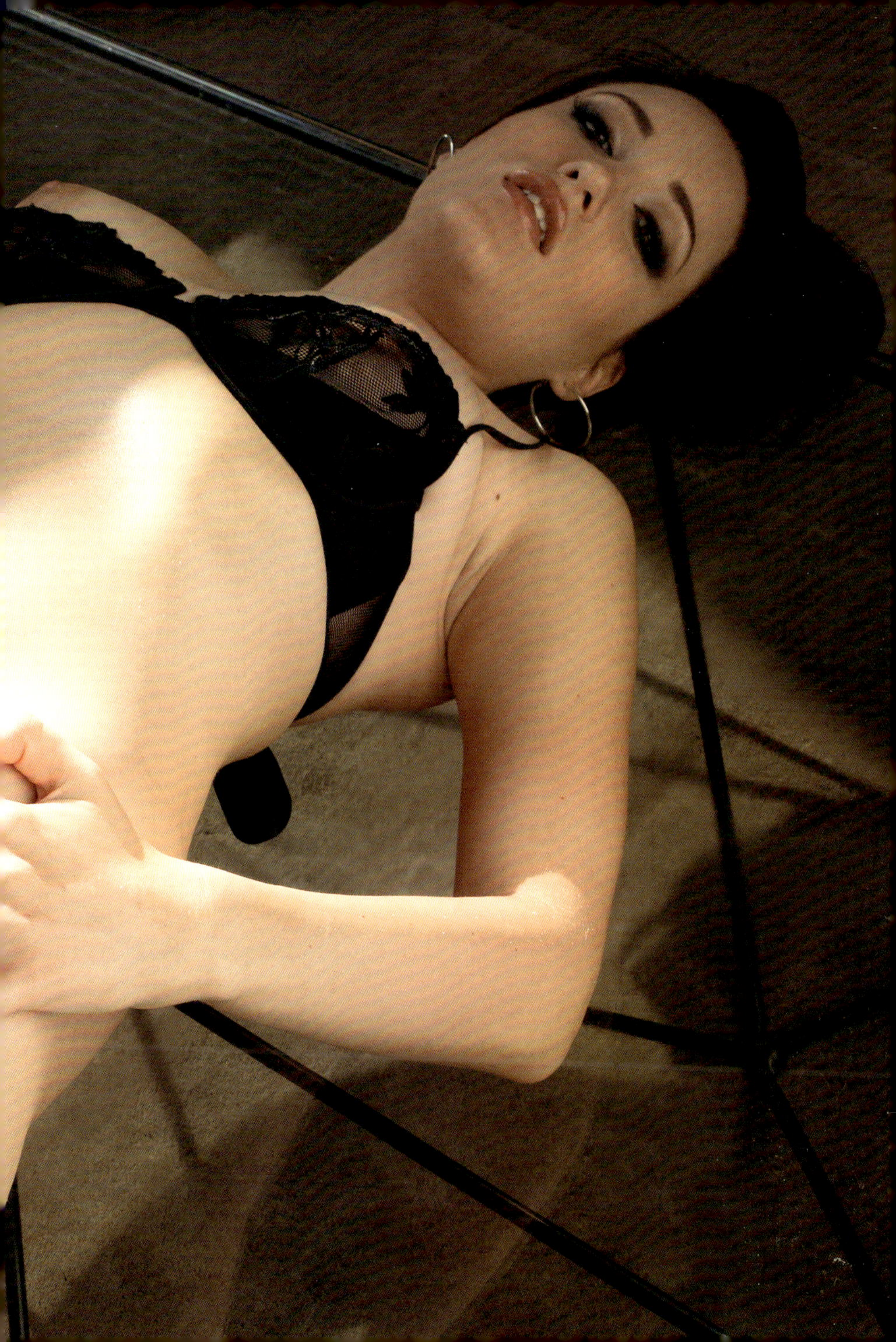

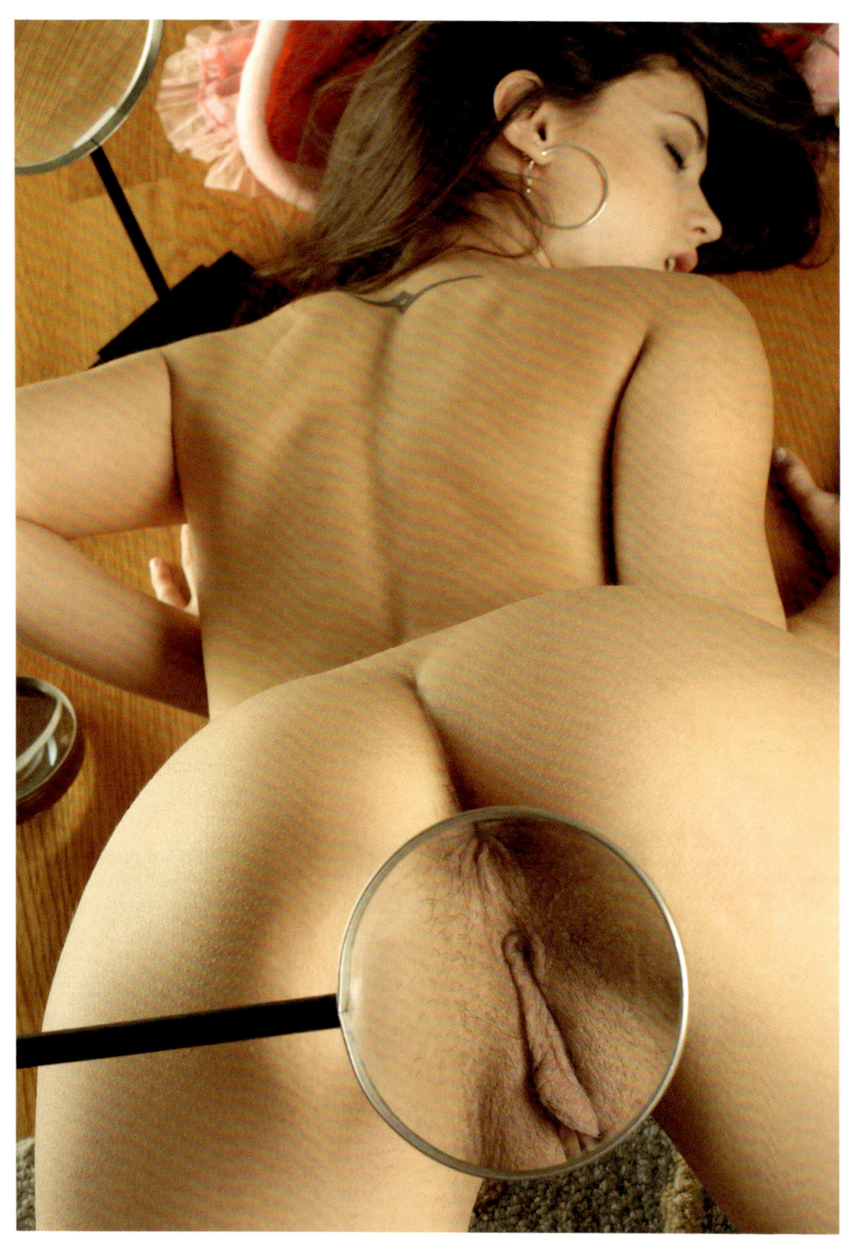

ABOVE **Georgia Jones** OPPOSITE **Roxy DeVille**

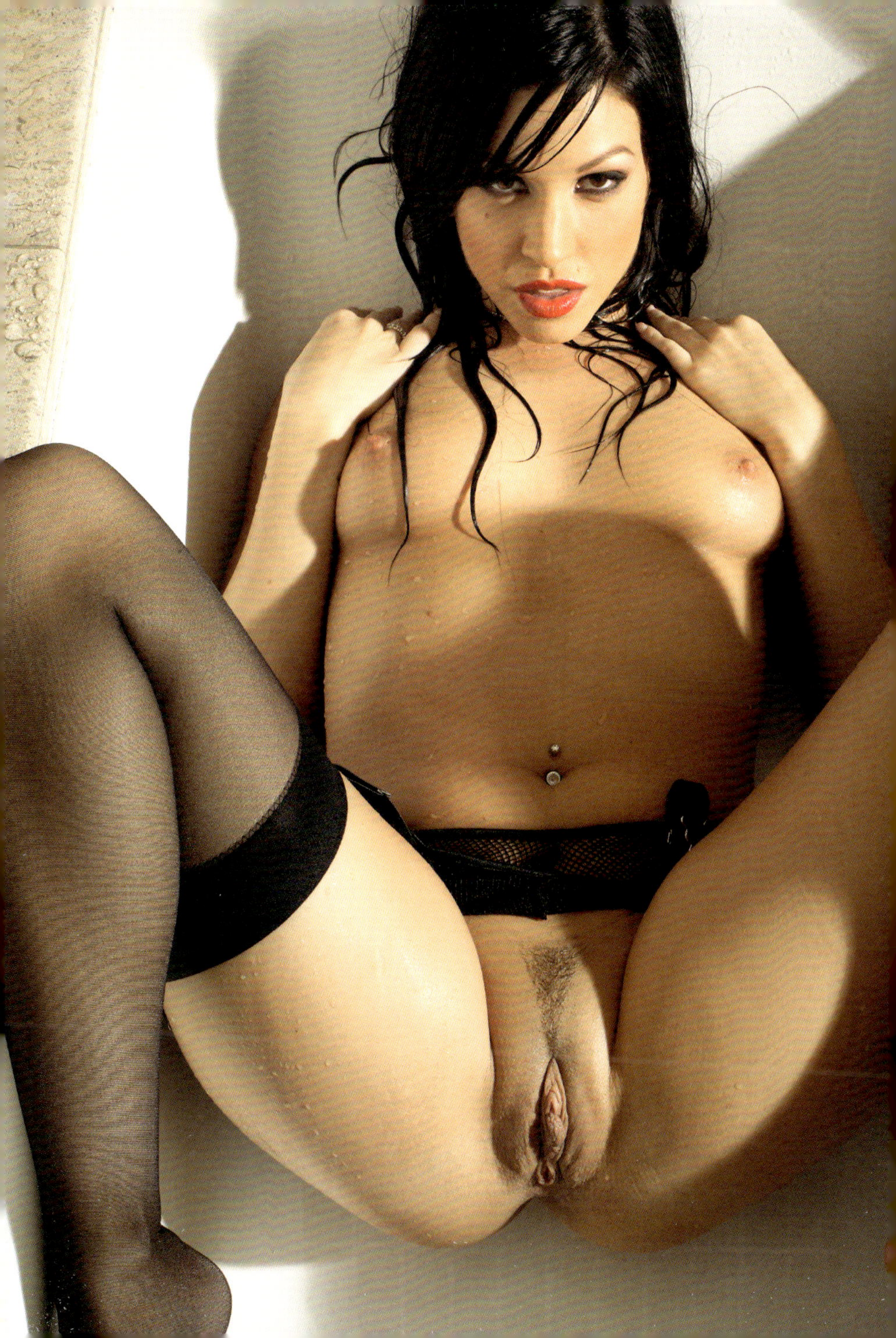

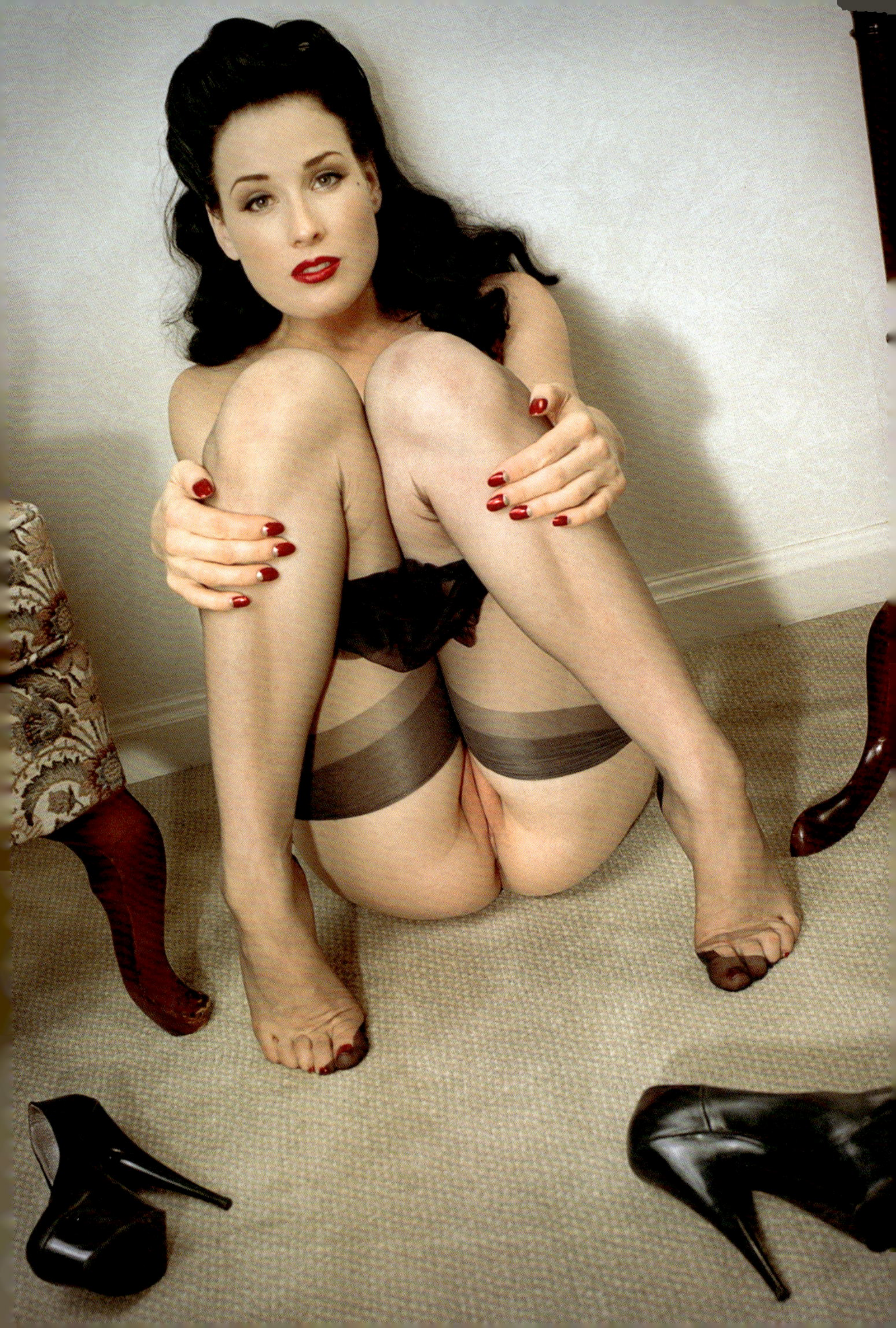

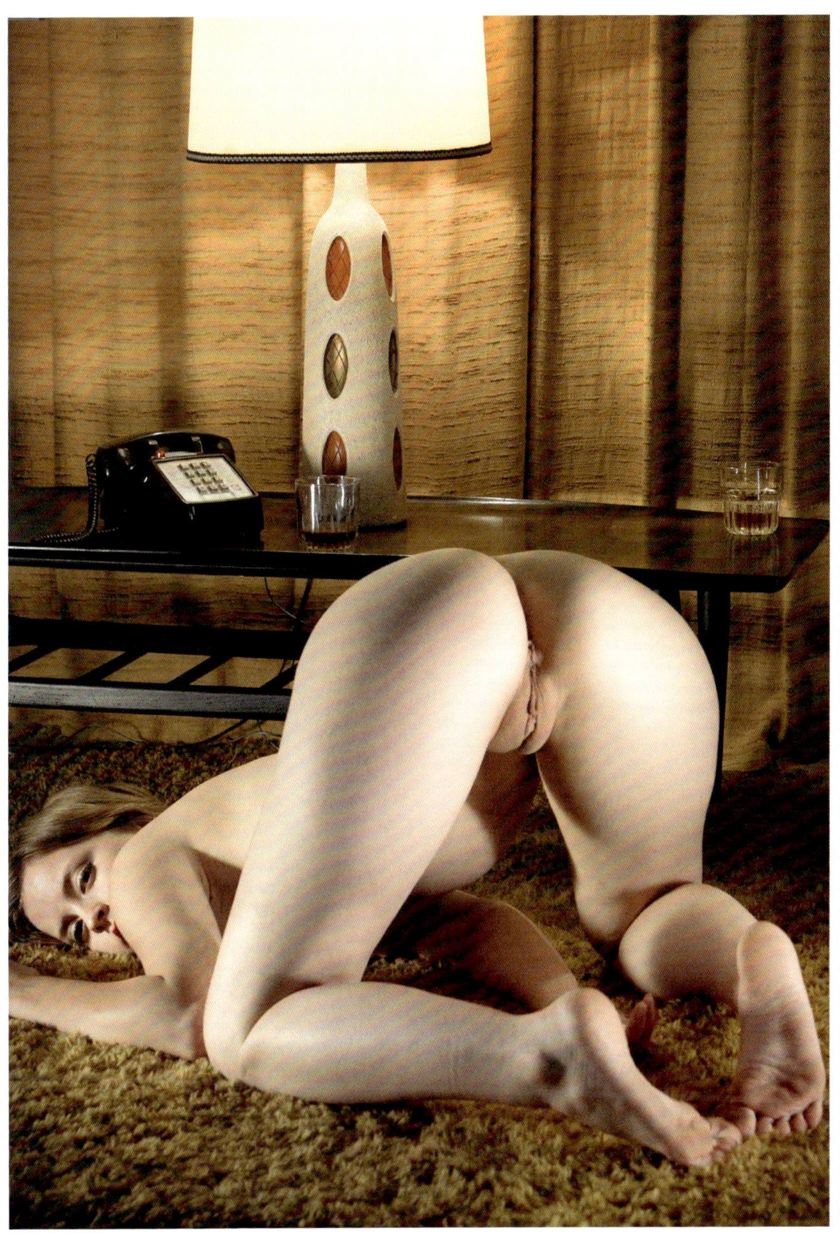

OPPOSITE **Dita Von Teese**   ABOVE **Erin Hulme**

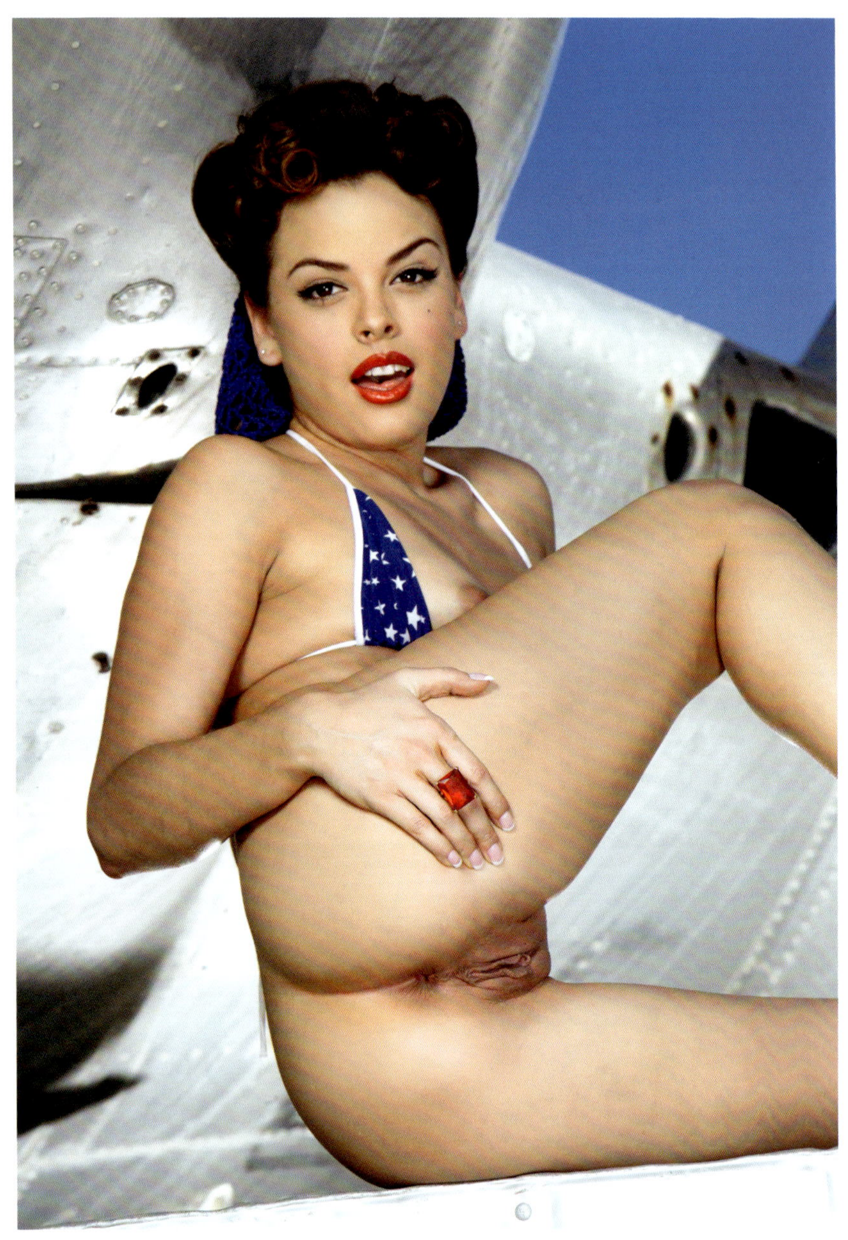

Renee Perez

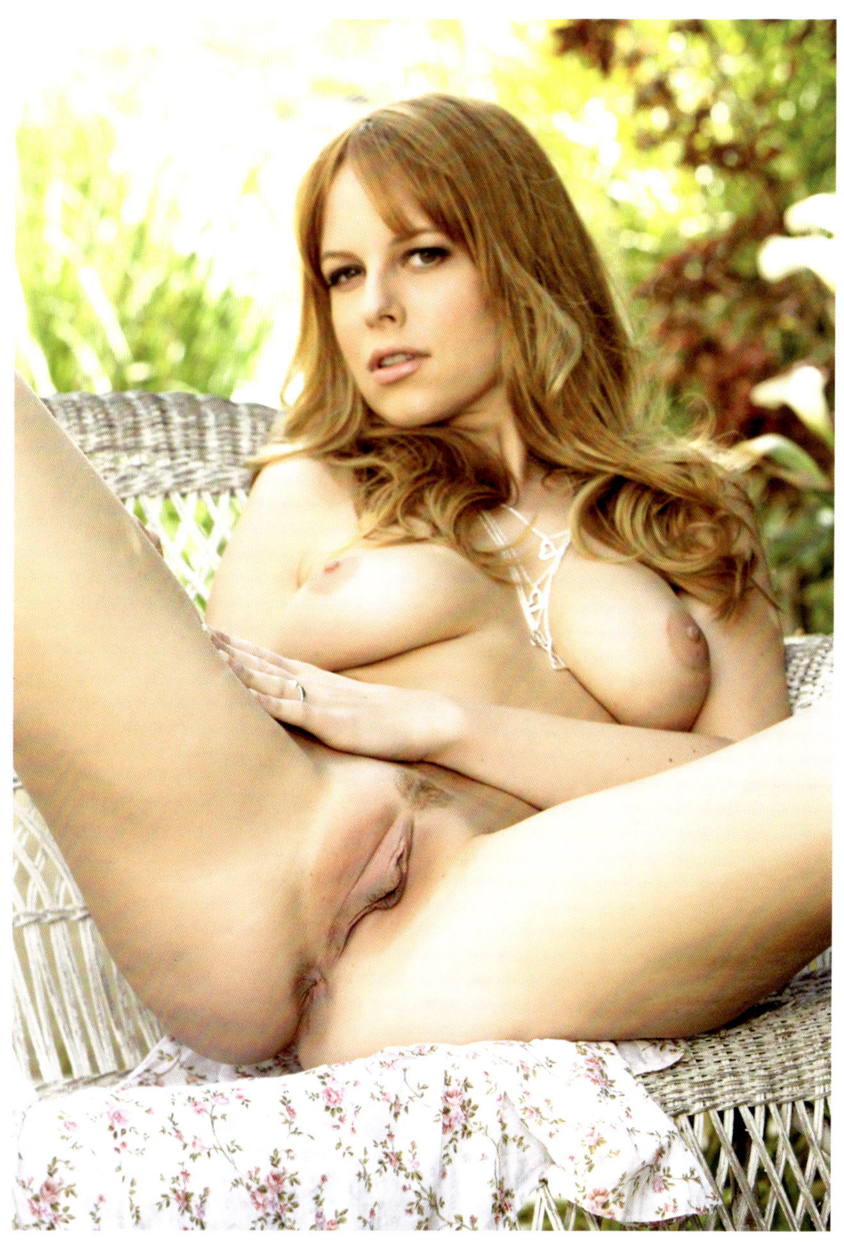

ABOVE **Andie Valentino** PAGES 176-177 **Heather Vandeven**

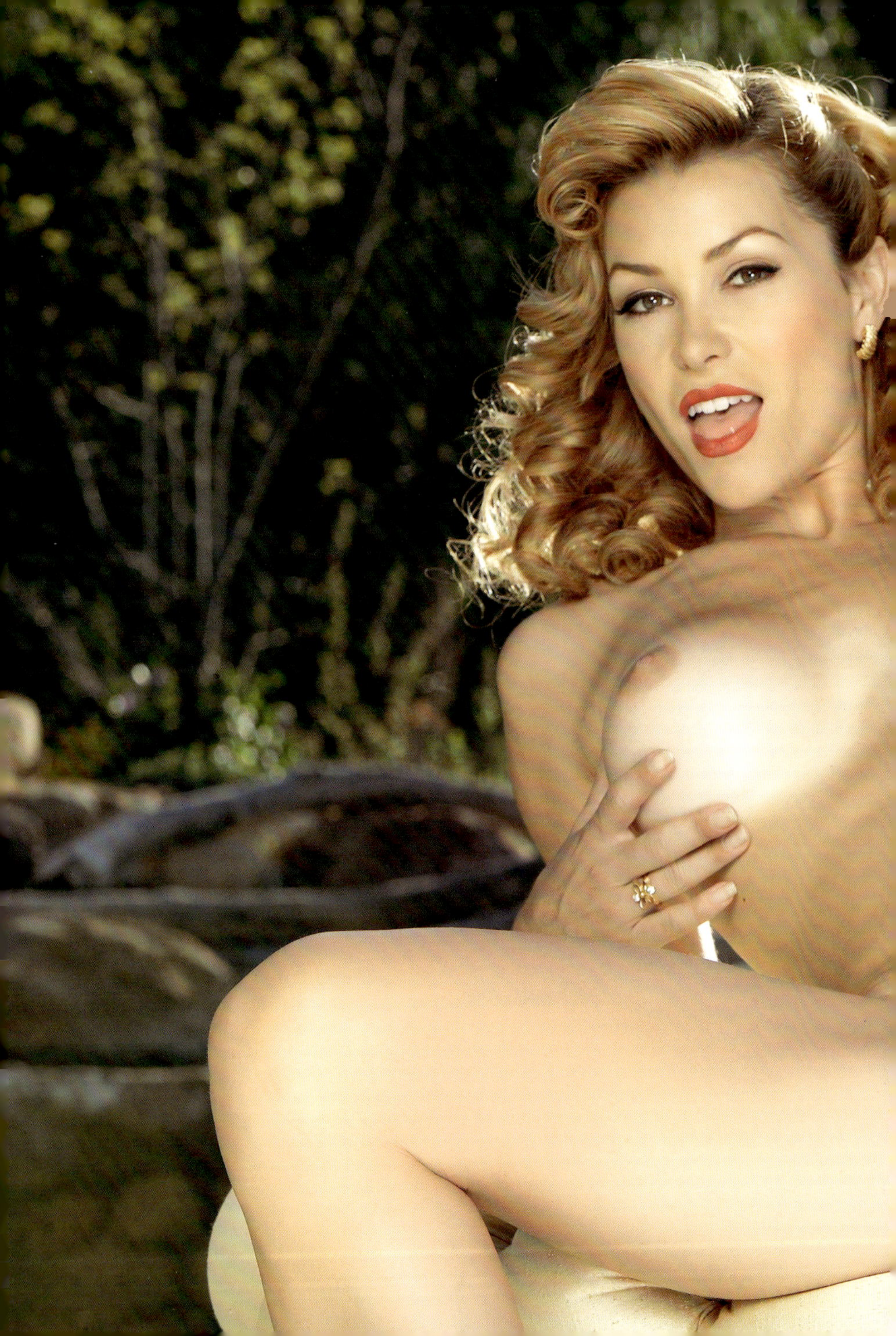

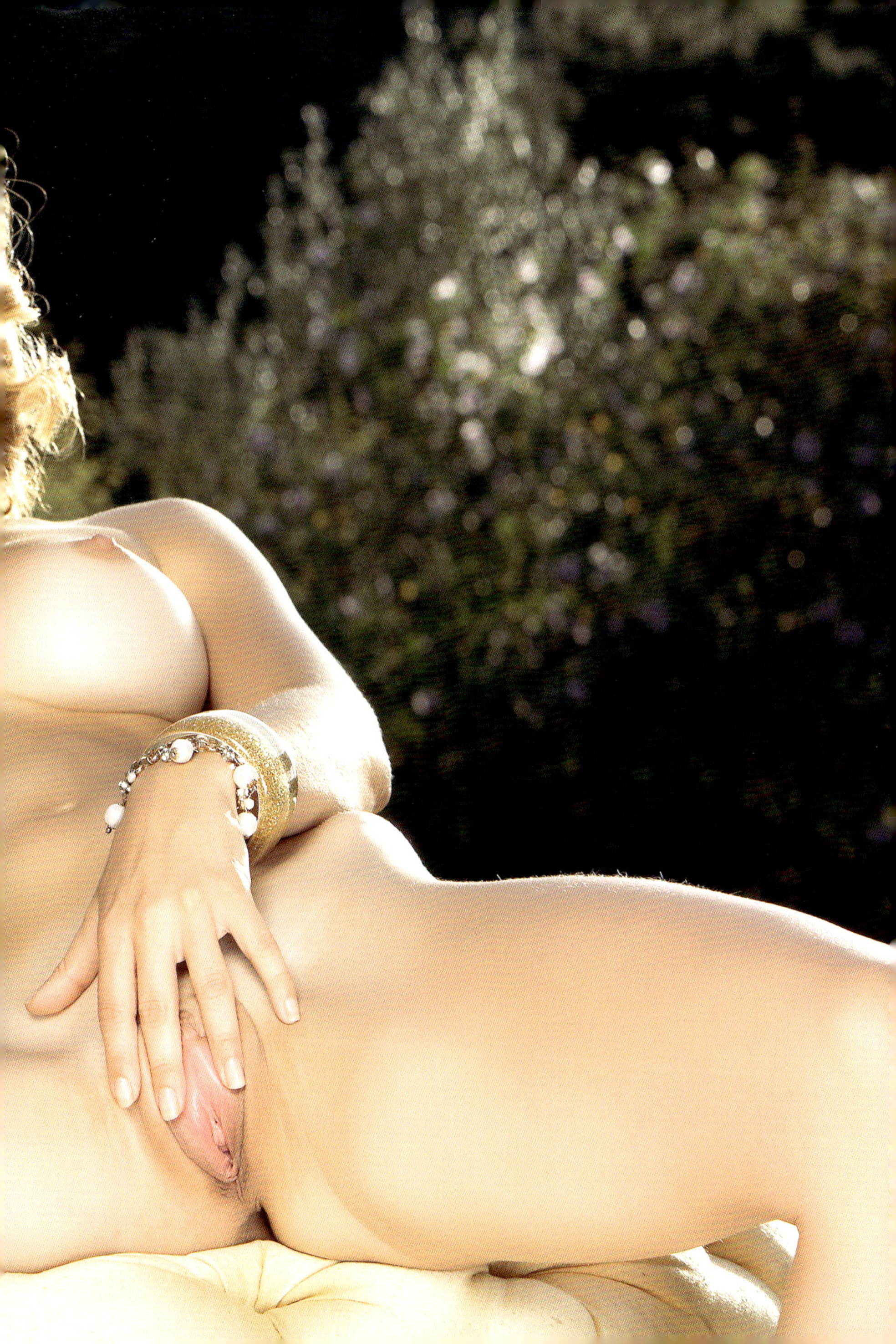

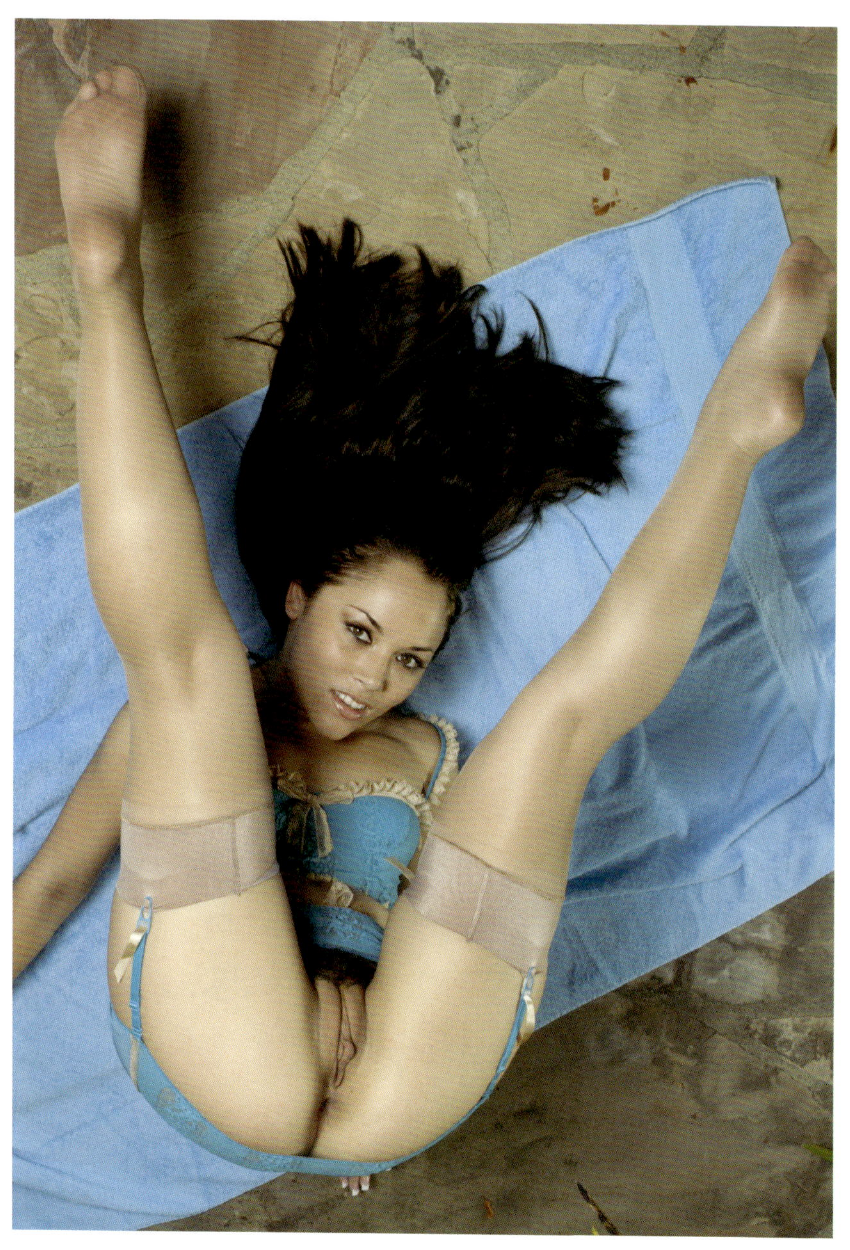

ABOVE **Unknown**   OPPOSITE **Heatherton**

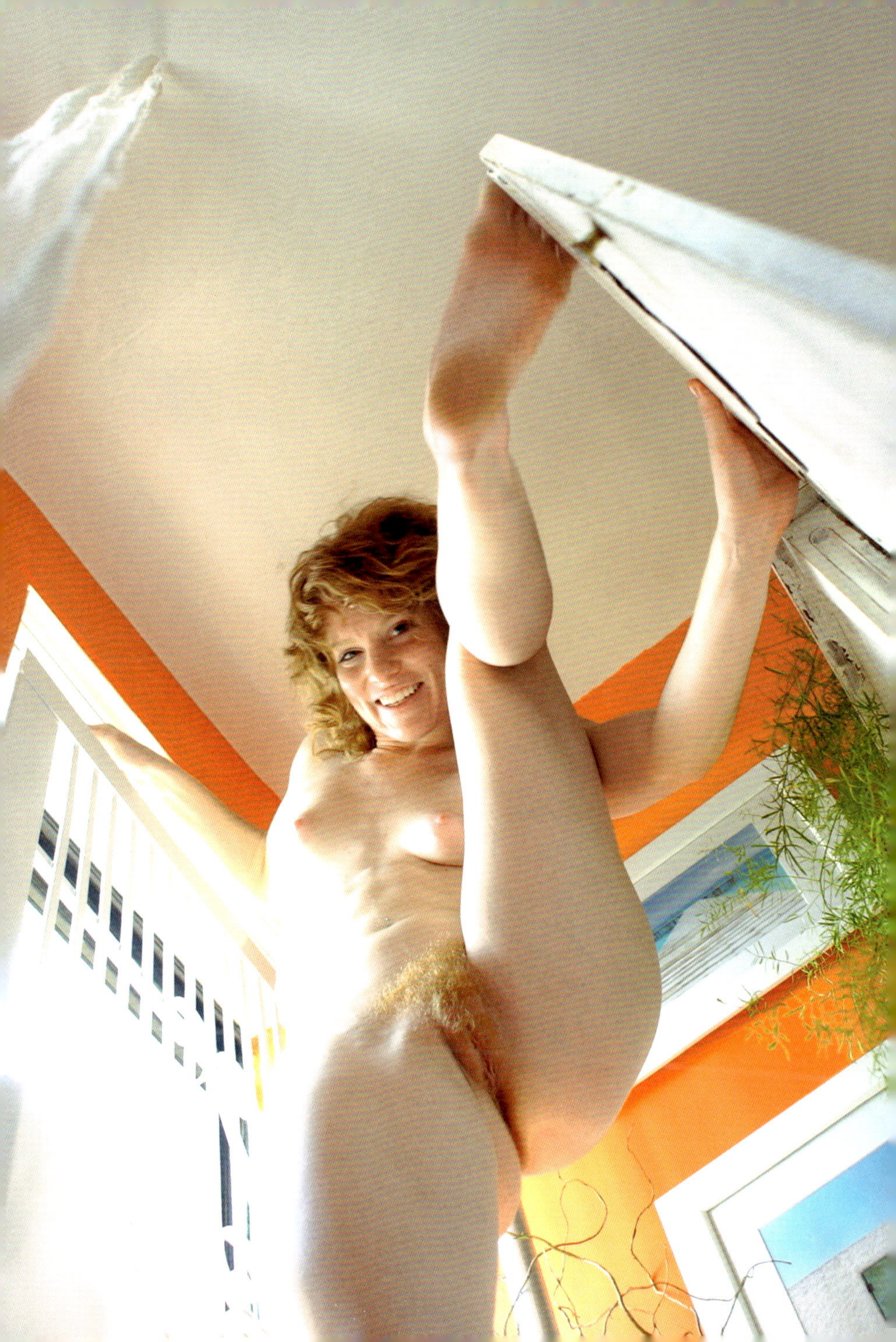

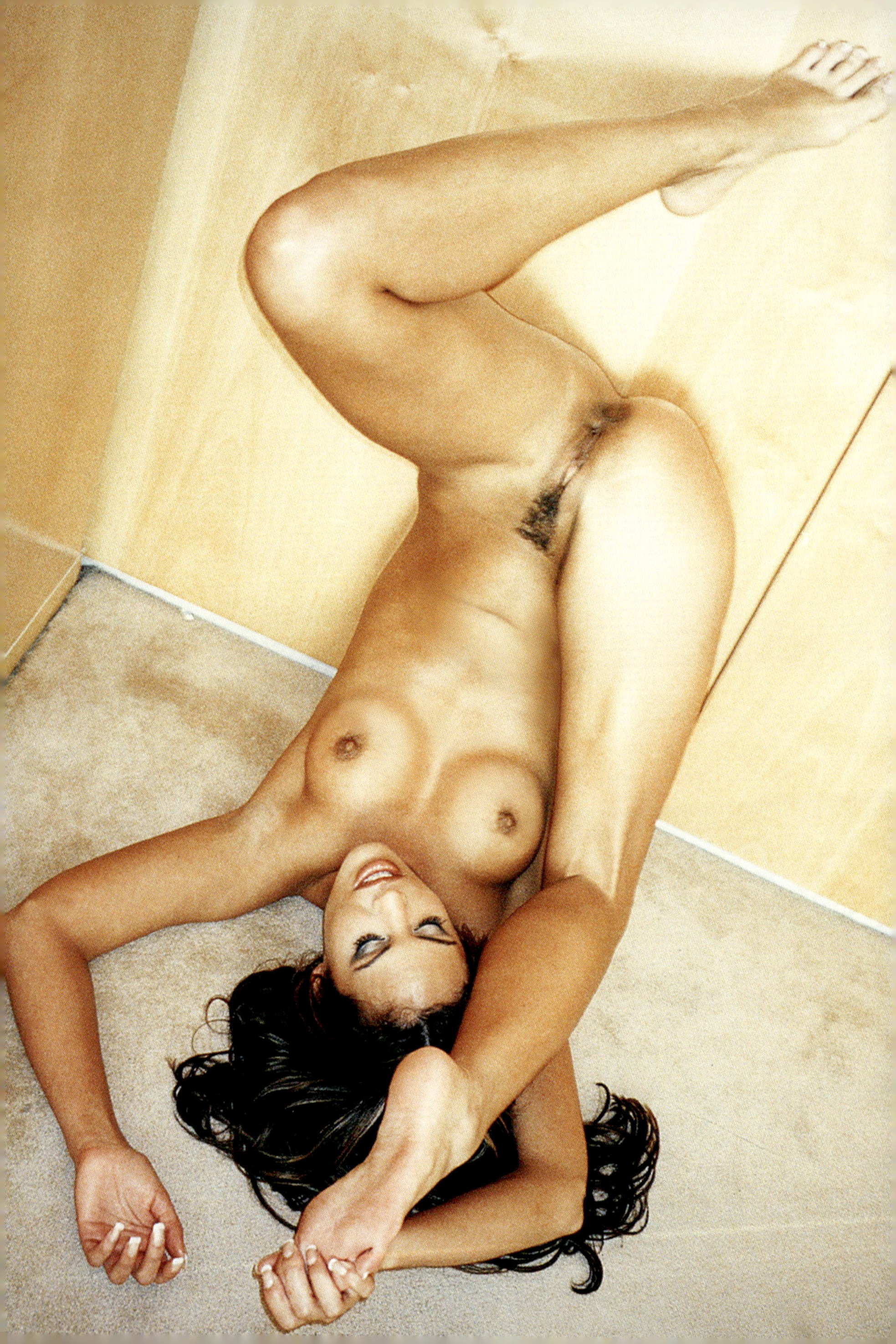

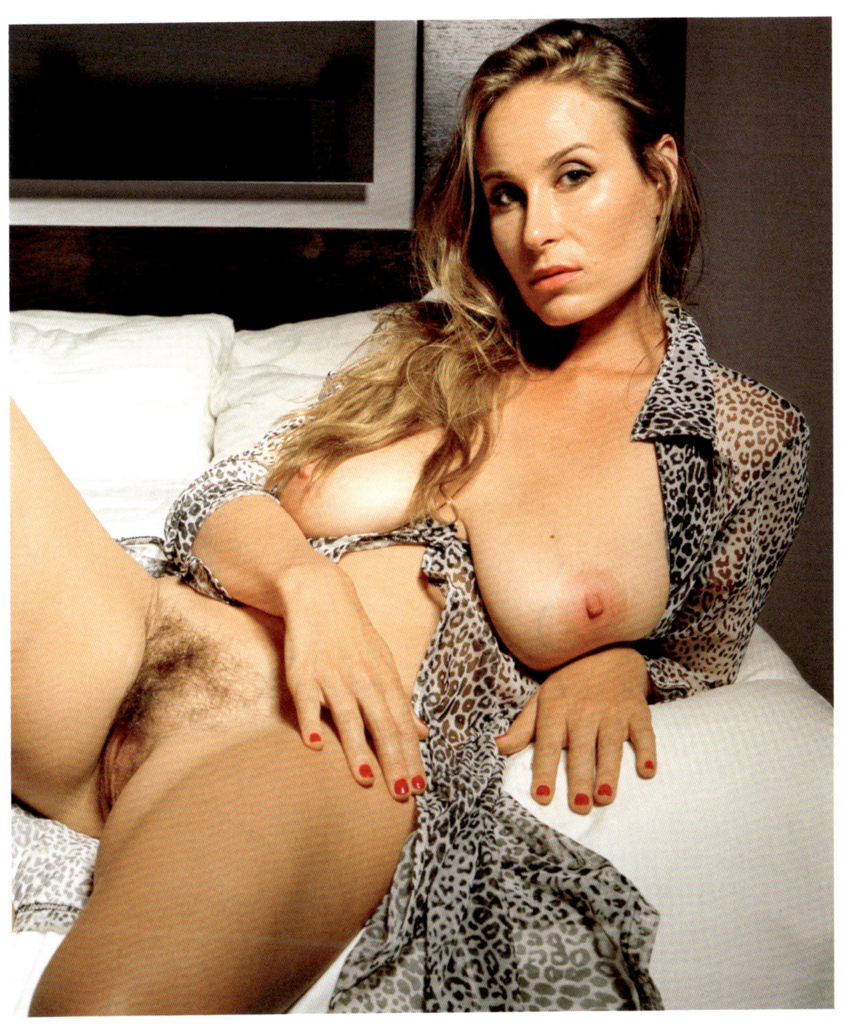

OPPOSITE **Dahlia Grey**   ABOVE **Vassanta**, GEORGE PITTS

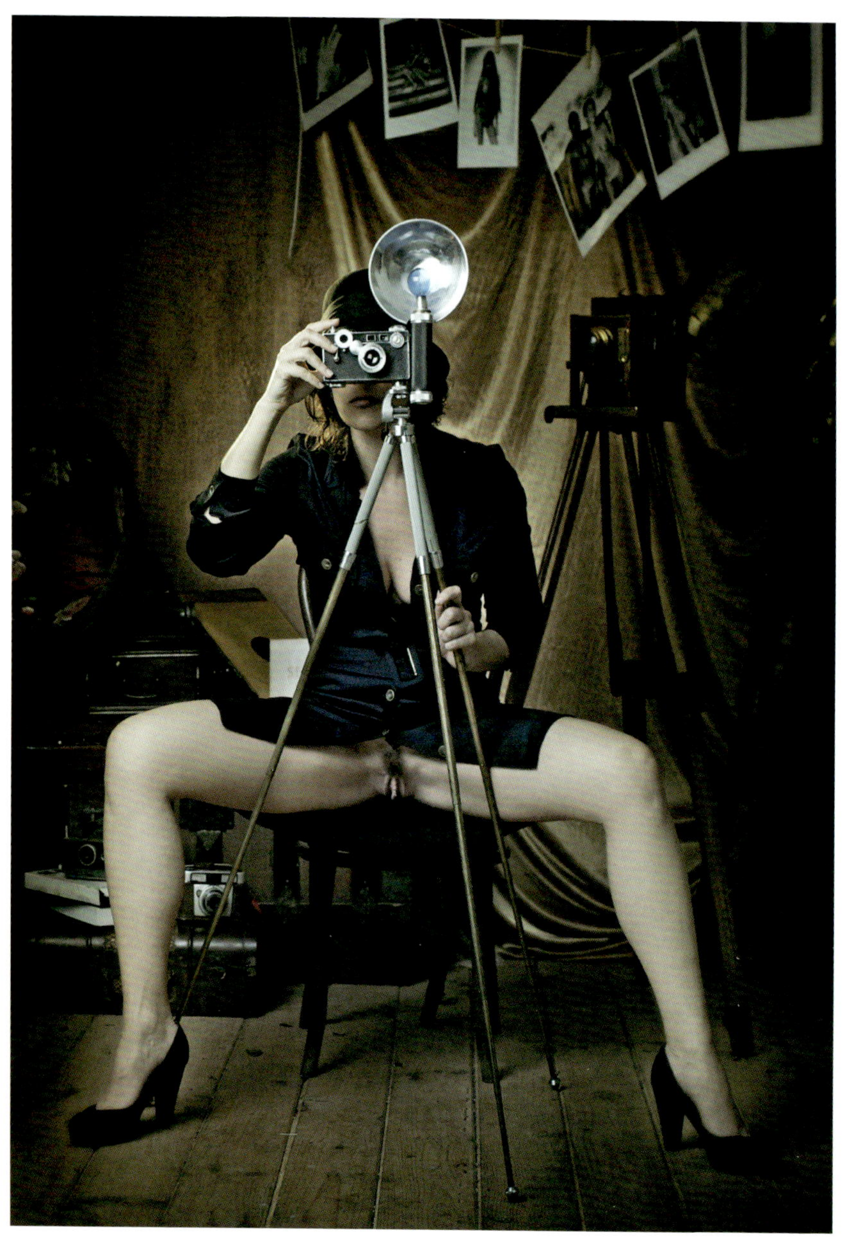

The Photographer

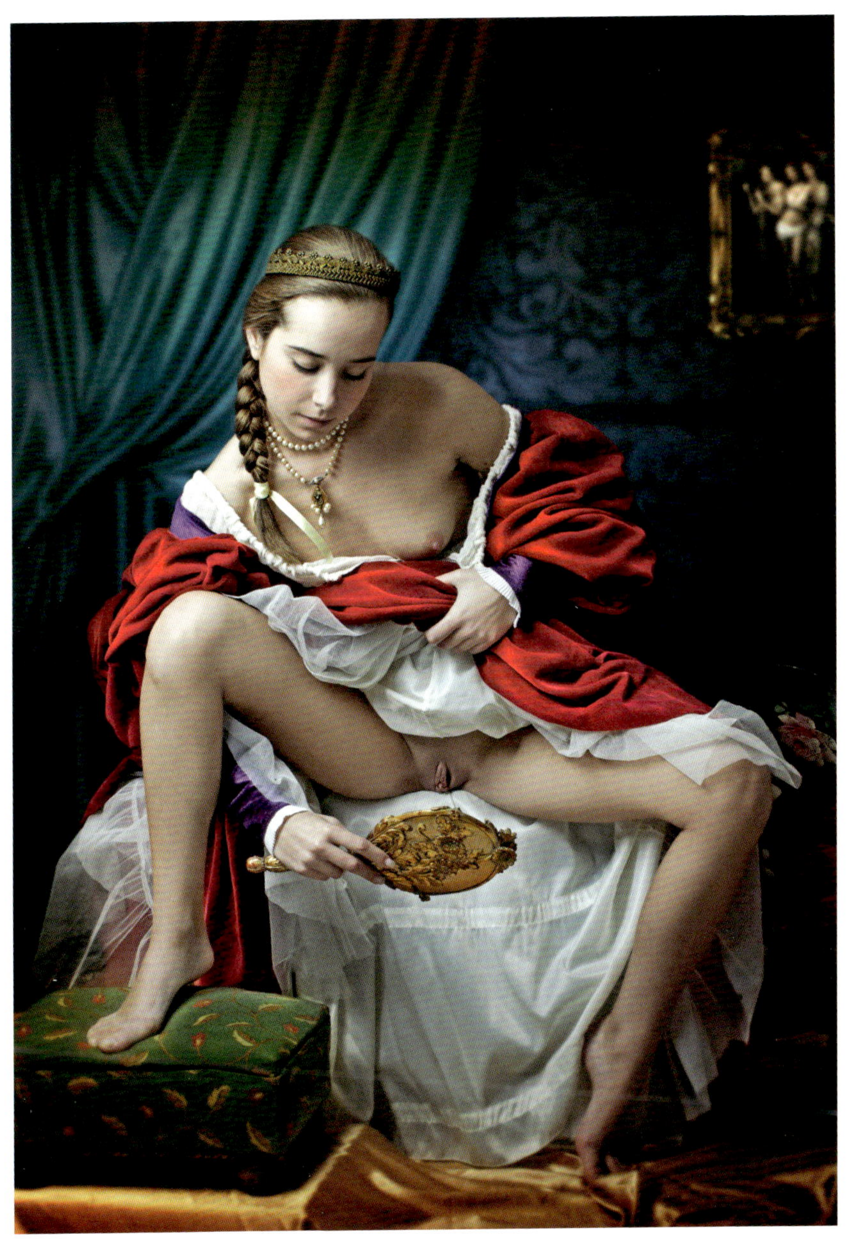

Young Woman with Mirror

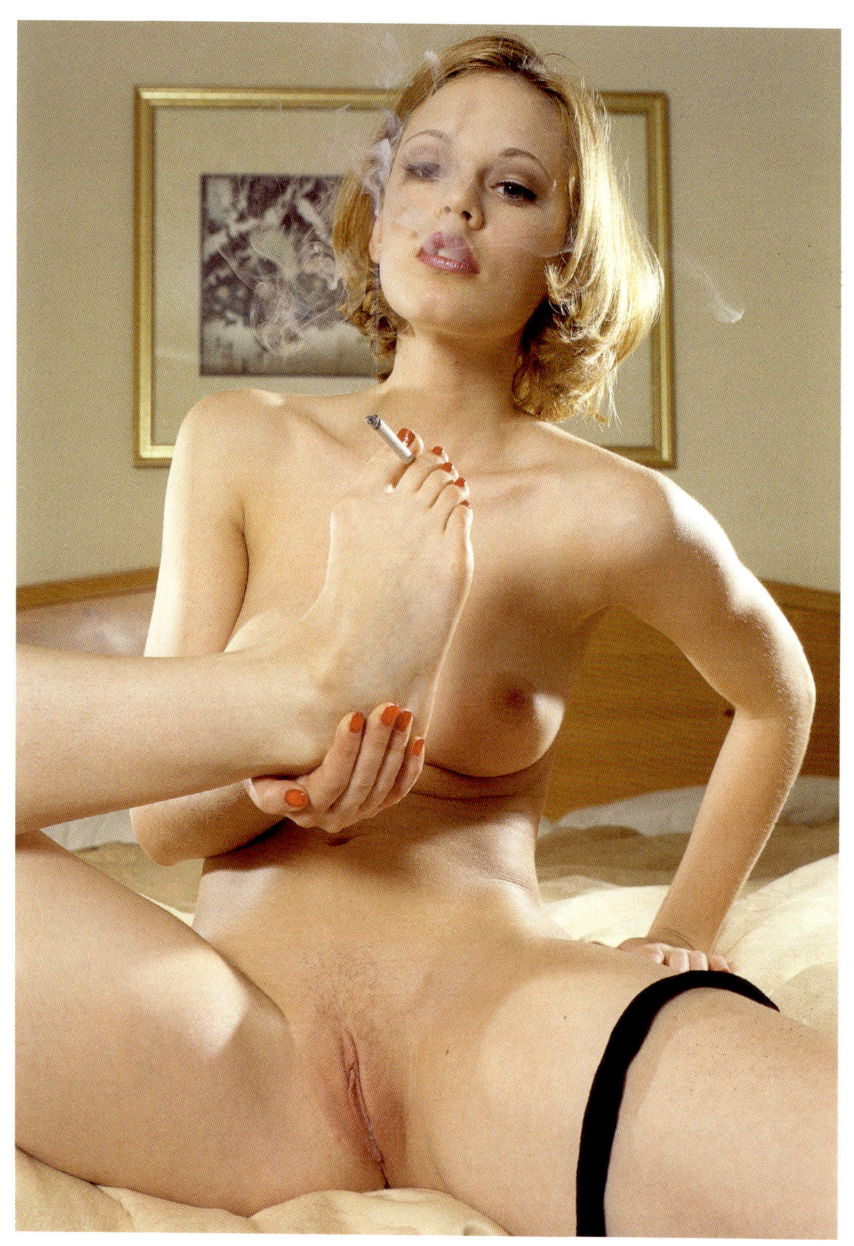

ABOVE **Unknown** OPPOSITE **Darian**

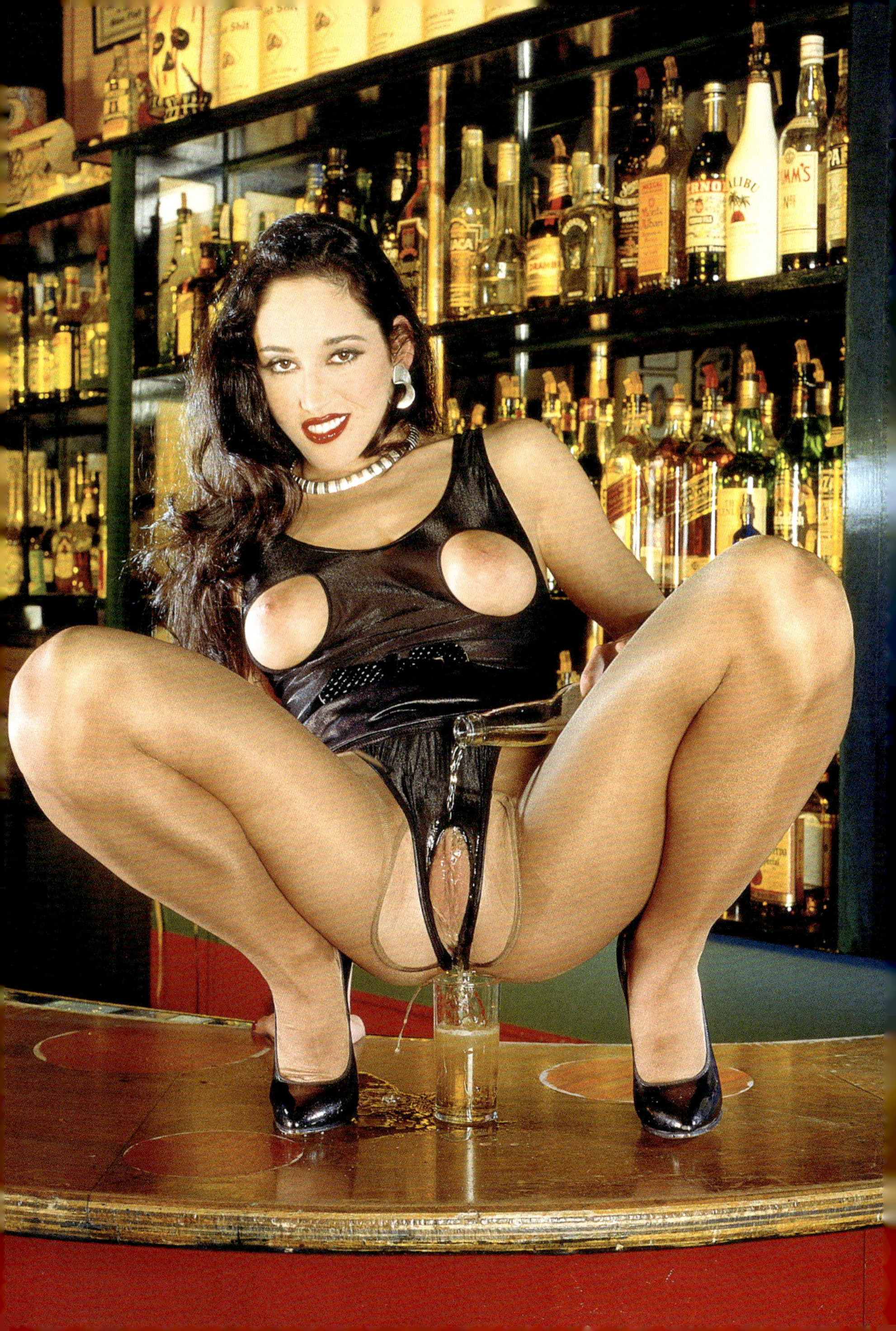

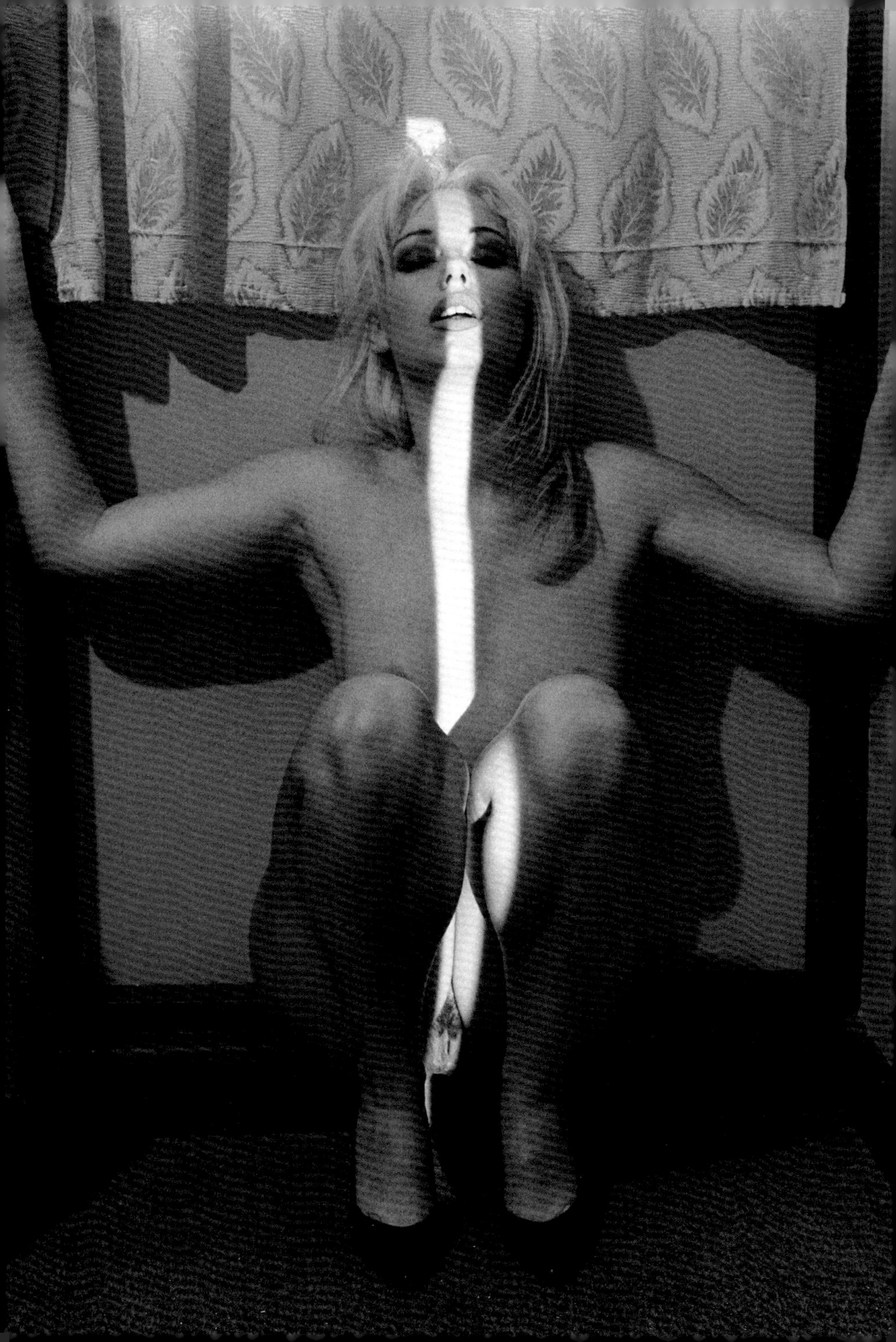

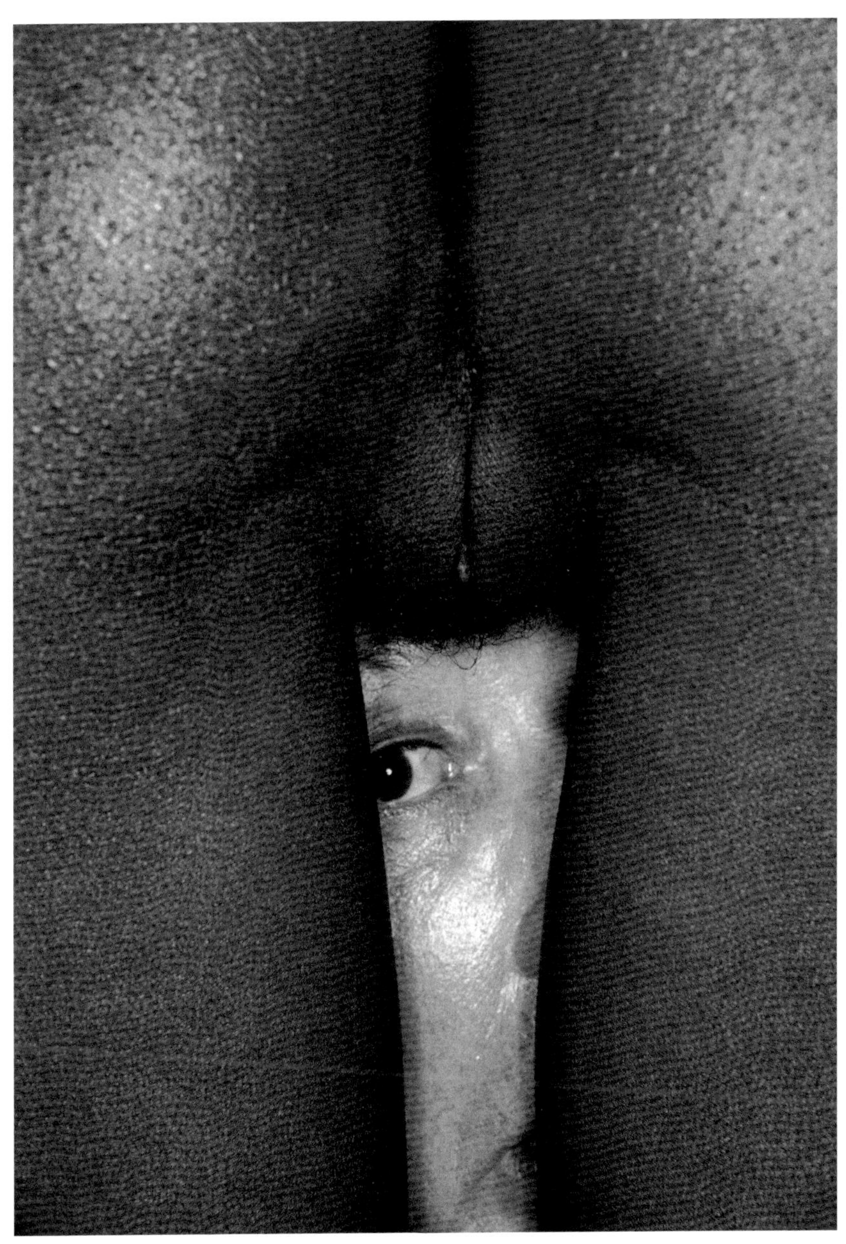

OPPOSITE **Debbie**   ABOVE **Peep Hole**   PAGES 188-189 **Mason Moore**

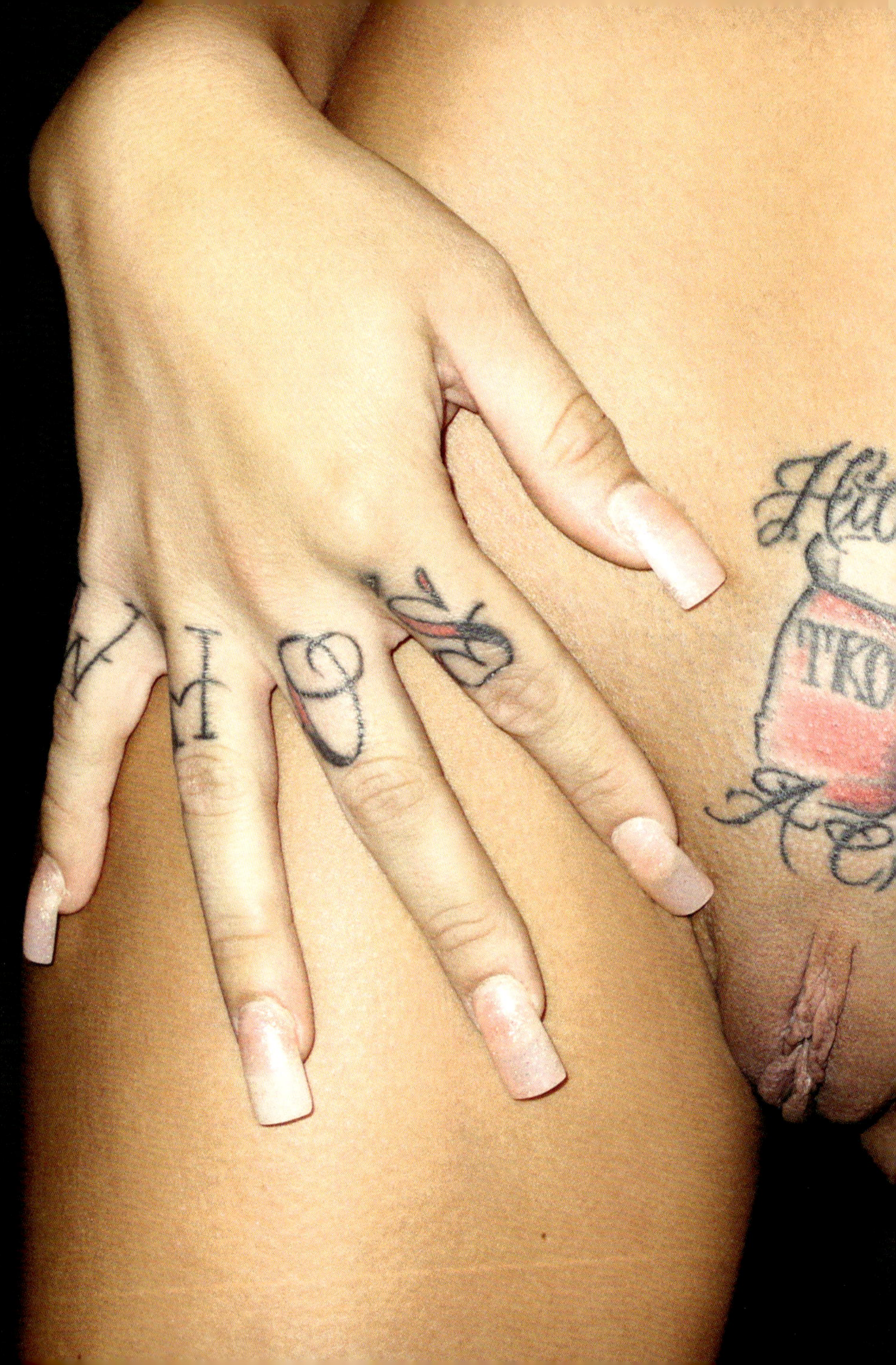

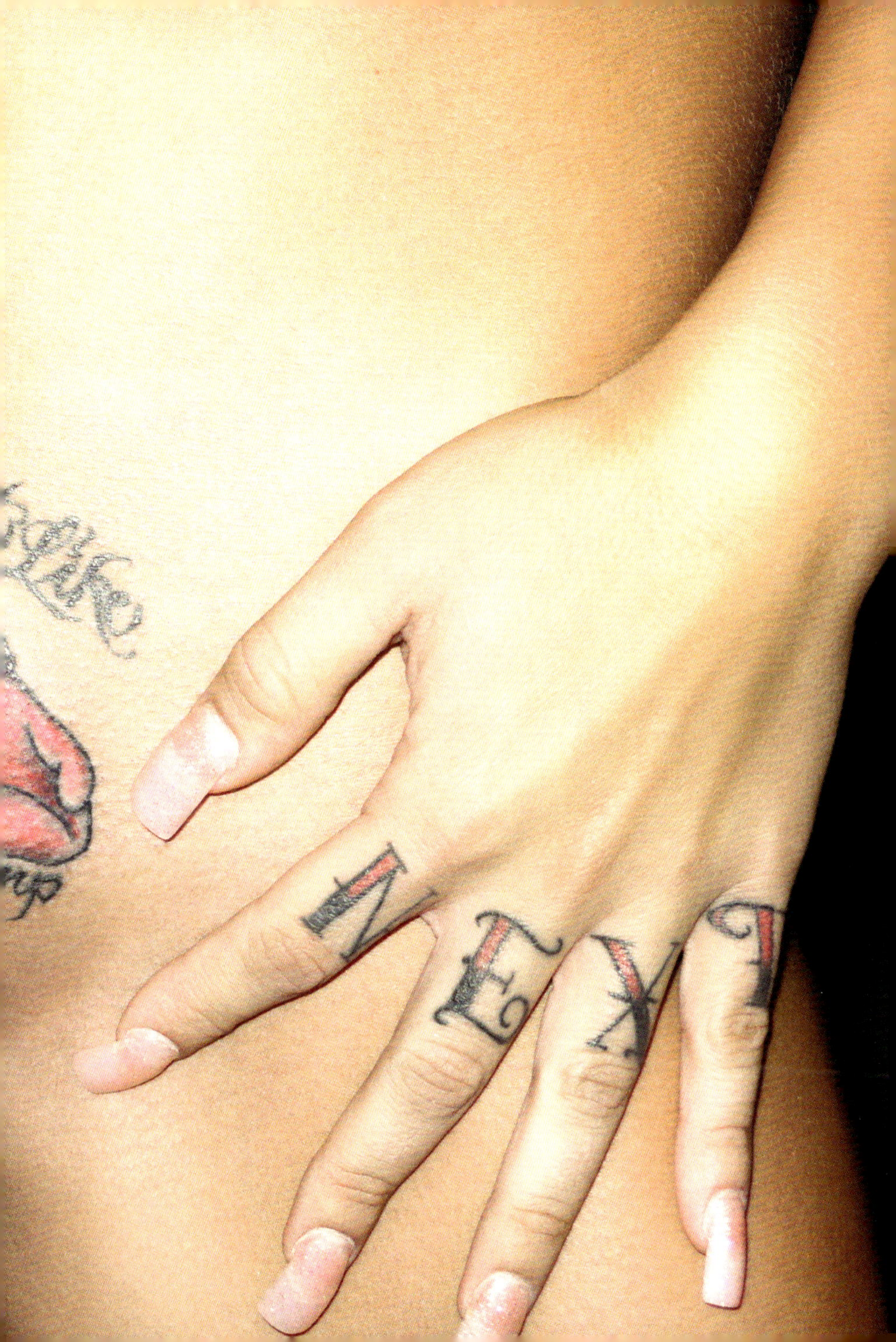
NEXT

Acknowledgments

Most of the photographs in this book were obtained from the massive archive of A. R. S. Inc., sellers of vintage erotica for over 25 years. They may be contacted by email at yesgirls@yesterdaygirls.com. Endpaper photos by Frannie Adams. Photo on page 149 by John Allum. Photos on pages 186 and 187 by Alva Bernadine. Photo on page 180 by Andrew Blake. Photos on pages 32/33 and 34 courtesy Serge Bramly. Photos on pages 148 and 150 by John Copeland. Photo on page 179 by Andrew Einhorn. Photo on pages 188/189 by Rick Shameless. Photos on front and back covers and on pages 168/169, 170, and 171 by Ed Fox. Photos on pages 39 and 40/41 courtesy Eric Godtland. Photos on pages 2, 9, 10, 15, 16, 17, 18, 28, 29, 30, 31, 35, 48, 49, 51, 53, 59, 72, 78/79, 84/85, 103, 108/109, 110, 116, 124, 140/141, 143, and 191 courtesy Dian Hanson. Photo on pages 36/37 courtesy Steven Kasher Gallery, New York. Photos on pages 184 and 185 by Richard Kern. Photo on page 129 by Lance Kincaid. Photos on pages 172 and 173 by Chas Ray Krider. Photo on page 142 by Tony LaSala. Photos on pages 24, 151, 156, 158/159, and 160 by Tommy Malibu. Photo on page 155 by Hal McQueeney, courtesy Ralph Bowman. Photo on page 178 by Dave Naz. Photo on page 1 by Jennifer Patrick. Photo on page 181 by George Pitts. Photos on pages 25, 62, 63, 107, 145, 154, and 162 courtesy Private magazine/Fraserside Holdings Ltd. Photos on pages 174, 175, and 176/177 by Holly Randall. Photos on pages 152/153, 162, 164/165, 166, and 167 by Suze Randall. Photos on pages 44, 45, and 46/47 by Charles West. Over-painted photos on page 14 by Eric Stanton. Photo on page 157 by Warren Tang. Memento on page 7 courtesy of Winter Works on Paper, New York. Photos on pages 182 and 183 by Mariano Vargas. Photo on page 55 courtesy Joe Zinatto.

Special thanks to Serge Bramly and Steven Kasher for going above and beyond, to cover girl Kimberly Kane for tolerating our demands, to Josh Baker, Francesco Belvedere, Jessica Sappenfield, and Marco Zivny for design and layout, Martin Holz for editorial coordination, Jennifer Patrick for production, Doug Adrianson for proofreading, Wordsworth for transcription, Ultra Graphics for scanning, and, as always, to Benedikt Taschen.

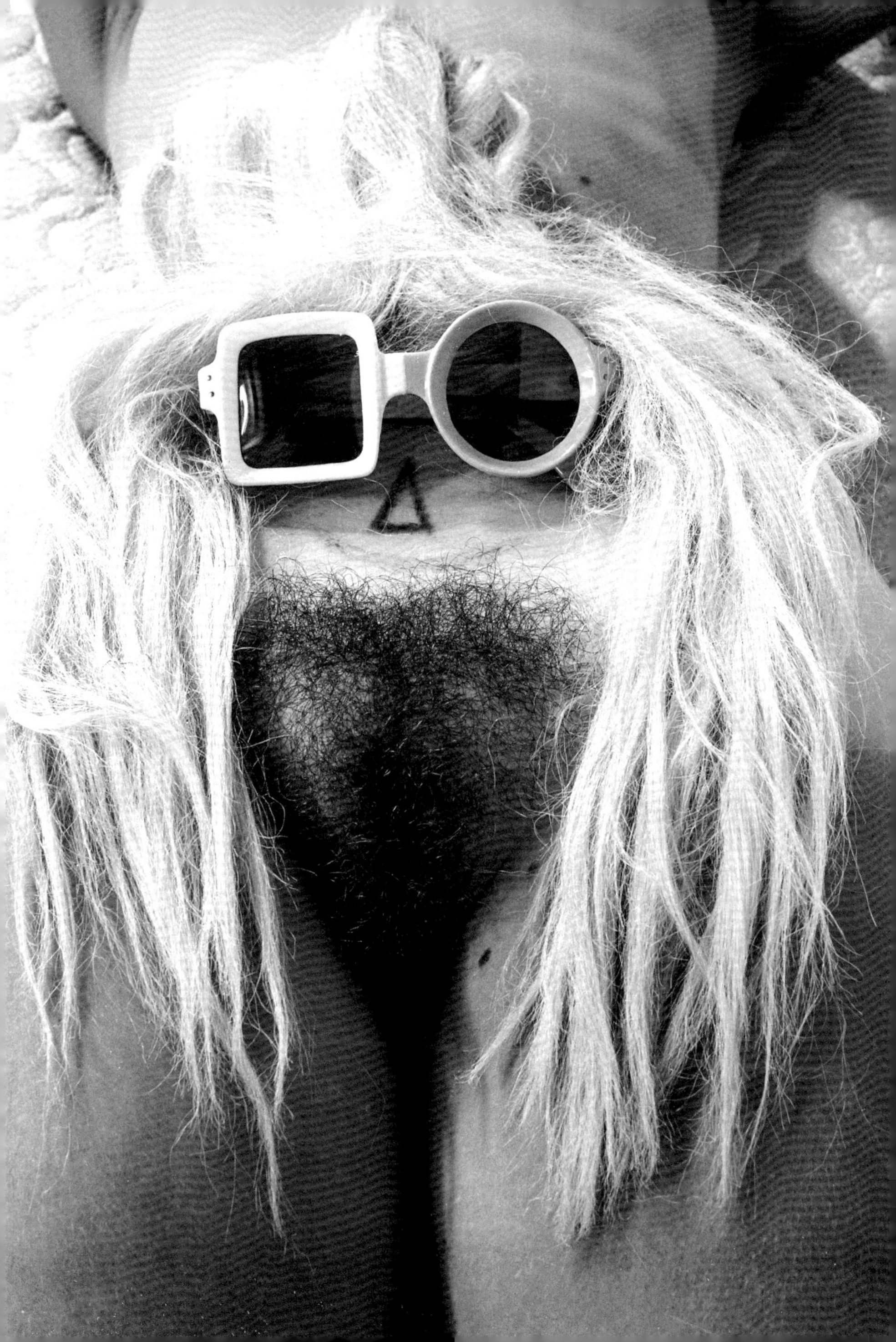

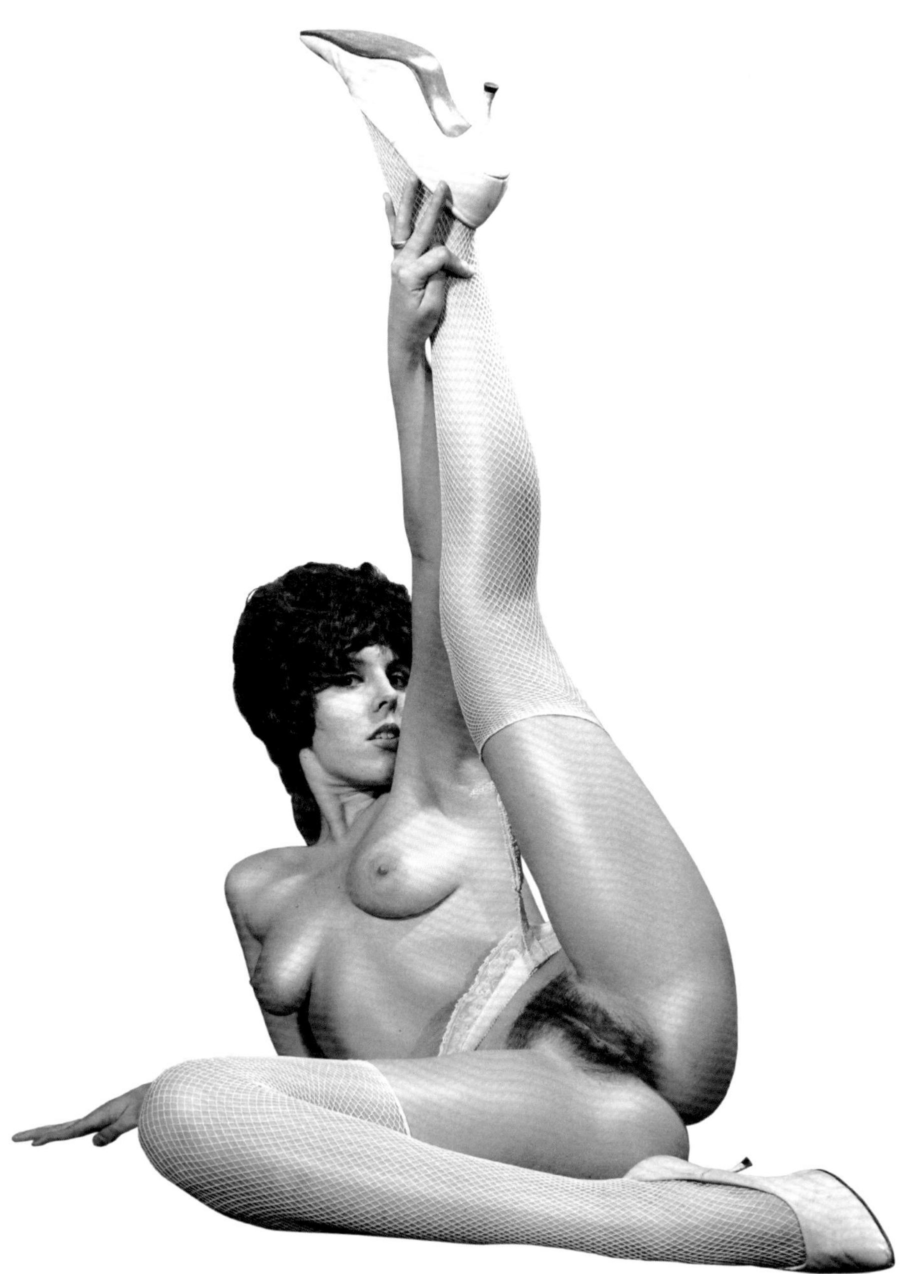

FRONT AND BACK COVERS Photographs of Kimberly Kane ©Ed Fox, 2011. See more of Kimberly at KaneArmy.com and follow her on X at x.com/KIMBERLYKANE.
ENDPAPERS Match the Pussy, by Frannie Adams
PAGE 1 Maneki-neko, the Japanese "beckoning cat," is believed to bring good luck.
PAGE 2 Unknown model, circa 1975.
PAGE 191 Creative use of pubic hair, circa 1975.
LEFT Dinda Evans, c. 1968.

EACH AND EVERY TASCHEN BOOK PLANTS A SEED!
Each year, we offset our annual carbon emissions with carbon credits at the Instituto Terra, a reforestation program in Minas Gerais, Brazil, founded by Lélia and Sebastião Salgado. To find out more about this ecological partnership, please check: taschen.com/institutoterra
Inspiration: unlimited. Carbon footprint: (almost) zero.

Want to see more? Visit taschen.com to view our current publications, browse our latest magazine, and subscribe to our newsletter.

© 2025 TASCHEN GmbH
Hohenzollernring 53, D–50672 Köln
taschen.com

German translation by Egbert Baqué, Berlin
French translation by Alice Pétillot, Bayonne

Printed in Italy
ISBN 978-3-8365-7893-6

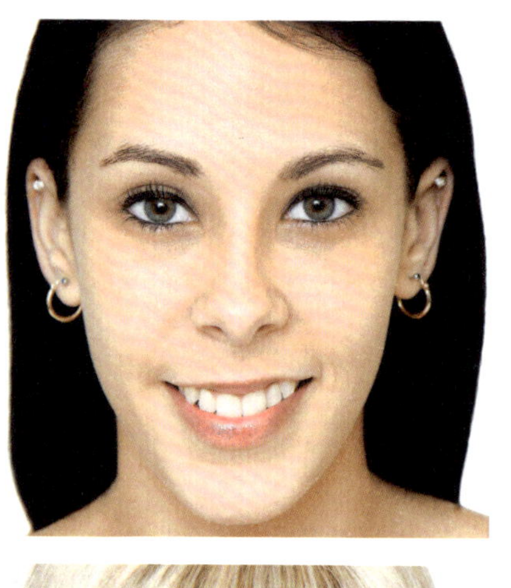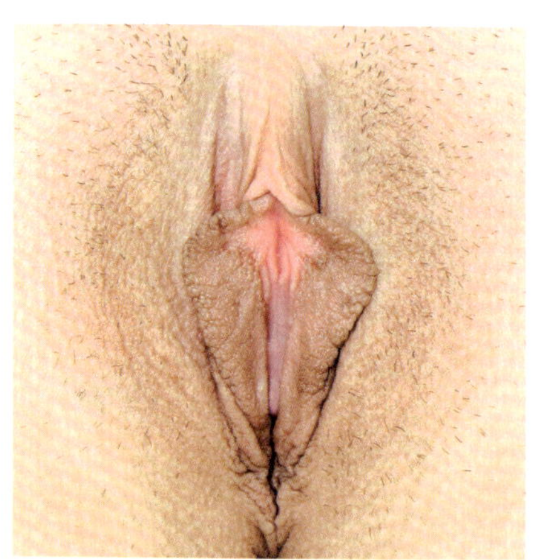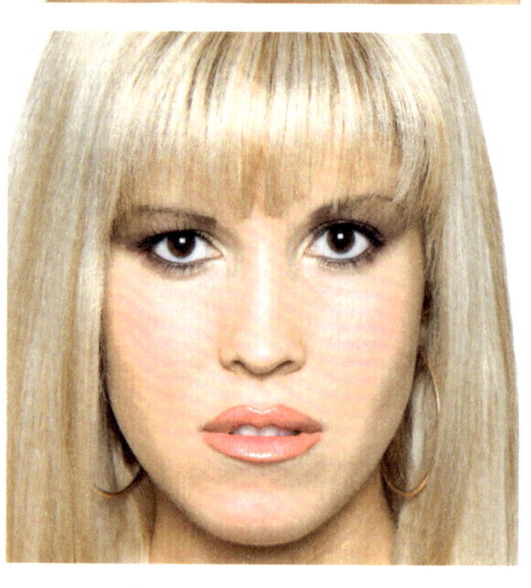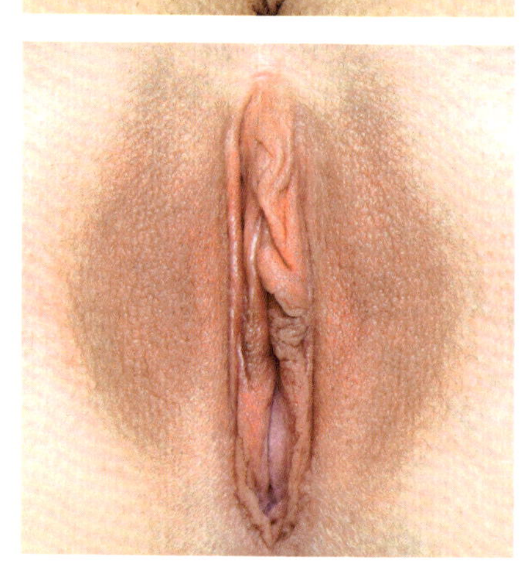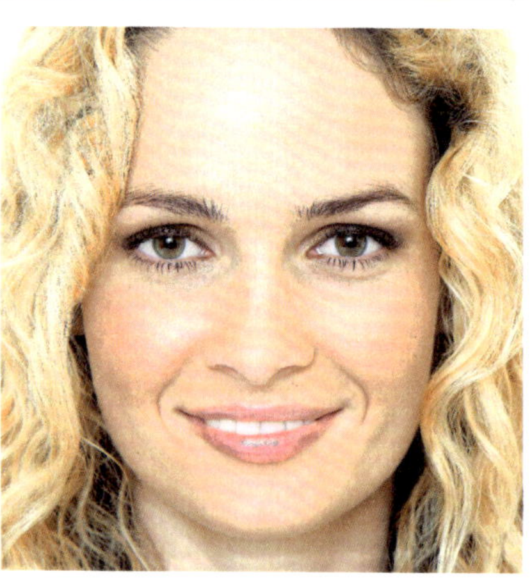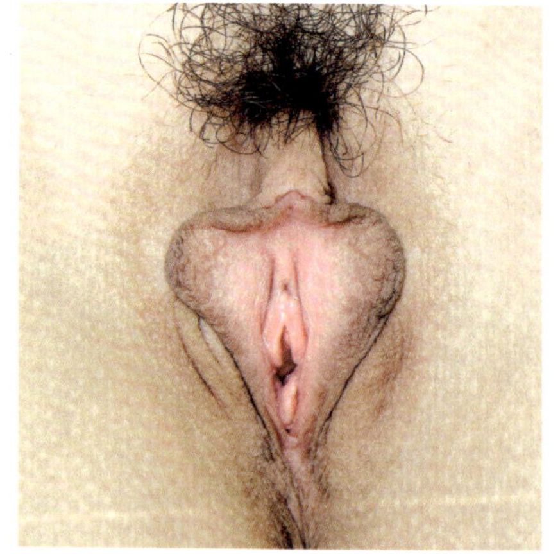